I0752861

SMITHSONIAN CONTRIBUTIONS TO KNOWLEDGE.

METEOROLOGICAL OBSERVATIONS

IN THE

ARCTIC SEAS.

BY

ELISHA KENT KANE, M. D., U. S. N.

MADE DURING THE SECOND GRINNELL EXPEDITION IN SEARCH OF SIR JOHN FRANKLIN, IN 1853, 1854, AND 1855, AT VAN RENSSELAER HARBOR, AND OTHER POINTS ON THE WEST COAST OF GREENLAND.

REDUCED AND DISCUSSED,

BY

CHARLES A. SCHOTT,
ASSISTANT U. S. COAST SURVEY.

[ACCEPTED FOR PUBLICATION, MAY, 1858.]

COLLINS, PRINTER,
PHILADELPHIA.

CONTENTS.

INTRODUCTORY LETTER.

WASHINGTON, *May* 17, 1858.

PROFESSOR JOSEPH HENRY, LL.D.,

Secretary of the Smithsonian Institution:

DEAR SIR: The records of the meteorological observations made under the direction of Dr. Kane, in the second expedition to the Arctic regions, were placed in my hands by his late lamented father, Judge Kane, in December last.

Dr. Kane had selected Assistant Charles A. Schott, of the Coast Survey, for the reduction of a considerable portion of the observations made in that expedition; and I, therefore, placed these in Mr. Schott's possession for reduction and discussion. The work has been faithfully performed, and I recommend it for publication in the "Smithsonian Contributions to Knowledge." It is proper to state that the instruments were furnished in part by the Smithsonian Institution, and that the computations have been made at its expense.

Very respectfully, yours,

A. D. BACHE.

PART I.

TEMPERATURES.

RECORD AND DISCUSSION OF TEMPERATURES.

THE vessel of the exploring expedition entered the winter quarters at Van Rensselaer Harbor, on the eastern trend of the coast of Greenland from Smith's Strait, on the 8th of September, 1853.[1] From the first of that month, she had not changed her position a mile, and the record and discussion of the observations for temperature will therefore commence, in the present paper, with September 1st, and be continued to January the 24th, 1855. This is the last day of entry in the original log-book in my possession. The temperatures after that date, and extending to the last of April, 1855, have been taken from Appendix No. XII. of the second volume of the narrative of the expedition.

The bay, surrounded by cliffs, is open towards the north and west, and the harbor is in latitude 78° 37′, and in longitude 70° 53′[2] west of Greenwich.

By the 28th of September, 1853, the erection of the meteorological observatory on the floe had been completed. It was a wooden structure, placed 140 yards from the ship, on the open ice-field, latticed and pierced with auger-holes on all sides, so as to allow the air to pass freely, and was firmly cemented to the ice at the base by freezing. To guard against the fine and almost impalpable drift which insinuates itself everywhere, and which would interfere with the observation of minute and sudden changes of temperature, a series of screens were placed at right angles to each other, so as to surround the inner chamber. The thermometers were suspended within the central chambers; a pane of glass permitted the light of the lanterns to reach them from a distance, and a lens and eyeglass were so fixed as to allow observing the instruments without going inside the screens. One of them—a three-feet spirit standard, by Tagliabue, of New York, graduated to 70° minus—was of sufficiently extended scale to be read, by rapid inspection, to tenths of a degree. It was not desired absolutely to neutralize the influence of the winds, but to make the exposure to them so uniform as to give comparable results for every quarter of the compass.[3]

The expedition was well supplied with thermometers. Thirty-six mercurial thermometers were received from the National Observatory at Washington, D. C. Their corrections near the freezing point were determined at the observatory, and

---

[1] See Narrative of the Expedition, Vol. II. p. 394.

[2] The result of a new reduction of the moon culminations.

[3] See Narrative, Vol. I. p. 117.

again by Mr. Sonntag, by means of Mr. Tagliabue's standard. Besides these, there were four maximum and four minimum thermometers, and two dozen spirit thermometers of various sizes, including two standards with a register 36 inches in length.[1] By one of these, and a mercurial standard of the same length, most of the temperatures of the air were noted.

Dr. Kane remarks:[2] "The temperature on the floes was always somewhat higher than at the island, the difference being due, as I suppose, to the heat conducted by the sea-water, which was at a temperature of +29°, the suspended instruments being affected by radiation."

This was on the 17th of January, 1854. On another page, he says:[3] "Upon the ice-floes, commencing with a surface temperature of —30°, I found, at two feet deep, a temperature of —8°, and at four feet +2°, and at eight feet +26°." This was in midwinter, on the largest floe in the open way off Cape Stafford. This subject will again be referred to.

Comparison of Thermometers.—The different readings of the instruments, particularly at temperatures below —40°, made their frequent comparison, in order to obtain corrective elements, a matter of great importance. Appendix No. XI. of the second volume of the narrative, contains a full exposition of the unreliable indications of the instruments at very low temperatures, and to this appendix the reader may be referred for further details.[4] Whether these anomalies be due to irregularities in the diameter of the tubes, or to unequal contraction of colored fluids of different specific gravity, it is admissible to suppose that the errors for a number of instruments, compared at the same temperature, may be as frequently in excess as in defect, provided they keep within a certain limit, beyond which the indications become useless. The mean reading of all thermometers compared at a certain temperature has, therefore, been taken for the true temperature, and, by comparing each result with this mean, a series of corrections has been obtained for each instrument. The same view was taken by Dr. Kane.

From the comparisons of February 5th, 6th, and 9th, 1854, I was led to suspect that some or all of the spirit thermometers, designated in the original log-book Nos. 1, 2, 3, 4, 5, were probably identical with those in the table of Appendix No. XI. in Vol. II. of the narrative, there named C, B, No. 4, A, No. 12, respectively. The numerous comparisons given in that appendix, and to which a few more have been added, made it unnecessary to use the observations from the above numbers in the first set of comparisons between the temperatures —68° and —20°. In the following table, arranged according to temperatures, S denotes the 36 inch spirit standard, upon which instrument the temperatures determined by the expedition mainly depend; $S_{(2)}$, a second similar standard; M, the 36 inch mercurial standard; the rest are alcoholic thermometers, from twelve to eighteen inches in length of scale. Fahrenheit's scale is used throughout.

---

[1] The expedition was also provided with one or more ether thermometers, of which I could find no further account.

[2] See Narrative, Vol. I. p. 154.

[3] Narrative, Vol. I. p. 267.

[4] An extract from this appendix will be found at the end of this article.

COMPARISON OF THERMOMETER READINGS BETWEEN THE TEMPERATURES —68° AND —20°, MADE IN 1854.

Therm. No.	Feb. 5th.	Feb. 5th.	Feb. 4th.	Jan. 20th.	Feb. 5th.	March 14th.	Feb. 6th.	March 3d.	Feb. 6th.	March 12th.	Feb. 9th.	March 3d.	Feb. 9th.	March 3d.	March 3d.	March 16th.
	°	°	°	°	°	°	°	°	°	°	°	°	°	°	°	°
12	—80.0	—77.9	—78.2	—73.0	—71.0	—64.4	—57.8	—58.0	—57.3	—56.2	—58.0	—54.5	—54.0	—47.5	—46.7	—44.1
1	—75.5	...	...	...	...	...	...	...	...	...	...	...	...	...	...	...
4	—75.0	—72.7	—74.0	—66.5	—63.0	—58.7	—55.5	—53.5	—55.0	—53.0	—53.5	—53.5	—53.5	—46.1	—45.5	—43.2
2	—72.0	—69.0	...	...	...	...	...	...	...	...	...	...	...	...	...	...
8	—70.5	—67.5	...	...	...	...	...	...	...	...	...	...	...	...	...	...
9	—68.4	...	...	...	...	...	...	...	...	...	...	...	...	...	...	—41.4
C	—64.6	—62.5	—63.0	—57.0	—54.0	...	—45.0	...	—44.0	...	—42.7	—43.0	—43.0	—40.5	—40.2	—38.8
S	—60.3	—58.3	—57.8	—54.8	—53.0	—50.2	—46.6	—45.5	—46.3	—43.8	—44.8	—45.0	—44.8	—41.2	—40.8	—39.1
$S_{(2)}$	...	...	...	...	...	...	...	...	...	...	—44.8	...	...	...	...	...
A	—57.0	—56.0	—56.2	—53.0	—50.0	—47.2	—44.5	—42.9	—44.0	—41.8	—43.0	—42.9	—42.5	—40.0	—39.7	—37.6
B	—56.4	—55.5	—56.0	—52.5	—51.0	—46.7	—43.6	—42.0	—43.0	—41.0	—42.0	—42.0	—42.0	—39.9	—39.0	—37.2
Means	—68.0	—64.9	—64.2	—59.5	—57.0	—53.4	—48.8	—48.4	—48.3	—47.2	—47.0	—46.8	—46.6	—42.5	—42.0	—40.2

Therm. No.	March 16th.	Feb. 25th.	Feb. 25th.	Feb. 26th.	Feb. 7th.	Feb. 14th.	Feb. 24th.	Feb. 18th.	Feb. 23d.	Feb. 20th.	Feb. 19th.	Feb. 12th.	Feb. 15th.	Feb. 19th.	Feb. 18th.	Feb. 17th.
	°	°	°	°	°	°	°	°	°	°	°	°	°	°	°	°
12	—43.7	—46.2	—41.0	—37.7	—35.0	—35.8	—33.8	—33.2	—31.7	—27.9	—27.0	—25.7	—25.0	—23.8	—22.7	—21.7
4	—42.9	—43.3	—40.6	—37.0	—34.2	—35.4	—33.3	—32.6	—31.2	—27.5	—27.0	—25.0	—24.3	—23.5	—21.9	—21.7
2	...	...	...	...	—32.4	...	...	...	...	...	...	...	...	...	...	...
8	...	...	...	...	—32.9	...	...	...	...	...	...	...	...	...	...	...
9	—41.0	...	—38.9	—35.7	—33.0	...	—32.0	...	—30.2	...	—26.0	...	—24.0	—23.3	—21.2	—21.0
C	—38.2	...	—35.6	—32.8	—29.5	—29.8	—29.0	—28.8	—27.3	—24.4	—23.6	—22.2	—22.0	—21 0	—20.0	—19.6
S	—38.7	—36.6	—36.6	—34.0	—31.8	—31.7	—31.0	—30.2	—29.0	—26.9	—24.5	—22.6	—22.1	—21.2	—20.0	—19.4
$S_{(2)}$	...	...	...	...	...	—31.8	...	—30.2	...	...	...	—22.6	...	...	...	...
M	—38.4	—36.1	—36.3	—33.8	—31.3	—31.2	—30.4	—29.6	—28.6	—25.2	—23.9	—22.0	—21.5	—20.8	—19.5	—19.1
A	—37.7	—34.8	—35.2	—32.9	—30.2	—29.7	—29.5	—29.0	—28.0	—24.7	—24.2	—21.6	—21.6	—20.8	—19.7	—19.3
B	—37.2	—36.0	—34.8	—32.2	—29.8	—29.2	—29.0	—28.5	—27.5	—24.3	—23.5	—22.2	—22.0	—21.3	—20.2	—19.6
Means	—39.7	—38.8	—37.4	—34.5	—32.0	—31.8	—31.0	—30.5	—29.2	—25.8	—25.0	—23.0	—22.8	—22.0	—20.7	—20.2

From the preceding comparisons, the following corrections have been deduced:—

Readings of *S*.	Corrections.	Readings of *S*.	Corrections.	Readings of *S* and *M*.	Corrections to *S*.	Corrections to *M*.	Readings of *S* and *M*.	Corrections to *S*.	Corrections to *M*.
—60°	—7°.5	—50°	—3°.1	—40°	—1°.2	—1°.5	—30°	—0°.1	—0°.6
—59	—7.0	—49	—2.9	—39	—1.1	—1.3	—29	—0.1	—0.7
—58	—6.4	—48	—2.6	—38	—1.0	—1.2	—28	0.0	—0.6
—57	—5.9	—47	—2.4	—37	—0.9	—1.1	—27	0.0	—0.6
—56	—5.4	—46	—2.3	—36	—0.7	—1.0	—26	0.0	—0.6
—55	—4.8	—45	—2.1	—35	—0.6	—0.8	—25	—0.1	—0.7
—54	—4.4	—44	—2.0	—34	—0.5	—0.7	—24	—0.3	—1.0
—53	—4.0	—43	—1.7	—33	—0.3	—0.7	—23	—0.4	—1.0
—52	—3.7	—42	—1.4	—32	—0.2	—0.7	—22	—0.6	—1.0
—51	—3.4	—41	—1.3	—31	0.0	—0.6	—21	—0.7	—1.2
...	...	...	...	...	...	...	—20	—0.8	—1.2

The corrections between temperatures of —20° and —40° for the two standards are small, and hardly exceed 1° at the lower limit, but beyond this point, for the lower temperatures, a regular increase is observed in the correction to the spirit standard. The caliber of most of the spirit thermometers was tested before leaving New York, and the differences exhibited in the table of comparisons for the several instruments arise, perhaps, principally from the unequal contraction of colored and not chemically pure alcohol. At these extreme low temperatures, the fluid appears to change its condition, and the coloring matter, with a falling temperature, remains adhering to the sides of the tube.

In order to test his thermometers, Dr. Kane provided himself with chemically pure mercury, and noted the temperatures at which it became solid. The following notes have been extracted from the log:—

Nov. 25, 1853. The mercury was exposed upon the floe at the meteorological observatory, and remained liquid with the spirit standard at —42°.0.

Dec. 8, 1853. At two o'clock, the mercury exposed was found frozen at —40°.5 of the spirit standard, the mercurial standard being at —39°.8.

Dec. 14, 1853. The mercury froze around the edges of the saucer containing it; *S* at —41°.0, and *M* at —40°.0.

Jan. 16, 1854. Mercury in bulb ceased to record at —43°.5; observed frozen at —38°.0.

Jan. 29, 1854. The mercury in the standard instrument, after registering —43°.0, descended in the bulb; at another time it registered, after being frozen, —44°.0, and then became stationary.

Nov. 29, 1854. Mercury congealed at —43°.0 of spirit standard, and resumed its fluidity at —38°.0.

If we refer the readings of the spirit standard to those of the mercurial standard by adding +0°.3, we obtain the following observed temperatures for the freezing point of mercury:—

—40°.2 —39°.8 —40°.7 —40°.0 —38°.0 and —42°.7 Mean, —40°.2

Similar differences in the freezing point of mercury have been noticed by other observers; Parry, for instance, saw the mercury liquid at —43°. The above mean being so near to what is generally assumed (—40°) as the point of congelation, I thought it best to apply no correction to the readings of the mercurial standard, and to diminish that of the spirit standard, for temperatures lower than —40°, by the apparent difference, at that temperature, between the indications of the mercurial and all other thermometers compared with it, or by the constant 1°.5; thus the maximum correction to the spirit standard becomes —6°.0 at —60°.

Thus applying the proper corrections to the spirit standard *S*, according to observations of February 4, 1854, spirit of naphtha became solid at —57°, oil of sassafras at —46°, bisulphuret of carbon at —26°; oil of wintergreen clouded at —40°, and remained liquid at the maximum temperature of that day, viz: —63°; the ethers likewise remained unchanged. On the following day, aqua ammonia F. F. froze solid from two hours exposure at a temperature of —52°, chloric ether became solid, and, after four hours of exposure, chloroform was covered with a granular follicle at —66°.

TABLE OF CORRECTIONS TO SPIRIT STANDARD *S*, OF TEMPERATURES BETWEEN —60° AND —40°.

Scale.	Corrections.	Scale.	Corrections.	Scale.	Corrections.	Scale.	Corrections.
—60°	—6°.0	—54°	—2°.9	—49°	—1°.4	—44°	—0°.5
—59	—5.5	—53	—2.5	—48	—1.1	—43	—0.2
—58	—4.9	—52	—2.2	—47	—0.9	—42	+0.1
—57	—4.4	—51	—1.9	—46	—0.8	—41	+0.2
—56	—3.9	—50	—1.6	—45	—0.6	—40	+0.3
—55	—3.3						

CORRECTIONS TO *S*, FOR TEMPERATURES BETWEEN —40° AND —20°.							
Scale.	Corrections.	Scale.	Corrections.	Scale.	Corrections.	Scale.	Corrections.
—40°	+0°.3	—34°	+0°.2	—29°	+0°.6	—24°	+0°.7
—39	+0.2	—33	+0.4	—28	+0.6	—23	+0.6
—38	+0.2	—32	+0.5	—27	+0.6	—22	+0.4
—37	+0.2	—31	+0.6	—26	+0.6	—21	+0.5
—36	+0.3	—30	+0.5	—25	+0.6	—20	+0.5
—35	+0.2						

For temperatures between —20° and +15°, the following table of corrections has been constructed. The third column contains the number of comparisons.

Scale.	Corrections.	Comparisons.	Scale.	Corrections.	Comparisons.	Scale.	Corrections.	Comparisons.
—20°	+0°.5	24	+1°	+0°.5	...	+ 7°	+0.2°	...
—15	+0.5	24	+2	+0.4	...	+10	+0.3	19
—10	+0.6	25	+3	+0.3	...	+12	+0.2	...
— 5	+0.5	17	+4	+0.2	...	+14	+0.1	...
0	+0.5	24	+5	+0.1	57	+15	0.0	6

In the absence of direct comparisons for temperatures of +16° and upwards, I have adopted Mr. Sonntag's corrections, as found by comparing the daily means for May, June, and July, in the log-book, with the corresponding means in Appendix XII. of Vol. II. of the narrative. They have, however, all been diminished by 0°.7, the correction, according to his table, applicable at +15°.0, for which temperature I have found that no correction was required. The last set of corrections to the spirit standard becomes then—

Scale.	Corrections.	Scale.	Corrections.
+15°.0	0°.0	+30°.0	—0°.7
+18.0	—0.1	+35.0	—0.5
+20.0	—0.3	+40.0	—0.4
+15.0	—0.5	+45.0	—0.4

In the following abstract of the hourly record of the atmospheric temperatures from September 1st, 1853, to January 24th, 1855, observed at Van Rensselaer Harbor, the *corrected* figures have been inserted in accordance with the previous investigation; foot notes contain any additional information that may be required.

These temperatures refer to the level of the sea. The observations were made by the officers and men on duty, and are referred to mean local time. Occasional short interpolations were effected by means of the known diurnal variation, and the gradual change in the absolute temperature; in all cases, accordingly, the means given are *corrected* for any such omission in the record. The hourly series in my possession terminates with January 24th, 1855; the daily means up to April 30th, 1855, have been extracted from the second volume of the narrative. Before these numbers were set down, the difference in the system of corrections, as adopted by Mr. Sonntag, and in the present paper was applied.

That the temperature was lower in winter in exposed positions at the astronomical observatory, and in the outer bay or channel, than at the meteorological observatory on the floe in the harbor, there can be no doubt; but, owing to non-compared instruments, the exact amount cannot be ascertained. November 23d, 1853, on the floe outside, the temperature was 10° lower, and again, December 20th, 1853, it was 6½° lower than inside. On the 19th of January, 1854, the spirit standard on the floe inside indicated —50°, and at the astronomical observatory the temperature was —58°.

To the local difference, in winter, of the temperature of the air incumbent on land, and on ice-floes resting on a sea with a temperature not far from its freezing-point, I have already alluded. During the first winter, the temperatures were observed on the floe, but, during the second, on board the brig; the mean difference, for the five coldest months in the two years, amounts to 1°.5, and for the absolute minima it is but 0°.9—the first being the colder in either case. This result, together with the statement (p. 405, Vol. II. of the Narrative) that *local* radiations were guarded against as far as possible, leaves no doubt that the recorded temperatures during the coldest months of the first season are not sensibly affected by any local radiation; at the same time, it must be admitted that, in winter, the ice-covered sea is, nevertheless, a source of heat which, propagated through this cover, is expended by radiation into the colder atmosphere.

Occasional omissions in the hourly record have been supplied by interpolation; these values are always indicated by being inclosed between brackets. The process of interpolation will be found illustrated by an example at the end of the record.

Temperature of the Air in Shade observed at Van Rensselaer Harbor,

In September, 1853, in Lat. 78° 37′, Long. 70° 53′ W. of Greenwich.

Expressed in degrees of Fahrenheit's scale. On deck the brig Advance and at meteorological observatory on floe.[1]

Hour.	1st.	2d.	3d.	4th.	5th.	6th.	7th.	8th.	9th.	10th.	11th.	12th.	13th.	14th.	15th.	16th.
	°	°	°	°	°	°	°	°	°	°	°	°	°	°	°	°
1h.	+28.6	+28.6	+28.1	+28.1	+28.3	+27.6	+30.6	+20.6	+18.9	+15.6	+15.1	+13.7	+17.6	+11.8	+12.0	+ 8.5
2	30.1	28.6	27.6	28.1	28.1	27.1	31.1	19.6	19.1	15.1	15.1	13.0	15.8	11.8	13.2	9.1
3	30.1	28.6	27.6	28.1	28.1	27.1	31.1	19.6	18.9	14.6	15.1	12.3	14.6	12.3	13.7	9.4
4	29.6	28.6	28.9	28.1	27.8	27.1	31.6	19.3	18.6	14.3	14.6	12.3	13.9	12.3	13.4	9.9
5	29.6	28.6	28.6	28.3	27.6	27.6	31.1	18.1	18.6	14.1	15.1	12.3	13.7	12.3	13.2	10.4
6	29.6	28.6	28.6	28.3	27.8	27.8	30.6	18.6	19.6	19.1	15.6	14.6	14.2	12.4	13.2	10.9
7	29.6	28.3	28.6	28.3	27.6	28.1	30.8	20.1	21.1	17.1	16.1	16.6	17.8	13.2	13.0	11.8
8	29.6	28.6	28.6	28.6	27.8	28.1	31.6	19.6	22.1	21.6	16.6	20.6*	21.6	13.2	13.7	13.2
9	30.3	28.6	28.6	28.6	28.1	28.1	31.6	19.8	19.9	17.6	17.6	26.1	23.6	14.7	14.2	13.9
10	30.3	29.6	28.6	28.6	28.1	28.6	31.6	19.6	19.4	18.4	19.4	25.1	21.6	15.3	14.2	14.6
11	30.3	29.6	28.6	29.6	27.6	29.1	31.6	19.6	19.4	19.2	17.3	20.1	17.6	15.8	14.6	16.1
Noon	28.6	30.1	28.6	29.6	28.1	29.6	31.6	20.6	19.3	18.7	17.2	20.1	16.6	14.9	14.6	15.1
13	30.6	30.6	28.6	28.6	28.1	30.6	29.3	21.1	19.6	18.6	17.6	20.1	14.8	14.6	17.3	18.1
14	30.6	30.3	28.1	28.1	28.1	30.6	26.6	21.1	19.6	18.6	17.6	20.6	13.9	14.3	16.1	20.8*
15	30.6	30.3	28.1	28.6	28.1	30.6	24.6	21.1	19.1	17.6	18.1	20.6	15.6	15.1	16.4	19.6
16	30.6	30.1	27.6	28.6	28.1	29.3	25.1	21.6	19.1	17.1	17.1	19.6	14.6	15.3	16.6	15.6
17	30.1	28.1	27.6	28.6	28.1	29.8	24.3	21.6	19.6	16.6	17.1	20.6	14.2	16.1	14.6	15.1
18	29.6	27.6	28.1	28.1	27.6	28.6	23.6	21.1	18.6	16.6	17.6	19.6	14.6	16.1	13.0	15.1
19	30.1	27.6	28.6	28.3	27.6	(28.1)	23.1	21.1	19.1	16.1	17.6	19.8	13.2	14.2	12.3	15.6
20	29.6	27.6	28.6	28.3	27.6	27.6	22.1	21.1	18.6	15.6	16.6	19.9	12.2	14.2	11.5	15.6
21	29.6	27.6	28.6	28.1	27.6	28.6	21.8	20.8	18.8	15.9	16.2	19.5	12.2	13.2	10.7	15.6
22	29.1	27.6	28.6	28.1	27.1	28.6	21.6	20.4	18.5	15.8	15.1	19.3	13.7	12.6	11.1	14.6
23	29.1	27.6	27.6	28.6	27.1	29.1	21.3	19.4	17.6	15.5	13.9	18.8	12.7	12.0	10.9	13.7
Midn't	+29.1	+27.6	+27.6	+28.6	+27.1	+29.6	+20.8	+18.8	+16.3	+15.0	+13.9	+18.3	+12.7	+11.3	+10.2	+13.7
Means	+29.79	+28.71	+28.28	+28.45	+27.80	+28.62	+27.46	+20.18	+19.14	+16.85	+16.38	+18.48	+15.54	+13.71	+13.49	+14.00

Hour.	17th.	18th.	19th.	20th.	21st.	22d.	23d.	24th.	25th.	26th.	27th.	28th.	29th.	30th.		Means.
	°	°	°	°	°	°	°	°	°	°	°	°	°	°		°
1h.	+14.6	+ 8.0	+ 6.7	+ 5.0	+ 5.2	+ 4.5	+19.6	+18.6	+18.6	+17.1	+11.8	+ 8.9	+ 9.3	+ 9.8	...	+16.38
2	14.6	8.2	6.0	4.0	5.2	4.0	17.6	17.1	17.6	15.6	11.8	9.4	9.2	9.7	...	16.08
3	12.7	7.5	6.0	3.7	5.0	4.0	17.6	17.1	17.6	13.7	11.6	9.3	9.0	9.8	...	15.86
4	11.8	6.2	5.0	3.7	4.0	4.2	18.1	16.6	16.1	12.7	11.3	8.4	8.6	9.3	...	15.54
5	11.2	6.2	4.5	4.0	3.7	5.0	18.1	18.3	17.1	8.9	10.4	9.0	7.7	4.7	...	15.27
6	11.2	6.2	5.5	5.5	6.0	5.2	18.6	19.3	19.1	9.4	11.3	8.6	8.0	5.0	...	15.95
7	11.8	8.0	7.0	7.5	8.2	11.8	18.6	19.8	19.1	9.6	11.3	8.6	7.6	4.0	...	16.70
8	15.6	12.3	7.0	11.4	10.6	13.7	18.9	19.8	19.1	16.6	11.3	8.9	7.8	3.7	...	18.06
9	(15.2)	15.6	9.0	10.9	10.1	16.6	19.6	19.6	20.6	16.6	11.8	8.6	8.2	5.1	...	18.63
10	(14.8)	17.6	10.0	11.4	14.2	19.1	19.6	18.6	21.6	19.6	13.2	9.3	8.9	6.1	...	19.23
11	(14.4)	18.6	11.0	10.9	14.6	18.6	23.1	18.6	21.6	15.6	13.2	9.8	9.1	9.3	...	19.15
Noon	(14.0)	12.7	11.0	14.1	13.7	17.3	23.6	18.8	23.6	13.2	12.7	10.3	9.3	9.5	...	18.90
13	13.7	12.7	10.5	11.1	13.7	17.8	23.1	17.1	23.3	12.2	12.3	10.5	9.8	9.3	...	18.84
14	12.7	12.3	11.7	11.1	14.6	18.1	23.1	19.6	23.3	10.0	11.8	10.5	10.0	9.0	...	18.76
15	11.8	11.3	11.1	14.8	11.8	19.1	23.8	14.9	23.3	9.6	11.2	10.6	11.0	10.7	...	18.64
16	12.7	11.3	12.0	14.6	11.6	19.1	23.1	14.6	21.8	9.6	10.4	10.4	10.0	10.3	...	18.25
17	13.0	9.9	11.1	13.7	11.4	18.6	21.6	14.1	21.6	9.4	8.5	10.3	10.1	7.2	...	17.75
18	13.2	8.0	10.4	12.7	10.9	17.6	20.6	12.7	21.6	11.8	7.5	10.2	10.1	3.3	...	17.20
19	10.4	7.2	9.9	11.4	8.9	17.6	20.6	10.9	20.8	12.3	7.0	10.2	10.2	0.8	...	16.85
20	9.9	7.0	8.4	9.4	8.0	17.4	22.6	10.9	20.6	12.3	7.0	10.0	10.0	+ 0.3	...	16.35
21	9.0	(7.0)	7.0	8.4	6.7	17.1	19.8	12.5	20.6	12.3	6.5	9.8	10.1	— 0.3	...	16.04
22	9.0	7.0	7.0	9.9	6.7	18.6	19.3	14.6	21.1	8.7	6.2	9.8	10.1	— 0.3	...	15.98
23	9.9	6.0	6.0	9.7	6.5	18.6	18.8	16.6	20.1	8.7	9.4	9.7	10.1	— 0.7	...	15.81
Midn't	+ 9.9	+ 5.5	+ 6.0	+ 5.0	+ 4.7	+19.6	+18.8	+18.3	+19.3	+12.5	+ 8.9	+ 9.0	+ 9.7	— 0.7	...	+15.57
Means	+12.38	+ 9.68	+ 8.33	+ 9.33	+ 9.00	+14.30	+20.34	+16.63	+20.38	+12.42	+10.35	+ 9.59	+ 9.33	+ 5.62	...	+17.16

[1] The observations upon the floe commence Sept. 28th. From Aug. 18th to Sept. 27th, inclusive, mercurial thermometer No. 6 was used; its scale correction, determined by two standards, is, —0°.2 and —0°.7 (at +39°), mean —0°.4. On and after Sept. 27th, the spirit standard *S* was used. A second correction has been applied, to refer the temperatures on deck to the temperatures on floe, viz: at +30° and +15° none, at +10°, +0°.3, and at +5° and 0°, +0°.4; deduced from 27 comparisons.

* Value deduced from temperature 80 feet above deck.

Note.—The mean temperature of the air given in Appendix No. XII. of the narrative, refers to days of nautical reckoning, commencing and ending with noon; on and after September 11, 1853, civil reckoning was adopted.

Temperature of the Air in Shade observed at Van Rensselaer Harbor,

In October, 1853, in Lat. 78° 37′, Long. 70° 53′ W. of Greenwich.

Expressed in degrees of Fahrenheit's scale. At meteorological observatory on floe.[1]

Hour.	1st.	2d.	3d.	4th.	5th.	6th.	7th.	8th.	9th.	10th.	11th.	12th.	13th.	14th.	15th.	16th.
	°	°	°	°	°	°	°	°	°	°	°	°	°	°	°	°
1h.	—0.8	+1.0	+ 0.5	+14.0	+12.7	+13.9	+13.1	+12.2	+ 4.6	+3.0	—5.3	+ 5.2	+12.7	+12.2	+13.2*	+6.1
2	—1.0	+0.5	+ 1.5	+13.5	+11.8	+14.7	+13.4	+11.9	+ 6.3	+1.7	—5.5	+ 8.2	+12.4	+13.3	+12.6*	+4.9
3	+0.3	+0.3	+ 1.8	+13.2	+13.5	+14.0	+13.6	+11.6	+ 7.6	+1.5	—5.5	+10.5	+12.3	+13.3	+11.8*	+3.7
4	+2.0	0.0	+ 2.1	+13.1	+15.2	+13.4	+14.0	+11.2	+10.5	+0.3	—5.5	+12.2	+12.2	+13.2	+11.6*	+2.4
5	+2.1	+2.4	+ 1.5*	+14.8	+14.9	+13.6	+13.2	+10.3	+10.3	—0.5	—6.5	+12.2	+12.6	+13.6	+10.3	+2.2
6	+2.6	+3.2	+ 3.0	+15.5	+14.5	+13.6	+10.4	+10.3	+ 9.3	—1.5	—6.5	+12.0	+12.8	+13.7	+10.5	+2.2
7	+2.9	+5.1	+ 3.3	+15.5	+14.8	+14.3	+ 9.1	+ 9.8	+ 7.7	—0.5	—7.3	+12.0	+13.3	+14.1	+10.8	+2.0
8	+3.5	+5.1	+ 3.3	+15.5	+14.3	+14.6	+ 9.8	+10.3	+ 7.1	—0.5	—7.3	+12.4	+13.1	+14.6	+11.7	+1.5
9	+5.1	+5.0	+ 4.3	+15.9	+15.2	+15.8	+10.1	+ 9.5	+ 7.1	—0.5	—7.0	+13.8	+13.3	+14.8	+13.0*	+1.9
10	+5.1	+4.9	+ 5.2	+16.2	+15.3	+16.2	+10.3	+ 9.8	+ 6.2	—1.1	—5.5	+13.1	+13.3	+14.8	+13.2*	+1.7
11	+6.1	+4.7	+ 6.3	+16.2	+16.2	+16.8	+ 9.4	+10.2	+ 6.1	—1.5	—5.0	+12.7	+14.1	+14.8	+14.6*	+2.3
Noon	+6.1	+4.7	+ 7.7	+16.0	+17.5	+17.0	+ 8.3	+ 9.5	+ 6.2	0.0	—4.5	+12.2	+14.1	+14.6	+16.6*	+2.8
13	(+4.7)	+4.7	+ 8.9	+14.5	+15.5	+14.7	+ 7.2	+ 8.5	+ 6.2	—0.5	—2.5	+12.6	+13.6	+14.5	+14.2	+2.8
14	+3.3*	+3.8	+ 8.3	+15.3	+16.0	+14.7	+ 7.2	+ 8.6	+ 6.2	—2.5	—2.5	+(12.3)	+10.8	+14.7	+14.2	+1.5
15	+3.3*	+1.3	+ 9.1	+16.6	+12.5	+14.1	+ 8.4	+ 8.7	+ 4.7	—1.5	—2.7	+12.0	+11.3	+14.8	+13.7	+3.3
16	+3.2*	+1.5	+10.1	+18.6	+12.8	+14.1	+ 8.5	+ 8.7	+ 3.3	—3.3	—3.2	+10.3	+11.2	+14.4	+13.4	+2.9
17	+2.5*	+0.7	+10.3	+18.2	+12.1	+13.2	+10.3	+ 8.7	+ 3.3	—3.6	—2.6	+10.8	+11.9	+14.2	+14.8*	+2.4
18	+1.8	—0.5	+10.3	+17.8	+13.8	+12.4	+10.7	+ 8.2	+ 3.3	—4.5	—2.2	+11.3	+11.3	+14.1	+14.6*	+1.8
19	—0.3	—1.5	+11.7	+17.0	+13.6	+13.0	+10.7	+ 7.9	+ 2.8	—5.4	—1.1	+12.2	+11.1	+14.3	+14.6*	+1.0
20	—1.5	—1.5	+13.1	+16.0	+13.4	+13.0	+10.8	+ 7.3	+ 2.4	—5.6	—0.6	+12.4	+10.6	+14.6	+13.6*	+0.5
21	—1.7	—1.0	+11.9	+14.8	+13.4	+12.9	+10.0	+ 7.2	+ 1.8	—5.5	0.0	+13.2	+ 9.6	+14.0	+11.2	+1.0
22	—1.0	—0.4	+12.4	+15.3	+12.4	+14.2	+ 9.3	+ 7.2	+ 1.9	—5.3	0.0	+12.7	+ 9.8	+13.8	+ 9.8	+3.8
23	—0.2	—0.4	+13.3	+14.8	+13.6	+14.4	+ 8.5	+ 6.2	+ 2.1	—5.5	—1.2	+12.7	+10.8	+13.6	+ 8.7	+4.9
Midn't	+1.2	0.0	+15.3	+14.7	+13.9	+14.1	+12.0	+ 4.8	+ 3.0	—4.4	—1.1	+12.7	+11.7	+13.4	(+7.4)	+5.8
Means	+2.05	+1.82	+ 7.26	+15.54	+14.12	+14.28	+10.35	+ 9.11	+ 5.42	—1.97	—3.80	+11.74	+12.08	+14.06	+12.50	+2.73

Hour.	17th.	18th.	19th.	20th.	21st.	22d.	23d.	24th.	25th.	26th.	27th.	28th.	29th.	30th.	31st.	Means.
	°	°	°	°	°	°	°	°	°	°	°	°	°	°	°	°
1h.	+5.8	— 2.4	+14.1	—0.9	— 4.7	—14.8	—20.0	—1.5	+ 8.2	+8.3	— 1.5	—16.7	—15.5	—15.5	—10.4	+1.96
2	+5.1	— 1.5	+15.8	—1.3	— 5.5	—16.5	—20.5	—1.5	+ 8.2	+7.2	— 1.5	—16.0	—16.5	—16.0	—10.9	+1.57
3	+5.1	— 0.9	+17.1	—1.4	— 6.5	—16.6	—21.6	+0.5	+ 8.3	+6.2	+ 0.5	—13.7	—17.5	—16.7	—10.9	+1.79
4	+5.1	— 0.4	+17.5	—3.1	— 6.8	—17.1	—22.4	+0.1	+ 9.3	+7.0	+ 0.5	—13.5	—17.8	—17.5	— 9.4	+1.92
5	+3.8	— 1.1	+16.3	—2.5	— 7.5	—11.0	—20.0	+0.4	+ 9.5	+6.7	— 2.0	—16.5	—18.5	—17.3	—10.8	+1.82
6	+4.2	— 2.0	+16.2	—2.5	—10.4	—18.8	—20.4	+1.8	+ 9.6	+5.3	— 2.3	—16.9	—18.3	—16.8	—11.5	+1.38
7	+4.7	— 0.1	+17.5	—3.0	—11.4	—18.7	—18.5	+1.6	+11.1	+5.6	— 5.0	—16.9	—17.5	—16.6	—12.5	+1.52
8	+4.7	— 0.5	+17.2	—3.4	— 9.4	—19.9	—18.7	+1.5	+ 9.8	+5.1	— 7.4	—16.5	—17.8	—16.4	—13.5	+1.41
9	+4.0	+ 2.7	+16.8	—3.8	— 8.7	—19.1	—12.5	+2.6	+ 9.5	+2.5	— 8.8	—16.5	—18.0	—16.2	—13.8	+1.87
10	+2.7	(+3.7)	+16.5	—5.2	— 6.0	—18.0	—15.9	+2.9	+ 9.3	+2.0	— 8.1	—15.6	—18.5	—17.0	—15.5	+1.81
11	+2.0	(+4.7)	+15.0	—6.1	— 5.5	—17.6	—14.2	+4.7	+ 9.3	+2.2	—10.6	—15.5	—18.0	—16.1	—16.0	+2.01
Noon	+1.0	(+5.7)	+15.0	—6.4	— 5.5	—18.9	—13.5	+6.6	+ 9.5	+2.4	—12.0	—16.1	—16.2	—15.6	—15.7	+2.23
13	—0.5	(+6.7)	+15.0	—7.4	— 9.2	—19.3	—12.5	+7.4	+ 8.8	+3.3	—12.0	—10.7	—17.5	—14.8	—15.0	+2.00
14	(—0.8)	+ 7.7	+16.2	—7.9	— 8.0	—19.3	—11.4	+7.7	+ 8.8	+3.3	—13.5	— 9.4	—18.1	—13.7	—14.6	+1.90
15	—1.1	+11.3	+15.0	—7.9	— 7.0	—20.0	— 8.4	+9.8	+ 8.0	+3.3	—14.5	— 9.4	—18.2	—12.5	—14.7	+2.04
16	—1.0	+11.7	+14.8	—5.0	— 9.8	—19.9	— 4.0	+8.7	+ 5.6	+0.5	—14.5	—12.8	—18.2	—11.9	—15.5	+1.78
17	0.0	+10.3	+12.4	—5.5	—10.6	—18.9	— 5.3	+9.2	+ 4.2	—0.5	—13.5	—12.8	—18.4	—11.4	—15.0	+1.66
18	—2.5	+11.2	+12.4	—4.8	—13.0	—18.2	— 5.0	+9.6	+ 4.3	—1.5	—14.5	—12.7	—18.7	—11.2	—15.7	+1.38
19	—2.0	+11.5	+11.8	—4.0	—13.0	—19.9	— 4.1	+9.4	+ 5.3	—2.5	—15.3	—14.5	—18.7	—10.5	—15.9	+1.26
20	—2.1	+12.3	+10.5	—3.8	—11.2	—19.9	— 2.7	+9.2	+ 5.3	—3.5	—16.7	—14.7	—17.8	—10.9	—15.9	+1.18
21	—0.9	+12.2	+ 8.5	—2.2	—10.0	—18.5	— 0.5	+8.7	+ 7.2	—4.9	—16.5	—15.7	—17.5	—10.9	—14.5	+1.20
22	—0.5	+12.8	+ 0.5	—1.0	—13.0	—20.6	— 0.5	+7.7	+ 7.6	—5.5	—15.6	—15.0	—17.0	—10.4	—14.0	+1.01
23	—0.5	+13.3	+ 0.2	—0.5	—11.0	—21.2	— 1.5	+7.7	+ 8.3	—6.6	—16.1	—14.7	—17.5	—10.4	—14.0	+1.02
Midn't	—1.0	+13.2	0.0	—0.5	—11.0	—20.5	— 1.5	+7.4	+ 8.5	—7.1	—16.3	—16.5	—16.0	—10.4	—14.3	+1.21
Means	+1.47	+ 5.92	+13.01	—3.75	— 8.95	—18.47	—11.48	+5.09	+ 8.06	+1.62	— 9.88	—14.55	—17.65	—14.03	—13.33	+1.62

[1] Observations by spirit standard *S*.

* Supplied from observations on deck, and referred to floe.

Oct. 25th. Astronomically, the upper limb of the sun would, by calculation, graze the horizon at noon. The sun was last seen on the 15th, on account of hills and clouds obstructing the view.

TEMPERATURE OF THE AIR IN SHADE OBSERVED AT VAN RENSSELAER HARBOR,

In November, 1853, in Lat. 78° 37′, Long. 70° 53′ W. of Greenwich.

Expressed in degrees of Fahrenheit's scale. At meteorological observatory on floe.[1]

Hour.	1st.	2d.	3d.	4th.	5th.	6th.	7th.	8th.	9th.	10th.	11th.	12th.	13th.	14th.	15th.	16th.
	°	°	°	°	°	°	°	°	°	°	°	°	°	°	°	°
1h.	—12.7	—20.3	—21.2	—14.8	—10.9	—23.5	—20.9	—10.3	—26.2	—25.0	— 8.7	—15.6	—16.0	—22.5	—26.5	—29.0
2	13.3	20.5	21.3	14.0	9.4	22.5	20.5	10.1	24.8	27.0	8.7	16.7	16.0	22.5	27.2	29.0
3	11.5	21.0	22.0	14.3	10.5	18.0	20.7	10.8	22.0	27.0	10.0	16.7	16.5	23.5	25.0	29.4
4	11.7	21.5	21.5	14.5	10.5	18.1	20.8	10.7	23.1	21.0	9.6	16.7	17.5	24.0	26.6	28.5
5	8.7	20.0	20.4	15.2	10.3	24.0	22.4	10.3	25.0	19.8	8.4	14.7	18.2	24.7	27.2	29.0
6	8.6	20.1	20.4	17.0	10.0	23.5	21.8	10.2	26.2	26.9	7.2	10.7	19.0	25.0	27.5	29.0
7	8.7	20.2	21.0	18.2	9.8	21.5	21.0	10.4	28.0	26.5	7.0	6.5	18.0	21.6	28.1	28.6
8	9.4	20.0	19.8	17.7	10.0	20.5	21.3	12.8	27.0	26.8	7.5	5.5	18.3	21.3	27.4	28.9
9	9.2	20.2	19.5	17.2	10.1	21.4	19.0	14.6	28.7	25.5	8.6	4.2	18.2	24.2	26.6	28.0
10	9.2	20.0	20.0	18.0	10.2	19.3	16.4	17.0	27.5	28.8	10.2	4.3	18.6	24.3	26.8	27.5
11	9.2	21.0	19.8	18.2	10.5	18.5	16.0	17.0	27.0	25.5	17.0	2.0	18.8	24.4	26.9	27.9
Noon	9.3	20.3	19.8	17.6	11.1	16.0	10.0	20.6	26.8	22.0	17.4	1.8	19.5	24.8	26.5	27.6
13	9.4	19.5	19.0	17.7	11.5	14.4	10.0	21.8	26.7	22.2	19.6	4.5	18.2	24.5	27.5	29.8
14	9.9	19.5	19.3	17.5	11.9	14.0	9.7	24.0	26.0	16.5	22.5	8.7	19.1	25.0	27.0	27.2
15	10.4	20.0	19.8	16.3	13.7	14.0	9.7	19.0	27.0	16.5	23.0	11.0	19.8	24.7	27.2	25.5
16	13.0	20.6	19.4	13.7	13.9	15.8	9.7	17.0	22.5	18.3	19.0	11.5	19.5	25.8	28.0	25.6
17	15.5	20.2	18.7	13.5	13.0	15.8	9.8	18.0	21.6	7.5*	16.5	11.0	20.0	27.5	28.2	26.0
18	16.3	20.0	17.5	13.2	11.5	16.7	9.5	19.5	22.8	9.2	16.8	11.6	20.5	27.4	28.0	27.5
19	18.0	20.2	17.5	14.8	12.1	16.7	9.5	19.4	23.7	8.6	17.4	13.3	21.1	26.8	28.0	27.0
20	18.7	20.5	17.5	16.2	11.9	16.0	9.8	19.5	24.2	9.2	17.6	14.7	21.7	25.8	28.4	26.0
21	19.2	21.4	19.5	15.5	16.5	14.8	10.1	17.1	25.6	7.8	19.1	12.8	22.4	25.6	27.5	25.6
22	20.0	21.4	19.3	13.4	18.4	14.0	10.4	17.6	25.2	7.8	18.4	15.2	21.8	26.8	27.8	27.9
23	19.0	21.3	18.2	11.8	20.8	18.0	10.4	21.0	25.6	7.8	18.0	16.1	22.9	26.2	28.0	26.4
Midn't	—20.0	—21.5	—16.2	—11.2	—20.8	—20.5	—10.7	—24.2	—23.2	— 6.5	—17.2	—16.6	—23.8	—26.5	—27.9	—26.4
Means	—12.95	—20.47	—19.53	—15.48	—12.47	—18.23	—14.63	—16.37	—25.27	—18.32	—14.39	—10.93	—19.39	—24.80	—27.32	—27.64

Hour.	17th.	18th.	19th.	20th.	21st.	22d.	23d.	24th.	25th.	26th.	27th.	28th.	29th.	30th.	31st.	Means.
	°	°	°	°	°	°	°	°	°	°	°	°	°	°	°	°
1h.	—28.5	—27.6	—33.0	—35.0	—26.5	—36.8	—36.5	—39.5	—38.1	—22.0	—25.0	—16.3	— 1.5	—9.0	...	—22.65
2	28.0	28.7	33.0	35.0	27.0	36.1	36.0	39.7	38.0	20.5	28.3	16.2	— 2.0	7.7	...	—22.66
3	27.6	27.6	31.5	35.0	28.5	35.2	36.2	39.5	37.5	20.0	28.5	17.1	+ 0.5	5.0	...	—22.27
4	28.0	30.5	31.0	35.0	28.5	34.9	35.0	40.0	35.7	16.8	25.5	18.2	+ 0.5	4.5	...	—21.98
5	27.5	30.5	33.2	34.0	29.6	35.5	37.5	40.6	37.1	24.1	24.0	20.0	0.0	4.8	...	—22.56
6	27.1	30.4	33.7	34.0	28.0	37.5	37.8	41.8	37.7	25.4	23.6	21.0	0.0	4.2	...	—22.84
7	27.3	31.2	33.2	34.9	29.6	36.7	37.5	40.0	37.2	26.9	23.1	20.8	+ 0.5	6.2	...	—22.65
8	28.0	31.3	32.8	34.0	29.3	37.0	36.8	40.0	34.8	26.9	20.4	19.1	+ 0.5	5.8	...	—22.33
9	27.0	32.1	32.2	33.8	30.4	36.5	36.5	38.5	32.5	27.5	21.0	17.0	+ 1.0	3.5	...	—22.09
10	26.4	32.6	33.0	31.6	30.6	36.5	36.5	39.0	32.0	29.5	21.0	16.0	+ 0.6	5.8	...	—22.27
11	27.9	32.1	33.0	31.0	31.5	36.5	37.0	38.0	30.5	29.4	21.5	14.8	— 3.0	5.0	...	—22.36
Noon	29.0	32.6	33.1	33.0	31.8	36.5	36.0	38.0	31.5	29.6	21.0	14.5	— 5.5	5.0	...	—22.27
13	30.0	31.0	34.2	33.2	33.0	36.5	37.0	39.2	31.7	28.2	20.0	14.0	— 6.3	5.0	...	—22.52
14	29.5	31.5	32.5	32.5	33.0	37.5	38.0	38.3	28.0	26.4	21.7	12.5	—10.2	3.5	...	—22.43
15	29.5	31.0	35.0	33.0	33.5	35.5	38.2	37.5	27.6	27.4	21.7	12.0	—12.5	4.0	...	—22.53
16	26.8	31.0	35.1	33.8	35.7	32.7	38.0	36.5	27.5	28.0	22.5	9.5	—14.2	4.8	...	—22.31
17	24.5	33.1	35.8	33.0	35.0	31.5	38.5	36.2	28.5	26.2	20.9	5.7	—13.5	5.0	...	—21.67
18	26.6	33.6	35.5	30.8	34.8	31.5	38.0	37.8	25.7	27.2	21.8	5.4	—13.5	5.8	...	—21.87
19	25.5	33.0	35.2	29.6	33.5	31.0	37.0	37.9	25.1	27.6	22.2	8.1	—14.5	6.0	...	—22.01
20	25.8	33.2	34.0	29.7	34.0	31.5	38.0	37.2	24.1	25.2	23.0	7.0	—17.0	7.6	...	—22.17
21	22.4	32.2	35.1	28.4	36.2	35.5	39.0	38.0	23.5	26.3	22.5	6.5	—21.5	8.5	...	—22.54
22	22.5	32.1	35.2	28.1	36.0	34.5	37.7	38.0	20.0	29.4	22.5	5.2	—23.0	8.2	...	—22.59
23	22.9	32.2	35.2	28.0	36.1	36.0	40.0	38.0	20.0	29.5	23.0	5.2	—24.0	10.5	...	—23.07
Midn't	—23.2	—32.9	—35.3	—27.0	—36.3	—36.0	—39.0	—37.5	—21.5	—29.6	—19.8	— 2.0	—17.0	—11.0	...	—22.71
Means	—26.73	—31.42	—33.78	—32.22	—32.02	—35.23	—37.40	—38.61	—30.24	—26.23	—22.69	—12.67	— 8.15	— 6.10	...	—22.39

[1] Temperatures noted by spirit standard *S*, till Nov. 2d, 4h.; after this hour, and throughout the month, the indications of the mercurial standard (*M*) are given.

* Corrected by 20°.

NOTES.—Nov. 5th. Thermometers were read at 2 o'clock P. M. without a light. Nov. 10th. At noon, the thermometers could no more be read without the use of a lantern; on the 14th inst., they were again read at 11 and 12 A. M., during bright moonlight. Nov. 22d. The darkness is now complete, being barely able to read at noonday; upper limb of sun below the horizon 7° 53′. Nov. 23d. The thermometer was 10° lower outside (or at —48°) than in the harbor; at this temperature, whiskey froze in the tent.

TEMPERATURE OF THE AIR IN SHADE OBSERVED AT VAN RENSSELAER HARBOR,

In December, 1853, in Lat. 78° 37′, Long. 70° 53′ W. of Greenwich.

Expressed in degrees of Fahrenheit's scale. At meteorological observatory on floe.[1]

Hour.	1st.	2d.	3d.	4th.	5th.	6th.	7th.	8th.	9th.	10th.	11th.	12th.	13th.	14th.	15th.	16th.
	°	°	°	°	°	°	°	°	°	°	°	°	°	°	°	°
1h.	—16.5	—29.5	—33.5	—25.0	— 8.5	—30.5	—26.4	—39.5	—35.0	—26.0	—13.5	—30.0	—27.5	—39.0	—42.5	—39.5
2	20.5	33.4	31.5	26.5	9.5	29.5	26.0	39.5	34.0	25.5	13.5	28.5	28.7	39.5	42.5	40.4
3	23.5	35.0	31.5	26.4	13.5	27.0	26.0	39.5	34.0	24.5	15.5	29.5	29.5	39.4	43.5	42.5
4	26.6	34.6	29.7	27.3	14.0	27.0	24.0	41.0	34.5	23.5	18.5	29.6	29.5	39.5	43.5	41.5
5	29.5	28.2	29.0	26.4	15.5	23.8	32.5	41.5	34.8	22.1	21.2	26.6	27.0	38.2	41.0	40.2
6	31.0	27.3	26.5	25.0	21.0	23.4	31.0	43.2	36.0	19.6	23.1	23.9	27.5	39.0	42.5	40.5
7	32.5*	24.7	26.5	23.0	17.0	26.1	31.6	41.9	33.0	19.0	23.0	24.9	29.0	37.4	41.0	40.4
8	31.7	25.2	24.5	22.2	20.5	29.2	32.0	42.5	31.5	17.8	20.5	25.4	30.5	39.4	41.5	42.0
9	28.0	24.5	25.5	26.4	24.0	31.5	37.0	41.5	34.6	15.0	20.0	26.0	30.0	40.0	42.5	42.5
10	32.0	26.0	25.5	23.6	26.5	32.0	38.3	42.5	34.0	15.0	23.8	25.8	31.5	39.8	42.9	42.7
11	30.5	24.5	26.0	23.0	28.4	32.7	37.8	42.0	34.5	12.5	24.6	26.5	34.8	40.5	43.0	41.5
Noon	24.5	22.5	26.0	20.8	28.5	33.2	38.5	43.5	31.5	10.5	26.0	26.5	34.5	40.5	42.5	41.5
13	20.9	21.0	27.1	12.0	27.4	33.7	36.9	43.5	28.8	10.3	26.4	26.5	35.0	39.5	41.6	42.0
14	23.0	22.5	26.1	12.0	27.2	33.7	37.8	43.9	25.4	10.5	27.4	27.5	35.4	38.5	41.6	39.5
15	23.1	24.5	26.2	12.5	28.2	33.5	40.8	43.9	26.8	10.0	27.9	27.0	34.0	37.5	41.4	40.5
16	22.2	26.0	27.7	14.5	27.2	33.0	42.0	44.0	26.3	9.5	27.9	25.5	35.2	40.0	39.4	40.5
17	23.0†	25.5	29.5	18.0	32.5	33.0	38.5	44.0	24.5	10.5	30.5	25.3	37.0	42.6	39.5	34.5
18	23.0	26.0	30.5	18.5	33.5	33.5	37.1	44.0	26.5	12.2	31.0	26.3	38.0	42.0	39.5	37.5
19	20.5	25.5	31.0	19.0	33.5	33.0	39.5	44.0	24.5	12.4	29.5	28.3	39.5	41.5	40.5	41.5
20	29.5	28.5	32.5	16.5	31.5	32.5	41.0	44.0	24.0	11.0	28.5	28.6	38.5	41.8	39.0	41.0
21	23.0	26.8	31.0	10.9	32.5	32.8	39.5	39.4	20.5	10.8	31.0	29.2	36.5	40.4	39.8	40.2
22	23.5	26.8	28.5	12.1	31.0	31.5	38.0	35.8	21.5	11.2	31.0	29.5	35.5	41.3	37.5	40.9
23	27.0	26.8	27.5	11.0	30.8	30.0	38.5	36.1	21.8	13.0	29.5	28.2	37.0	41.0	37.5	41.0
Midn't	—31.0	—30.4	—26.0	— 9.5	—29.5	—26.4	—40.0	—35.0	—23.5	—13.2	—28.5	—27.8	—37.5	—41.5	—38.0	—42.2
Means	—25.69	—26.90	—28.30	—19.25	—24.65	—30.52	—35.45	—41.49	—29.23	—15.23	—24.68	—27.20	—33.30	—39.99	—41.01	—40.69

Hour.	17th.	18th.	19th.	20th.	21st.	22d.	23d.	24th.	25th.	26th.	27th.	28th.	29th.	30th.	31st.	Means.
	°	°	°	°	°	°	°	°	°	°	°	°	°	°	°	°
1h.	—41.5	—39.5	—21.5	—30.0	—35.0	—34.8	—28.7	—13.5	—19.0	—26.5	—14.5	+13.0	— 0.8	—19.5	—11.5	—25.35
2	42.3	38.0	21.0	30.5	33.5	35.6	27.5	13.5	19.7	23.0	14.0	+13.0	— 0.8	19.5	10.0	—25.32
3	43.5	36.0	20.5	29.5	33.8	36.0	21.5	14.8	19.5	27.5	13.5	+13.5	— 0.8	20.5	10.0	—25.64
4	42.3	37.8	19.5	29.5	33.0	36.8	18.0	15.5	20.0	25.6	13.0	+15.8	— 0.8	21.7	9.5	—25.53
5	43.4	36.6	18.8	27.7	34.8	36.8	11.5	11.2	18.0	23.2	12.2	+16.5	+ 1.4	21.6	8.5	—24.64
6	42.5	32.8	19.8	31.6	31.0	37.5	11.9	11.4	19.4	23.2	13.9	+16.0	— 0.5	21.5	8.2	—24.83
7	42.0	31.9	17.5	34.2	31.1	38.0	11.1	10.8	20.8	22.5	14.4	+ 8.7	— 1.5	20.3	8.2	—24.73
8	37.5	29.5	17.9	35.0	32.0	37.2	16.0	11.5	22.5	22.5	13.3	+ 7.0	— 2.4	21.0	6.9	—24.99
9	39.0	28.5	16.4	31.0	32.0	37.3	14.0	11.6	23.3	21.6	12.5	+ 8.5	— 6.6	22.0	7.5	—25.28
10	39.2	27.5	16.7	32.4	31.6	37.5	12.3	12.2	22.2	21.0	12.5	+ 8.5	— 8.0	21.3	8.0	—25.67
11	39.5	25.8	16.8	33.5	31.0	37.2	12.4	12.0	23.4	21.3	12.6	+ 9.8	—12.5	20.3	8.1	—25.79
Noon	41.0	25.0	16.5	30.0	32.3	33.9	11.5	12.3	23.6	21.5	12.0	+ 9.0	—14.5	19.5	8.5	—25.29
13	40.5	25.5	18.0	35.3	34.5	33.2	9.7	12.3	28.5	20.3	12.0	+ 9.5	—16.3	17.1	6.5	—24.93
14	41.0	24.5	21.7	34.3	37.8	32.0	10.3	12.2	28.7	20.4	11.8	+11.0	—16.8	16.7	7.3	—25.05
15	42.0	26.5	23.3	36.6	37.5	35.0	12.0	12.0	29.0	20.5	11.2	+ 7.7	—16.9	15.8	7.5	—25.67
16	38.4	27.5	26.5	36.5	39.5	35.5	15.0	12.0	30.1	19.5	10.2	+ 6.5	—17.2	16.5	7.6	—26.01
17	41.0	25.5	23.6	36.2	39.9	39.0	14.8	10.2	29.0	19.2	9.1	+ 4.9	—13.6	14.2	7.5	—26.01
18	41.5	25.2	24.6	38.2	40.0	32.8	14.0	10.1	29.5	19.0	8.4	+ 4.2	—12.4	13.6	8.0	—26.20
19	41.5	25.4	28.2	40.0	39.4	36.5	12.1	10.1	29.1	19.0	7.5	+ 2.5	—15.1	13.5	8.0	—26.73
20	41.5	25.0	30.1	40.2	37.0	34.6	12.2	11.0	27.4	18.5	5.2	+ 2.0	—16.4	12.5	7.8	—26.64
21	38.7	22.8	34.0	33.6	28.6	31.0	13.0	13.0	26.0	18.5	4.6	+ 1.1	—18.0	12.6	11.0	—25.44
22	38.7	22.0	34.9	30.8	28.5	31.0	12.6	13.0	27.5	17.8	3.5	+ 1.8	—20.2	12.8	10.8	—25.09
23	38.5	23.0	35.0	32.5	35.0	30.2	12.2	13.0	26.8	16.8	5.8	+ 2.2	—18.2	10.8	9.3	—25.18
Midn't	—37.5	—22.6	—30.5	—32.8	—31.6	—29.0	—12.0	—13.0	—26.5	—16.5	— 6.4	+ 1.8	—18.8	—12.5	— 5.5	—24.95
Means	—40.60	—28.52	—23.05	—33.41	—34.18	—34.93	—14.43	—12.18	—24.56	—21.06	—10.59	+ 8.10	—10.32	—17.39	— 8.40	—25.46

[1] Temperatures noted by the mercurial standard (*M*); readings between —40°.0 and —44°.0 checked by spirit standard (*S*), or noted by the latter instrument.

* Temperature falling 21°.8 in eight hours.

† Corrected by 10°.

Dec. 20th. At 3½ P. M., the temperature at the floe was —36°.5; the party at skirts of bay obtained, for the same hour, —43°.0.

Dec. 22d. Maximum depression of the sun below the horizon, at noon and for the upper limb, 11° 7′.

Dec. 28th. First heavy gale experienced since the closure of the winter harbor; wind from the S. E. (magnetic). Rise of temperature, between 0h. and 1h., 19°.4—the most sudden change yet noted.

TEMPERATURE OF THE AIR IN SHADE OBSERVED AT VAN RENSSELAER HARBOR,
In January, 1854, in Lat. 78° 37′, Long. 70° 53′ W. of Greenwich.
Expressed in degrees of Fahrenheit's scale. At meteorological observatory on floe.[1]

Hour.	1st.	2d.	3d.	4th.	5th.	6th.	7th.	8th.	9th.	10th.	11th.	12th.	13th.	14th.	15th.	16th.
	°	°	°	°	°	°	°	°	°	°	°	°	°	°	°	°
1h.	—4.5	+ 2.0	+7.0	—11.6	— 8.0	—4.5	—4.8	—12.6	—23.0	—30.0	—29.6	—36.0	—21.8	—25.0	—43.2	—38.0
2	—4.5	+ 2.0	+4.0	11.8	10.5	4.7	4.8	16.7	23.5	30.0	34.1	36.5	25.5	25.0	44.5	39.5
3	—3.5	+ 2.0	+3.8	12.5	13.5	5.5	6.0	16.6	24.5	29.2	36.2	36.5	25.7	25.1	43 8	43.2
4	—3.5	— 1.0	+3.0	13.0	14.5	6.5	7.2	17.6	26.0	30.2	37.0	36.0	23.6	24.0	44.5	44.5
5	—3.5	— 2.4	+4.1	11.1	15.7	8.8	6.4	15.5	27.0	31.9	36.0	35.2	23.5	25.0	41.9	44.5
6	—2.1	+ 3.0	+3.6	10.4	14.0	9.2	6.8	17.0	26.8	32.8	36.2	35.3	23.7	26.5	43.2	45.0
7	—2.0	+ 0.9	+3.6	10.6	13.6	9.0	8.0	16.8	29.0	33.5	37.5	33.7	23.6	29.0	41.9	45.0
8	—2.0	+ 0.9	+3.5	10.8	13.0	11.1	8.0	19.5	29.2	32.8	37.4	32.5	23.0	29.0	42.3	45.8
9	—1.5	+ 0.4	+4.7	11.7	9.5	11.0	9.0	20.6	29.7	32.2	39.5	35.7	23.4	28.8	41.9	47.3
10	—2.1	+ 1.0	+4.7	11.5	10.2	9.0	7.5	24.5	29.2	31.9	39.5	30.0	23.0	29.0	45.2	47.3
11	—1.4	+ 5.0	+4.4	11.5	10.0	8.8	9.5	23.0	28.3	33.1	38.7	28.0	23.5	30.5	45.2	48.5
Noon	—1.3	+ 9.0	+3.2	12.0	8.2	7.5	4.9	18.5	28.5	29.4	38.0	32.8	22.9	31.0	45.8	46.8
13	—0.5	+11.5	+3.2	11.0	10.5	9.7	9.8	17.8	30.2	34.5	38.5	28.6	23.0	32.8	47.3	47.9
14	0.0	+ 9.7	+2.8	11.7	7.0	9.7	8.2	17.0	29.5	34.0	38.3	28.0	25.0	34.5	45.1	48.1
15	+1.6	+ 8.0	+1.2	14.0	9.0	12.0	8.5	23.8	28.1	35.0	35.5	26.1	27.0	34.7	43.2	48.5
16	+1.2	+ 8.5	+1.8	12.0	10.5	10.5	9.8	23.5	28.8	36.0	35.4	24.8	26.8	34.5	42.4	50.4
17	+1.8	+10.1	+1.5	10.8	10.8	7 0	7.6	24.9	31.0	36.0	35.2	25.0*	29.5	36.8	39.0	50.4
18	+1.5	+ 9.5	+0.4	10.2	13.5	6.0	7.6	25.6	31.0	38.5	35.8	23.0*	27.5	36.8	35.5	51.1
19	+1.0	+ 7.2	—0.2	9.8	13.4	2.2	9.0	25.2	32.0	38.5	32.8	24.1	29.0	38.4	34.5	50.4
20	+2.0	+ 7.2	—0.2	9.6	12.8	2.6	9.0	25.5	32.0	37.5	32.4	23.1	28.5	36.4	35.5	50.4
21	+1.5	+ 7.0	0.0	9.5	13.0	4.0	7.0	26.5	28.5	36.5	36.0	22.0	25.0	41.1	34.3	45.6
22	+0.5	+ 6.8	0.0	9.5	9.0	3.8	8.2	23.5	30.0	35.0	37.0	21 5	26.5	41.1	35.5	47.9
23	+0.5	+ 6.5	0.0	9.0	8.8	5.6	8.2	23.5	34.2	34.0	37.8	21.5	26.5	41.0	36.3	49.7
Midn't	+2.0	+ 5.0	—4.5	— 9.0	— 5.5	—6.0	—8.8	—23.5	—30.5	—28.0	—37.6	—21.0	—25.5	—41.0	—36.4	—48.5
Means	—0.78	+ 4.99	+2.32	—11.03	—11.02	—7.28	—7.69	—20.80	—28.77	—33.35	—36.33	—29.04	—25.12	—32.38	—41.18	—46.85

Hour.	17th.	18th.	19th.	20th.	21st.	22d.	23d.	24th.	25th.	26th.	27th.	28th.	29th.	30th.	31st.	Means.
	°	°	°	°	°	°	°	°	°	°	°	°	°	°	°	°
1h.	—48.9	—39.5	—48.1	—52.5	—44.5	—26.5	—31.9	—29.5	—38.5	—21.5	—35.5	—28.5	—45.6	—47.3	—40.5	—27.82
2	49.3	42.1	47.1	52.9	39.0	27.9	38.6	29.5	36.3	21.0	32.5	28.5	45.6	49.3	43.2	—28.66
3	49.1	44.5	48.5	53.6	39.0	25.0	35.5	32.5	33.2	21.0	32.0	27.0	43.2	50.4	44.5	—28.87
4	49.1	47.1	47.9	54.2	37.0	22.9	34.5	33.5	30.0	19.5	29.6	29.0	46.8	47.9	41.9	—28.94
5	48.1	49.8	47.9	56.2	37.5	23.5	37.5	32.0	28.0	19.0	30.0	28.5	47.3	44.5	43.9	—28.97
6	47.9	48.7	47.9	56.9	37.5	23.5	37.5	33.0	27.5	19.0	30.8	26.4	42.4	47.2	44.7	—28.82
7	43.8	49.1	51.6	58.3	37.0	24.5	40.5	30.8	32.0	19.0	31.0	29.5	43.2	47.0	40.2	—29.23
8	44.2	46.2	51.6	55.5	35.2	22.5	38.5	31.5	28.5	19.2	31.0	30.0	43.4	46.3	41.0	—28.92
9	42.5	48.5	51.2	56.6	34.5	24.5	37.2	33.7	32.0	19.5	33.8	29.2	42.0	51.6	37.2	—29.38
10	40.3	46.8	52.9	58.0	36.2	25.5	31.2	32.3	32.8	20.1	35.0	37.0	43.5	46.8	33.7	—29.24
11	38.7	46.8	54.2	54.9	38.0	31.4	31.0	28.5	33.2	20.5	36.0	38.3	43.4	39.7	31.0	—28.91
Noon	35.3	49.1	52.9	53.4	36.0	36.0	30.5	34.5	29.0	22.5	37.5	38.0	44.5	41.9	28.7	—28.55
13	34.5	46.2	51.0	50.4	37.5	38.4	36.5	36.5	26.9	24.7	35.5	40.5	45.0	46.1	31.5	—29.31
14	30.7	43.8	52.2	51.6	37.5	40.5	36.5	36.5	23.0	26.5	35.5	41.8	46.4	47.3	32.5	—29.22
15	40.5	46.2	51.8	51.6	37.7	40.6	32.0	37.5	23.0	28.5	34.0	44.5	44.5	47.4	37.0	—30.05
16	43.2	45.6	53.5	50.4	39.5	39.7	36.0	37.0	23.0	32.5	31.0	45.6	43.2	46.0	39.6	—30.31
17	45.6	44.5	51.6	45.0	39.0	40.5	30.5	36.0	23.5	33.5	29.7	46.3	46.8	36.0	40.2	—29.65
18	41.3	41.9	49.1	45.6	35.5	39.5	30.6	38.0	24.2	32.5	28.6	43.8	48.5	37.5	40.2	—29.27
19	41.9	44.5	50.4	45.3	40.3	41.0	28.0	38.7	23.0	32.5	28.0	47.3	48.5	37.0	39.9	—29.60
20	41.3	44.7	52.9	50.0	41.5	41.0	30.5	39.0	22.0	33.5	26.0	45.6	47.3	39.0	40.0	—29.70
21	39.8	45.9	52.5	45.6	35.0	41.0	28.5	37.8	21.5	33.2	28.5	45.8	45.8	43.2	40.0	—29.18
22	39.0	47.9	53.2	48.5	37.0	39.0	26.8	38.9	22.0	34.1	28.0	45.3	45.0	40.2	40 0	—29.23
23	36.8	48.5	53.5	48.5	31.0	44.6	29.5	39.4	22.0	32.6	28.2	46.5	46.8	40.5	43.2	—29.70
Midn't	—40.7	—48.4	—52.2	—47.9	—29.0	—40.0	—30.4	—39.3	—22.5	—33.6	—29.3	—46.3	—47.0	—41.2	—44.7	—29.40
Means	—42.19	—46.10	—51.07	—51.81	—37.16	—33.31	—33.34	—34.83	—27.40	—25.81	—31.54	—37.88	—45.24	—44.22	—39.14	—29.21

[1] Temperatures above —40°, noted by (*M*); lower temperatures, by (*S*). * Readings changed by 10°.

Jan. 4th. To-day at noon a distinct zone of illumination was seen to the south, clearly defining the highest hills. Upper limb of sun still 10° 25′ below the horizon. The largest print is illegible at noon.

Jan. 7th. The increased illumination of the southern horizon is distinctly visible; we cannot yet read large print. (K.) Same remark on Jan. 18th.

Jan. 19th. To-day I read the title-page of my prayer-book, by turning the type towards the illuminated sky to the southward. Upper limb depressed below the horizon at noon 7° 55′.

Jan. 22d. Spirit standard read at 12 o'clock without artificial light. At 2 P. M. dark, with a faint streak of light to the south.

TEMPERATURE OF THE AIR IN SHADE OBSERVED AT VAN RENSSELAER HARBOR,

In February, 1854, in Lat. 78° 37′, Long. 70° 53′ W. of Greenwich.

Expressed in degrees of Fahrenheit's scale. At meteorological observatory on floe.[1]

Hour.	1st.	2d.	3d.	4th.	5th.	6th.	7th.	8th.	9th.	10th.	11th.	12th.	13th.	14th.	15th.
	°	°	°	°	°	°	°	°	°	°	°	°	°	°	°
1h.	—46.8	—41.0	—56.0	—46.2	—52.9	—51.3	—55.5	—24.5	—49.1	—48.5	—30.0	—34.3	—28.7	—24.5	—31.7
2	47.9	41.0	56.2	46.8	56.9	51.6	54.2	27.2	45.1	43.2	29.7	33.5	30.5	20.7	31.5
3	44.5	43.7	56.9	49.1	58.0	53.2	41.9	29.2	43.2	43.2	29.2	32.7	30.6	21.0	29.2
4	44.5	39.0	52.2	52.2	60.2	54.2	31.7	23.5	45.6	44.5	31.0	32.3	32.5	22.0	29.7
5	44.5	42.0	53.4	56.0	62.1	56.9	26.5	31.5	45.8	45.6	31.5	30.8	34.5	26.2	30.0
6	39.5	42.8	51.2	60.4	65.0	49.1	27.0	31.7	46.5	43.4	31.2	23.5	34.6	28.3	30.0
7	38.5	42.9	47.4	61.9	66.0	46.8	23.2	31.7	45.8	37.8	31.5	22.5	34.5	30.4	29.5
8	38.8	45.1	44.3	62.9	65.0	46.1	22.0	31.1	44.8	34.0	31.5	21.0	35.0	31.6	28.5
9	47.1	42.5	50.4	62.9	66.4*	44.5	25.0	30.2	45.0	22.0	31.7	22.5	33.7	32.0	22.0
10	47.1	44.7	46.8	51.6	64.5	45.8	21.3	31.7	45.6	21.0	32.2	22.5	36.0	34.2	22.0
11	43.7	45.7	45.6	61.4	64.5	45.6	21.4	31.7	46.2	21.3	33.7	22.5	36.2	34.2	21.0
Noon	39.5	46.2	47.9	61.4	55.5	47.4	20.5	33.0	46.3	21.0	33.5	22.5	35.3	31.5	20.2
13	39.3	43.5	45.4	62.9	54.2	48.5	21.2	33.0	44.5	19.3	33.2	21.9	35.0	29.7	13.5
14	39.0	45.0	44.5	59.9	52.9	49.1	22.0	33.1	42.5	20.0	33.2	20.5	34.8	29.0	13.7
15	39.5	44.1	44.5	56.9	52.2	48.7	22.5	34.5	41.7	20.0	33.0	21.2	34.0	28.5	13.5
16	40.5	48.3	45.1	54.2	49.1	45.6	22.5	36.0	41.3	22.0	32.7	20.1	34.1	29.7	13.5
17	39.5	49.1	46.3	51.6	51.7	47.8	24.0	43.5	45.8	21.5	31.5	20.7	33.5	28.5	10.0
18	39.2	44.5	46.8	48.7	53.9	49.8	21.7	44.1	47.0	21.5	29.0	22.2	32.5	27.5	10.0
19	38.4	46.8	45.6	49.4	51.6	52.9	22.0	40.3	46.5	21.6	30.8	23.3	32.5	28.0	10.0
20	35.2	46.8	47.1	45.6	50.7	54.9	25.0	42.0	45.6	22.3	29.0	25.0	33.0	29.0	10.0
21	37.0	50.7	36.8	49.1	50.8	52.9	20.8	45.6	44.7	23.8	29.6	26.5	33.0	30.5	11.0
22	42.0	49.1	37.8	51.6	50.4	51.6	21.4	50.0	46.1	26.6	32.0	27.4	29.0	32.5	11.5
23	38.7	51.6	38.8	54.2	51.2	57.7	21.9	42.4	46.8	29.5	33.5	25.9	26.0	33.6	11.5
Midn't	—38.0	—55.5	—40.8	—56.2	—51.6	—58.3	—22.4	—43.4	—47.0	—30.0	—30.8	—24.8	—25.5	—33.6	—11.0
Means	—41.20	—45.48	—46.99	—54.59	—56.36	—50.55	—26.57	—35.20	—45.35	—29.32	—31.46	—25.00	—32.71	—29.03	—19.35

Hour.	16th.	17th.	18th.	19th.	20th.	21st.	22d.	23d.	24th.	25th.	26th.	27th.	28th.		Means.
	°	°	°	°	°	°	°	°	°	°	°	°	°		°
1h.	—13.2	—11.0	—22.0	—20.0	—26.8	—31.5	—22.0	—27.7	—33.8	—25.6	—37.2	—38.0	—30.6	...	—34.30
2	13.7	12.2	23.5	19.6	27.6	31.6	20.8	29.5	33.5	24.1	38.7	38.0	30.6	...	—34.26
3	14.2	13.0	25.8	19.0	25.9	30.7	21.0	30.5	33.8	25.0	39.0	38.5	32.5	...	—34.09
4	14.5	12.5	25.8	16.2	27.8	30.0	22.5	29.6	33.3	25.0	31.3	38.5	35.5	...	—33.49
5	14.5	12.5	25.8	16.0	27.5	29.2	23.0	29.5	32.4	26.0	30.1	38.2	34.6	...	—34.16
6	14.0	12.5	25.8	13.6	27.5	26.9	23.0	31.5	32.4	24.5	32.5	37.0	35.0	...	—33.59
7	13.4	15.0	24.6	17.4	23.5	26.7	23.5	32.5	32.5	23.0	32.8	35.3	38.0	...	—33.16
8	14.0	17.0	23.8	17.0	24.0	27.2	22.5	32.0	34.0	25.0	30.0	35.8	35.7	...	—32.85
9	14.8	14.4	22.0	18.6	24.0	24.5	22.0	32.0	33.5	29.4	30.5	35.2	34.7	...	—32.62
10	15.5	15.3	21.0	18.9	20.8	23.0	22.0	32.9	32.3	29.4	31.0	33.0	36.5	...	—32.09
11	14.5	14.7	18.8	20.0	24.0	25.0	22.8	34.0	32.3	29.3	33.0	31.0	33.6	...	—32.42
Noon	15.0	14.5	18.8	21.0	20.8	25.2	22.5	32.4	33.5	30.5	31.5	29.3	33.3	...	—31.79
13	15.7	15.0	18.7	16.5	22.8	25.2	22.5	33.0	36.5	29.2	32.7	31.0	32.6	...	—31.30
14	16.2	17.0	17.0	16.5	25.2	25.4	24.0	34.0	31.4	33.0	32.0	31.4	34.0	...	—31.30
15	16.2	16.7	17.3	18.5	25.3	24.0	24.6	36.0	29.6	34.7	35.2	32.1	35.7	...	—31.45
16	15.0	16.5	16.0	19.8	24.0	24.5	25.7	34.5	31.2	36.3	34.6	33.4	36.8	...	—31.54
17	15.7	15.9	17.0	20.0	25.1	24.6	25.8	32.5	28.2	35.8	34.0	34.9	36.0	...	—31.80
18	14.0	15.9	18.5	20.7	26.8	25.5	26.2	33.2	27.6	38.0	34.3	32.0	35.6	...	—31.67
19	11.7	13.6	17.6	20.8	29.5	25.6	26.4	33.0	27.0	38.8	33.0	32.6	36.2	...	—31.62
20	10.3	13.5	17.0	21.0	28.6	23.0	27.4	36.9	27.5	39.2	36.0	31.5	36.5	...	—31.77
21	11.1	14.0	19.0	24.1	28.5	21.5	27.4	37.5	29.0	40.8	37.4	31.6	37.0	...	—32.20
22	11.3	16.3	20.5	25.5	29.5	24.9	28.0	38.0	29.0	40.8	39.0	31.9	37.9	...	—33.27
23	11.5	18.0	21.4	26.3	29.5	23.7	28.0	35.0	29.5	40.5	38.0	31.5	36.5	...	—33.31
Midn't	—11.3	—20.4	—21.6	—26.9	—30.0	—24.0	—27.0	—35.2	—30.0	—38.9	—37.5	—33.5	—35.2	...	—33.59
Means	—13.80	—14.89	—20.80	—19.75	—26.04	—25.98	—24.19	—33.04	—31.41	—31.78	—34.22	—33.97	—35.03	...	—32.65

[1] Temperatures noted by *M*, down to —40°; lower temperatures by *S′*.

* Minimum temperature observed this winter.

Feb. 3d. Thermometers read at 9 o'clock without the use of a lantern.

Feb. 7th. Between the hours of 2 and 4 A. M., the temperature was elevated 22°.5. Wind from the south, and blowing a gale.

Feb. 16th. By calculation, the upper limb of the sun would graze the horizon at noon. Two days later, a mist prevented its visibility. On the 20th, at noon, his rays shine on the cliffs, on the eastern side of the bay.

TEMPERATURE OF THE AIR IN SHADE OBSERVED AT VAN RENSSELAER HARBOR,

In March, 1854, in Lat. 78° 37′, Long. 70° 53′ W. of Greenwich.

Expressed in degrees of Fahrenheit's scale. At meteorological observatory on floe.[1]

Hour.	1st.	2d.	3d.	4th.	5th.	6th.	7th.	8th.	9th.	10th.	11th.	12th.	13th.	14th.	15th.	16th.
	°	°	°	°	°	°	°	°	°	°	°	°	°	°	°	°
1h.	—37.4	—35.2	—38.6	—41.2	—42.4	—44.7	—47.0	—48.5	—40.5	—48.1	—47.1	—45.6	—47.6	—51.0	—50.4	—27.8
2	36.0	35.2	34.8	42.3	41.9	41.3	47.5	48.2	27.0	48.8	46.8	48.3	49.8	49.9	51.6	34.0
3	37.5	35.8	33.0	42.3	42.4	40.0	46.7	47.6	26.0	49.4	48.5	48.7	51.8	51.0	51.6	34.0
4	37.5	35.5	33.4	42.0	44.6	44.5	45.6	45.6	26.5	50.6	47.9	49.1	50.4	53.3	48.3	33.5
5	38.5	36.5	33.5	45.0	44.5	44.5	45.6	46.8	28.0	50.4	47.9	49.8	49.1	54.2	41.3	33.0
6	37.0	37.5	32.5	44.5	45.6	44.5	48.5	48.5	31.1	49.4	46.9	49.1	49.8	51.8	40.5	32.5
7	36.2	38.5	32.5	46.1	46.8	45.0	49.1	46.8	32.5	49.0	46.8	48.4	49.8	51.0	38.9	31.5
8	39.5	38.5	33.0	45.6	46.8	44.5	49.1	46.8	30.5	47.9	46.8	48.4	50.4	49.1	38.4	30.5
9	41.0	36.5	34.7	45.4	45.4	41.0	46.9	39.3	30.0	47.6	46.3	47.9	51.2	47.9	32.0	30.0
10	40.7	37.1	32.7	45.6	45.8	40.6	46.2	39.5	30.5	45.6	45.9	49.1	46.0	47.4	30.5	30.0
11	36.0	35.0	33.0	43.8	44.0	41.7	45.0	42.3	32.0	44.7	43.4	46.8	43.4	43.5	30.0	30.0
Noon	36.5	36.7	34.0	45.6	43.8	44.5	45.6	43.0	28.0	42.0	44.5	43.2	42.4	44.0	30.0	30.3
13	33.0	36.3	36.5	46.2	43.2	41.5	45.2	44.3	27.3	42.5	45.6	45.0	43.7	40.8	29.8	29.2
14	31.5	37.0	37.5	45.2	44.4	45.6	39.9	45.6	29.3	41.9	44.8	39.7	42.6	41.0	28.7	28.5
15	32.2	37.4	38.2	46.8	40.5	45.8	45.6	42.5	38.3	44.5	43.5	45.6	39.7	39.3	36.3	28.0
16	30.5	37.4	37.0	44.4	45.4	46.8	47.2	42.3	41.5	46.3	45.9	48.5	43.8	46.1	39.7	30.5
17	30.5	36.5	37.5	43.8	45.6	46.2	47.2	42.5	41.5	46.2	45.8	48.7	45.6	45.6	37.5	31.0
18	30.5	37.5	38.0	45.1	46.8	46.8	47.9	42.5	42.5	46.2	46.5	48.1	46.8	47.2	37.0	32.5
19	31.5	38.0	38.5	45.6	47.9	46.8	47.3	42.0	42.6	46.8	46.8	47.4	47.9	46.8	35.5	33.5
20	33.5	38.0	39.0	46.1	48.5	46.8	45.6	42.0	44.5	46.8	47.3	46.8	48.2	47.9	34.0	35.0
21	33.5	36.0	41.6	45.0	46.2	46.2	43.8	41.8	45.8	46.2	47.3	46.8	49.5	48.5	30.5	40.0
22	33.2	37.7	42.4	44.6	46.8	45.6	43.9	41.8	47.4	47.0	46.8	48.7	50.0	49.0	30.0	42.0
23	34.7	37.4	44.1	43.8	49.1	45.8	46.2	41.0	47.6	47.3	45.3	48.7	49.8	49.1	30.0	42.0
Midn't	—35.7	—38.0	—42.4	—42.6	—48.5	—45.6	—47.9	—41.4	—47.9	—47.9	—45.7	—48.6	—49.9	—50.0	—31.6	—44.1
Means	—35.17	—36.88	—36.60	—44.53	—45.29	—44.43	—46.27	—43.86	—35.78	—46.80	—46.25	—47.38	—47.47	—47.72	—36.84	—33.06

Hour.	17th.	18th.	19th.	20th.	21st.	22d.	23d.	24th.	25th.	26th.	27th.	28th.	29th.	30th.	31st.	Means.
	°	°	°	°	°	°	°	°	°	°	°	°	°	°	°	°
1h.	—45.0	—47.0	—39.7	—39.5	—22.5	—17.0	—7.0	—14.5	—28.5	—40.5	—40.3	—36.8	—43.4	—45.1	—41.5	—38.76
2	45.0	47.3	42.8	39.0	22.0	—13.0	7.8	13.3	31.0	44.5	39.5	35.5	44.5	45.6	41.9	—38.58
3	43.2	46.8	43.0	41.9	21.0	—14.0	5.5	14.3	31.5	43.9	39.5	36.6	44.5	46.3	43.4	—38.77
4	46.1	47.9	45.0	42.0	20.5	—14.5	5.3	14.6	32.2	45.1	40.8	34.2	44.6	45.8	42.1	—39.00
5	46.8	47.9	43.2	41.9	20.0	—16.1	5.3	14.4	32.7	46.2	38.0	34.0	45.1	44.8	41.9	—38.93
6	45.6	46.8	44.6	40.8	19.8	—17.1	4.9	14.6	33.2	46.0	37.2	33.5	43.9	41.0	41.0	—38.70
7	44.5	44.5	47.2	42.0	19.2	— 6.0	5.8	14.5	33.6	44.5	36.8	32.0	42.5	41.0	34.6	—37.99
8	43.2	41.9	47.0	37.3	18.0	— 6.0	7.0	14.5	34.0	43.2	34.5	31.0	42.5	40.0	39.2	—37.58
9	40.0	39.7	44.5	41.8	17.2	— 2.5	9.0	13.0	31.5	41.0	33.0	29.5	42.5	39.0	37.0	—36.27
10	41.5	39.7	44.5	39.3	19.2	— 2.0	8.0	15.8	30.0	40.5	32.0	31.0	39.0	37.0	34.0	—35.70
11	40.5	40.9	43.2	34.8	16.2	— 0.5	8.4	15.6	30.0	39.0	28.7	30.2	37.0	37.0	33.4	—34.52
Noon	40.0	38.0	40.5	33.0	16.2	— 0.7	6.5	13.5	30.5	36.4	29.5	31.5	33.0	36.5	33.2	—33.97
13	38.5	36.8	40.8	30.5	15.0	+ 2.5	7.2	14.1	32.0	37.5	28.2	31.2	33.4	35.0	33.5	—33.59
14	38.5	34.8	39.9	30.5	15.0	+ 1.5	7.0	14.5	32.5	37.5	28.0	31.5	30.8	34.3	32.0	—33.18
15	38.7	38.3	37.2	34.0	14.5	— 2.2	5.0	16.0	28.3	37.0	28.0	31.2	28.3	34.5	31.0	—33.82
16	39.5	37.7	36.0	33.5	15.0	— 2.5	5.7	16.5	31.5	37.5	28.2	31.2	31.5	32.5	30.2	—34.91
17	39.5	41.0	37.8	31.5	15.5	— 2.9	8.4	18.0	33.5	41.2	28.5	32.5	35.5	35.5	30.3	—35.59
18	39.7	41.1	37.8	29.5	17.0	— 3.4	5.8	18.8	37.8	41.5	29.6	35.0	35.3	38.1	30.5	—36.22
19	39.7	41.8	37.9	29.5	18.2	— 3.9	6.9	20.6	38.4	44.5	29.2	38.0	34.5	39.9	30.9	—36.74
20	41.9	43.4	38.4	29.5	18.4	— 4.4	9.5	22.0	38.8	44.5	31.0	40.5	39.5	43.2	31.3	—37.62
21	45.1	43.3	38.6	25.0	19.5	— 2.2	10.7	22.1	39.0	43.2	34.0	43.2	41.0	43.2	31.5	—37.75
22	45.8	42.8	39.0	25.0	19.2	— 2.0	11.8	22.6	40.0	41.9	34.5	44.1	39.5	43.2	29.8	—38.00
23	47.9	35.7	39.0	24.5	19.0	— 6.0	12.0	25.0	41.8	43.2	36.0	44.5	40.3	41.5	27.2	—38.24
Midn't	—48.6	—37.0	—39.4	—21.0	—19.0	— 7.8	—12.4	—29.0	—41.0	—41.9	—35.4	—44.5	—41.0	—41.0	—24.0	—38.41
Means	—42.70	—41.75	—41.13	—34.06	—18.21	— 5.95	— 7.62	—17.16	—33.89	—41.76	—33.35	—35.13	—38.88	—40.04	—34.39	—36.79

[1] Temperatures above —40° noted by *M*; below —40°, by *S*.

March 5th. The sun shows upon our observatory on the floe at 10 o'clock A. M. Noticed an effect on the exposed thermometers during sunshine.

March 8th. Sun sunk below the hills at half-past two P. M.

March 9th. Between the hours of one and two A. M., the temperature rose from —40°.5 to —27°.0. At close of the watch, a fresh breeze from the eastward.

March 22d. Temperature rises between six and seven A. M. 11°.1; wind S. E.

TEMPERATURE OF THE AIR IN SHADE OBSERVED AT VAN RENSSELAER HARBOR,

In April, 1854, in Lat. 78° 37′, Long. 70° 53′ W. of Greenwich.

Expressed in degrees of Fahrenheit's scale. At meteorological observatory on floe.[1]

Hour.	1st.	2d.	3d.	4th.	5th.	6th.	7th.	8th.	9th.	10th.	11th.	12th.	13th.	14th.	15th.	16th.
	°	°	°	°	°	°	°	°	°	°	°	°	°	°	°	°
1h.	—20.0	—19.5	(—35.5)	—39.9	—12.6	—13.2	—26.0	—34.0	—20.0	—11.3	—17.4	—25.4	—11.0	+3.4	—4.6	+8.5
2	20.0	19.8	(35.8)	36.4	12.0	12.0	25.8	33.8	19.5	12.0	20.0	23.5	—12.1	+4.0	—4.3	+8.0
3	19.6	20.5	(36.4)	37.2	11.6	11.6	25.0	33.0	20.0	12.8	19.0	24.0	—12.4	+3.7	—7.2	+7.5
4	19.0	21.0	(36.3)	35.7	11.8	11.0	25.0	33.5	20.0	13.3	18.0	23.0	—12.5	+3.4	—6.5	+6.3
5	18.8	21.6	(35.6)	26.7	11.0	10.3	23.7	30.5	17.5	12.0	20.0	20.5	—12.0	+3.9	—6.0	+6.5
6	18.5	18.5	(35.2)	25.5	12.3	11.0	22.0	28.0	17.3	11.0	18.0	19.5	— 9.0	+4.0	—5.5	+6.2
7	18.0	20.2	(33.9)	19.8	11.5	9.5	22.0	23.8	16.2	10.0	17.6	18.0	— 7.5	+3.8	—5.5	+7.9
8	17.8	21.2	(32.6)	17.5	13.5	10.5	21.5	24.2	13.8	7.5	14.5	18.0	— 4.0	+3.0	—3.0	+8.5
9	17.2	21.0	(30.3)	13.5	9.0	9.0	23.8	21.0	10.3	3.8	17.0	12.0	+ 2.8	+2.8	—1.8	+7.5
10	16.5	21.0	(29.1)	13.1	8.7	10.8	25.0	20.0	8.3	5.0	14.5	10.5	+ 2.2	+3.5	—1.6	+7.5
11	15.9	20.5	(27.6)	12.5	10.0	10.0	23.0	18.0	5.0	4.3	13.0	11.0	+ 3.5	+4.5	+1.2	+7.5
Noon	15.5	20.5	(26.7)	11.5	11.6	11.0	23.0	18.0	2.3	3.2	12.5	11.5	+ 4.0	+4.8	+1.5	+7.5
13	15.2	21.5	26.9	12.0	12.0	10.5	23.0	18.0	3.0	3.0	11.5	9.7	+ 4.6	+4.2	+2.0	+7.0
14	15.0	21.0	26.5	8.6	12.6	11.0	25.0	16.8	2.5	3.2	11.5	9.0	+ 4.0	+3.7	+5.5	+7.2
15	14.7	21.2	24.0	9.0	12.5	12.2	27.0	14.0	2.8	4.0	12.0	8.7	+ 3.7	+4.0	+4.0	+8.2
16	15.5	22.3	25.8	9.8	12.5	14.3	28.0	16.5	3.0	4.5	16.0	7.0	+ 3.0	+4.1	+2.5	+8.0
17	17.5	23.0	29.0	11.0	10.7	14.5	24.8	16.5	3.5	4.5	18.0	1.5	+ 2.5	+4.0	+3.6	+6.4
18	17.5	25.0	30.4	12.6	10.5	18.0	26.0	16.6	4.6	7.5	17.0	3.0	+ 3.0	+4.2	+3.0	+6.0
19	18.8	28.0	33.0	13.7	11.2	19.5	31.2	16.5	4.8	10.0	20.0	3.4	+ 2.7	+4.0	+3.6	+1.5
20	18.5	27.0	35.3	13.2	11.0	22.2	31.9	16.2	5.5	10.0	21.5	4.3	+ 2.3	+3.0	+8.0	+0.5
21	18.8	(29.9)	38.0	13.2	10.4	24.0	33.5	18.5	9.0	12.0	22.3	5.8	+ 2.0	—0.5	+7.0	0.0
22	18.8	(31.7)	39.2	13.5	13.0	27.7	36.5	18.5	9.0	13.0	23.3	6.9	+ 1.0	—3.5	+6.9	—5.5
23	18.8	(32.8)	40.0	12.5	13.0	27.0	34.0	18.5	10.0	14.5	23.0	8.8	— 0.5	—5.8	+6.8	—5.5
Midn't	—19.0	(—34.2)	—41.7	—12.5	—13.0	—27.0	—34.2	—20.0	—11.0	—15.8	—25.3	—13.0	+ 1.0	—4.5	+6.8	—6.8
Means	—17.70	—23.45	—32.70	—17.95	—11.58	—14.91	—26.70	—21.85	— 9.95	— 8.67	—17.62	—12.33	—1.61	+2.57	+0.68	+4.85

Hour.	17th.	18th.	19th.	20th.	21st.	22d.	23d.	24th.	25th.	26th.	27th.	28th.	29th.	30th.		Means.
	°	°	°	°	°	°	°	°	°	°	°	°	°	°		°
1h.	— 7.0	—14.3	—15.0	—16.6	— 9.0	— 4.0	—3.2	—10.0	—5.5	—4.0	—1.0	0.0	—2.3	+ 4.8	...	—12.19
2	— 7.2	—13.7	—14.3	—15.5	—13.3	— 3.2	—2.5	—10.3	—6.4	—3.8	—5.0	0.0	—2.5	+ 6.8	...	—12.20
3	— 7.1	—12.0	—13.0	—14.4	—13.0	—11.0	—3.7	—10.0	—6.3	—3.5	—8.0	—0.7	—3.0	+ 6.5	...	—12.61
4	— 6.8	—12.0	—12.7	—13.5	—11.0	—10.0	—2.3	— 8.0	—6.0	—3.3	—2.0	—1.0	—2.3	+ 5.5	...	—12.08
5	— 5.0	—11.5	—15.5	—14.1	—11.0	— 7.0	—0.5	— 9.5	—4.0	+3.3	—1.5	—7.3	—4.2	+ 6.4	...	—11.24
6	— 4.0	—10.8	—12.7	—13.4	—11.0	— 6.5	+2.4	— 8.5	—8.0	+3.2	—1.5	—5.6	—4.0	+ 4.4	...	—10.57
7	— 6.3	— 8.0	—10.2	—12.4	— 8.5	— 4.5	0.0	— 7.5	—4.0	+3.7	—1.0	—5.6	—4.2	+ 4.6	...	— 9.52
8	— 7.5	— 8.0	—10.0	— 6.6	— 9.2	— 3.0	+4.5	— 7.8	—4.0	+4.0	—1.2	—5.0	+1.8	+ 4.9	...	— 8.44
9	— 6.5	— 5.8	— 7.8	— 6.0	— 7.0	+ 3.0	+4.8	— 3.2	—4.5	+4.0	—1.5	—4.0	+3.0	+ 5.3	...	— 6.76
10	— 6.5	— 5.0	— 5.0	— 2.6	— 3.5	+ 4.8	+6.0	— 1.2	—5.0	+4.2	—1.0	—4.2	+1.0	+ 6.5	...	— 6.08
11	— 6.0	— 3.8	— 4.0	0.0	— 5.0	+ 6.0	+7.2	— 1.0	—3.0	+5.3	—0.5	—3.8	+3.0	+ 6.3	...	— 5.11
Noon	— 5.0	— 3.5	— 3.0	+ 1.7	— 3.4	+ 5.8	+4.5	— 0.2	—2.5	+7.7	0.0	+4.5	+3.0	+ 6.0	...	— 4.46
13	— 3.0	— 3.5	— 2.0	+ 1.0	— 2.0	+ 7.2	+4.5	+ 2.5	—2.5	+8.1	+0.5	+5.2	+5.0	+ 7.0	...	— 4.02
14	— 1.0	— 2.0	0.0	+ 2.5	+ 0.5	+ 7.5	+4.5	+ 2.0	0.0	+8.1	+4.4	+5.0	+4.0	+10.9	...	— 3.20
15	— 2.3	— 3.0	+ 3.0	+ 2.5	— 1.0	+ 8.4	+4.5	+ 2.4	+1.0	+8.5	+5.6	+4.2	+5.2	+11.0	...	— 3.07
16	— 2.8	— 3.5	+ 2.5	+ 4.0	— 3.0	+15.0	+4.5	+ 2.3	+1.5	+9.2	+6.0	+5.0	+5.5	+10.2	...	— 3.37
17	— 1.5	— 4.5	+ 2.0	+ 3.0	+ 0.5	+11.2	+4.0	+ 3.4	+2.0	+8.3	+7.2	+5.5	+3.5	+ 8.8	...	— 3.49
18	— 3.5	— 4.8	+ 0.1	+ 0.5	+ 3.8	+ 8.5	+3.5	+ 3.2	+2.0	+8.0	+7.0	+4.0	+2.5	+ 7.0	...	— 4.36
19	— 4.0	— 7.0	— 2.0	+ 2.5	+ 0.8	+ 7.0	+2.0	+ 1.2	+1.0	+7.7	+6.4	+4.0	+2.0	+ 4.0	...	— 5.76
20	— 5.8	— 8.7	— 5.3	— 3.0	— 1.4	+ 4.4	+0.5	0.0	—1.0	+7.1	+5.2	+3.5	+2.4	+ 3.0	...	— 6.73
21	— 8.5	— 8.5	— 5.5	— 5.0	— 2.0	+ 6.5	—2.5	— 2.3	—1.5	+6.0	+2.3	+1.0	+2.3	+ 3.0	...	— 8.05
22	—12.0	— 9.5	— 6.8	— 6.0	— 3.5	+ 5.0	—5.0	— 2.2	—1.9	+5.2	0.0	—3.0*	+2.1	+ 2.1	...	— 9.59
23	—13.5	—12.2	— 6.7	— 6.5	— 5.0	+ 4.0	—7.0	— 4.0	—2.1	0.0	—0.5	—3.0*	+2.0	+ 2.5	...	—10.33
Midn't	—14.2	—13.8	—16.7	— 8.0	— 5.8	— 0.1	—9.3	— 4.5	—2.7	0.0	—1.3	—2.3*	+2.3	+ 3.0	...	—11.45
Means	— 6.12	— 7.89	— 6.69	— 5.25	— 5.12	+ 2.29	+0.89	— 3.05	—2.64	+4.04	+0.77	—0.15	+1.17	+ 5.85	...	— 7.69

[1] Temperatures noted by mercurial standard.

* Sign — supplied.

For the interpolation on the 2d and 3d, the parameter of the diurnal variation was found 1.6 and 1.9 of the mean value from six observations before and six observations after the interval. The change in the mean temperature during the same time amounted to 5°.3.

April 12th. Sun rises at half-past 3 o'clock. On the 17th inst., the sun was up at 1 A. M.

April 19th. The sun was refracted above the horizon at midnight.

Temperature of the Air in Shade observed at Van Rensselaer Harbor,

In May, 1854, in Lat. 78° 37′, Long. 70° 53′ W. of Greenwich.

Expressed in degrees of Fahrenheit's scale. At meteorological observatory on floe.[1]

Hour.	1st.	2d.	3d.	4th.	5th.	6th.	7th.	8th.	9th.	10th.	11th.	12th.	13th.	14th.	15th.	16th.
	°	°	°	°	°	°	°	°	°	°	°	°	°	°	°	°
1h.	+ 2.5	+ 6.8	—5.8	—6.0	—5.0	—4.5	+ 5.6	+6.4	+ 5.1	+ 5.9	+ 5.1	+ 1.5	—7.3	+0.5	+4.2	+ 5.1
2	4.6	+ 6.0	—6.5	—6.0	—7.5	—4.0	6.4	8.0	5.3	6.4	5.7	1.8	—7.1	0.5	4.2	4.2
3	6.4	+ 5.3	—5.8	—5.5	—4.8	—3.5	7.0	10.0	5.5	6.9	7.6	0.5	—5.3	2.4	4.2	4.5
4	8.5	+ 2.4	—4.5	—5.2	—4.0	—3.4	7.6	10.6	5.7	7.2	6.4	2.4	—3.1	3.3	4.2	6.4
5	13.5	+ 3.1	—3.8	—5.1	0.0	—3.3	8.2	10.8	6.2	7.2	4.4	2.9	+3.3	3.3	6.1	8.5
6	12.8	+ 5.2	—2.4	—2.5	+1.5	—4.6	9.3	11.2	6.8	7.8	5.1	3.3	+2.9	3.5	7.0	9.8
7	14.8	+ 7.0	—2.2	—2.2	+1.5	—3.6	9.8	11.7	6.5	9.3	6.1	4.7	+2.4	3.8	8.2	10.3
8	18.4	+10.0	—1.4	—1.5	+2.3	—2.0	11.7	12.2	5.5	12.7	9.3	6.1	+1.5	3.8	10.3	10.8
9	17.1	+ 9.4	—0.5	—1.0	+2.5	+0.5	12.4	12.6	6.5	14.6	12.6	7.2	+1.5	3.8	3.3	11.7
10	19.5	+ 7.6	—0.2	0.0	+2.3	+1.2	12.2	12.9	7.3	13.3	13.2	7.8	+3.1	4.0	5.1	11.4
11	16.2	+ 6.7	+0.8	+0.2	+2.1	+1.6	12.2	14.0	7.7	11.6	14.1	7.6	+4.2	5.2	7.4	11.9
Noon	14.2	+ 6.4	+1.0	+0.7	+2.2	+2.0	10.3	15.5	8.6	9.6	14.8	8.0	+5.1	7.4	8.4	12.5
13	16.0	+ 7.2	+2.3	+2.0	+2.7	+3.1	9.8	16.2	9.8	10.8	14.1	8.4	+5.3	8.1	9.0	13.5
14	18.2	+ 7.3	+2.7	+4.5	+4.0	+2.8	10.3	16.0	10.3	10.3	13.6	9.2	+5.4	8.6	10.7	14.1
15	16.3	+ 7.0	+3.3	+4.0	+4.7	+4.1	12.5	16.5	11.7	10.9	11.5	9.7	+6.7	8.2	12.5	14.6
16	15.5	+ 6.6	+3.2	+5.2	+4.5	+3.9	14.3	17.5	11.5	10.3	11.0	10.3	+7.2	8.5	14.4	15.2
17	13.2	+ 5.3	+2.0	+5.0	+4.3	+3.7	14.1	17.1	11.3	9.9	9.3	10.5	+7.4	10.3	13.7	15.0
18	10.2	+ 4.5	0.0	+4.1	+4.5	+3.5	12.2	16.3	11.5	9.7	8.5	10.3	+7.2	11.4	13.1	14.5
19	10.0	+ 3.4	—1.2	0.0	+3.0	+3.3	12.0	15.4	11.7	9.2	7.2	7.5	+7.0	10.3	11.9	14.1
20	10.4	+ 2.1	—3.0	—1.0	+1.3	+3.3	11.7	14.1	11.3	9.0	6.5	5.1	+6.7	9.8	10.3	11.2
21	10.5	0.0	—5.5	—1.5	+0.2	+2.8	11.4	12.5	10.8	8.4	5.1	3.3	+5.4	8.9	9.4	10.3
22	10.0	— 1.0	—5.8	—3.0	0.0	+2.9	11.2	10.5	10.3	8.0	4.2	2.4	+4.3	10.1	7.6	9.7
23	10.0	— 1.5	—6.0	—3.4	—0.5	+1.9	10.5	5.6	8.2	5.7	3.8	1.7	+1.9	8.1	5.4	9.2
Midn't	+10.1	— 3.0	—6.4	—3.0	—1.0	+5.1	+ 9.6	+5.1	+ 7.2	+5.4	+3.3	+0.5	+0.5	+5.1	+4.7	+ 8.9
Means	+12.45	+ 4.74	—1.90	—0.88	—0.87	+0.70	+10.51	+12.45	+ 8.43	+9.17	+8.44	+5.53	+2.76	+6.20	+8.14	+10.72

Hour.	17th.	18th.	19th.	20th.	21st.	22d.	23d.	24th.	25th.	26th.	27th.	28th.	29th.	30th.	31st.	Means.
	°	°	°	°	°	°	°	°	°	°	°	°	°	°	°	°
1h.	+13.3	+11.4	+ 5.3	+ 6.3	+ 9.8	+ 8.3	+13.6	+13.2	+19.0	+23.5	+30.4	+31.4	+24.5	+28.8	+20.2	+ 9.00
2	11.6	16.3	5.8	7.5	10.3	9.0	13.8	12.8	18.6	24.5	30.4	31.9	26.4	28.8	19.8	+ 9.34
3	9.5	17.6	7.4	8.6	10.7	10.6	13.8	15.4	18.3	24.5	30.9	31.4	26.4	31.5	17.9	+10.00
4	10.0	17.9	8.1	10.4	11.8	12.6	14.4	16.2	17.9	25.5	31.4	31.9	26 9	29.5	17.9	+10.55
5	9.8	19.3	9.6	9.8	12.2	13.9	15.5	19.0	21.0	26.0	33.0	33.2	29.3	31.9	18.6	+11.85
6	10.3	20.0	10.3	10.3	14.0	17.4	17.1	18.4	19.7	28.6	34.6	36.0	31.4	30.5	19.7	+12.74
7	10.1	19.8	10.8	13.3	14.3	17.9	18.1	17.9	21.2	27.7	35.3	38.0	34.5	30.7	20.7	+13.50
8	9.3	20.7	13.5	15.3	16.4	14.5	19.1	19.7	19.7	28.1	37.0	34.4	37.5	31.4	21.2	+14.44
9	8.9	18.4	13.2	12.6	18.1	15.8	17.1	14.4	21.9	28.3	37.6	34.5	36.6	30.9	22.6	+14.36
10	9.6	19.0	15.5	16.0	18.2	17.2	14.4	15.0	22.7	30.5	38.6	34.2	37.6	31.7	25.5	+15.05
11	9.8	13.4	18.7	13.4	17.9	18.4	15.4	17.6	23.8	32.6	36.5	34.5	37.6	34.5	29.3	+15.35
Noon	10.5	12.6	19.1	12.9	18.6	22.1	18.6	17.3	24.5	31.4	35.5	40.1	39.0	34.5	29.3	+15.89
13	9.8	11.6	20.3	13.7	19.0	22.1	20.2	17.1	24.9	32.9	35.7	34.2	35.6	36.0	28.3	+16.12
14	9.8	12.2	20.8	14.3	18.5	22.1	20.7	18.2	25.5	32.4	35.1	34.9	33.4	32.4	28.8	+16.36
15	11.5	12.4	19.7	15.0	19.4	22.7	17.4	17.9	26.4	32.6	34.5	34.8	32.4	31.7	27.6	+16.46
16	14.1	13.1	19.3	16.0	18.5	23.1	17.0	19.7	24.7	31.9	34.7	33.8	33.4	32.6	28.3	+16.75
17	12.2	12.8	17.4	16.4	17.9	22.6	18.2	20.1	24.5	30.9	32.4	34.1	32.9	29.3	27.4	+16.17
18	9.7	12.5	12.8	16.2	17.8	19.7	17.9	19.3	25.1	30.9	32.0	32.6	31.8	28.3	27.4	+15.34
19	8.2	11.8	12.2	15.5	16.9	17.4	17.4	20.2	24.7	29.9	31.8	30.9	31.4	28.3	27.9	+14.49
20	7.8	11.5	11.5	13.8	15.5	16.0	16.7	20.7	24.0	31.3	31.4	29.3	30.8	26.4	26.9	+13.63
21	7.4	9.9	10.9	13.2	14.2	15.0	16.0	20.5	23.5	32.6	32.4	29.0	29.4	24.5	26.4	+12.80
22	7.6	7.7	10.0	10.8	10.5	14.5	15.3	19.0	22.9	29.8	30.4	28.9	29.4	21.7	22.6	+11.69
23	9.9	4.7	6.6	10.3	10.3	13.4	15.5	18.6	23.3	29.7	29.3	28.1	28.4	20.7	20.7	+10.65
Midn't	+10.6	+ 4.2	+ 5.1	+ 9.8	+ 8.6	+13.4	+15.4	+18.2	+23.8	+30.9	+28.3	+27.4	+28.4	+20.7	+19.7	+10.21
Means	+10.05	+13.78	+12.66	+12.56	+14.97	+16.65	+16.61	+17.77	+22.57	+29.46	+33.30	+32.90	+31.88	+29.47	+23.94	+13.45

[1] Up to the 5th, inclusive, the temperatures noted by *M*; after the 5th, by *S*.

May 20th. The sun is now acquiring power in the middle of the day sufficient to soften the snow on the surface, and black objects lying upon it sink quite fast—a tarpaulin sinking about two inches in a day.

May 26th. The thermometer indicates a temperature above the freezing point of water, for the first time in the season.

Temperature of the Air in Shade observed at Van Rensselaer Harbor,

In June, 1854, in Lat. 78° 37′, Long. 70° 53′ W. of Greenwich.

Expressed in degrees of Fahrenheit's scale. At meteorological observatory on floe.[1]

Hour.	1st.	2d.	3d.	4th.	5th.	6th.	7th.	8th.	9th.	10th.	11th.	12th.	13th.	14th.	15th.	16th.
	°	°	°	°	°	°	°	°	°	°	°	°	°	°	°	°
1h.	+23.5	+22.8	+26.2	+25.5	+21.1	+19.5	+21.1	+21.2	+24.5	+22.9	+27.7	+22.6	+22.1	+25.0	+22.6	+25.6
2	23.0	23.9	25.9	25.5	22.1	19.2	21.2	20.7	24.6	26.4	25.5	22.6	22.1	23.9	22.6	25.6
3	23.5	25.0	26.7	24.5	19.7	18.4	22.1	26.4	24.7	26.6	25.5	22.1	21.6	24.0	23.6	25.0
4	23.5	25.5	27.4	24.5	21.8	18.8	24.0	25.5	24.8	26.6	28.3	22.1	20.7	22.8	25.5	25.0
5	23.5	28.3	(28.1)	(24.7)	22.2	24.1	24.5	25.5	25.4	25.5	26.9	22.7	24.5	26.0	26.0	28.5
6	19.9	29.3	(28.8)	(24.9)	22.4	24.3	24.7	26.0	25.6	26.3	28.7	24.7	21.6	27.4	28.0	28.3
7	19.7	31.4	(29.5)	(25.1)	22.6	24.5	24.7	26.4	26.3	27.7	26.5	26.5	24.5	30.8	29.8	28.1
8	21.6	33.0	(30.2)	(25.3)	23.2	25.5	25.0	27.3	26.5	27.4	28.7	27.5	24.5	34.7	29.5	27.4
9	24.5	34.5	30.9	25.5	22.9	26.1	24.0	27.9	27.4	31.4	27.4	23.5	25.5	28.4	27.4	29.3
10	25.1	32.6	29.3	26.4	23.0	26.4	24.0	28.3	27.9	26.0	28.4	25.5	26.4	28.6	28.3	31.4
11	25.3	31.9	27.4	26.4	23.5	25.5	24.0	29.8	30.3	31.9	28.8	25.7	27.4	28.7	27.8	31.9
Noon	25.8	30.8	28.3	26.4	23.7	25.5	25.0	34.5	29.3	35.5	28.3	25.7	28.4	29.3	27.6	35.5
13	26.4	31.0	28.8	25.9	23.8	25.5	25.0	34.5	29.4	35.4	28.3	26.0	28.8	29.4	28.8	35.5
14	26.7	30.7	29.8	26.3	25.0	25.9	28.0	32.4	32.4	33.5	27.4	26.4	28.7	30.5	29.3	34.5
15	26.9	31.0	30.3	26.6	27.1	26.4	28.4	29.3	31.4	28.3	28.4	26.4	30.2	32.5	29.3	33.4
16	27.3	31.3	30.3	26.1	27.4	27.1	27.4	27.9	27.6	28.3	26.1	27.4	28.3	31.4	30.3	34.5
17	27.3	31.3	29.3	25.5	27.5	26.4	26.9	27.9	26.9	28.3	29.6	27.4	28.4	29.3	30.9	34.5
18	27.3	30.3	27.4	25.5	26.5	25.9	26.9	28.0	26.3	28.3	28.3	28.3	28.3	29.3	30.9	35.0
19	26.9	30.8	26.9	25.5	25.5	25.5	28.3	26.4	27.4	29.3	27.4	25.5	28.3	30.3	29.3	32.4
20	26.4	30.3	27.4	24.5	25.5	28.3	26.4	25.5	25.9	28.3	27.4	24.5	26.4	29.3	30.3	33.4
21	25.8	29.8	26.9	24.5	22.6	27.4	24.5	25.5	25.9	27.4	26.4	26.4	25.4	27.4	30.3	32.9
22	25.5	29.3	26.4	24.5	22.6	27.4	22.6	24.5	24.5	27.0	25.4	23.6	25.4	29.3	30.3	31.4
23	23.5	28.3	26.4	21.6	22.6	23.5	22.6	24.5	23.6	26.5	24.5	23.6	19.7	28.4	29.3	30.3
Midn't	+21.6	+27.4	+26.0	+21.6	+21.6	+22.6	+22.6	+24.5	+23.6	+26.0	+24.5	+23.6	+22.6	+28.4	+24.5	+29.3
Means	+24.60	+29.60	+28.11	+25.12	+23.58	+24.57	+24.75	+27.10	+26.76	+28.37	+27.27	+25.01	+25.41	+28.55	+28.55	+30.78

Hour.	17th.	18th.	19th.	20th.	21st.	22d.	23d.	24th.	25th.	26th.	27th.	28th.	29th.	30th.		Means.
	°	°	°	°	°	°	°	°	°	°	°	°	°	°		°
1h.	+31.9	+30.9	+30.3	+29.3	+29.0	+29.3	+29.3	+29.1	+31.9	+32.4	+29.1	+32.9	+34.0	+37.1	...	+27.01
2	32.1	27.9	30.8	28.9	29.8	29.3	29.3	30.8	31.4	33.4	28.3	32.8	34.2	37.4	...	+27.06
3	32.0	27.9	30.8	27.9	32.3	29.8	30.3	30.8	31.4	33.4	26.9	32.8	33.8	37.5	...	+27.23
4	35.0	30.9	30.8	26.1	29.8	28.8	30.3	30.8	31.9	33.4	28.4	32.2	34.5	37.1	...	+27.56
5	35.0	32.4	33.8	27.5	29.8	31.4	27.9	33.5	36.3	34.5	31.4	31.7	37.2	36.6	...	+28.85
6	34.9	36.0	33.6	27.5	31.1	34.2	28.6	33.6	36.5	34.6	32.9	32.9	38.0	39.6	...	+29.50
7	35.0	38.3	36.2	27.9	31.5	35.1	28.5	33.7	36.5	34.6	35.7	33.6	38.6	41.6	...	+30.36
8	34.5	40.1	37.8	31.9	32.9	35.7	29.3	34.2	38.6	40.7	39.4	34.1	39.1	42.6	...	+31.61
9	35.0	32.1	38.6	28.3	28.4	34.8	29.7	37.5	36.6	35.5	39.1	34.5	37.6	40.6	...	+30.83
10	35.0	34.4	39.6	29.3	29.3	33.4	30.3	36.5	37.0	36.6	39.4	35.0	37.6	40.1	...	+31.04
11	35.5	34.9	37.1	30.3	30.3	35.3	30.3	37.3	36.6	36.6	39.4	35.5	37.2	39.6	...	+31.41
Noon	34.5	34.4	35.5	30.3	38.1	35.3	31.9	39.6	36.6	38.6	39.1	36.3	37.1	38.6	...	+32.18
13	34.5	34.5	35.0	30.9	37.6	36.0	32.4	39.1	35.5	38.6	39.1	37.0	37.1	40.1	...	+32.33
14	33.7	35.5	35.5	30.3	35.5	32.4	32.9	38.6	35.0	38.1	(37.5)	36.0	38.1	40.1	...	+32.21
15	34.5	35.0	35.5	28.3	35.0	31.9	32.9	38.1	35.0	38.1	36.0	34.5	37.1	39.6	...	+31.91
16	35.0	34.5	35.5	28.3	34.5	32.4	34.0	37.6	34.7	36.6	35.5	34.0	37.6	39.1	...	+31.60
17	34.8	34.5	35.0	28.8	35.0	30.9	34.1	37.6	33.4	37.1	34.5	34.0	37.6	37.6	...	+31.41
18	34.5	34.8	35.0	29.8	34.5	31.4	34.0	37.0	32.9	36.6	35.5	33.6	38.1	35.5	...	+31.19
19	34.5	34.5	35.0	29.5	33.5	31.4	34.5	34.5	32.4	35.0	35.5	34.5	38.1	35.2	...	+30.79
20	35.5	34.5	33.4	29.4	33.7	31.4	34.0	34.5	32.4	35.0	35.5	34.5	38.1	35.2	...	+30.56
21	34.5	34.0	33.4	29.6	33.2	30.9	29.3	34.5	32.4	34.9	35.5	33.4	38.1	34.5	...	+29.91
22	33.4	33.4	32.4	29.7	32.4	29.3	30.3	34.3	32.2	34.7	35.5	33.4	38.3	35.5	...	+29.48
23	32.4	32.4	31.4	28.8	31.6	29.5	31.3	33.5	32.4	34.5	34.5	32.9	38.1	35.0	...	+28.57
Midn't	+32.4	+31.3	+30.3	+30.0	+31.2	+29.5	+30.3	+33.5	+32.4	+34.5	+34.0	+32.9	+37.9	+34.8	...	+28.18
Means	+34.17	+33.71	+34.26	+29.11	+32.50	+32.06	+31.09	+35.01	+34.25	+35.75	+34.90	+33.96	+37.21	+37.94	...	+30.12

[1] Temperatures noted by spirit standard *S*.

TEMPERATURE OF THE AIR IN SHADE OBSERVED AT VAN RENSSELAER HARBOR,

In July, 1854, in Lat. 78° 37′, Long. 70° 53′ W. of Greenwich.

Expressed in degrees of Fahrenheit's scale. At magnetical observatory on Fern Rock Island.[1]

Hour.	1st.	2d.	3d.	4th.	5th.	6th.	7th.	8th.	9th.	10th.	11th.	12th.	13th.	14th.	15th.	16th.
	°	°	°	°	°	°	°	°	°	°	°	°	°	°	°	°
1h.	+35.0	+39.1	+36.0	+42.6	+39.5	+43.0	+34.0	+36.0	+32.0	+34.0	+34.0	+34.0	+35.0	+34.0	+39.0	+(33.9)
2	35.3	40.1	35.9	42.6	40.0	42.0	34.0	36.5	31.0	32.0	34.0	35.0	37.0	37.5	38.0	(34.3)
3	34.5	41.6	37.0	43.6	40.3	40.5	34.0	36.5	31.5	35.0	34.0	35.0	37.0	35.0	37.0	(34.5)
4	34.5	41.1	36.5	44.6	40.0	40.5	34.0	35.0	34.0	36.0	34.5	38.0	37.5	35.0	37.0	(34.7)
5	36.5	45.6	36.5	46.6	39.5	40.0	35.0	36.0	34.5	33.0	34.0	36.0	36.0	35.0	38.5	+34.0
6	36.0	46.1	37.5	47.6	39.5	40.0	35.0	36.5	35.0	33.0	35.0	37.0	36.0	36.0	38.0	36.2
7	36.0	45.6	39.5	43.6	40.0	42.0	35.5	36.0	35.0	34.0	35.5	37.0	36.5	36.8	37.0	36.0
8	36.5	45.1	39.0	44.6	40.0	42.0	36.0	36.0	36.0	35.0	37.0	37.0	37.0	38.0	36.6	35.5
9	36.5	49.6	39.0	48.6	41.0	41.0	38.0	37.0	37.0	36.0	37.0	38.0	38.0	39.8	37.0	36.0
10	37.2	49.6	38.5	48.6*	41.0	43.0	39.0	37.0	37.0	37.0	37.0	38.0	38.0	44.0	36.5	36.2
11	37.6	48.4	38.5	48.1	42.0	40.0	39.0	38.0	39.0	39.0	37.5	39.0	38.0	45.0	36.0	36.7
Noon	38.3	48.4	38.0	46.6	42.0	42.0	37.0	40.0	39.0	39.0	37.5	40.0	38.0	47.0*	35.0	37.0
13	38.6	48.6	36.5	48.6	39.0	41.0	37.0	39.0	39.0	39.0	38.0	41.0	40.0	48.0*	37.0	37.0
14	40.6	38.1	39.5	44.6†	38.0	38.0	37.0	36.0	39.0	43.0	38.5	41.0	41.0	49.0*	38.0	37.0
15	41.6	39.6	37.5	42.6	39.0	41.0	36.0	38.0	40.0	40.0	37.0	41.0	42.0	48.0	37.0	36.0
16	41.6	36.0†	36.5	46.6	42.0	40.0	35.0	37.0	37.0	40.0	38.0	41.0	43.0	45.0	37.0	36.5
17	39.6	39.6	36.5	44.6	41.0	35.0	35.5	36.0	36.0	39.0	39.0	38.0	41.0	45.0	38.0	37.0
18	39.6	39.9	35.5	45.6	39.0	35.0	36.0	37.0	36.0	38.0	37.0	37.0	38.0	44.0	39.0	34.8
19	42.6	37.5	35.5	43.9	42.0	34.5	36.0	36.0	35.0	37.0	36.0	37.0	37.5	43.0	39.5	33.9
20	42.6	38.5	36.5	40.1	41.0	35.0	35.5	35.0	36.0	37.0	37.0	36.0	37.0	40.0	38.0	36.2
21	39.6	39.5‡	42.5	39.1	41.0	33.0	35.0	35.0	37.0	33.0	34.0	35.0	36.0	38.7	36.0	36.4
22	39.6	35.0	37.6§	37.6	41.0	35.0	34.0	35.0	35.0	34.0	33.0	34.0	36.0	37.5	34.2	35.8
23	41.6	35.9	38.6	39.6	42.0	34.0	33.0	34.0	34.0	34.0	32.0	34.0	35.5	37.0	33.5	36.0
Midn't	+40.6	+36.5	+39.6	+40.1	+41.0	+35.0	+34.0	+33.0	+32.0	+35.0	+32.0	+34.0	+35.0	+36.0	+33.0	+36.5
Means	+38.42	+41.87	+37.68	+44.19	+40.45	+38.86	+35.60	+36.31	+35.71	+36.33	+35.77	+37.21	+37.75	+40.59	+36.91	+35.75

Hour.	17th.	18th.	19th.	20th.	21st.	22d.	23d.	24th.	25th.	26th.	27th.	28th.	29th.	30th.	31st.	Means.
	°	°	°	°	°	°	°	°	°	°	°	°	°	°	°	°
1h.	(+37.1)	(+35.7)	(+35.9)	+34.0	+35.0	+41.0	+39.0	+43.0	+38.0	+38.0	+38.5	+35.0	+39.0	+33.0	+31.0	+36.65
2	(37.4)	(35.6)	(35.6)	35.2	36.0	40.0	40.0	43.0	39.0	37.0	38.0	36.5	37.3	33.0	30.0	+36.74
3	(37.9)	(35.4)	(35.1)	36.0	35.5	39.5	40.0	44.5	39.0	36.0	36.8	38.0	36.0	34.0	29.3	+36.77
4	(38.2)	(35.3)	(34.7)	36.7	35.5	38.3	39.5	41.0	39.0	35.0	37.0	39.0	35.0	34.9	28.0	+36.77
5	+39.0	+35.2	+33.5	40.5	35.0	38.5	40.0	41.0	37.0	35.0	38.0	40.5	35.0	35.0	29.0	+36.93
6	40.0	33.0	34.0	48.0	35.0	38.5	40.5	41.5	35.5	35.0	38.0	41.0	37.0	34.0	30.0	+37.59
7	41.0	37.0	34.0	41.0	36.0	39.5	41.0	41.0	37.0	36.0	38.0	41.5	36.0	35.5	30.0	+37.76
8	38.0	36.5	35.0	40.0	37.0	40.0	43.0	43.0	38.0	37.0	38.0	43.5	44.0	37.0	30.0	+38.43
9	38.2	37.0	35.0	40.0	36.2	40.0	47.0	46.0	39.0	39.0	39.0	45.0	44.0	37.0	30.0	+39.42
10	37.7	37.0	36.5	39.2	36.0	40.0	51.0	47.0	40.0	40.5	38.0	45.0	44.0	38.0	31.0	+39.63
11	38.0	36.5	37.0	38.7	35.5	41.0	51.0	46.0	41.0	41.5	38.0	45.0	37.0	38.0	34.0	+40.00
Noon	37.0	38.0	37.0	39.0	36.5	41.0	50.0	42.0	41.0	45.0	38.0	46.0	33.0	36.0	37.0	+40.04
13	36.0	36.0	37.0	38.5	37.0	40.0	48.0	39.0	42.0	44.0	37.0	47.0	34.0	36.0	36.0	+39.83
14	37.0	38.0	37.5	39.0	37.0	40.0	48.0	40.2	43.0	40.0	37.5	48.0	35.0	35.0	37.0	+39.69
15	35.0	39.0	40.0	40.0	37.0	39.0	49.0	41.0	41.0	39.0	38.0	46.0	34.0	38.0	37.0	+39.65
16	36.0	39.0	45.0	41.0	38.5	41.0	47.0	43.0	39.0	39.0	36.5	45.0	34.0	36.0	37.0	+39.65
17	36.0	39.0	42.0	41.0	39.0	38.0	46.0	39.0	38.0	40.0	36.5	41.0	34.2	38.0	36.0	+38.85
18	37.0	38.0	40.0	40.0	40.0	38.5	46.0	38.0	38.0	39.0	36.7	41.5	34.5	39.0	36.1	+38.51
19	37.0	38.8	39.0	39.0	39.5	38.0	44.0	39.0	38.0	38.0	36.0	40.8	34.8	41.0	35.5	+38.24
20	+36.5	37.5	37.5	39.0	40.0	37.0	42.0	39.0	37.0	38.0	35.5	40.5	34.0	38.0	35.0	+37.67
21	(36.2)	37.4	38.0	39.0	40.0	37.0	41.0	39.0	41.0	36.0	35.0	41.0	34.0	35.0	34.0	+37.24
22	(36.2)	37.5	37.0	37.0	39.0	38.2	42.0	40.0	40.5	36.0	35.7	41.5	33.0	35.0	34.0	+36.67
23	(36.1)	37.0	35.0	36.0	39.5	36.5	44.0	40.0	41.0	36.1	35.8	42.0	39.0	36.0	33.0	+36.83
Midn't	(+36.0)	+36.2	+35.0	+36.0	+39.0	+37.0	+45.0	+39.8	+40.0	+35.8	+36.0	+41.0	+37.0	+36.0	+32.0	+36.94
Means	+37.28	+36.90	+36.93	+38.91	+37.28	+39.06	+44.33	+41.58	+39.25	+38.16	+37.15	+42.14	+36.45	+36.18	+33.00	+38.19

[1] The instruments were removed from the floe to Fern Rock Island magnetic observatory on the first of the month.
* The readings of the sun and shade thermometers have evidently been exchanged in the log; the above abstract contains the correct figure.
† Original record corrected by 10°.
‡ Observations from 21 hours to the same hour (inclusive) on the following day, made on board the brig. Correction to brig thermometer from comparison with two standards at +37°, —0°.7, and —0°.4; mean adopted (for mercurial thermometer No. 9), —0°.5.
§ From 22h. July 3d to Aug. 15th, mercurial thermometer No. 15 was used, according to Mr. Sonntag's notes. Comparisons with the two standards at +36°, —0°.8, and —1°.4; adopted —1°.0. On July 4th, the column in the log is still headed spirit st. I have, therefore, applied the correction on that day accordingly. The scale of No. 15 is divided from 2 to 2 degrees; the readings are generally to the nearest half degree.
July 16th. Some thermometers were broken, the tent being blown down. July 22d. First six hours supplied from dry bulb readings. July 23d. At 10 and 11 o'clock, highest temperature of the season, +51°.0.

TEMPERATURE OF THE AIR IN SHADE OBSERVED AT VAN RENSSELAER HARBOR,

In August, 1854, in Lat. 78° 37′, Long. 70° 53′ W. of Greenwich.

Expressed in degrees of Fahrenheit's scale.[1]

Hour.	1st.	2d.	3d.	4th.	5th.	6th.	7th.	8th.	9th.	10th.	11th.	12th.	13th.	14th.	15th.	16th.
	°	°	°	°	°	°	°	°	°	°	°	°	°	°	°	°
1h.	+33.0	+29.0	+35.5	+34.0	+34.3	+35.0	+32.5	+31.5	+33.0	+33.0	+32.0	+29.0	+31.0	+29.0	+32.2	+24.7
2	33.0	29.0	36.0	34.0	33.0	36.2	32.0	31.5	36.0	34.0	33.0	31.0	31.0	28.0	32.2	25.2
3	32.0	29.1	36.0	33.0	32.0	37.0	31.0	32.0	38.0	33.5	34.5	32.0	31.0	28.0	31.2	24.7
4	33.0	29 0	37.0	34.0	33.1	35.0	30.0	32.0	41.0	33.0	35.0	31.0	31.0	28.0	32.2	26.2
5	33.5	31.0	35.0	36.0	34.0	33.0	33.0	32.0	35.0	33.0	34.0	29.0	30.5	28.0	30.7	28.2
6	34.0	34.0	33.0	37.0	37.0	34.1	35.0	33.0	36.0	34.0	33.0	29.0	30.0	29.0	31.2	30.2
7	37.0	35.0	32.0	38.0	35.0	34.8	37.0	33.0	36.0	35.0	33.0	29.0	31.0	30.0	31.2	32.2
8	41.0	36.0	32.0	39.0	35.0	34.7	43.0	39.0	37.0	35.0	32.0	30.0	31.0	31.0	31.7	36.2
9	45.0	38.0	34.0	40.0	37.0	34.7	41.0	40.0	38.0	36.0	33.0	32.0	31.0	30.0	31.7	35.2
10	49.0	39.0	35.0	39.5	36.0	35.5	44.0	41.0	39.0	37.0	37.0	33.0	31.0	34.0	32.2	36.2
11	42.0	41.0	35.0	39.0	37.0	36.1	36.0	41.0	40.0	37.5	42.0	32.0	31.0	34.0	33.2	37.2
Noon	41.0	43.0	35.2	39.0	37.0	36.5	33.0	40.0	41.0	39.0	38.0	31.0	31.0	33.0	34.2	38·2
13	37.0	40.0	37.0	38.5	39.0	37.0	35.0	41.0	39.0	40.0	38.0	31.0	31.0	34.0	33.2	37.2
14	36.0	39.0	35.0	38.5	40.0	37.0	35.0	42.0	38.0	41.0	37.0	33.0	31.0	36.0	35.2	37.2
15	37.0	40.0	31.0	39.0	39.0	39.0	36.0	41.0	37.0	40.0	37.0	33.0	31.0	33.0	35.2	37.7
16	37.5	37.0	33.0	39.0	39.5	35.0	35.0	41.0	37.0	39.0	36.0	33.0	31.0	32.0	33.2	37.2
17	36.0	35.0	35.0	39.0	37.0	35.0	33.0	40.0	37.0	38.3	37.0	32.0	31.0	31.0	34.2	37.2
18	35.0	34.0	35.0	38.5	37.0	34.8	34.0	39.0	36.0	38.0	38.0	32.0	31.0	31.5	34.2	38.2
19	37.0	38.0	34.7	38.0	36.5	35.0	35.0	36.0	35.5	37.0	38.0	32.0	31.0	32.0	33.2	33.2
20	35.0	37.0	34.5	35.0	36.0	35.0	35.0	33.0	34.0	36.0	39.0	32.0	31.0	32.0	33.2	41.2
21	35.0	36.5	32.0	33.0	36.0	35.0	35.0	34.0	35.0	38.0	37.0	32.0	31.0	32.5	32.2	35.2
22	31.7	34.8	33.0	34.0	36.0	34.0	35.0	34.0	34.0	38.0	36.0	31.0	31.0	32.0	31.2	28.2
23	30.5	33.0	34.0	34.5	37.0	34.0	32.0	34.0	33.0	39.0	35.0	30.5	31.0	31.5	30.2	28.2
Midn't	+28.2	+32.5	+35.0	+34.0	+39.0	+33.0	+33.0	+34.0	+33.0	+36.0	+34.0	+30.5	+31.0	+32.0	+29.2	+28.2
Means	+36.22	+35.41	+34.37	+36.81	+36.35	+35.27	+35.02	+36.46	+36.60	+36.68	+35.77	+31.25	+30.94	+31.31	+32.43	+33.05

Hour.	17th.	18th.	19th.	20th.	21st.	22d.	23d.	24th.	25th.	26th.	27th.	28th.	29th.	30th.	31st.	Means.
	°	°	°	°	°	°	°	°	°	°	°	°	°	°	°	°
1h.	+29.7	+28.2	+27.2	+33.7	+28.2	+25.2	+19.2	+19.2	+23.7	+26.2	(+28.2)	(+23.8)	+23.2	+31.2	+30.2	+29.22
2	30.2	28.2	28.2	31.7	28.2	25.2	19.2	19.2	24.2	26.2	(28.1)	(24.2)	27.2	31.2	29.2	+29.53
3	30.8	29.2	28.2	31 7	28.2	21.2	20.2	19.2	24.2	26.2	(27.9)	(23.9)	27.2	31.7	28.2	+29.45
4	31.2	32.2	29.2	32.2	28.2	22.7	20.2	19.2	25.2	26.2	(27.6)	(24.1)	27.2	31.2	27.7	+29.83
5	27.2	30.2	28.2	33.2	29.2	21.2	22.2	19.2	27.2	27.2	+27.2	(23.6)	29.2	31.2	28.2	+29.69
6	29.2	29.2	26.2	34.2	29.2	23.2	23.2	20.2	28.2	26.2	26.7	(24.8)	30.2	30.2	29.2	+30.31
7	29.2	30.2	29.2	33.2	30.2	25.2	23.2	22.2	28.7	27.2	26.2	(25.9)	30.2	29.2	30.2	+30.95
8	30.2	30.2	28.2	32.2	31.2	27.2	23.2	25.2	29.7	27.2	26.2	(28.3)	30.2	28.2	29.2	+31.94
9	30.2	31.2	28.2	32.2	31.2	30.2	23.2	33.2	30.7	27.2	28.2	+31.2	30.2	29.2	31.2	+33.04
10	30.2	32.2	29.2	31.7	30.7	31.2	23.2	32.2	31.2	26.7	29.2	33.2	30.7	29.4	31.2	+33.89
11	30.5	33.2	30.2	32.2	30.7	32.2	25.2	31.2	31.2	26.2	30.2	34.2	31.7	30.2	32.2	+34.04
Noon	33.2	33.7	33.2	34.2	29.2	32.2	28.2	31.2	31.2	26.2	31.2	31.2	31.7	31.2	32.2	+34.20
13	32.2	35.2	34.2	33.2	28.2	31.2	28.2	32.2	31.7	30.4	32.7	29.2	32.2	(30.0)	32.7	+34.24
14	32.2	35.2	33.2	33.2	29.2	30.2	27.2	32.2	31.7	31.2	30.2	28.2	34.2	(29.9)	32.7	+34.25
15	34.2	35.2	33.7	32.2	26.2	29.2	26.2	30.2	31.2	30.7	29.2	29.2	33.2	(29.8)	32.7	+33.84
16	33.2	35.2	33.7	31.2	27.2	28.2	26.2	28.2	30.7	31.2	29.2	30.2	33.2	(29.3)	30.0*	+33.30
17	32.2	35.2	34.2	30.7	28.2	26.2	(24.1)	31.2	29.2	31.7	30.2	29.2	34.2	(29.2)	30.0*	+33.01
18	31.2	34.2	33.2	30.2	29.2	25.2	23.2	31.2	29.2	30.2	29.2	29.7	32.2	(28.9)	(24.4)	+32.50
19	30.2	34.0	33.2	29.2	28.2	25.2	22.7	31.2	28.2	30.2	29.2	29.2	31.2	(28.9)	(22.5)	+32.11
20	30.2	33.2	33.2	28.2	29.2	24.2	23.2	30.2	27.2	(29.9)	27.2	29.2	30.7	(28.9)	(20.8)	+31.75
21	29.7	32.2	33.7	27.7	29.2	25.2	22.2	30.2	28.2	(29.6)	26.2	31.2	29.2	29.0*	22.2	+31.45
22	29.7	32.2	32.2	27.7	29.2	24.2	22.2	30.2	28.2	(29.2)	25.2	31.2	29.2	29.0*	21.2	+30.80
23	30.2	31.7	33.2	28.2	28.2	23.2	21.7	27.2	27.2	(29.0)	25.2	31.2	29.2	29.0*	21.2	+30.42
Midn't	+30.2	+29.2	+32.2	+27.4	+27.2	+23.2	+20.2	+24.2	+26.2	(+28.6)	+25.2	+30.2	+29.2	+29.0*	+20.2	+29.84
Means	+30.72	+32.11	+31.05	+31.31	+28.91	+26.35	+23.24	+27.08	+28.51	+28.37	+28.16	+28.60	+30.28	+29.79	+27.90	+31.82

[1] According to entries by Mr. Sonntag on Aug. 15th, and by Dr. Kane on Oct. 11th, mercurial thermometer No. 12 seems to have been used as shade thermometer between these dates. Its scale is divided from 2 to 2 degrees. Correction by two standards, —1°.1 and 0°.4; mean adopted, —0°.8. Mr. Sonntag applied the same correction in the tables, p. 420 of the narrative, vol. ii., after Sept. 1st.

* Supplied from the dry bulb readings.

Temperature of the Air in Shade observed at Van Rensselaer Harbor,

In September, 1854, in Lat. 78° 37′, Long. 70° 53′ W. of Greenwich.

Expressed in degrees of Fahrenheit's scale. On deck of the brig Advance.

Hour.	1st.	2d.	3d.	4th.	5th.	6th.	7th.	8th.	9th.	10th.	11th.	12th.	13th.	14th.	15th.	16th.
	°	°	°	°	°	°	°	°	°	°	°	°	°	°	°	°
1h.	+21.2	(+18.0)	+16.2	+ 7.2	+ 3.2	+ 7.7	+10.2	+ 8.2	+ 7.2	+ 9.2	+ 9.2	+ 1.5	—3.8	+ 0.2	+11.2	+ 3.2
2	19.2	(16.5)	15.7	8.8	6.2	8.2	8.2	7.7	6.2	9.7	8.2	+ 0.7	—2.8	2.2	+11.2	3.7
3	18.2	+15.2	15.2	8.2	4.2	8.2	7.2	8.7	9.2	9.7	7.2	+ 0.2	—2.8	3.2	+11.2	3.2
4	17.2	17.2	15.2	8.2	4.2	8.2	7.2	8.7	9.2	9.7	4.2	— 0.8	—1.8	3.7	+11.2	5.2
5	17.2	19.2	15.2	10.2	6.2	9.2	8.2	9.2	11.2	10.2	5.2	+ 2.2	—2.8	4.2	+12.2	7.2
6	17.7	19.2	15.2	13.2	8.2	10.2	8.2	9.2	12.2	10.2	5.2	+ 3.2	—4.8	6.2	+11.2	7.2
7	17.2	20.2	16.2	13.2	8.5	14.2	9.2	12.2	14.7	12.2	8.2	+ 5.2	+1.2	8.2	(+11.5)	7.2
8	21.2	20.2	18.2	16.2	8.7	17.2	8.7	13.2	13.7	15.2	15.2	+ 9.2	+6.2	8.2	(+11.8)	9.2
9	21.2	21.2	17.2	17.2	10.2	18.2	9.2	15.2	14.2	21.2	17.2	+10.2	+9.2	9.2	+12.2	12.2
10	23.2	21.2	17.2	17.2	11.2	19.2	9.2	16.2	15.2	21.2	17.2	+12.2	+9.7	11.2	+12.2	13.2
11	27.2	22.2	17.2	18.2	15.2	21.2	12.2	17.2	16.2	22.2	18.2	+12.2	+8.7	14.2	+14.2	12.2
Noon	22.2	24.2	19.2	24.2	16.2	22.2	15.2	15.2	19.2	22.2	19.2	+12.2	+9.2	13.2	+15.2	11.2
13	27.2	24.2	17.2	26.2	17.2	21.2	17.2	13.2	18.2	21.2	19.2	+11.2	+9.2	12.2	+16.2	11.2
14	26.2	23.2	18.2	27.2	15.2	20.2	16.2	13.2	19.2	21.2	16.2	+11.2	+6.2	13.2	+16.2	12.2
15	26.2	22.2	17.7	25.2	12.2	19.7	14.2	13.7	18.2	20.2	14.7	+ 9.2	+6.2	13.2	+16.2	12.2
16	25.2	22.2	17.2	24.2	11.2	17.2	13.2	12.2	17.2	18.2	15.2	+ 8.2	+7.2	12.2	+15.2	11.2
17	25.2	21.2	17.2	23.2	10.2	17.2	(12.6)	12.2	17.2	17.2	11.2	+ 7.2	+9.2	11.2	+12.2	12.2
18	25.2	21.2	17.2	20.2	10.2	15.2	(12.0)	11.2	17.2	13.2	7.7	+ 4.2	+8.2	11.2	+ 9.2	11.2
19	21.2	20.2	16.2	19.2	10.2	14.2	(11.4)	11.2	17.2	11.2	6.7	+ 3.2	+7.2	11.2	+ 7.2	10.2
20	21.2	19.2	13.2	17.2	9.7	11.2	(10.8)	11.2	16.2	9.2	5.2	+ 3.7	+8.2	11.2	+ 5.2	9.2
21	20.2	20.2	13.2	9.2	9.2	11.2	10.2	11.4	15.2	8.2	5.2	— 0.3	+8.7	12.2	— 0.8	8.2
22	19.2	17.2	9.2	6.2	8.7	11.2	9.2	10.2	15.2	6.2	3.2	— 0.8	+8.2	12.2	— 2.8	7.2
23	19.2	17.2	8.2	4.2	8.2	10.2	7.2	8.2	10.7	7.2	2.2	— 1.8	+7.7	12.2	+ 1.2	4.7
Midn't	+19.2	+16.2	+ 8.2	+ 5.2	+ 5.2	+10.2	+ 8.2	+ 8.2	+10.7	+ 7.7	+ 2.2	— 2.8	+3.2	+11.7	+ 2.2	+ 4.7
Means	+21.60	+19.95	+15.45	+15.39	+ 9.57	+14.28	+10.64	+11.54	+14.20	+13.91	+10.14	+ 5.02	+4.78	+ 9.49	+10.11	+ 8.72

Hour.	17th.	18th.	19th.	20th.	21st.	22d.	23d.	24th.	25th.	26th.	27th.	28th.	29th.	30th.		Means.
	°	°	°	°	°	°	°	°	°	°	°	°	°	°		°
1h.	+ 2.2	+1.2	+1.2	—6.8	+4.7	+ 2.2	—3.3	— 0.8	+15.2	+12.2	+13.2	+ 4.2	+ 7.2	— 0.3	...	+ 6.07
2	+ 4.2	+2.2	+2.2	—6.8	4.2	+ 4.2	—2.3	— 2.8	14.2	15.2	12.2	10.2	6.2	+ 0.2	...	+ 6.[illegible]3
3	+ 4.2	+8.2	+2.2	—5.8	3.2	+ 3.2	—1.8	+ 0.2	14.2	17.2	11.2	10.2	6.2	17.2	...	+ 7.20
4	+ 3.2	+9.2	+1.2	—5.8	3.2	+ 3.2	—2.8	+ 4.2	14.2	15.2	12.2	11.2	7.2	17.2	...	+ 7.32
5	+ 3.2	+8.2	+0.7	—7.3	2.2	+ 1.2	—0.8	+ 1.2	13.2	15.2	11.2	11.2	7.2	16.2	...	+ 7.57
6	+ 5.2	+7.2	+1.2	—8.8	3.2	+ 3.0	+1.2	+ 3.2	15.2	13.2	11.2	13.2	7.2	15.2	...	+ 8.08
7	+11.2	+6.2	—0.8	—4.8	2.2	+ 3.0	+1.2	+ 7.2	15.2	13.2	11.2	11.2	8.7	15.2	...	+ 9.31
8	+13.2	+9.2	+3.2	—1.8	1.7	+ 7.0	+0.2	+ 7.2	14.2	14.2	9.2	10.2	9.2	14.2	...	+10.78
9	+11.2	+6.2	+5.2	—1.8	2.2	+ 9.2	— 0.8	+ 7.2	11.2	15.2	12.2	11.2	11.2	15.2	...	+11.67
10	+13.2	+3.2	+7.2	—0.8	3.2	+11.2	—2.8	+ 9.2	13.2	15.2	13.2	11.2	11.2	17.2	...	+12.38
11	+13.2	(+3.8)	+7.2	+0.2	1.2	+13.2	—2.8	+ 9.7	13.2	16.2	12.2	12.2	11.2	16.2	...	+13.19
Noon	+13.2	(+4.4)	+9.2	(+1.2)	9.2	+11.2	—1.8	+11.2	13.2	16.2	10.2	13.2	10.2	16.2	...	+13.91
13	+14.2	(+5.0)	+7.2	(+2.2)	5.2	+12.2	+0.2	+11.2	14.2	16.2	9.2	13.2	13.2	16.2	...	+14.06
14	+11.2	(+5.6)	+6.2	(+3.2)	7.2	+10.2	—4.8	+11.2	13.2	15.2	8.2	11.2	12.2	16.2	...	+13.38
15	+ 7.2	+6.2	+2.2	+4.2	4.2	+ 7.2	—3.8	+12.2	13.2	15.2	7.2	10.2	12.7	16.2	...	+12.52
16	+ 7.2	+4.2	+1.2	+3.7	5.2	+ 4.2	—4.8	+11.2	12.2	15.2	6.2	11.2	13.2	16.2	...	+11.78
17	+ 6.2	—2.3	—0.8	+3.2	7.2	+ 2.2	—3.8	+11.2	11.2	12.2	6.2	11.2	13.2	17.2	...	+11.03
18	+ 6.2	+1.2	+3.7	+3.2	6.2	+ 3.2	—2.8	+12.2	11.2	13.2	5.2	12.2	12.2	17.2	...	+10.63
19	+ 0.2	—1.8	—1.3	+3.2	7.2	— 2.8	—1.8	+13.2	10.2	13.2	5.2	10.2	11.2	17.2	...	+ 9.37
20	— 3.8	+1.2	—0.8	+3.2	6.2	— 2.8	—1.8	+13.2	11.2	13.2	4.2	11.2	11.2	17.2	...	+ 8.82
21	— 5.8	+7.2	—0.8	+3.2	6.2	— 2.8	(—1.6)	+15.2	13.2	14.2	7.2	10.2	11.2	15.2	...	+ 8.45
22	— 2.8	+8.2	—3.8	+4.2	5.7	— 2.8	(—1.4)	+15.2	13.2	13.2	6.2	11.2	9.2	14.2	...	+ 7.65
23	— 6.8	+7.7	—7.8	+3.2	5.2	— 2.8	(—1.2)	+13.2	12.2	12.2	3.2	6.2	6.2	13.2	...	+ 6.35
Midn't	— 7.8	+8.2	—8.8	+3.2	+4.2	— 2.8	(—1.0)	+11.2	+12.2	+12.2	+ 2.2	+ 5.2	+ 6.2	+13.2	...	+ 5.93
Means	+ 5.12	+4.99	+1.51	—0.38	+4.60	+ 3.92	—1.88	+ 8.64	+13.08	+14.33	+ 8.74	+10.53	+ 9.78	+14.55	...	+ 9.74

Sept. 30th. First part of the day, wind blowing in heavy squalls.

Temperature of the Air in Shade observed at Van Rensselaer Harbor,

In October, 1854, in Lat. 78° 37′, Long. 70° 53′ W. of Greenwich.

Expressed in degrees of Fahrenheit's scale. On deck of the brig Advance.

Hour.	1st.	2d.	3d.	4th.	5th.	6th.	7th.	8th.	9th.	10th.	11th.	12th.	13th.	14th.	15th.	16th.
	°	°	°	°	°	°	°	°	°	°	°	°	°	°	°	°
1h.	+14.2	+ 4.2	+17.2	+21.2	+17.2	+13.2	—1.8	+6.2	— 7.8	—24.8	—28.2	—4.5	— 1.5	— 6.0	+13.5	—10.5
2	14.2	4.2	16.7	21.2	18.2	+13.2	—0.8	+7.2	8.8	23.8	27.5	—3.5	— 0.5	— 6.0	+ 8.5	11.5
3	15.2	9.2	16.2	22.2	17.2	+13.2	—1.8	+3.2	7.8	22.8	26.5	—4.5	— 0.5	— 5.5	+ 4.5	10.5
4	13.2	9.2	16.2	22.2	18.2	+14.7	—2.8	+3.2	7.8	24.8	27.5	—2.5	+ 0.5	— 6.8	+ 4.9	11.5
5	14.2	9.2	18.2	21.2	19.2	+11.2	—4.8	+3.2	7.8	25.8	26.5	—2.5	+ 0.5	— 6.5	+ 4.5	11.5
6	12.2	9.2	19.2	20.2	21.2	+10.2	—3.8	+3.2	8.8	24.8	25.5	—1.5	— 1.0	— 7.5	+ 5.5	7.5
7	13.2	9.2	17.2	20.2	21.2	+ 9.2	—3.8	+3.2	10.8	25.3	22.5	—2.0	— 1.5	— 1.5	+ 7.5	7.5
8	13.2	10.2	19.2	22.2	19.2	+10.2	—3.8	+4.7	14.8	24.8	18.5	—1.0	— 1.5	— 1.5	+ 5.5	9.5
9	13.2	11.2	21.2	23.2	19.2	+10.2	—4.8	+2.2	11.8	25.8	16.5	+1.5	— 3.5	— 1.5	+ 3.5	8.5
10	15.2	10.7	21.2	23.2	19.2	+10.2	—6.8	+3.2	11.8	24.8	14.5	+3.5	— 4.5	+ 1.5	+ 2.5	9.5
11	14.2	9.2	21.2	23.2	20.2	+13.2	—7.3	+4.2	13.8	22.8	13.5	+3.3	— 4.5	— 1.5	— 2.5	9.5
Noon	15.2	10.2	21.7	23.2	19.2	+ 2.2	—5.8	—0.8	12.8	23.8	12.5	+3.3	— 7.0	— 1.5	— 3.5	12.5
13	15.2	11.7	21.2	23.2	19.2	+ 4.2	—4.8	+1.2	13.8	23.8	12.5	+4.5	— 7.0	— 1.8	— 3.7	14.5
14	13.2	12.2	23.2	23.2	20.2	+ 3.2	—2.8	—0.8	14.8	22.8	13.5	+4.5	— 9.0	— 1.5	— 4.3	15.5
15	10.2	13.2	23.2	21.2	20.7	+ 3.2	—3.3	—1.8	15.8	22.8	12.5	+1.7	—11.0	+ 0.1	— 4.5	18.0
16	10.2	14.7	23.2	20.2	19.7	+ 4.2	+0.2	—2.8	17.8	22.8	14.5	+1.7	—11.0	+ 0.1	— 5.5	15.5
17	9.2	17.2	21.2	17.2	19.2	+ 4 2	—1.8	—3.8	17.8	22.8	14.0	+0.5	—12.5	+ 1.5	— 7.5	17.5
18	8.2	16.2	19.2	16.2	19.2	+ 4.2	+0.2	—3.8	18.8	25.8	12.0	—2.0	—13.5	+ 2.5	— 7.5	17.5
19	9.2	17.2	18.2	15.2	19.2	+ 2.2	+1.2	—4.8	20.8	26.8	11.5	—1.5	—13.5	+ 3.5	— 7.5	19.0
20	9.2	16.2	20.2	17.2	19.2	+ 1.2	+0.2	—6.8	21.8	27.8	11.0	—1.5	—12.5	+ 4.5	— 7.0	19.5
21	9.2	15.2	21.2	18.2	17.2	+ 1.2	—0.8	—8.8	23.8	27.8	10.0	—1.5	—11.5	+ 1.5	— 6.5	17.5
22	8.7	15.2	22.2	20.2	17.2	— 0.8	—0.3	—6.8	22.8	28.8	10.0	—2.5	— 9.5	+ 1.5	— 6.8	18.0
23	7.2	14.2	22.2	19.2	16.2	— 1.8	+1.2	—8.8	23.8	29.3	5.5	—2.5	— 9.0	+12.5	— 8.5	18.0
Midn't	+ 6.2	+14.2	+21.2	+18.2	+13.2	— 1.8	+1.2	—8.8	—23.3	—29.3	— 5.5	—2.5	— 8.0	+12.5	— 8.5	—17.7
Means	+11.80	+11.80	+20.08	+20.53	+18.74	+ 6.43	—2.40	—0.57	—14.99	—25.20	—16.34	—0.48	— 6.38	— 0.31	— 0.97	—13.68

Hour.	17th.	18th.	19th.	20th.	21st.	22d.	23d.	24th.	25th.	26th.	27th.	28th.	29th.	30th.	31st.	Means.
	°	°	°	°	°	°	°	°	°	°	°	°	°	°	°	°
1h.	—14.5	—11.5	—14.5	— 9.5	—21.5	(—16.2)	(—20.7)	—13.5	—16.0	—24.0	—25.5	—34.5	—27.0	—26.5	—22.0	— 8.89
2	14.5	8.5	10.5	12.3	21.5	(—14.8)	(—22.4)	14.0	16.0	24.5	25.6	32.5	27.0	22.3	21.0	— 8.59
3	15.5	8.2	7.9	13.5	22.0	—13.5	—24.0	10.0	17.0	25.5	26.0	36.5	29.0	22.0	22.0	— 8.76
4	15.5	8.0	6.7	15.5	21.5	13.0	23.5	9.0	18.0	26.5	27.0	34.5	27.0	20.0	21.0	— 8.65
5	14.5	8.0	6.5	13.5	19.2	13.2	24.0	5.0	18.0	26.5	28.0	35.5	24.0	20.0	20.0	— 8.38
6	13.5	7.9	6.0	13.5	19.5	13.4	24.0	3.0	22.0	18.0	28.0	37.8	23.0	19.0	20.0	— 8.00
7	11.5	7.5	6.5	13.5	20.0	16.0	18.0	4.0	22.5	17.0	31.0	37.0	27.0	18.0	19.5	— 7.84
8	14.0	8.5	6.5	14.0	21.7	15.0	14.0	7.5	22.0	15.0	32.0	37.0	27.0	18.0	20.0	— 7.85
9	13.5	12.5	6.5	14.0	20.5	13.0	13.0	9.0	22.0	17.0	34.0	34.0	23.5	18.3	21.0	— 7.70
10	14.5	8.5	6.8	13.2	20.0	10.5	12.5	9.5	23.0	23.0	33.5	25.0	20.0	17.5	22.5	— 7.15
11	14.5	8.5	10.0	16.7	19.5	9.0	12.0	9.5	25.0	27.0	34.8	20.0	20.0	19.5	23.0	— 7.60
Noon	14.5	8.5	7.5	17.9	19.5	8.0	11.0	9.0	26.0	30.0	34.5	19.5	20.0	20.0	22.0	— 8.16
13	15.5	10.5	7.5	18.0	19.0	8.0	11.0	9.0	26.0	32.5	34.0	15.5	20.0	21.0	22.0	— 8.10
14	16.5	13.5	8.0	17.5	18.5	8.0	12.0	7.0	25.5	32.0	34.5	14.7	22.0	22.5	22.0	— 8.37
15	18.0	14.0	3.5	18.5	17.5	8.5	11.0	5.5	24.5	29.0	34.0	16.0	21.0	23.0	18.0	— 8.33
16	19.5	14.9	3.5	19.0	18.5	9.5	13.0	3.0	22.0	22.0	34.0	18.0	23.0	24.0	19.0	— 8.34
17	18.5	13.5	4.5	17.0	18.5	11.0	13.0	4.5	23.4	24.0	33.5	14.0	24.0	25.3	19.5	— 8.76
18	18.5	17.5	4.5	17.5	18.5	9.0	14.0	5.3	24.0	26.0	31.0	19.0	21.0	26.3	20.0	— 9.26
19	20.5	17.5	8.7	19.7	18.5	11.0	14.0	6.5	27.0	26.0	29.0	22.5	26.0	27.0	22.0	—10.17
20	19.5	18.0	8.0	19.9	17.5	12.0	13.0	7.5	25.5	24.0	30.0	26.0	27.0	27.0	24.5	—10.30
21	15.5	18.5	7.5	20.5	17.5	13.0	13.0	7.0	22.0	24.5	30.0	27.0	30.0	25.5	24.0	—10.32
22	14.0	14.5	6.8	21.5	17.0	13.5	15.0	7.5	21.0	24.0	34.5	27.0	29.5	24.0	28.0	—10.29
23	12.5	13.5	6.5	20.5	18.5	18.0	15.0	9.0	18.0	25.0	36.0	28.0	29.0	24.0	30.0	—10.26
Midn't	—11.5	—11.5	— 7.5	—21.5	—17.5	—19.0	—15.0	—10.5	—23.0	—26.0	—36.0	—27.0	—30.0	—23.0	—30.5	—10.59
Means	—15.44	—11.81	— 7.18	—16.59	—19.31	—12.34	—15.75	— 7.72	—22.06	—24.54	—31.52	—26.60	—24.88	—22.24	—22.23	— 8.78

Oct. 11th. Shade thermometer No. 12 was withdrawn, and mercurial thermometer *B* substituted. From four comparisons with the spirit standard on shore, I deduced the correction +1°.5. This thermometer was used for 11 days.

Oct. 18th. The sun at meridian no longer reaches our brig.

Oct. 22d. Spirit thermometer *A* was used from this date. This thermometer was uniformly exposed in a wind protected case, suspended near foremast, 16 feet above water-line. From 16 comparisons, I deduce the correction +2°.0.

Temperature of the Air in Shade observed at Van Rensselaer Harbor,

In November, 1854, in Lat. 78° 37′, Long. 70° 53′ W. of Greenwich.

Expressed in degrees of Fahrenheit's scale. On deck of the brig Advance.

Hour.	1st.	2d.	3d.	4th.	5th.	6th.	7th.	8th.	9th.	10th.	11th.	12th.	13th.	14th.	15th.	16th.
	°	°	°	°	°	°	°	°	°	°	°	°	°	°	°	°
1h.	—30.5	—37.7	—24.0	...	...	...	...	...	...	...	—12.0	—20.5	—20.5	—28.5	—31.0	—32.0
2	31.0	35.5	27.0	...	...	...	...	...	...	...	12.5	21 0	20.0	28.0	32.0	29.0
3	29.0	35.5	26.5	...	...	...	...	...	...	...	12.0	22.0	19.0	28.0	31.0	29.0
4	30.0	35.5	26.5	...	...	...	...	...	...	...	13.0	22.6	21.0	30.0	32.0	28.0
5	31.0	36.5	26.0	...	...	...	...	...	...	...	13.0	21.0	21.1	28.0	33.3	37.0
6	31.0	38.0	26.2	...	...	...	...	...	...	...	13.0	19.0	21.4	29.0	34.3	37.5
7	30.0	33.0	26.7	...	...	...	...	...	...	...	12.8	21.0	19.8	27.0	34.4	33.0
8	32.0	31.5	25.0	...	...	...	...	...	...	...	19.3	21.5	23.9	25.5	35.3	33.5
9	24.0	32.0	31.0	...	...	...	...	...	...	...	21.5	16.6	23.0	25.5	34.0	34.8
10	27.0	33.0	30.0	...	...	...	...	...	...	...	22.0	17.5	22.1	22.5	36.0	35.0
11	19.0	31.0	27.0	...	...	...	...	...	...	...	19.0	16.5	25.5	25.5	35.5	35.0
Noon	18.5	31.0	23.5	...	...	...	...	...	...	...	20.5	14.5	26.0	26.0	33.5	35 0
13	18.0	24.0	26.0	...	...	...	...	...	...	...	22.0	14.6	24.0	27.0	37.0	36.0
14	18.0	24.5	28.0	...	...	...	...	...	...	...	22.0	15.0	24.5	27.0	38.0	37.0
15	18.5	27.0	30.0	...	...	...	...	...	...	...	21.5	17.0	25.0	27.0	38.5	37.0
16	18.5	29.5	28.0	...	...	...	...	...	...	...	21.8	18.0	26.0	26.0	39.0	37.5
17	23.0	30.5	30.0	...	...	...	...	...	...	...	22.0	15.8	28.0	26.4	38.0	36.0
18	25.0	29.0	32.0	...	...	...	...	...	...	...	23.0	13.5	29.0	27.2	38.0	36.4
19	29.2	31.0	34.0	...	...	...	...	...	...	...	21.5	15.5	24.3	28.7	39.0	38.0
20	31.0	30.5	35.5	...	...	...	...	...	...	...	22.0	16.0	26.0	30.0	37.0	38.2
21	32.0	33.0	36.5	...	...	...	...	...	...	...	21.0	16.0	27.0	32.0	37.0	39.0
22	30.0	34.0	37.0	...	...	...	...	...	...	...	21.0	15.0	26.5	32.5	37.0	38.0
23	35.0	36.0	38.0	...	...	...	...	...	...	...	21.0	15.0	25.0	33.0	34.0	40.0
Midn't	—36.0	—35.0	—39.0	...	...	...	...	...	...	...	—20.0	—16.5	—26.0	—32.0	—33.0	—40.0
Means	—26.97	—32.26	—29.72	—28.35 *	—26.98 *	—25.61 *	—24.23 *	—22.86 *	—21.48 *	—20.11 *	—18.73	—17.57	—23.94	—28.01	—35.33	—35.50

Hour.	17th.	18th.	19th.	20th.	21st.	22d.	23d.	24th.	25th.	26th.	27th.	28th.	29th.	30th.	Means.	Corrected means.
	°	°	°	°	°	°	°	°	°	°	°	°	°	°	°	°
1h.	—38.5	—31.0	— 5.5	— 6.5	— 9.0	—16.0	—3.5	+7.0	0.0	— 5.7	—11.8	—18.0	—23.3	—36.8	—18.93	—19.90
2	39.0	33.0	6.0	— 3.0	10.0	14.0	—2.0	+6.5	— 2.0	6.7	15.0	19.9	23.3	35.7	—19.09	—20.03
3	41.0	33.0	7.0	— 2.0	12.0	14.3	—3.0	+3.0	1.5	6.7	17.5	21.5	21.7	35.1	—19.36	—20.28
4	41.5	31.0	6.0	— 2.0	13.0	14.5	—3.5	+3.0	2.0	8.8	17.9	20.5	20.5	35.2	—19.65	—20.54
5	41.0	(28.8)	10.3	— 2.0	15.8	12.0	—2.0	0.0	3.5	10.4	19.3	24.4	20.5	35.7	—20.55	—21.35
6	40.0	(26.6)	10.6	— 1.0	15.0	11.0	—2.0	+1.0	4.0	13.5	22.9	24.4	21.6	37.3	—20.80	—21.62
7	38.0	24.5	15.5	+ 1.0	15.0	12.0	—5.0	0.0	4.0	9.9	23.5	25.4	26.4	38.8	—20.64	—21.41
8	36.0	24.0	17.0	+ 1.0	17.0	12.0	—7.0	—4.0	3.0	13.0	22.0	25.6	23.8	40.1	—21.35	—22.05
9	36.0	25.0	18.0	0.0	17.5	11.5	—6.0	—1.5	5.0	11.8	21.5	25.6	24.9	40.8	—21.20	—21.90
10	35.0	24.5	19.0	+ 2.0	18.5	9.8	—7.0	—1.5	5.8	12.0	21.0	25.8	26.4	41.8	—21.36	—22.01
11	35.5	13.5	15.0	— 0.3	19.0	9.5	—3.3	—1.5	6.3	12.0	19.8	24.9	24.9	39.7	—19.97	—20.77
Noon	34.0	5.0	15.1	— 2.3	21.0	9.5	—4.7	—1.0	6.8†	15.5	19.5	24.4	26.4	37.8	—19.63	—20.48
13	36.0	4.0	15.0	— 0.7	24.0	9.0	—4.0	—0.5	8.0	17.0	18.9	24.4	30.4	43.2	—20.16	—20.98
14	34.0	3.5	17.5	— 1.0	24.0	8.8	—2.0	—0.5	7.5	17.0	19.5	25.8	31.5	39.7	—20.27	—21.09
15	32.0	3.5	18.0	— 1.5	23.0	8.0	+4.0	0.0	9.4	15.5	19.3	25.4	35.8	38.8	—20.33	—21.14
16	25.0	4.0	21.4	— 2.0	19.0	8.0	+2.0	0.0	14.3	15.5	19.4	25.5	41.9	39.7	—20.78	—21.58
17	25.0	2.1	22.0	— 2.0	16.0	7.0	+1.0	—2.0	14.5	17.5	19.0	24.7	43.2	41.6	—21.10	—21.90
18	24.0	4.0	23.0	— 4.0	16.0	7.6	+2.0	+1.0	14.5	17.0	19.3	27.7	43.7	42.1	—21.43	—22.23
19	25.5	4.5	15.0	— 5.0	16.0	7.4	+5.0	+1.0	11.4	16.5	19.5	28.4	45.6	45.6	—21.55	—22.39
20	26.0	5.0	16.0	— 7.0	19.0	6.0	+6.0	+1.0	9.9	11.4	19.7	29.1	47.9	39.7	—21.56	—22.43
21	34.0	4.7	18.0	— 6.5	19.7	6.0	+5.0	+0.5	11.4	11.4	19.2	26.9	47.3	39.3	—22.28	—23.10
22	32.0	4.0	16.3	— 7.3	19.0	6.7	+5.0	0.0	9.1	10.9	19.5	23.3	43.2	37.8	—21.53	—22.40
23	34.0	4.0	8.0	— 8.0	20.5	7.0	+5.4	—1.0	7.4	14.5	19.5	23.3	38.8	37.9	—21.55	—22.42
Midn't	—34.0	— 4.0	—12.0	—10.0	—21.0	— 6.0	+5.0	—0.5	— 7.4	—14.5	—22.0	—19.5	—35.7	—37.8	—21.60	—22.49
Means	—34.04	—14.47	—14.47	— 2.92	—17.50	— 9.73	—0.61	+0.42	— 7.03	—12.70	—19.44	—24.35	—32.03	—39.08	[—20.70]	—21.52

* Mean daily temperatures not given in Appendix XII. Vol. II. of the narrative. The above values are interpolated. On account of this, a correction was applied to the mean daily values (—0°.82). Besides this correction, a small one was applied to the hourly means to refer them to the middle of the month.

† From noon, Nov. 25th, the second spirit standard was used. From a number of comparisons, its corrections were found the same as those made out for spirit standard *S*.

Nov. 11th. The thermometer can hardly be observed at noonday without a light. Nov. 15th. Can read Parry's type at noon, but with great difficulty. Nov. 19th. Could not read the type at noon. Nov. 20th. Spirit standard and long ether thermometer on shore, and long mercurial standard on board, broken by last night's gale. Nov. 29th. Mercury congealed at —42°.7; resumes its fluidity at —38°.

TEMPERATURE OF THE AIR IN SHADE OBSERVED AT VAN RENSSELAER HARBOR,

In December, 1854, in Lat. 78° 37′, Long. 70° 53′ W. of Greenwich.

Expressed in degrees of Fahrenheit's scale. On deck of the brig Advance.

Hour.	1st.	2d.	3d.	4th.	5th.	6th.	7th.	8th.	9th.	10th.	11th.	12th.	13th.	14th.	15th.	16th.
	°	°	°	°	°	°	°	°	°	°	°	°	°	°	°	°
1h.	—35.7	—22.4	—35.7	—32.6	—40.8	—39.7	(—48.6)	(—43.2)	(—44.8)	(—41.7)	(—26.8)	(—52.8)	(—49.4)	—46.3	—47.9	—37.2
2	34.7	30.4	34.7	33.8	41.9	38.8	(41.7)	(42.6)	(44.0)	(41.8)	(27.1)	(51.6)	—50.4	43.2	47.2	37.3
3	43.2	29.5	35.7	32.6	41.9	40.8	—34.8	(42.0)	—43.2	—41.9	—27.4	—50.4	50.4	45.0	48.0	39.7
4	43.2	28.0	34.3	32.6	39.9	41.9	38.8	(41.4)	41.9	42.5	28.4	46.8	52.9	47.0	48.8	50.7
5	41.9	26.9	32.6	36.2	39.2	42.5	40.8	—40.8	(42.8)	(42.0)	27.4	41.8	51.6	47.9	48.2	42.3
6	39.7	26.8	31.5	34.2	37.8	42.6	41.9	41.8	(43.6)	(41.4)	29.5	40.0	45.0	47.3	48.0	41.8
7	43.7	34.8	29.0	35.8	44.4	42.8	41.4	41.2	44.5	40.8	25.9	31.9	37.8	46.1	51.6	45.6
8	44.5	35.7	27.3	36.8	38.2	43.2	41.6	43.2	43.8	38.7	25.6	31.5	38.2	46.1	49.4	45.0
9	43.2	29.5	22.4	35.8	37.2	41.9	38.8	45.9	42.7	41.1	29.1	32.5	39.0	49.1	47.9	49.3
10	41.9	29.5	20.5	34.8	37.3	39.0	40.8	44.6	42.8	41.3	29.5	31.0	38.8	49.5	47.9	50.4
11	40.8	30.0	23.3	37.5	35.8	38.8	39.3	43.2	40.8	40.0	32.0	27.9	37.8	51.2	48.6	46.8
Noon	39.3	31.5	20.0	35.8	33.1	43.7	40.5	43.2	39.0	39.7	35.1	26.9	35.0	52.4	47.9	46.0
13	43.2	35.7	15.5	35.8	32.6	44.7	40.8	42.3	38.3	39.7	37.8	28.4	35.7	53.3	46.8	46.8
14	43.2	33.8	17.0	36.8	32.6	45.6	42.5	41.3	41.9	37.5	39.1	28.7	37.8	52.9	46.4	47.5
15	36.8	41.3	18.7	37.2	31.5	45.0	43.4	40.3	(42.5)	37.3	40.8	28.7	37.2	50.0	47.3	47.6
16	32.5	41.9	18.5	37.8	30.5	44.4	44.2	34.8	(43.1)	37.6	48.4	30.8	37.8	50.4	41.4	47.3
17	32.5	41.9	19.5	39.0	29.7	43.6	44.5	31.1	43.7	38.0	49.1	30.8	38.1	51.6	40.2	47.3
18	33.2	43.2	20.0	35.2	29.5	45.1	44.0	29.2	44.6	32.0	49.1	31.5	38.8	52.1	39.7	45.2
19	33.5	42.5	20.5	36.8	30.5	44.5	44.1	34.5	41.9	36.8	50.7	31.8	39.1	51.6	44.5	45.6
20	29.0	38.5	19.5	38.6	31.5	44.5	—46.2	37.8	43.2	37.1	53.2	37.8	39.3	48.2	—50.8	45.9
21	26.1	37.8	29.0	38.3	31.8	44.5	(45.6)	40.2	41.2	27.7	56.2	42.5	52.1	46.0	(48.1)	45.6
22	21.5	36.2	32.6	38.1	32.5	44.8	(45.0)	42.3	—41.3	—25.9	—56.4	—46.3	46.5	42.5	(45.4)	45.1
23	17.5	37.6	32.8	40.2	35.8	51.8	(44.4)	43.2	(41.4)	(26 2)	(55.2)	(47.3)	40.3	41.3	(42.7)	39.7
Midn't	—16.7	—35.7	—32.8	—39.7	—38.0	—55.5	(—43.8)	—45.6	(—41.5)	(—26.5)	(—54.0)	(—48.4)	—39.7	—43.2	(—40.0)	—38.8
Means	—35.73	—34.42	—25.98	—36.33	—35.58	—43.74	—42.40	—40.65	—42.44	—37.30	—38.91	—37.42	—42.03	—48.09	—46.45	—44.77

Hour.	17th.	18th.	19th.	20th.	21st.	22d.	23d.	24th.	25th.	26th.	27th.	28th.	29th.	30th.	31st.	Means.
	°	°	°	°	°	°	°	°	°	°	°	°	°	°	°	°
1h.	—36.8	—38.1	— 8.9	—19.7	—25.9	—19.7	—47.2	(—49.0)	—54.4	—47.9	—47.9	—29.0	—34.8	—18.5	—43.2	—37.63
2	33.8	38.8	12.5	20.0	24.4	18.1	47.6	—48.3	(50.6)	47.9	48.2	28.5	34.2	19.7	44.5	—37.36
3	29.5	40.8	13.0	24.8	23.8	18.0	(48.1)	50.4	46.8	46.1	47.9	28.2	35.8	20.5	44.8	—37.58
4	25.4	39.7	12.2	25.0	22.9	18.8	48.7	54.4	46.6	46.3	47.9	29.0	38.3	21.5	43.2	—38.03
5	29.4	35.3	11.0	24.3	22.4	22.4	49.4	51.6	47.5	44.8	47.6	26.4	37.8	19.5	40.1	—37.24
6	31.8	39.7	17.0	24.0	23.3	26.4	48.3	49.1	41.9	40.8	48.1	24.6	38.1	16.8	37.1	—36.77
7	43.9	40.9	12.0	23.0	23.3	37.8	51.6	46.8	39.7	39.7	47.9	22.4	38.8	15.0	32.6	—37.18
8	44.5	40.8	20.0	26.3	23.3	37.8	52.9	47.1	35.1	39.1	48.6	21.7	38.0	14.5	29.6	—37.04
9	42.6	24.1	22 2	23.0	22.9	41.8	52.9	47.3	33.1	38.3	45.6	21.4	37.3	14.0	26.3	—36.07
10	42.5	23.3	25.0	23.5	22.6	41.3	53.1	48.1	32.6	39.0	43.7	20.8	31.0	14.5	25.4	—35.68
11	42.5	21.6	25.3	22.7	21.6	43.2	52.9	49.1	29.5	39.7	42.5	20.5	27.4	16.5	24.0	—35.25
Noon	43.5	14.5	24.5	23.3	19.8	42.5	55.2	49.7	29.2	44.5	41.8	19.0	20.0	18.0	23.8	—34.79
13	46.2	14.0	23.3	34.0	17.5	41.8	52.9	49.1	29.2	44.5	42.3	19.5	20.4	19.5	23.4	—35.32
14	47.1	9.8	24.0	35.3	13.8	43.5	54.6	50.4	30.5	43.5	43.2	17.0	22.6	22.4	23.7	—35.84
15	47.9	7.0	25.5	34.8	11.4	41.8	54.5	51.0	33.2	45.6	42.3	15.8	24.9	28.9	22.8	—35.90
16	47.4	7.4	26.6	35.5	13.0	42.3	51.8	51.6	35.2	47.9	40.8	14.5	26.4	38.1	21.4	—36.17
17	45.6	8.0	26.2	35.7	14.1	43.7	50.7	54.0	35.1	48.3	41.1	17.4	23.3	41.6	22.7	—36.39
18	48.1	8.5	27.5	35.9	15.9	43.7	49.7	54.8	36.6	47.9	46.8	15.5	23.6	40.8	23.3	—36.48
19	45.6	9.4	27.0	35.8	18.5	45.0	51.0	58.3	40.2	47.3	34.8	19.5	22.4	42.5	23.6	—37.09
20	42.5	10.4	27.5	36.0	18.5	45.6	49.6	57.3	41.3	46.8	32.6	20.0	21.0	45.6	22.7	—37.05
21	43.2	11.6	(27.4)	37.0	(23.0)	45.6	(50.5)	56.9	43.4	46.3	31.5	22.4	19.5	45.6	22.4	—38.03
22	45.9	—12.7	(27.2)	34.8	27.4	45.6	51.3	59.1	43.7	45.8	29.0	22.8	17.5	45.6	24.4	—38.23
23	47.0	(11.4)	(27.1)	31.7	25.4	46.2	50.4	59.9	45.6	45.6	25.4	32.6	17.5	46.8	26.4	—37.95
Midn't	—44.5	(—10.1)	—26.0	—26.9	—21.9	—46.1	—49.8	—59.9	—47.2	—46.7	—28.5	—33.6	—17.9	—46.8	—26.4	—37.84
Means	—41.55	—21.58	—21.66	—28.88	—20.69	—37.45	—51.03	—52.22	—39.51	—44.60	—41.50	—22.59	—27.85	—28.05	—29.08	—36.79

Dec. 19th. From 3h. to 20h., the readings were supplied from thermometer *A*.

Dec. 20th. From 1h. to 14h., the readings were supplied from thermometer *A*.

Temperature of the Air in Shade observed at Van Rensselaer Harbor,

In January, 1855, in Lat. 78° 37′, Long. 70° 53′ W. of Greenwich.

Expressed in degrees of Fahrenheit's scale. On deck of the brig Advance.

Hour.	1st.	2d.	3d.	4th.	5th.	6th.	7th.	8th.	9th.	10th.	11th.	12th.	13th.	14th.	15th.	16th.
	°	°	°	°	°	°	°	°	°	°	°	°	°	°	°	°
1h.	—25.4	—45.6	—38.4	—39.2	(—47.6)	(—34.4)	(—51.6)	—65.5*	—55.8	—40.8	—41.3	—44.9	—26.4	—19.5	—36.8	—31.5
2	25.4	43.7	37.8	39.4	—48.3	(34.6)	(52.2)	64.5	55.5	42.8	43.2	45.6	26.4	21.5	37.3	35.1
3	25.7	42.3	37.1	40.4	48.5	—34.8	—52.9	65.0	55.9	43.2	42.5	47.1	27.4	20.5	35.8	34.1
4	26.4	43.2†	37.3	41.8	48.7	34.2	54.8	64.5	55.9	41.8	42.3	47.9	27.0	20.7	35.8	34.8
5	26.9	43.7†	36.8	43.7	49.1	35.2	51.6	63.7	55.5	39.8	40.8	48.3	26.4	21.5	36.1	35.1
6	29.0	45.6†	37.1	44.8	48.3	38.1	50.0	62.9	57.6	39.0	39.0	49.1	25.7	22.4	35.3	35.3
7	30.5	47.9	37.3	46.8	47.9	43.7	47.3	63.1	58.7	39.2	34.8	50.4	24.9	23.7	33.8	35.8
8	22.7	47.6	36.8	46.6	44.5	43.2	50.4	58.3	58.3	35.7	30.0	49.7	23.4	24.4	37.1	38.3
9	34.1	46.8	36.3	49.4	42.3	43.2	50.7	56.2	56.0	35.2	24.4	47.9	24.4	23.4	30.5	41.4
10	34.8	47.1	35.7	49.6	43.5	45.0	51.1	55.5	56.9	35.0	23.4	45.6	17.5	23.4	31.0	39.7
11	36.3	47.3	35.7	51.3	42.3	49.9	50.9	55.8	57.5	34.8	21.5	43.2	14.5	23.4	31.5	39.3
Noon	37.1	42.5	36.8	49.6	41.8	54.6	50.4	55.8	57.7	35.1	18.5	41.8	10.4	23.4	30.5	36.7
13	37.5	43.2†	37.1	48.3	39.2	54.8	50.4	55.5	56.9	34.8	21.5	41.8	11.0	23.7	30.0	(35.5)
14	38.3	43.5†	37.8	48.1	38.8	54.6	51.0	55.5	56.6	35.1	27.3	41.8	10.7	23.4	29.5	(34.4)
15	38.8	43.7†	38.0	46.8	38.3	55.5	51.6	54.8	54.8	35.7	32.9	41.1	11.5	24.9	31.8	(33.2)
16	39.2	44.5†	38.3	47.1	37.8	56.1	52.9	54.6	54.2	36.8	36.3	40.8	11.8	25.4	32.6	(32.0)
17	38.8	44.5	39.2	45.6	36.0	56.2	53.5	54.2	51.6	37.1	38.9	41.8	12.8	25.7	33.0	(30.9)
18	38.1	46.5	39.7	45.0	35.7	58.5	56.9	55.0	48.5	37.8	39.7	42.5	14.0	26.4	32.0	(29.8)
19	34.8	43.2†	40.7	45.0	35.2	58.3	61.4	56.2	49.9	38.8	41.0	40.8	16.5	26.9	31.5	28.7
20	35.1	41.3†	41.0	46.2	32.6	56.2	61.6	53.5	51.5	39.2	43.2	40.8	17.8	27.7	32.0	28.5
21	34.0	40.8	40.8	48.1	32.4	56.9	64.4	52.9	49.7	37.8	43.2	46.0	18.5	(29.5)	(31.9)	28.0
22	34.8	41.1	40.8	46.2	34.8	(54.9)	64.3	53.5	47.4	39.7	44.5	34.8	19.0	(31.3)	(31.8)	27.9
23	40.1	39.2	40.8	46.8	34.6	52.9	64.4	53.8	43.2	40.2	44.5	31.0	19.0	(33.1)	(31.7)	37.7
Midn't	—46.0	—39.0	—39.7	—47.0	—34.2	—51.0	—65.3	—55.1	—40.0	—40.8	—44.5	—27.8	—19.3	(—34.9)	(—31.6)	(—35.1)
Means	—33.74	—43.91	—38.21	—45.95	—40.93	—48.20	—54.65	—57.77	—53.57	—38.17	—35.80	—43.02	—19.01	—25.03	—32.95	—34.12

Hour.	17th.	18th.	19th.	20th.	21st.	22d.	23d.	24th.	25th.	26th.	27th.	28th.	29th.	30th.	31st.	Means.	Corrected means.
	°	°	°	°	°	°	°	°	°	°	°	°	°	°	°	°	°
1h.	—32.5	—23.3	—25.9	—18.5	—36.3	—26.4	—35.0	—24.4	...	...	...	...	...	...	...	—36.13	—28.28
2	30.5	18.5	26.2	20.5	36.4	27.9	34.9	22.4	...	...	...	...	...	...	...	—36.27	—28.40
3	30.0	17.5	23.5	27.4	33.8	31.5	33.8	21.4	...	...	...	...	...	...	...	—36.34	—28.44
4	27.4	19.5	23.3	25.9	33.8	32.0	33.1	22.4	...	...	...	...	...	...	...	—36.44	—28.47
5	27.7	(19.7)	(23.7)	(26.5)	(33.2)	(33.0)	(32.6)	20.5	...	...	...	...	...	...	...	—36.30	—28.41
6	26.9	(19.8)	(24.0)	(27.0)	(32.5)	(33.9)	(32.0)	20.5	...	...	...	...	...	...	...	—36.49	—28.64
7	26.4	20.0	24.4	(27.5)	(31.9)	(34.9)	(31.5)	20.0	...	...	...	...	...	...	...	—36.77	—28.85
8	26.9	20.5	22.9	(28.0)	(31.2)	(35.8)	(31.0)	19.5	...	...	...	...	...	...	...	—35.95	—27.98
9	26.4	22.4	21.4	28.5	30.5	36.8	30.5	18.5	...	...	...	...	...	...	...	—35.72	—27.76
10	25.4	21.5	21.9	28.5	30.5	36.8	31.5	17.5	...	...	...	...	...	...	...	—35.35	—27.37
11	6.5‡	23.3	22.4	28.5	28.4	36.8	32.5	15.5	...	...	...	...	...	...	...	—34.55	—26.59
Noon	5.0	23.8	23.3	27.4	27.9	37.6	33.8	13.5	...	...	...	...	...	...	...	—33.96	—25.98
13	(6.2)	(22.8)	(23.0)	(27.7)	(27.4)	(38.2)	34.0	12.5	...	...	...	...	...	...	...	—33.88	—25.79
14	(7.4)	(21.8)	(22.6)	(28.0)	(26.9)	(38.8)	33.8	11.0	...	...	...	...	...	...	...	—34.03	—25.92
15	(8.5)	(20.7)	(22.2)	(28.3)	(26.4)	(39.5)	34.0	8.6	...	...	...	...	...	...	...	—34.23	—26.09
16	(9.7)	(19.7)	(21.8)	(28.7)	(25.9)	(40.1)	33.8	7.4	...	...	...	...	...	...	...	—34.48	—26.32
17	(10.9)	18.6	21.4	29.0	25.4	40.8	34.3	(—6.3)	...	...	...	...	...	...	...	—34.44	—26.32
18	(12.1)	19.5	22.0	29.5	24.9	41.4	33.8	(—5.2)	...	...	...	...	...	...	...	—34.77	—26.68
19	(13.3)	16.5	(22.6)	(30.5)	(25.1)	(40.5)	(32.5)	(—4.1)	...	...	...	...	...	...	...	—34.33	—26.16
20	(14.5)	17.3	(23.2)	(31.5)	(25.3)	(39.6)	(31.3)	(—3.0)	...	...	...	...	...	...	...	—34.75	—26.61
21	15.7	(19.0)	(23.8)	(32.4)	(25.5)	(38.7)	30.0	(—1.9)	...	...	...	...	...	...	...	—35.08	—26.94
22	17.5	(20.7)	24.4	(33.4)	(25.7)	(37.8)	28.6	(—0.8)	...	...	...	...	...	...	...	—34.82	—26.72
23	28.4	(22.4)	26.7	(34.4)	(26.0)	(36.8)	27.2	(+0.3)	...	...	...	...	...	...	...	—35.61	—27.55
Midn't	—22.4	(—24.1)	—25.4	(—35.3)	(—26.2)	(—35.9)	26.9	(+1.4)	...	...	...	...	...	...	...	—35.25	—27.21
Means	—19.05	—20.12	—23.42	—28.45	—29.05	—36.31	—32.18	—12.30	+14.62 §	—0.98 §	+3.30 §	+6.45 §	+4.72 §	—7.20 §	—19.08 §	[—35.25]	—27.23

* Lowest temperature observed this winter. † Readings supplied from thermometer *C*. ‡ Blowing hard between 10h. and 12h.

§ Means supplied from the second volume of the narrative, the values being corrected by +1°.34, from comparisons on Jan. 13th.

The constant correction applied to the last vertical column is —27°.23 +35°.25 = +8°.02, to which has been added small corrections to refer the diurnal variation and the means to the middle of the month.

The following is an example (of a somewhat extreme case) of the method of interpolation adopted in the preceding abstract. Required, the hourly temperatures between, 1854, April 2d, 20h., and April 3d, 13h.. The monthly means of each hour (omitting the observations on the 2d and 3d) were first compared with their monthly mean, when the mean diurnal variation (for the 15th of the month) became known. In like manner, the variation for the preceding month was obtained; and then, by a simple interpolation, the mean diurnal variation for the time between the 2d and 3d was found. Let $v_1\ v_2\ v_3\ v_4 \cdots - v_{24}$ equal the hourly values of the diurnal variation, t equal the mean temperature, and T resulting or interpolated temperatures; then $T = t + v\,p$, where p a factor depending principally on the transparency of the atmosphere. To find the hourly values of t and p for the above interval, we select a convenient number of consecutive observations before and after the interval, which, in the present case, gives the equations—

April 2, 15h.	$-21.2 = t + 3.7\,p$	April 3, 13h.	$-26.9 = t + 3.4\,p$
16	$-22.3 = t + 3.2\,p$	14	$-26.5 = t + 4.0\,p$
17	$-23.0 = t + 2.8\,p$	15	$-24.0 = t + 3.7\,p$
18	$-25.0 = t + 2.1\,p$	16	$-25.8 = t + 3.2\,p$
19	$-28.0 = t + 1.1\,p$	17	$-29.0 = t + 2.8\,p$
20	$-27.0 = t + 0\ 2\,p$	18	$-30.4 = t + 2.1\,p$
Mean	$-24.4 = t + 2.2\,p$		$-27.1 = t + 3.2\,p$
And from comparison with each equation	$t = -29.1$, $p = 2.14$ for $17\frac{1}{2}$h.		$t = -36.8$, $p = 3.03$ for $15\frac{1}{2}$h.

Hence, hourly variation in t —0°.35, and in p —0°.04.

The above sets of equations were then corrected for this hourly change of t and p, when the following corrected results were obtained:—

$t = -27.9$ $p = 1.60$ $t = -33.2$ $p = 1.90$

These values, when substituted in the equations, leave the following residuals:—

In first set	—0.1	—0.1	+0.2	—0.3	—1.3	+1.5	Prob. error of each ±0°.6
In second set	—1.1	—1.5	+2.0	+1.5	—0.5	—0.3	" " ±1.0

The true hourly variation in t becomes —0°.24
" " p " —0.01

The following table contains the interpolated values of t and p, and the resulting hourly temperatures for the interval.

1854	t	v	p	T	1854	t	v	p	T
April 2, 21h.	—28°.7	—0°.7	1°.65	—29°.9	April 3, 5h.	—30°.6	—2°.9	1°.75	—35°.6
22	—29.0	—1.6	1.66	—31.7	6	—30.9	—2.4	1.77	—35.2
23	—29.2	—2.1	1.68	—32.8	7	—31.1	—1.6	1.79	—33.9
24	—29.5	—2.8	1.69	—34.2	8	—31.3	—0.7	1.80	—32.6
April 3, 1	—29.7	—3.4	1.70	—35.5	9	—31.6	+0.7	1.82	—30.3
2	—29.9	—3.4	1.72	—35.8	10	—31.8	+1.5	1.83	—29.1
3	—30.2	—3.6	1.73	—36.4	11	—32.0	+2.4	1.85	—27.6
4	—30.4	—3.4	1.74	—36.3	12	—32.3	+3.0	1.86	—26.7

Which values in the last column will be found in their proper place in the preceding abstract.

Diurnal Variation.—Before giving the table of the diurnal change of the atmospheric temperatures, it will be proper to remark that, astronomically, the upper limb of the sun ceases to be visible at noon on Oct. 25th, and reappears at noon Feb. 16th; between April 19th and Aug. 24th, the lower limb will continue above the horizon without setting. On account of the considerable annual variation of the temperature, the figures in the last vertical column of each month in the preceding abstracts, headed "mean," require a small correction for the effect of the annual change during twenty-four hours; they will then represent the diurnal variation for the middle of each month. Thus, for September, 1853, the effect of the annual change during twenty-four hours is 0°.50 decreasing, hence the maximum corrections applied are —0°.25 and +0°.25 for $1^{h.}$ and $24^{h.}$ respectively; and for the intermediate hours an aliquot part of this is applied, according to the interval from noon, where the correction is zero. The following table presents the summary of the diurnal variation for each month of the year; for the first five months, the figures are the mean from two sets. The highest and lowest values, for better distinction, are placed between parentheses.

MEAN DIURNAL VARIATION OF THE TEMPERATURE FOR THE MIDDLE OF EACH MONTH OF THE YEAR.

Hour.	Sept.	Oct.	Nov.	Dec.	Jan.	Feb.	March.	April.	May.	June.	July.	August.
	°	°	°	°	°	°	°	°	°	°	°	°
1	(+10.92)	—3.76	—21.51	—31.54	—28.04	(—34.36)	—38.56	—11.77	(+ 9.31)	(+27.21)	+36.67	(+28.99)
2	10.97	3.79	21.54	31.39	28.49	34.32	38.40	11.82	9.62	27.25	36.76	29.33
3	11.28	3.74	21.46	31.65	28.62	34.14	38.61	(12.26)	10.26	27.40	36.79	29.27
4	11.21	3.58	21.42	(31.82)	28.67	33.54	(38.86)	11.77	10.78	27.71	36.78	29.67
5	11.23	3.47	22.00	30.97	28.66	34.20	38.81	10.96	12.05	28.98	36.94	29.55
6	11.85	3.47	(22.35)	30.83	28.71	33.62	38.60	10.33	12.91	29.61	37.60	30.17
7	12.87	3.29	22.13	30.97	(29.02)	33.19	37.91	9.32	13.64	30.46	37.76	30.83
8	14.32	3.32	22.27	31.04	28.43	32.87	37.52	8.28	14.56	31.69	38.43	31.84
9	15.07	3.00	22.06	30.69	28.56	32.63	36.23	6.64	14.45	30.89	39.42	32.96
10	15.75	(2.72)	22.18	30.68	28.29	32.10	35.68	6.00	15.11	31.08	39.63	33.83
11	16.15	2.81	21.68	30.52	27.75	32.42	34.51	5.07	15.38	31.43	40.00	34.00
Noon	16.40	2.97	(21.37)	(30.04)	(27.26)	31.79	33.97	4.46	15.89	32.18	(40.04)	34.20
13	(16.47)	3.03	21.73	30.12	27.55	31.30	33.60	4.05	16.09	(32.31)	39.83	34.26
14	16.12	3.18	21.72	30.44	27.57	(31.29)	(33.20)	3.27	16.31	32.17	39.69	(34.29)
15	15.65	3.08	21.77	30.77	28.08	31.44	33.86	(3.17)	16.38	31.85	39.65	33.90
16	15.11	3.18	21.86	31.08	28.32	31.52	34.97	3.51	(16.65)	31.52	39.65	33.38
17	14.51	3.43	21.69	31.18	28.00	31.78	35.67	3.67	16.04	31.31	38.85	33.11
18	14.07	3.79	21.93	31.32	28.00	31.64	36.32	4.57	15.17	31.08	38.50	32.62
19	13.28	4.28	22.06	31.53	27.87	31.58	36.85	6.01	14.29	30.66	38.23	32.25
20	12.78	4.36	22.14	(31.81)	28.18	31.73	37.75	7.01	13.41	30.41	37.66	31.91
21	12.46	4.34	(22.64)	31.74	28.09	32.15	37.90	8.37	12.56	29.75	37.22	31.63
22	12.07	4.38	22.30	31.62	28.01	33.22	38.17	9.94	11.43	29.30	(36.65)	31.00
23	11.36	4.34	22.54	31.51	(28.66)	33.25	38.42	10.71	10.37	28.38	36.81	30.63
Midn't	+11.05	(-4.39)	—22.37	—31.35	—28.34	—33.53	—38.61	—11.87	+ 9.90	+27.98	+36.92	+30.07
Mean	+13.45	—3.57	—21.95	—31.12	—28.22	—32.65	—36.79	— 7.70	+13.45	+30.12	+38.19	+31.82
Amplitude	5.55	1.67	*1.00	*1.65	*1.55	3.07	5.66	9.09	7.34	5.10	3.37	5.30

* The amplitude for November, December, and January, was derived from a graphical representation of the hourly values through which a curve was thrown with a free hand in order to eliminate the effect of the accidental variations, which, during these months, approach in magnitude to the range of the diurnal variation itself.

According to the preceding table, the epoch of the diurnal maximum temperature occurs in the months of October and November (when the diurnal amplitude is a minimum) about one hour before noon, and in April and May (when the diurnal amplitude is a maximum) about three hours after noon, the whole mean range (obtained graphically) being four hours during the year. In the months of November, December, and January, there are two minima, one at about 6 A. M. (whether this represents the primary or secondary minimum cannot well be decided from these observations alone), and the other at about 9 P. M. During the remaining months of the year, there is but one minimum during twenty-four hours, which occurs at 1 A. M.

At about 7½ in the morning, and a little before 8 in the afternoon, the temperature equals the mean temperature of the day, excepting the months of November, December, and January. The greatest deviations from these hours are ±1½ hours. For the remaining three months, the means are reached at 9½ in the morning, and also between 4 and 10 in the afternoon; the latter (as well as another hour at about 4 A. M.) being very irregular.

For three months of the year, the diurnal variation is exhibited graphically.

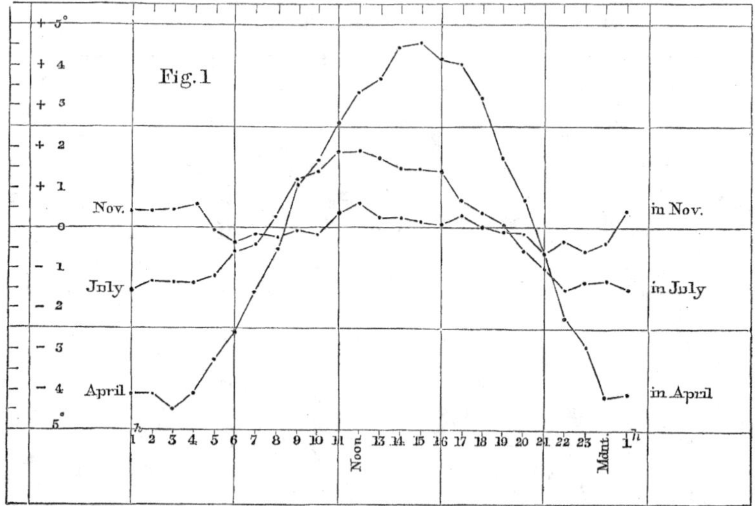

The diagram shows the maximum diurnal variation in the month of April, the secondary minimum variation in the month of July, and the diurnal variation in the month of November when nearest to its absolute minimum. ± indicates a {higher / lower} temperature than the mean of the day. The month of November exhibits considerable anomalies. In July the sun never set, and in November he never rose above the horizon.

In the following diagram, I have exhibited the annual march of the diurnal amplitude for each month.

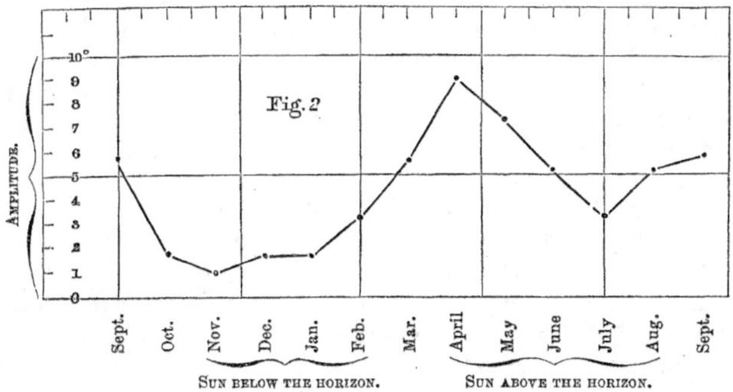

The absolute maximum value of the amplitude was observed in April (9°.09), and the absolute minimum in November (1°.00); the diurnal variation never disappearing altogether, although the sun remained for 2⅔ months below the horizon. A secondary minimum was reached in July (3°.37), somewhat later than the middle of the time the sun made his circuit round the points of the compass without setting.[1] The mean amplitude of the diurnal variation during the whole year is 4°.20—the maximum rising 4°.9 above, and the minimum falling 3°.2 below. The daily range of the effect of the thermal wave propagated northward during the long arctic darkness, may be set down to 1°.6 on the average.

For the purpose of comparing with similar results at other stations, I add a table of the mean daily variation during the year. Each figure is simply the mean of the twelve values corresponding to the same hour, and was taken from the preceding table. No attention was paid to the small anomalies noticed in three winter months, which cannot sensibly affect the means. The second column contains the mean values, and the third the same after the general mean has been subtracted from each of them, and, consequently shows the mean variation proper, $\pm$ indicating a {higher / lower} value than the mean. The fourth column exhibits the hourly differences of the variation.

Mean Diurnal Variation for the Year, derived from its Monthly Values.

Hour.	Mean temperature.	Diurnal variation.	Its hourly difference.	Hour.	Mean temperature.	Diurnal variation.	Its hourly difference.
1	—4°.70	—1°.79	—0°.05	13	—1.°04	+1°.87	—0°.03
2	—4.65	—1.74	—0.03	14	—1.01	+1.90	+0.22
3	—4.62	—1.71	—0.16	15	—1.23	+1.68	+0.28
4	—4.46	—1.55	—0.27	16	—1.51	+1.40	+0.29
5	—4.19	—1.28	—0.38	17	—1.80	+1.11	+0.38
6	—3.81	—0.90	—0.45	18	—2.18	+0.73	+0.44
7	—3.36	—0.45	—0.62	19	—2.62	+0.29	+0.45
8	—2.74	+0.17	—0.57	20	—3.07	—0.16	+0.40
9	—2.17	+0.74	—0.32	21	—3.47	—0.56	+0.46
10	—1.85	+1.06	—0.37	22	—3.93	—1.02	+0.39
11	—1.48	+1.43	—0.38	23	—4.32	—1.41	+0.23
Noon	—1.10	+1.81	—0.06	Midn't	—4.55	—1.64	+0.15

[1] A more complete understanding of the diurnal variation can only be had in connection with hygrometric observations.

Accordingly the mean is reached at 7h..7 A. M. and 7h..6 P. M; the maximum at 2 P. M., and the minimum at 1 A. M. The mean range equals 3°.69, a quantity necessarily smaller than the mean amplitude for the whole year as given above. Maximum mean hourly difference or change 0°.62 between 7h. and 8h. A. M., and 0°.45 between the same hours P. M.

We now return to the last vertical columns of the general monthly abstracts, and examine the

Observed Hours of Mean Daily Temperature.—The following table contains the hours of the day when the temperature equals its mean daily value, made out for each month of the year. Also shows their difference, or the "critical interval." These values are derived directly from the general abstracts of observed temperatures, and, for the first five months, are mean values derived from two sets of observations in the first and second years.

Month.	Morning hour.	Evening hour.	Critical interval.	Month.	Morning hour.	Evening hour.	Critical interval.
September . .	7.4	18.4	11h.0	April	8.4	20.7	12.3
October . . .	Uncertain,	17.1	11.1	May	6.9	20.2	13.3
November . .	probably one	Uncertain, one		June	6.7	20.7	14.0
December . .	near 3h., the	near 15h., the	12.0	July	7.6	19.1	11.5
January . . .	other near 9h.	other near 21h.		August . . .	7.9	19.8	11.9
February . .	8.9	21.4	12.5				
March . . .	8.5	19.1	10.6	Means . . .	7.2	19.2	12.0

In the following table, I have exhibited the greatest absolute changes of temperature observed between any two successive hours, between the highest and lowest of any day of 24 consecutive hours, any month, and for the whole year.

Month.	Hourly.	Daily.	Monthly.	Month.	Hourly.	Daily.	Monthly.
September . . .	7°.0	15°.6	32°.3	June	8°.0	15°.0	24°.2
October	8.0	24.1	41.0	July	8.0	14.6	23.0
November . . .	10.8	25.0	42.8	August	8.0	20.8	29.8
December . . .	19.4	30.4	60.5	September . . .	16.0	24.0	36.0
January	8.1	21.8	69.8	October	11.0	25.0	61.0
February . . .	12.3	37.8	56.4	November . . .	11.0	32.0	54.9
March	13.5	24.1	56.7	December . . .	16.7	41.1	52.9
April	10.0	33.1	56.7	January	18.9	35.6	81.6
May	7.8	17.8	46.5				
				Means	11.4	25.7	48.6

The following values are the absolute maximum and minima observed:—

Minimum in winter, 1853–54	—66°.4,	observed on	Feb. 5th
Maximum in summer, 1854	+51.0,	"	July 23d
Minimum in winter, 1854–55	—65.5,	"	Jan. 8th

Absolute maximum difference, 117°.4 Fahr.

Mean Monthly Temperatures and Annual Variation.—In the following recapitulation of the mean monthly temperatures, the values have been taken directly from the general abstracts. The means for the months of February, March, and April, of 1855, have been added by means of the table given in Vol. II. of the Narrative, p. 425, corrected from ten comparisons of monthly means between —14° and —34°, so as to refer the quantities to the same system of corrections as used in the present paper. This correction, from consistent separate values, is +0°.99. On account of the occasional omissions of observations in the hourly abstract, the daily means in the Narrative for these three months are probably not reliable, the calculator, as has been found on other occasions, having paid no attention to such omissions in taking his mean; the monthly means may, nevertheless, be nearly correct.

Mean Monthly Temperatures at Van Rensselaer Harbor.

(Degrees of Fahrenheit's scale.)

1853	September	+17°.16	1854	July	+38°.19
	October	+ 1.62		August	+31.82
	November	—22.39		September	+ 9.74
	December	—25.46		October	— 8.78
1854	January	—29.21		November	—21.52
	February	—32.65		December	—36.79
	March	—36.79	1855	January	—27.23
	April	— 7.69		February	—20.22
	May	+13.45		March	—32.98
	June	+30.12		April	—13.01

If we unite the temperatures for the same months in one mean, we obtain the following mean temperatures for each month of the year:—

1853–54	September	+13.°45	1854–55	March	—34°.88
	October	— 3.58		April	—10.35
	November	—21.95	1854	May	+13.45
	December	—31.12		June	+30.12
1854–55	January	—28.22		July	+38.19
	February	—26.43		August	+31.82

These values, when thrown into a curve, present a great regularity during the summer months; not so, however, during the winter months, when the direct effect of the sun is very feeble, and the winds probably become the main source of the variability of temperature. To exhibit this difference in the variation of the summer and winter temperatures, I have graphically presented the half monthly means, when the steadiness of the summer curve becomes very striking.

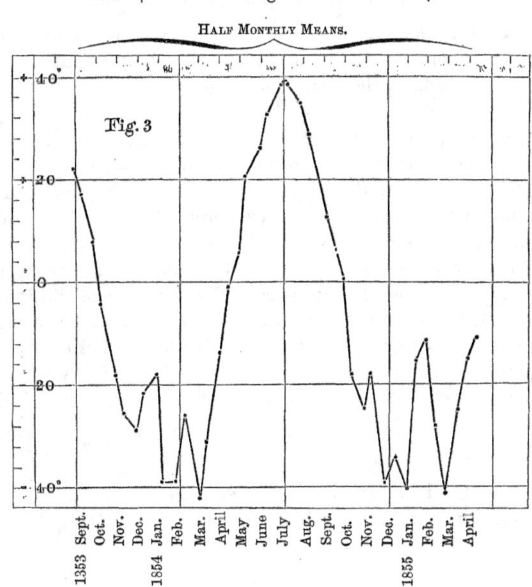

It must be considered a fortunate circumstance that the observations extend over *two* winters, and thus give us a more exact mean temperature for that season.

The warmest month is July, and the coldest is March; the temperature of December, however, does not differ much from it, and December actually was the coldest month in the second winter. The highest mean monthly temperature seems to fall almost exactly to the middle of July, and the lowest would probably occur in February, if we had a longer series of observations extending over several winters. From the observations on hand, we find the December temperature only 3¾° higher than the March temperature. The range of the mean temperature for the warmest and coldest month is 73°.07. The temperatures for the meteorological seasons—December, January, and February being regarded as winter—become as follows:—

Winter	—28°.59	Mean temperature for the whole year, —2°.46.
Spring	—10.59	
Summer	+33.38	
Autumn	— 4.03	

The mean annual temperature is reached in the middle of spring (April), and again in the middle of autumn (October). The difference in the winter and summer temperature is 61°.97.

The seasons of the second year compare with the corresponding ones of the first as follows:—

Autumn in the second year colder by	5°.65
Winter " " warmer by	1.03
First two months of spring colder by	0.76

The lowest mean monthly temperature of the first winter (March, —36°.79) was precisely the same as that of the second winter (December, —36°.79), both months falling in the year 1854.

For the purpose of continuing the discussion of the atmospheric temperatures, it becomes necessary to express the annual variation analytically. On account of the great range of this variation, I have first applied a small correction to the preceding monthly means, in order to refer them to the middle of months of average length of 30d..4 in common, and 30d..5 in leap years. Thus, the mean temperature of January, 1854, refers to (noon) 15d..5, when it ought to refer to 15d..2; difference, 0d..3. The fifteenth part of the difference of the January half monthly means is —1°.40; hence the correction +0°.40. For convenience of reference, the number of days for which a correction is to be applied to refer the means of the true to an average month are here inserted. Commencing with January, these numbers for the several months in their proper order become—

—0d..3	+0.6	+1.5	+1.5	+1.4	+1.3	+1.2	+0.7	+0.6	+0.5	+0.4	+0d..3
—0.2	+0.2	+0.8	+0.8	+0.8	+0.8	+0.8	+0.2	+0.2	+0.2	+0.2	+0.2

The first line is for a common year, the second for a leap year. The maximum correction applied was +1°.34 (to the mean of March). To the following monthly means, referring to months of an average length, I have added the probable uncertainty obtained by comparison with the daily means.

Month	Mean	Uncertainty	Month	Mean	Uncertainty
January . . .	—28°.26	±1°.5	July	+38°.18	±0°.3
February . . .	—26.53	±1.4	August . . .	+31.59	±0.4
March . . .	—33.54	±1.3	September . .	—13.15	±0.6
April . . .	— 9.48	±1.2	October . . .	— 4.13	±1.1
May . . .	+14.78	±1.2	November . . .	—21.96	±0.9
June . . .	+30.76	±0.5	December . . .	—31.00	±0.9
Annual mean from 12 average months				— 2 20	±0.3

For the purpose of interpolation, and for the representation of the annual variation, a function involving terms of the sine or cosine of multiples of an angle is usually adopted. In the present case, I prefer a form of discussion which makes the law of the change of the monthly temperatures analogous to that of a falling body. This method was adopted by Mr. J. Wiessner, and applied to the discussion of the Washington observations. (See p. 322 of the Annual Report of the Regents of the Smithsonian Institution for 1857.) The annual variation may thus be represented by a parabolic wave. The diurnal variation has previously been represented by others by parabolic arcs. Whatever form of expression we may adopt, the winter curve is so irregular, owing to the short number of observations, that no continuous law can be deduced; the temperatures during this season will, therefore, be treated separately. If the observations were continued for several years, it is probable that the lowest temperature would fall in February, near the time of sunrise; as it is, we have a slight increase of temperature during January and February.

A uniformly retarded motion is represented by $s = ct - \frac{1}{2} gt^2$, and the condition for the turning point is $o = c - gt$, corresponding to the middle of July, or the third month, commencing with the middle of April as zero. For $t = 3$, $c = 3g$, and, putting for convenience $g = 2$, we find $c = 6$; hence, if t = number of months after the middle of April, the arguments for the several months become—

0 1 2 3 2 1 0 —1 —2 —3 —2 —1 0

the temperature in April being the same as in June, etc. Substituting these numbers successively in the formula $s = 6t - t^2$, we find the values (R) 0, 5, 8, 9, 8 ..... for the months of April, May, June — .... Each month furnishes an equation of the form $T = t_m + Rp$, where t_m = the mean temperature and p a factor depending on the amplitude of the annual variation. t_m and p, when found for spring, summer, and autumn, are found to vary, and hence an interpolation is made for each month. We have next to introduce a second term to allow for a shifting of the epoch. Let x be the quantity addition to the arguments 0 1 2 3 2, etc., for the change in the epoch, and expressed in parts of a month, we have for—

$0 + x$	$s = 6\ (0 + x) - (0 + x)^2$	or $s = 0 + 6x$
$1 + x$	$6\ (1 + x) - (1 + x)^2$	$5 + 4x$
$2 + x$	$6\ (2 + x) - (2 + x)^2$, etc.	$8 + 2x$, etc.

omitting terms containing the second power of x. Putting $px = q$, we obtain, in place of the first expression for the temperature—

$$T = t_m + Rp + Q_q$$

For the day or summer period we thus obtain the equations:—

May	$+14^\circ.78 = t_m + 5p + 4q$	Whence $t_m = -15^\circ.73$, $p = 5.918$, and $q = +0.12$ as resulting from the normal equations.
June	$+30.76 = t_m + 8p + 2q$	
July	$+38.18 = t_m + 9p$	$T = -15^\circ.73 + 5.918\,R + 0.12\,Q \pm 0^\circ.7$
August	$+31.59 = t_m + 8p - 2q$	
September	$+13.15 = t_m + 5p - 4q$	

For the spring months:—

March	$-33^\circ.54 = t_m - 5p + 4q$	
April	$-9.48 = t_m + 6q$	$T = -9^\circ.18 + 4.832\,R - 0.05\,Q$
May	$+14.78 = t_m + 5p + 4q$	

For the autumn months:—

September	$+13^\circ.15 = t_m + 5p - 4q$	
October	$-4.13 = t_m - 6q$	$T = -4.91 + 3.510\,R - 0.13\,Q$
November	$-21.96 = t_m - 5p - 4q$	

The above 3 values for t_m, p, and q are represented by the formulæ:—

$$t_m = -15.73 + 0.71n + 0.96n^2$$
$$p = +5.918 - 0.220n - 0.1942n^2$$
$$q = +0.12 - 0.01n - 0.022n^2$$

Where n = number of months from the middle of July. For March $n = -2$; for Nov. $+2$.

The following table contains their computed values for each month (under discussion).

Month.	t_m	p	q		Obs. — comp. temperatures.
March	—13°.31	4.082 (—0.750)	+0.06	If we now compare the com-	—0.°20
April	— 9.18	4.832 (—0.750)	—0.05	puted and observed tempera-	—0.14
May	—13.31	5.582	+0.06	tures for each month, we yet	—0.20
June	—15.48	5.944 Differences.	+0.11	find a constant correction to	—1.67
July	—15.73	5.918	+0.12	t_m of $+0^\circ.14$. Applying it to	+0.51
August	—14.06	5.504	+0.09	the tabular quantities, the for-	+1.66
September	—10.47	4.701 (—1.191)	+0.02	mulæ represent the observa-	+0.06
October	— 4.91	3.510 (—1.191)	—0.11	tions as follows:—	—0.02
November	—10.47	2.319	+0.02		+0.04
Correct. to tabular t_m =	+ 0.14				

These differences between the observed and computed values are very nearly within the probable uncertainty as given in a preceding table.

For the winter season, the most simple interpolation seems to be the best that can be adopted. We find for December 1st the temperature —26°.5, the mean of the temperatures for November 15th and December 15th, and for March 1st, in like manner; the mean temperature —30°.0. The following table[1] was used for interpolation:—

Mean temperature Dec. 1st	—26°.5		
" Jan. 15th	—28.2	$\Delta = 1^\circ.7$
" March 1st	—30.0	1.8

[1] For the purpose of a ready comparison and uniformity of method, the following expression of the annual variation of the temperature at Van Rensselaer Harbor is here inserted; it compares directly with similar expressions for other stations given by Kämtz and inserted in the article (Sir John Herschel's)

Influence of Winds on Temperature.—To ascertain the temperature of the winds, the following method was employed. By means of the preceding formula, expressing the temperature, a set of tables was formed—partly by direct computation, partly by interpolation between these computed values—of the daily mean temperature throughout the year, and the same was set down opposite the respective hours of the day when the mean temperature is reached. Next, by means of the known diurnal variation, interpolated from its mean monthly value, for each day, these tables were completed by inserting the temperature for every hour of the day to the nearest whole degree. They were then compared, hour for hour, with the abstract of observed temperature, and the difference $\left\{ \begin{array}{l} + \text{for excess} \\ - \text{for defect} \end{array} \right\}$ placed in the column for the respective wind as observed at the same hour. For this latter purpose, an hourly abstract of the wind was prepared. The abstract of differences contains eight columns for each of the principal directions, and an additional one for calms. By this process, the effect of the annual and diurnal variation is at once eliminated, and the remaining differences can safely be left to their own compensation. The results for the months from September to January (both inclusive, have been combined for the two years. The following table exhibits the results of this somewhat lengthy process. The first column contains the magnetic directions of the wind, including a line for the calms; the second, the sum of the differences as explained above; the third, the number of times the wind blew from each of the eight directions during the seventeen months of registered hourly temperatures and winds; the sum total, or Σn, equals 11534, and the number by which it falls short of 12264, indicates the number of hours observations were wanting; the last figure in the column gives the number of hours during which the atmosphere was calm. The fourth column shows the values of $\frac{\Sigma \Delta}{n}$, or the quantity by which each wind affected the temperature, the sign + corresponding to an effect of raising the temperature above its mean.

"Meteorology," Vol. XIV. 8th edition of the *Encyclopædia Britannica.* The value $\theta = 0$ corresponds to January 1st and T is expressed in degrees of Fahrenheit's scale.

$$T = -2^\circ.20 + 35^\circ.39 \sin(\theta + 251^\circ 43') + 6^\circ.72 \sin(2\theta + 69^\circ 47') + 3^\circ.20 \sin(3\theta + 17^\circ 5').$$

The formula leaves the following differences (O.—C.) between the observed and computed monthly means:—

In January	$-0^\circ.2$	In July	$+1^\circ.2$
February	+3.4	August	+1.5
March	—4.9	September	—2.4
April	+2.7	October	+1.4
May	+0.3	November	+1.3
June	—2.5	December	—1.9

And a probable error of any single determination of $\pm 1^\circ.6$. The warmest day is accordingly July 8th, and the coldest March 1st. The mean temperature of the year is attained April 29th and October 12th. The mean diurnal variation for the whole year, as derived from its monthly values, is represented by the formula—

$$t = +1^\circ.85 \sin(\theta + 64^\circ 55') + 0^\circ.08 \sin(2\theta + 97^\circ) + 0^\circ.03 \sin(3\theta + 128^\circ),$$

with a probable error for any single hour of $\pm 0^\circ.03$, the angle θ counting from noon.

Mag. direction of wind.	Σ Δ	n	$\frac{\Sigma \Delta}{n}$	Mag. direction of wind.	Σ Δ	n	$\frac{\Sigma \Delta}{n}$
N.	+ 34	323	+0°.1	S. W.	+ 2729	955	+2°.9
N. E.	+ 138	92	+1.5	W.	+ 509	313	+1.6
E.	+ 220	159	+1.4	N. W.	+ 99	744	+0.1
S. E.	+2879	1182	+2.4	C.	—22923	6655	—3.4
S.	+2346	1111	+2.1				

These results are necessarily imperfect, on account of the impossibility of obtaining a correct mean temperature from so short a series of observations, yet their ratio may be depended upon. We notice that all winds tend to elevate the temperature, and the calms to lower the same. The frequency of the calms is greater than that of all the winds combined. The difference in the temperature of the warmest and coldest wind is 2°.8; N. E., E., and W. (magnetic) winds show a mean value; S. E., S., and S. W. winds are from 0°.6 to 1°.4 above, and N. and N. W. winds 1°.4 below, this mean temperature. The region included by the directions S. E. and S. W. (magnetic), or N. N. E. and E. S. E. (true),[1] being the quarter of the warmer winds, and the space between W. S. W. and S. S. W. (true) that of the colder winds. It must be remarked that, since a true north wind the longer it blows assumes a more and more easterly direction, the true directions between N. N. E. and E. point to a more northerly origin of the wind than actually indicated.[2]

Of the rise of temperature during certain gales, the explanatory foot-notes in the temperature abstract may be referred to; the more remarkable cases are the following ones:—

Gale of November 28, 1853,	from the	S. E.	(a little snow falling).
" December 10, "	"	S. E.	(not snowing).
" December 28, "	"	S. E. and S. W.	(no snow).
" February 7, 1854,	"	S.	(no snow).
" May 7–8, "	"	S'd	"
" November 20, "	"	S. W.	"
" December 18, "	"	S. E.	"
" January 29, 1855,	"	S. E.	"
" February 13–14, 1855,	"	S. E.	"

The reader may also be referred to pp. 17, 30, 39, 40, and 55, of the 2d vol. of the Narrative.

Effect of Snow (and Rain) on the Temperature.—If we combine in like manner the differences of observed and mean temperature of all hours during which snow fell, we find a great regularity in the monthly values expressing the elevation of temperature during the hours of the fall of snow, due to the conversion of latent into sensible heat. The following table exhibits in the first column the algebraic

---

[1] See my discussion of Dr. Kane's magnetical observations, in Vol. X. of the Smithsonian Contributions to Knowledge, 1858. The magnetic declination is found 108° west.

[2] The bearing of this investigation on an open (partially so) polar sea, can only be fully made out after the construction of a hygrometric and barometric wind-card. The direction of the warmer winds points towards the Spitzbergen Sea, and the relative colder winds come in a direction from the northernmost part of continental America.

sum of the above differences for the hours during which snow fell, the second column the number of hours, and the last column the rise of temperature above the mean. In 17 months, it snowed during 680 hours, and rained during 60 hours. This small quantity of rain fell in the month of July; snow also fell during 10 hours in this (warmest) month.

	ΣΔ	n			ΣΔ	n	
2 January . . .	+1403°	74	+19°.0	July	+ 50°	70	+ 0°.7
February . . .	+ 250	16	+15.6	August	+ 54	26	+ 2.1
March	+ 130	14	+ 9.3	2 September . .	+ 419	111	+ 3.8
April	+ 176	21	+ 8.4	2 October . . .	+ 623	80	+ 7.8
May	+ 534	136	+ 4.0	2 November . . .	+1323	79	+16.7
June	— 48	36	— 1.3	2 December . . .	+ 819	77	+10.6

On the average, during the whole year, the sensible heat was increased during the fall of snow by 7°.7.

The bearing of this source of change of the temperature on the alternation of relative cold and warm periods during the winter season, will be further illustrated in the following analyses of these undulations.

Recurrence of Maxima of Cold during Winter.—An alternate variation from comparatively warmer to colder extremes, taking weeks to perform their cycles, has before been noticed in the arctic regions of America. These returns of maxima of cold, their causes, periods, and amplitudes, now deserve our particular attention. Dr. Kane, from various notes in his log-book, seems to be inclined to consider the phases of the moon as intimately connected with the subject; on page 55, Vol. II. of the Narrative, he remarks: "There is a seeming connection between the increasing cold and the increasing moonlight." Under date Nov. 28th, 1854, he entered the following remark in the log: "The moon first appeared above the hills to S. and S. E. The depression of the temperature, and the general transparency of the atmosphere, is again noted as material for discussion." Dec. 1st, 1854, he says: "With the cessation of wind, the absence of cirri, and the increased brightness of the moon, the atmosphere grows sensibly colder. * * * This immediate influence of the moon is a matter of frequent observation. The full moon season, with cloudless nights is always in correspondence with the lowest mean temperatures of our meteorological record." The following discussion has been made in accordance with these notes.

To eliminate as much as possible disturbing influences, particularly those produced by the winds and precipitations, the average of the mean daily temperature of a number of consecutive days has been taken, and it was found, after trials with 3, 5, 6, and 7 days, that the period of 6 days answered best, that is, brought out in the plainest manner, the march of the temperature during the winter season, the general features of the curves being the same for any of the above periods.

The epoch of the 6 day period was so selected that the highest and lowest temperatures should, as near as may be, fall towards the middle of a period. These average values were next compared with the mean temperature deduced from the half monthly means in order to exhibit the deviation of the observed average values above or below the mean temperature, ± indicating $\left\{\begin{array}{c}\text{warmer}\\ \text{colder}\end{array}\right\}$ than the mean. These differences are herewith presented graphically by full lines; the phases of the moon are marked opposite the corresponding dates, the new moons being given at the top, the full moons at the bottom, of each diagram. The investigation commences with Nov. 3d, and ends with April 13th, for the winter 1853–54, and includes the time between Oct. 19th and April 16th of the second winter. Between these intervals, the mean half monthly temperatures are below —10°. Temperatures observed after Jan. 24th, 1855, have been taken from the abstract in Vol. II. of the Narrative (corrected for index error). They are probably subject to small corrections, and hence have been dotted in the diagram.

The wavy line above the zero line indicates the number of hours during which snow fell in the corresponding 6 day period; the numbers in the vertical column answering also for the hour scale. The wavy line below, or on the negative side of the temperatures, indicates the number of clear days in each 6 day period, and in order to use the side figures also for this day-scale, the number of clear days was doubled, 12 being the maximum indication of 6 clear days.

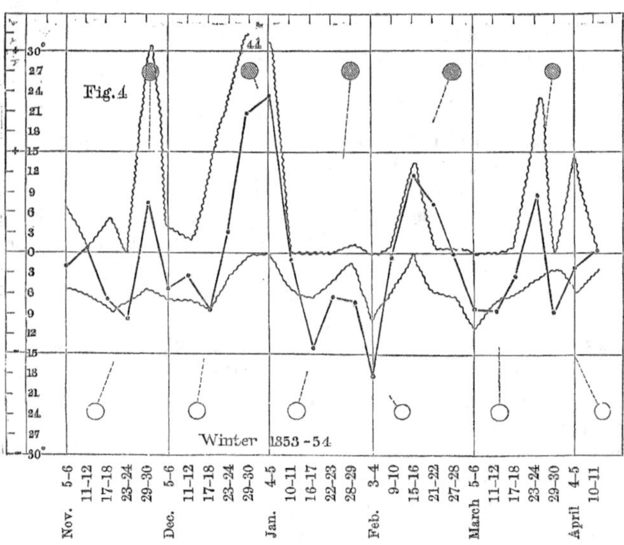

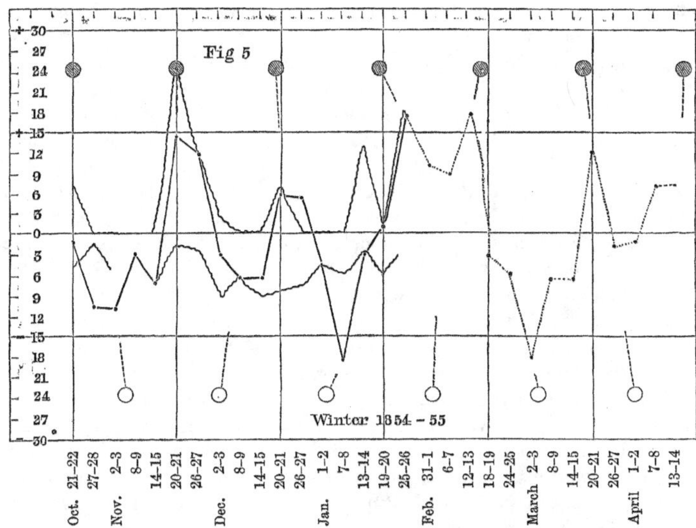

These diagrams fully bear out the observer's remarks, viz: that the lowest temperatures are reached about the time of full moon. Setting aside some small deviations in the regularity of the curves (of temperature), there is not a single exception to the correspondence of relative maxima of cold near the epoch of the full moon, and of relative minima of cold near the time of new moon. The period between any two consecutive maxima of cold from five intervals is $25^{d.}.2 \pm 1^{d.}.9$, and the same between the minima of cold from four intervals $28^{d.}.5 \pm 2^{d.}.4$, for the first winter, and $28^{d.}.8 \pm 1^{d.}.5$ (from five intervals), and $28^{d.}.8 \pm 3^{d.}.3$ (from five intervals), for the second winter, respectively. Combining these four values with the application of weights according to the respective probable errors, the resulting period for the recurrence of cold becomes $27^{d.}.7 \pm 1^{d}.0$. The synodic period of the moon is $29^{d.}.5$; somewhat longer than the period just deduced, but by no means incompatible therewith.

If we now follow the curve indicating the duration of the fall of snow, we find, in the two winters, maxima near the period of new moon, thus accounting, in conformity with the previous investigation, for the rise in the temperature; the average elevation above the mean temperature for the six winter months, during the hours of snow fall, being, according to the table, 13°. The superior maximum of Dec. 27th to Jan. 1st (first winter), when it snowed during 44 hours, is particularly instructive.

The lower wavy line indicates maxima in the amount of serenity of atmosphere near the time of full moon, better marked in the first than in the second winter. The above special case of Dec. 29–30, is again interesting as conspiring to an elevation of temperature by the nearly total obscurity of the atmosphere during the six days in question.

The mean amplitude of the wave in the winter 1853–54 is 19°.4, and in the winter 1854–55, 20°.1, or 19°.8 from an average during these two winters.

It has been remarked by an eminent astronomer that, if the moon emits any sensible heat, it is probably expended and becomes apparent by a tendency to disappearance of clouds under the full moon. Supposing this to be a fact, it would seem that the powerful radiating force of the earth's surface, called into activity under a clear sky, produces, as a secondary effect, the phenomenon of greatest cold at the time of full moon. The process is going on gradually, and, when combined with the tendency of a fall of snow about the period of new moon, would favor the production of the caloric waves observed during the winter season. These waves could not be explained either in range, duration, or regularity, by the effect of various winds and calms, since their total effect could only amount in maxima to 6½°, according to the previous investigation.

A maximum cold will be produced, as stated by Dr. Kane, by a concurrence of the time of full moon with a perfect calm and a great transparency of the atmosphere, during the middle of the winter season. The opposite effect requires, for its full development, a concurrence of the time of new moon with a continued fall of snow, a generally obscured atmosphere, and winds from a direction between N. N. E. and E. S. E. (true).

Enough has been shown to make these alternations of relative cold and warm periods in winter an interesting and instructive subject for further study, specially with a view of tracing out and confirming the apparent connection of the concurrence of the two principal lunar phases, with a tendency to obscurity and transparency of the atmosphere.

In accordance with Prof. Dove's investigations of the return of cold about the 11th of May, the mean daily temperature on May 13th (1854) of +2°.8 was 9°.3 lower than the computed (by preceding formula) temperature.[1]

Hourly Corrections for Periodic Variations.—The following table for reducing the mean of observations taken at any hour of the day to the true mean temperature of the day, has a similar arrangement, and was prepared for the same use, as those given for other stations in the Smithsonian *Miscellaneous Collections of Meteorological and Physical Tables*, by Prof. A. Guyot (2d edition, Washington, 1858). The figures necessarily present some anomalies, since they are derived directly from a series of hourly observations extending over seventeen months; they present, therefore, only the differences between the hourly and the true means.

---

[1] While this paper was going through the press, I received the March number (1859) of the *London, Edinburgh, and Dublin Philosophical Magazine*, containing J. Park Harrison's article on the "Lunar Influence on Temperature as connected with Serenity of the Sky." He states that, from 20 years of observations at Greenwich, the mean temperature is above the average at the period of the new moon (also at first quarter and before last quarter), it is below the average before and after full moon (also between new moon and first quarter, and at and after last quarter).

ARCTIC AMERICA—VAN RENSSELAER HARBOR, Lat. 78° 37′, Long. 70° 53′ W. of Greenwich.

Corrections to be applied to any hourly or set of hourly observations to obtain the mean temperature of the day. Degrees of Fahrenheit.

Hours.	Jan.	Feb.	March.	April.	May.	June.	July.	Aug.	Sept.	Oct.	Nov.	Dec.	Year.
	°	°	°	°	°	°	°	°	°	°	°	°	°
1 A. M.	+0.07*	+1.65	+1.97	+4.50	+4.45	+3.11	+1.54	+2.60	+2.22	—0.12	—0.68	+0.37	+1.81
2	+0.31	+1.61	+1.79	+4.51	+4.11	+3.06	+1.45	+2.29	+2.20	—0.07	—0.61	+0.22	+1.74
3	+0.44	+1.44	+1.98	+4.92	+3.45	+2.89	+1.42	+2.37	+1.92	—0.15	—0.68	+0.48	+1.71
4	+0.48	+0.84	+2.21	+4.39	+2.90	+2.56	+1.42	+1.99	+2.02	—0.22	—0.70	+0.66	+1.55
5	+0.47	+1.51	+2.14	+3.55	+1.60	+1.27	+1.26	+2.13	+2.03	—0.30	0.00	—0.18	+1.29
6	+0.49	+0.94	+1.91	+2.88	+0.71	+0.62	+0.60	+1.51	+1.44	—0.27	+0.27	—0.33	+0.90
7	+0.82	+0.51	+1.20	+1.83	—0.05	—0.24	+0.43	+0.87	+0.45	—0.42	+0.07	—0.17	+0.44
8	+0.23	+0.20	+0.79	+0.75	—0.99	—1.49	—0.24	—0.12	—0.97	—0.36	+0.23	—0.11	—0.17
9	+0.35	—0.03	—0.52	—0.93	—0.91	—0.71	—1.23	—1.22	—1.70	—0.66	+0.04	—0.45	—0.66
10	+0.09	—0.56	—1.09	—1.61	—1.60	—0.92	—1.44	—2.07	—2.35	—0.91	+0.18	—0.45	—1.07
11	—0.47	—0.23	—2.27	—2.58	—1.90	—1.29	—1.81	—2.72	—2.22	—0.79	—0.39	—0.60	—1.44
Noon	—0.95	—0.86	—2.82	—3.23	—2.44	—2.06	—1.85	—2.38	—2.96	—0.62	—0.58	—1.08	—1.83
1 P. M.	—0.67	—1.35	—3.20	—3.67	—2.67	—2.21	—1.64	—2.42	—3.00	—0.53	—0.20	—1.00	—1.88
2	—0.65	—1.35	—3.61	—4.49	—2.91	—2.09	—1.50	—2.43	—2.62	—0.35	—0.20	—0.68	—1.91
3	—0.15	—1.20	—2.97	—4.62	—3.01	—1.79	—1.46	—2.02	—2.13	—0.44	—0.12	—0.34	—1.69
4	—0.10*	—1.11	—1.88	—4.32	—3.30	—1.48	—1.46	—1.48	—1.57	—0.30	—0.01	—0.04	—1.42
5	—0.24	—0.85	—1.20	—4.20	—2.72	—1.29	—0.66	—1.19	—0.94	—0.03	—0.17	+0.07	—1.12
6	—0.24	—0.98	—0.57	—3.33	—1.89	—1.17	—0.32	—0.68	—0.47	+0.36	+0.09	+0.22	—0.75
7	—0.34	—1.03	—0.05	—1.93	—1.04	—0.67	—0.05	—0.29	+0.34	+0.87	+0.25	+0.78	—0.26
8	—0.07	—0.88	+0.83	—0.96	—0.18	—0.44	+0.52	+0.07	+0.86	+0.98	+0.35	+0.72	+0.15
9	—0.16	—0.45	+0.96	+0.36	+0.65	+0.21	+0.95	+0.37	+1.20	+0.98	+0.86	+0.61	+0.55
10	—0.24	+0.62	+1.21	+1.90	+1.76	+0.64	+1.52	+1.02	+1.63	+1.06	+0.54	+0.53	+1.02
11	+0.40	+0.66	+1.45	+2.64	+2.80	+1.55	+1.36	+1.40	+2.37	+1.04	+0.79	+0.44	+1.41
Midn't	+0.08	+0.94	+1.62	+3.76	+3.24	+1.94	+1.25	+1.98	+2.70	+1.11	+0.65	+0.27	+1.63
6, 6	+0.12	—0.02	+0.67	—0.22	—0.59	—0.27	+0.14	+0.44	+0.48	+0.04	+0.18	—0.05	+0.08
7, 7	+0.24	—0.26	+0.57	—0.05	—0.54	—0.45	+0.19	+0.29	+0.40	+0.22	+0.16	+0.31	+0.09
8, 8	+0.08	—0.34	+0.81	—0.11	—0.58	—0.96	+0.14	—0.02	—0.05	+0.31	+0.29	+0.30	—0.01
9, 9	+0.10	—0.24	+0.22	—0.28	—0.13	—0.25	—0.14	—0.42	—0.25	+0.16	+0.45	+0.08	—0.06
10, 10	—0.07	+0.03	+0.06	+0.15	+0.08	—0.14	+0.04	—0.52	—0.36	+0.07	+0.36	+0.04	—0.02
7, 2, 9	0.00	—0.43	—0.48	—0.77	—0.77	—0.71	—0.04	—0.40	—0.32	+0.07	+0.24	—0.08	—0.31
6, 2, 10	—0.13	+0.07	—0.16	+0.10	—0.15	—0.28	+0.21	+0.03	+0.15	+0.15	+0.20	—0.16	0.00
7, 2, 9, 9	—0.04	—0.43	—0.12	—0.49	—0.41	—0.48	+0.21	—0.20	+0.06	+0.30	+0.40	+0.09	—0.09
3, 9, 3, 9	+0.12	—0.06	—0.14	—0.07	+0.05	+0.15	—0.08	—0.12	—0.18	—0.07	+0.03	+0.08	—0.02

* The tabular quantities for 1 A. M. and 4 P. M., in January, are mean values of the directly observed values for these hours combined with those of the preceding and following hours.

The hours 7 A. M., 2 P. M., and 9 P. M., are those of the Mannheim Meteorological Society, adopted at the military posts of the United States and by the Smithsonian Institution; the hours 3 and 9 A. M. and 3 and 9 P. M., are those proposed by the Royal Society. Of the bi-hourly series, the observations at 10 A. M. and 10 P. M., will give a very close approximation; the sum of the squares of the tabular monthly values is a maximum, and the temperature at these hours does not change as rapidly as at other hours. Of the three-hour series, the hours 7, 2, and twice 9 are most convenient, but less accurate than the hours 6, 2, 10. The hours 3 and 9 A. M. and P. M., have the least sum of the squares of the monthly values; these hours are most suitable for cases having a sufficient number of observers, or for fully organized expeditions.

Solar Radiation.—After the return of light in the spring of 1854, a thermometer was exposed to the direct action of the sun. On and after April 10th, the statical measure by means of a black bulb thermometer was adopted. In connection with these observations, the estimated amount of solar light was also noted. From a note, Oct. 19th, 1854, it appears that the numbers expressive of the quantity of solar light have the following signification:—

1 Entirely clear.
2 Slightly obscured.
3 Clouded.
4 Misty and dark.
5 Excessive obscurity.

The sign 0, which occasionally occurs, probably indicates either no observation, or snowy or rainy atmosphere. There are a few apparent anomalies in the following tables, the temperature indicated by the black bulb being somewhat lower than that indicated by the shade thermometer with an overcast sky. These may arise from a slightly erroneous index error, or occasional observing errors, or different localities of exposure.

The following record of the observations of the temperature by the black bulb thermometer exposed to the solar rays, contains the corrected readings, which renders them directly comparable with the readings of the preceding general record, and has been inserted for the use of those who may desire to further investigate the subject.

Readings of the Black Bulb Thermometer, and corresponding Notes on the Solar Light, observed at Van Rensselaer Harbor,

In April, 1854, in Lat. 78° 37′, Long. 70° 53′ W. of Greenwich.

Expressed in degrees of Fahrenheit's scale. At meteorological observatory.

Hour.	10th.	11th.	12th.	13th.	14th.	15th.	16th.	17th.	18th.	19th.	20th.	21st.	22d.	23d.	24th.
	°	°	°	°	°	°	°	°	°	°	°	°	°	°	°
1h.	...	...	...	...	...	...	...	...	...	...	...	...	...	...	...
2	...	...	...	...	...	...	...	...	...	...	...	...	...	...	...
3	...	...	...	...	...	...	...	...	—10.0	...	...	— 8.0	— 8.0	...	...
4	...	...	...	...	...	...	...	...	...	— 1.0	...	+ 4.0	— 1.0	...	+1.0
5	...	— 7.0	—17.0	...	...	— 5.0	...	0.0	—10.0	+ 9.0	— 4.0	+ 2.0	+ 5.0	...	2.0
6	...	— 6 0	—10.0	...	...	— 4.5	+ 7.0	+ 5.0	— 2.0	+10.0	0.0	+12.0	+14.0	...	3.0
7	— 4.0	+ 5.0	— 6.0	...	...	— 4.5	16.0	4.0	+ 2.0	+ 8.0	+ 8.0	?	+ 7.0	+ 8.0	7.0
8	— 4.0	+10.0	— 2.0	...	...	+ 2.0	12.0	4.0	+ 5.0	+ 4.0	+12.0	?	+16.0	7.6	8.0
9	— 2.0	+ 6.0	*+1.0	+ 6.2	...	+ 4.5	12.0	6.0	+10.0	+ 5.5	+ 8.0	+20.0	+22.0	13.0	15.0
10	+ 0.5	+10.0	+ 1.0	6.0	...	+ 6.0	12.0	8.0	+11.0	+14.0	+14.0	+17.0	+13.5	13.0	15.0
11	+ 1.0	†+10.0	+ 2.0	12.0	+6.0	+ 9.0	‡15.0	8.0	+ 6.0	+17.5	+ 9.0	+ 4.0	+24.0	16.0	19.5
Noon	+ 2.0	+ 4.0	+ 2.3	10.0	+6.0	+10.0	?	...	+14.0	+24.0	+25.0	+18.0	+17.0	21.0	27.0
13	+ 1.8	+ 1.8	+ 5.0	12.0	...	+10.0	25.0	26.0	+ 8.0	+12.0	+16.0	+26.0	+27.0	20.0	23.0
14	— 0.6	+ 2.0	+ 7.0	10.0	+5.0	+ 6.0	25.0	24.0	+18.0	+15.0	+25.0	+18.0	+30.0	23.0	24.0
15	— 1.5	+ 3.5	+ 8.0	9.0	+4.5	+ 3.0	20.0	22.0	+10.0	+18.0	+22.0	+17.0	+33.0	30.0	20.0
16	— 2.0	+ 5.0	+ 7.0	+ 8.0	+5.0	+ 3.3	20.5	20.0	+ 9.0	+15.0	+20.0	+15.0	+28.0	21.0	14.0
17	— 2.5	— 8.0	— 1.0	...	+5.0	...	16.0	8.0	?	+15.0	+17.0	+14.2	+22.0	14.0	9.5
18	§—7.5	—11.0	— 1.9	...	+4.5	...	14.0	6.0	— 2.0	+ 8.0	+ 7.0	+14.0	+ 9.0	13.0	2.0
19	—10.0	—18.0	— 3.6	...	+4.0	...	+ 5.0	4.0	— 3.0	+ 3.0	+ 4.0	+11.0	+ 8.0	6.5	+3.0
20	— 9.0	—20.5	...	...	+2.0	...	0.0	+ 4.0	— 4.0	— 4.8	+ 3.0	+ 9.0	+ 2.0	3.0	...
21	...	...	...	...	—1.5	...	...	...	...	— 5.2	— 4.0	— 3.2	...	+ 1.8	...
22	...	...	...	...	...	...	...	...	...	?	— 4.5	— 3.0	...	0.0	...
23	...	...	...	...	...	...	...	...	...	?	...	...	...	...	...
Midn't	...	...	...	...	...	...	...	...	...	—13.9	...	...	...	...	...

Hour.	10th.	11th.	12th.	13th.	14th.	15th.	16th.	17th.	18th.	19th.	20th.	21st.	22d.	23d.	24th.
1h.	...	...	...	...	...	...	...	...	...	...	...	...	...	...	1
2	...	...	...	...	...	...	...	...	...	...	...	1	...	...	1
3	...	...	...	...	...	...	...	...	...	...	...	1	1	...	1
4	...	...	...	...	...	...	...	...	...	1	...	1	1	...	1
5	3	3	1	...	...	1	...	1	1	1	1	1	1	...	1
6	3	4	1	...	4	1	3	1	1	1	1	1	1	...	1
7	3	4	1	...	...	1	2	1	1	1	1	1	1	4	1
8	3	4	1	...	...	1	1	1	1	1	1	1	1	?	1
9	4	1	1	4	‖4	1	...	...	1	1	1	1	2	2	1
10	4	1	1	4	‖4	1	...	...	1	1	1	1	1	2	1
11	4	2	1	4	4	2	...	...	1	1	1	1	1	2	1
Noon	4	2	1	4	4	2	...	...	1	1	1	1	2	2	1
13	4	2	1	4	‖4	2	1	1	1	1	1	1	2	1	1
14	4	2	1	4	4	2	1	1	1	1	1	1	2	1	1
15	4	2	1	4	4	4	1	1	1	1	1	1	2	1	1
16	4	2	2	4	4	‖4	1	1	1	1	1	1	2	1	1
17	4	1	2	4	4	‖4	1	1	1	1	1	1	3	1	1
18	4	1	3	4	4	‖4	1	1	1	1	...	1	3	2	1
19	4	1	3	...	4	‖4	1	1	1	2	...	1	4	1	1
20	4	1	4	...	4	‖4	1	1	1	3	...	1	4	1	1
21	...	...	...	...	4	...	...	...	...	3	...	...	...	...	1
22	...	...	...	...	...	...	...	...	...	3	...	...	...	...	1
23	...	...	...	...	...	...	...	...	...	3	...	...	...	...	1
Midn't	...	...	...	...	...	...	...	...	...	4	...	...	...	...	1

* Corrected from 10° to 1°.0.

† In the original, it has the sign —.

‡ Changed from 5 to 15.

§ Corrected reading, the original being 9°.

‖ The original has 0; the column for clouds indicates 4, as above.

Note.—The observations are made with mercurial thermometer No. 1; by comparison with the observatory standard at +42°, its correction was —0°.1. It was not thought necessary to apply this small correction.

Readings of the Black Bulb Thermometer, and corresponding Notes on the Solar Light, observed at Van Rensselaer Harbor,

In April and May, 1854, in Lat. 78° 37′, Long. 70° 53′ W. of Greenwich.

Expressed in degrees of Fahrenheit's scale. At meteorological observatory.

Hour.	25th.	26th.	27th.	28th.	29th.	30th.	1st.	2d.	3d.	4th.	5th.	6th.	7th.	8th.	9th.
	°	°	°	°	°	°	°	°	°	°	°	°	°	°	°
1h.	...	...	...	+ 4.0	...	...	...	...	...	*—6.5	+ 2.1	...	...	+ 6.3	...
2	...	— 1.0	...	4.0	...	...	...	...	...	*—6.0	3.5	...	...	9.8	+14.0
3	+ 3.0	+ 1.0	— 3.8	3.0	+ 5.0	+ 7.0	+ 9.0	...	+ 1.0	*—4.5	5.0	+ 0.5	+ 7.5	9.7	17.0
4	4.0	4.0	+ 4.2	3.0	7.0	8.0	12.0	...	12.0	*—4.0	6.5	1.0	10.5	11.3	20.0
5	6.0	5.0	5.0	4.3	8.0	8.3	14.5	...	17.0	+ 2.0	7.0	6.0	10.0	16.0	22.0
6	7.5	7.0	5.6	5.5	10.0	8.0	24.0	...	18.0	+ 2.0	8.0	8.0	10.0	18.0	26.5
7	8.0	12.0	5.9	6.0	12.0	13.0	21.5	...	21.0	+ 1.5	8.0	14.0	13.0	20.0	26.0
8	11.0	16.0	6.8	8.5	13.0	14.0	29.0	...	19.0	+ 1.0	9.0	14.0	20.0	20.0	21.0
9	6.0	20.0	10.0	10.0	15.0	15.0	26.0	...	16.0	+ 5.0	10.0	10.0	26.0	18.0	16.0
10	8.0	25.0	12.0	16.0	16.0	25.0	28.0	...	20.0	+10.0	10.5	14.5	21.0	19.0	17.0
11	10.0	26.0	15.0	17.0	16.0	23.0	28.0	...	27.0	+16.0	11.0	20.1	18.0	23.0	28.0
Noon	12.0	30.0	18.0	20.0	16.0	22.0	19.0	...	32.0	+18.0	11.2	20.0	20.0	26.0	30.0
13	12.5	32.0	23.0	22.0	18.0	20.0	22.0	...	30.0	+19.0	11.5	17.5	16.0	27.0	28.0
14	12.0	28.0	24.0	24.0	22.0	21.0	29.0	...	27.0	+16.4	13.0	16.0	13.0	30.0	29.0
15	15.0	26.0	22.5	22.0	20.0	20.0	24.0	...	22.0	+13.0	11.5	12.4	13.0	29.0	30.0
16	18.0	25.0	22.0	14.0	18.0	22.5	20.0	...	21.0	+ 9.2	12.0	11.0	15.0	28.0	32.0
17	13.0	22.0	23.0	13.0	15.0	22.0	17.0	...	18.0	+ 9.0	13.0	7.0	13.0	25.0	30.0
18	8.0	20.0	20.0	12.0	15.0	11.0	14.0	...	14.5	+ 7.5	12.0	6.0	14.3	24.0	26.0
19	7.0	18.0	17.0	8.0	13.0	9.0	+10.0	...	+ 6.0	+ 5.0	10.0	5.0	13.0	22.0	27.0
20	+ 7.5	15.0	12.0	8.0	11.0	8.0	...	...	0.0	+ 2.0	+ 6.0	4.0	14.0	21.5	24.0
21	...	+ 8.0	+ 8.0	6.0	10.0	5.0	...	...	— 5.0	+ 1.5	— 1.0	3.8	11.5	16.0	13.0
22	...	...	0.0	+ 4.0	+ 9.0	+ 1.0	...	...	...	— 1.0	...	3.0	11.0	14.0	12.5
23	...	...	...	...	...	...	...	...	...	...	...	+ 2.8	+10.0	8.0	10.2
Midn't	...	...	...	...	...	...	...	...	...	...	...	...	...	+ 7.0	+11.0

Hour.	25th.	26th.	27th.	28th.	29th.	30th.	1st.	2d.	3d.	4th.	5th.	6th.	7th.	8th.	9th.
1h.	...	1	1	1	1	1	1	...	1	1	4	3	3	2	1
2	...	1	1	1	1	1	1	...	1	1	4	3	3	2	1
3	1	1	1	1	1	1	1	...	1	1	4	2	4	2	1
4	1	1	1	1	1	1	1	...	1	1	4	2	3	1	1
5	1	1	1	1	1	1	1	...	1	1	4	1	3	2	1
6	1	1	1	1	1	1	1	...	1	1	4	1	4	3	1
7	1	1	1	1	1	1	1	...	1	1	4	1	3	3	1
8	1	1	1	1	1	1	1	...	1	1	4	1	3	3	1
9	1	1	1	1	1	1	1	...	1	1	4	2	2	3	1
10	1	1	1	1	1	1	2	...	1	1	4	1	4	3	1
11	1	1	1	1	1	1	3	...	1	1	3	1	4	3	1
Noon	1	1	1	1	1	1	3	...	1	1	3	1	4	1	1
13	1	1	1	1	1	1	1	...	1	1	3	1	†4	2	1
14	1	1	1	1	1	1	1	4	1	1	3	2	†4	1	1
15	1	1	1	1	1	1	2	4	1	1	3	2	2	1	1
16	1	1	1	1	1	1	2	3	1	1	3	2	1	2	1
17	1	1	1	1	1	1	2	3	1	1	3	2	1	1	1
18	1	1	1	1	1	1	2	3	2	1	2	2	1	1	1
19	1	1	1	1	1	1	3	1	2	1	2	3	1	1	1
20	1	1	1	1	1	1	4	1	2	2	3	3	1	1	1
21	...	1	1	1	1	1	4	1	2	2	3	3	2	1	1
22	...	1	1	1	1	2	...	1	2	3	3	4	2	1	1
23	...	1	1	...	1	2	...	1	2	...	4	3	2	1	1
Midn't	...	1	1	...	1	2	...	1	1	...	4	4	2	1	1

* The sign is wanting in the original.

† Zeros in the abstracts.

On May 2d, the sun was obscured during the greater part of the day.

Readings of the Black Bulb Thermometer, and corresponding Notes on the Solar Light, observed at Van Rensselaer Harbor,

In May, 1854, in Lat. 78° 37′, Long. 70° 53′ W. of Greenwich.

Expressed in degrees of Fahrenheit's scale. At meteorological observatory.

Hour.	10th.	11th.	12th.	13th.	14th.	15th.	16th.	17th.	18th.	19th.	20th.	21st.	22d.	23d.	24th.
	°	°	°	°	°	°	°	°	°	°	°	°	°	°	°
1h.	+14.0	+ 5.0	+ 5.0	+ 6.0	+ 6.0	+ 9.0	+15.0	+14.0	...	+10.0	+13.0	+12.0	+11.0	+19.0	+17.0
2	15.0	7.6	4.0	7.0	7.0	10.0	20.5	13.0	...	12.0	16.5	13.5	12.0	17.0	18.0
3	18.0	7.7	2.0	10.8	12.0	9.0	23.0	15.0	...	13.0	23.2	14.8	16.0	22.0	26.0
4	20.0	8.0	5.0	13.0	14.0	13.0	20.0	15.0	...	14.0	27.0	16.0	22.0	20.0	26.0
5	23.0	6.2	8.0	14.0	17.0	13.0	18.0	16.0	...	20.0	30.2	17.0	28.0	21.0	36.0
6	23.2	7.0	9.6	14.5	18.5	18.0	20.0	16.5	...	30.0	38.0	20.0	30.0	24.0	21.0
7	22.8	9.0	11.0	16.0	22.2	20.0	21.0	18.0	...	36.0	36.0	28.0	40.0	28.0	28.0
8	23.0	11.5	13.2	16.8	23.8	24.0	22.0	19.5	...	39.0	35.0	30.0	34.0	32.0	38.0
9	23.0	13.5	15.0	18.0	29.0	17.0	30.3	21.0	...	31.0	27.0	28.0	27.5	27.0	32.1
10	20.0	17.5	20.0	20.0	31.5	20.0	28.0	24.0	...	34.0	29.5	30.0	34.0	34.0	32.0
11	15.0	20.0	26.0	27.0	31.0	22.5	34.0	31.0	...	33.0	30.0	30.0	39.0	31.5	35.0
Noon	11.5	25.0	32.0	24.0	30.2	24.0	40.0	40.0	...	38.6	30.5	30.0	48.0	34.0	31.0
13	13.0	26.0	34.0	22.0	32.0	25.5	36.0	36.0	...	43.1	32.0	30.0	40.0	31.0	32.5
14	11.5	28.0	38.0	24.0	31.0	26.0	29.0	23.0	...	46.0	38.0	29.0	44.0	29.0	35.0
15	13.2	24.0	34.0	24.0	31.5	28.5	27.0	23.5	...	40.0	36.0	31.0	43.0	24.0	39.4
16	13.1	18.0	20.0	22.0	29.0	29.0	23.0	25.0	...	30.7	37.0	27.0	35.0	23.0	34.0
17	12.0	14.0	21.0	21.0	29.0	27.0	24.5	24.0	...	29.0	33.0	24.0	31.5	25.0	39.0
18	11.0	13.5	17.0	17.0	30.4	25.0	23.5	17.5	...	23.0	32.0	23.0	29.5	28.0	29.0
19	9.0	12.3	12.0	14.5	25.0	22.0	22.0	+13.0	...	20.0	31.2	19.0	27.0	27.0	27.0
20	10.0	10.0	8.3	10.0	14.5	18.0	20.0	...	...	17.0	29.0	17.5	24.0	27.0	28.0
21	10.0	9.0	10.5	8.0	18.0	12.0	17.0	...	+10.0	15.0	20.0	16.2	21.0	18.0	+23.0
22	10.4	8.0	11.0	7.0	12.0	11.0	16.0	...	9.0	12.0	17.5	11.0	19.5	16.0	...
23	+ 9.0	7.0	13.0	3.0	14.0	10.5	14.5	...	8.0	9.0	17.0	11.0	18.0	18.0	...
Midn't	...	+ 8.0	+ 9.0	+ 2.0	+ 8.0	+ 8.0	+12.0	...	+ 9.0	+ 8.0	+13.4	+10.0	+14.0	+16.0	...

Hour.	10th.	11th.	12th.	13th.	14th.	15th.	16th.	17th.	18th.	19th.	20th.	21st.	22d.	23d.	24th.
1h.	1	*4	1	2	1	1	1	1	*4	2	1	2	1	1	2
2	1	*4	1	1	1	1	1	2	*4	2	1	2	1	1	2
3	1	*4	1	1	1	1	1	2	...	2	1	2	1	1	1
4	1	*4	1	1	1	1	1	2	...	2	1	2	1	1	1
5	2	4	1	1	1	1	1	2	...	2	1	2	1	1	2
6	2	4	1	1	1	1	1	2	...	1	1	2	1	1	3
7	3	4	1	1	1	1	1	2	...	1	1	2	1	1	2
8	3	3	1	1	1	2	1	2	...	1	1	2	1	1	1
9	3	3	1	1	1	2	1	2	...	2	1	2	1	1	1
10	4	4	1	1	1	1	1	2	*4	2	1	1	1	1	1
11	*4	4	1	1	1	1	1	2	4	4	1	1	1	2	1
Noon	*4	4	1	1	1	1	1	2	4	3	1	1	1	3	1
13	4	3	1	1	1	1	1	1	4	2	1	1	1	4	1
14	4	2	1	1	1	1	1	1	4	2	1	2	1	4	1
15	4	2	1	1	1	1	1	2	4	1	1	2	1	4	1
16	4	3	1	1	1	1	1	3	4	1	1	1	1	3	1
17	4	3	1	1	1	1	1	3	4	1	1	1	1	2	1
18	4	2	3	1	1	1	1	3	4	1	1	2	1	1	1
19	4	3	3	1	1	1	1	*4	4	1	1	2	1	1	1
20	4	3	4	1	1	1	1	*4	4	1	1	3	1	1	2
21	4	2	4	1	1	1	1	*4	3	1	1	2	1	1	3
22	4	1	4	1	1	1	1	*4	3	1	1	2	1	1	...
23	4	1	4	1	1	1	1	*4	3	1	1	1	1	1	...
Midn't	4	1	4	1	1	1	1	4	3	1	1	1	1	1	...

* The original has 0s.

May 14th. McGary returned, reporting open water at Fog Inlet as far as the eye could see across the channel.

May 20th. The sun is now acquiring power in the middle of the day sufficient to soften the snow on the surface, and black objects lying upon it sink quite fast.

READINGS OF THE BLACK BULB THERMOMETER, AND CORRESPONDING NOTES ON THE SOLAR LIGHT, OBSERVED AT VAN RENSSELAER HARBOR,

In May and June, 1854, in Lat. 78° 37′, Long. 70° 53′ W. of Greenwich.

Expressed in degrees of Fahrenheit's scale. At meteorological observatory.

Hour.	25th.	28th.	29th.	30th.	31st.	1st.	2d.	3d.	4th.	5th.	6th.	7th.	8th.	9th.	10th.
	°	°	°	°	°	°	°	°	°	°	°	°	°	°	°
1h.	...	+37.0	...	+31.0	+30.0	+25.0	+32.0	+30.0	+27.0	+28.0	+20.0	+23.0	+25.0	+26.0	+26.0
2	...	38.0	...	31.0	35.0	28.0	31.0	34.5	28.0	25.0	19.5	23.5	23.0	26.0	32.0
3	...	36.0	...	31.0	33.0	25.0	32.0	38.7	28.0	26.2	21.0	28.0	33.0	26.0	33.0
4	+20.5	37.5	...	32.0	31.0	32.0	33.0	42.0	28.0	28.0	22.0	34.0	35.0	26.0	38.0
5	...	...	...	32.0	30.0	32.0	38.0	...	...	32.0	24.0	38.3	36.0	27.5	36.0
6	...	...	...	36.0	32.0	26.4	40.0	...	...	31.6	24.0	29.1	37.3	28.3	37.0
7	...	...	...	40.0	36.0	29.0	50.0	...	...	31.3	30.0	30.0	38.0	29.2	38.0
8	...	45.0	+46.0	45.0	37.0	34.0	45.0	...	...	29.5	32.0	32.5	39.5	31.7	38.0
9	28.0	42.0	44.0	42.0	35.0	39.0	42.0	44.0	35.0	35.1	34.0	34.0	40.0	33.2	35.0
10	31.0	41.0	...	44.0	36.0	37.0	38.5	38.0	36.0	38.0	35.0	38.0	40.0	34.0	41.0
11	27.0	43.0	...	40.0	37.0	38.0	38.0	42.0	37.0	34.0	32.0	40.0	44.0	35.0	40.0
Noon	33.0	40.0	...	43.0	36.0	42.0	37.0	40.0	38.0	34.0	33.0	34.0	42.0	36.0	41.0
13	32.0	41.0	40.0	43.5	42.0	38.0	34.0	37.0	33.7	36.0	36.0	38.0	42.0	35.0	41.3
14	33.0	42.0	42.0	42.0	41.0	39.0	34.5	37.0	34.5	36.0	38.0	44.0	38.0	42.5	42.0
15	34.0	41.3	38.0	39.4	40.0	37.5	34.5	36.0	35.0	36.2	36.0	44.0	34.0	46.0	44.0
16	32.0	41.0	42.0	39.0	40.0	38.0	34.0	33.0	34.0	37.2	31.5	35.0	34.0	36.0	43.5
17	31.0	...	40.0	36.0	39.0	38.0	34.0	32.5	31.0	35.0	32.0	35.0	34.0	36.0	44.0
18	30.0	...	40.0	35.0	39.0	38.0	34.0	31.7	30.0	30.0	28.2	35.0	34.0	35.5	45.0
19	30.5	...	39.0	34.5	36.0	38.0	34.5	34.5	29.0	29.0	30.0	38.0	31.0	34.0	32.0
20	30.6	...	38.0	31.0	37.0	35.0	34.0	31.5	30.0	28.0	26.0	37.0	+30.0	28.0	31.0
21	30.0	...	31.0	30.0	37.0	34.0	33.0	28.0	30.0	26.0	28.0	36.0	...	34.0	29.0
22	29.0	...	30.5	26.0	34.0	34.0	32.0	28.0	29.0	29.0	27.0	30.0	...	30.0	28.0
23	25.0	...	+30.0	27.0	32.0	28.0	30.0	28.0	29.0	28.0	25.0	31.0	...	30.0	28.0
Midn't	+26.0	...	...	+25.0	+29.0	+27.5	+29.0	+28.0	+28.0	+24.0	+23.0	+24.0	...	+28.0	+27.0

Hour.	25th.	28th.	29th.	30th.	31st.	1st.	2d.	3d.	4th.	5th.	6th.	7th.	8th.	9th.	10th.
1h.	...	4	...	4	2	1	2	...	...	4	4	4	1	4	1
2	...	4	...	4	2	2	2	...	...	4	4	4	...	4	1
3	...	4	...	4	1	2	2	...	...	4	2	3	...	4	1
4	4	4	...	4	1	1	2	...	...	4	2	1	...	4	1
5	...	...	...	*4	1	1	1	...	...	...	...	...	...	...	...
6	...	...	...	4	1	1	1	...	...	...	...	...	...	...	...
7	...	...	...	3	1	2	1	...	...	...	...	...	...	...	...
8	...	4	2	3	1	2	2	...	...	...	...	...	...	...	...
9	4	4	4	2	1	2	2	1	...	...	3	1	...	...	...
10	4	4	*4	3	1	2	3	1	...	1	4	1	3	4	2
11	4	4	*4	3	1	3	3	1	...	4	2	2	3	4	2
Noon	4	4	*4	3	1	3	4	1	1	4	2	3	1	3	2
13	4	4	4	3	2	3	*4	1	1	4	3	1	1	...	2
14	4	4	3	3	2	3	*4	1	1	4	...	1	...	3	2
15	4	4	4	3	2	3	*4	1	1	1	3	1	2	3	2
16	4	4	*4	3	1	3	*4	1	...	1	4	...	2	2	2
17	4	...	*4	3	1	3	*4	1	...	1	4	...	2	2	2
18	4	...	*4	*4	1	2	*4	1	...	1	4	...	2	1	2
19	4	...	*4	*4	1	1	3	1	...	...	...	...	...	...	1
20	4	...	*4	4	1	1	3	*4	...	...	...	...	...	...	1
21	4	...	4	4	1	1	3	3	...	...	...	...	...	...	...
22	4	...	4	3	1	1	2	3	...	...	...	...	...	...	...
23	4	...	4	3	1	1	1	3	...	...	...	...	...	...	...
Midn't	4	...	4	2	1	1	1	4	...	...	...	...	...	...	...

* Zeros in the original.

No observations on the 26th and 27th.

May 26th. The effect of the higher temperature is very apparent on the snow and ice, rendering the former very soft, and the latter spongy and porous.

May 27th. The snow is melting fast, the water rising through the cracks in the ice foot, and forming large basins every tide.

May 28th. Ice foot decaying rapidly.

READINGS OF THE BLACK BULB THERMOMETER, AND CORRESPONDING NOTES ON THE SOLAR LIGHT, OBSERVED AT VAN RENSSELAER HARBOR,

In June, 1854, in Lat. 78° 37′, Long. 70° 53′ W. of Greenwich.

Expressed in degrees of Fahrenheit's scale. At meteorological observatory.

Hour.	11th.	12th.	13th.	14th.	15th.	16th.	17th.	18th.	19th.	20th.	21st.	22d.	23d.	24th.	25th.
	°	°	°	°	°	°	°	°	°	°	°	°	°	°	°
1h.	+28.0	+23.5	+25.0	+28.0	+40.0	+41.0	+33.0	+38.0	+33.0	+34.0	+31.0	+31.0	+31.5	+31.0	+34.0
2	27.0	25.0	25.0	30.0	43.5	29.0	34.0	36.0	33.0	36.0	31.5	31.0	31.5	34.0	33.0
3	27.0	25.0	24.0	30.0	48.0	28.0	34.0	36.0	33.5	36.0	33.0	31.0	31.5	33.0	33.0
4	30.0	25.0	24.0	29.5	35.0	28.0	40.5	42.0	33.5	37.0	33.6	30.0	31.5	37.3	34.0
5	32.1	28.0	29.0	34.0	...	36.0	40.4	39.0	40.0	38.0	33.6	38.1	28.0	38.0	39.0
6	32.2	29.7	29.0	34.8	...	34.5	40.1	38.8	42.1	34.3	34.0	35.7	29.5	39.7	40.0
7	32.0	30.6	29.8	33.4	?26.7	34.3	40.0	38.5	46.0	32.0	34.6	36.2	30.0	40.0	41.3
8	36.0	37.0	30.0	36.0	34.0	32.0	38.0	38.0	49.0	34.0	34.8	38.7	33.1	42.3	42.0
9	38.0	40.0	30.0	39.0	38.0	38.0	40.0	44.0	50.0	34.0	34.0	44.3	34.0	40.2	43.0
10	41.0	41.0	32.0	40.0	40.0	44.0	42.0	45.0	53.0	34.0	34.0	37.2	34.0	42.1	45.0
11	40.0	40.5	33.0	45.0	46.0	48.0	39.0	46.0	54.0	34.0	35.0	38.0	35.0	44.2	45.0
Noon	40.5	41.0	33.0	48.0	45.0	44.0	42.0	49.0	50.0	40.0	52.0	38.2	37.0	46.2	45.0
13	40.0	41.0	32.5	48.0	48.0	43.0	41.0	49.0	48.0	40.0	54.0	44.0	36.0	45.0	43.0
14	41.0	41.5	33.0	48.7	47.0	38.0	38.0	46.0	49.0	34.0	52.0	37.0	40.0	44.0	40.0
15	41.0	41.0	34.0	49.0	45.0	39.0	39.0	45.5	49.0	29.0	52.0	37.0	43.0	42.0	40.0
16	40.0	41.0	33.0	48.0	45.0	39.0	39.5	43.0	44.0	29.0	56.0	37.5	46.0	41.0	37.5
17	40.0	41.0	33.0	46.0	46.0	39.0	40.0	38.0	43.0	30.0	56.0	35.0	46.0	41.0	34.0
18	40.5	41.0	33.0	44.0	49.0	39.0	40.0	38.0	42.0	31.0	42.0	35.0	45.0	40.0	35.0
19	38.0	31.0	33.0	41.0	41.0	36.0	47.0	38.0	42.0	30.9	38.0	34.0	38.0	38.0	35.0
20	36.0	32.0	29.0	38.0	40.0	35.0	46.0	39.0	38.0	31.0	36.2	33.0	36.0	38.0	35.0
21	35.0	*32.0	29.0	38.0	41.0	34.0	44.0	38.0	38.0	31.0	33.5	33.0	31.0	37.0	34.5
22	34.0	26.0	29.0	38.0	40.0	32.0	40.0	34.5	40.0	32.0	?31.4	33.0	32.0	36.0	33.5
23	32.0	25.0	30.0	36.0	34.0	33.0	38.0	34.0	34.0	30.2	32.0	+32.0	33.0	35.0	34.0
Midn't	+33.0	+28.0	+31.0	+31.0	+40.0	+33.0	+38.0	+34.0	+34.0	+29.7	+32.0	...	+32.0	+35.0	+34.0

Hour.	11th.	12th.	13th.	14th.	15th.	16th.	17th.	18th.	19th.	20th.	21st.	22d.	23d.	24th.	25th.
1h.	4	4	3	1	1	1	2	1	4	1	4	4	4	2	3
2	4	4	2	1	1	3	2	1	4	1	4	4	4	2	3
3	...	3	3	1	1	4	2	1	4	1	4	4	4	2	3
4	...	3	4	1	1	4	1	1	4	1	4	4	4	...	2
5	4	3	2	1	1	3	1	1	4	1	4	4	4	...	2
6	4	2	2	1	1	2	1	1	4	1	4	4	4	...	2
7	3	2	2	1	1	2	1	1	4	1	4	4	4	...	2
8	4	2	2	1	1	2	...	1	3	1	4	4	4	...	2
9	2	2	3	1	1	2	...	2	1	1	...	4	1	3	1
10	2	2	3	1	1	2	...	2	1	1	...	...	1	3	1
11	2	3	3	1	1	1	2	2	1	1	...	...	1	3	2
Noon	2	4	3	1	1	2	1	2	1	2	1	...	1	3	2
13	2	4	2	1	1	2	1	2	1	2	1	...	4	2	2
14	2	4	3	1	1	2	1	2	1	4	1	4	4	3	1
15	2	4	3	1	1	2	1	2	1	4	2	4	4	2	2
16	2	4	3	1	1	2	1	2	1	4	3	4	2	2	2
17	1	4	3	1	1	2	1	4	1	4	4	4	1	3	2
18	1	4	3	1	1	2	1	4	1	4	4	4	1	3	...
19	...	...	4	1	1	2	1	4	1	4	4	4	2	3	3
20	...	...	4	1	1	3	1	4	1	4	4	4	2	3	3
21	...	...	4	1	1	3	1	4	1	4	4	4	2	3	3
22	...	...	4	1	1	3	1	4	1	4	4	4	2	3	3
23	...	...	4	1	1	3	1	4	1	4	4	4	2	3	3
Midn't	...	...	4	1	1	3	1	4	1	4	4	4	2	3	3

* Corrected from 23° to 32°.

Readings of the Black Bulb Thermometer, and corresponding Notes on the Solar Light, observed at Van Rensselaer Harbor,

In June and July, 1854, in Lat. 78° 37′, Long. 70° 53′ W. of Greenwich.

Expressed in degrees of Fahrenheit's scale. At meteorological observatory and Fern Rock Island.

Hour.	26th.	27th.	28th.	29th.	30th.	1st.	2d.	4th.	5th.	6th.	7th.	8th.	9th.	10th.	11th.
	°	°	°	°	°	°	°	°	°	°	°	°	°	°	°
1h.	+37.0	+36.5	+37.0	+38.0	+38.5	+36.0	+40.0	+50.0	+44.0	+45.0	+34.0	+37.0	+32.0	+36.0	+40.0
2	37.0	28.0	35.5	38.2	38.8	38.0	40.0	48.5	49.0	45.0	34.0	37.0	31.0	44.0	41.0
3	37.5	29.0	37.0	38.5	38.0	38.0	41.0	47.0	40.0	43.0	35.0	37.0	32.0	49.0	41.5
4	39.0	*47.0	37.0	40.0	39.0	38.0	41.0	48.0	48.0	43.0	34.0	36.0	36.0	44.0	49.5
5	39.0	37.0	35.0	45.2	40.0	39.0	...	53.0	45.0	44.0	34.0	...	36.0	39.0	50.0
6	39.0	39.0	35.1	45.2	46.0	39.5	...	66.0	47.0	41.0	35.0	...	37.0	40.0	49.0
7	39.0	38.0	35.1	45.0	48.0	38.0	...	56.0	50.0	45.0	36.0	...	38.0	46.0	52.0
8	40.0	41.0	36.2	45.0	51.0	38.0	...	67.0	53.0	44.0	36.5	...	38.5	44.0	51.0
9	39.5	43.0	38.0	46.0	50.0	40.0	...	61.0	60.0	46.5	37.0	38.0	38.0	44.0	49.0
10	39.5	44.0	39.0	46.0	52.0	41.0	...	54.0	64.0	?39.0	38.0	38.0	38.0	45.0	49.0
11	39.0	44.5	41.0	48.0	53.0	43.0	...	52.0	54.0	?39.0	39.0	38.0	40.0	43.0	47.0
Noon	44.0	46.0	41.5	49.0	53.0	43.0	...	49.0	49.0	40.0	37.5	39.0	41.0	43.0	46.0
13	54.0	49.0	44.0	51.0	53.0	48.0	...	49.0	48.0	40.0	37.0	?37.0	43.0	43.0	44.0
14	53.0	...	41.0	50.0	53.0	47.5	...	58.0	61.0	38.0	37.0	37.0	42.0	41.0	45.5
15	47.0	53.0	38.0	45.0	48.0	49.5	...	57.0	53.0	40.0	36.0	36.0	41.0	42.0	51.0
16	45.0	56.0	37.5	46.0	44.0	57.5	...	51.0	61.0	40.0	+34.0	37.0	39.0	41.0	47.0
17	45.0	51.0	37.3	42.0	43.0	54.0	...	51.0	†70.0	35.0	...	...	40.0	43.0	46.0
18	43.0	49.0	37.2	39.0	39.0	54.0	...	56.0	62.0	35.0	...	+53.0	44.0	44.0	41.0
19	41.0	50.0	34.5	39.5	37.5	46.0	...	59.0	57.0	36.0	...	...	42.0	42.0	40.0
20	40.0	49.0	34.5	38.0	35.5	?45.0	...	54.0	57.0	+35.0	...	...	42.0	42.0	39.0
21	41.0	49.0	34.0	38.5	35.0	40.5	...	51.0	50.0	...	...	...	41.0	38.0	+38.0
22	41.0	39.0	34.0	38.0	35.5	40.0	...	47.0	53.0	...	...	...	40.0	40.0	...
23	38.0	37.0	33.0	39.0	36.0	43.0	...	46.0	49.0	...	...	...	38.0	41.0	...
Midn't	+38.0	+37.0	+33.0	+38.0	+36.0	+37.0	...	+49.0	+43.0	...	...	...	+37.0	+42.0	...

Hour.	26th.	27th.	28th.	29th.	30th.	1st.	2d.	4th.	5th.	6th.	7th.	8th.	9th.	10th.	11th.
1h.	2	4	3	2	2	3	2	4	4	2	?0	?0	?0	3	2
2	2	2	3	2	2	2	2	4	4	3	?0	?0	?0	1	2
3	2	2	3	2	2	2	2	4	4	2	?0	?0	?0	1	2
4	2	4	3	2	2	2	2	3	4	1	?0	?0	3	1	1
5	2	4	2	2	...	3	3	1	4	3	?0	?0	?0	1	1
6	2	4	2	2	...	4	4	1	4	3	?0	?0	?0	1	1
7	2	4	2	2	...	3	5	4	4	4	4	?0	3	1	1
8	2	4	2	2	...	3	5	1	4	4	4	?0	2	1	1
9	1	4	1	1	2	3	4	1	3	2	4	4	3	1	2
10	1	4	1	1	2	2	4	1	2	3	4	4	3	1	1
11	3	4	2	1	2	2	4	1	3	4	4	4	2	1	2
Noon	2	4	2	1	2	2	3	1	2	4	4	4	2	1	1
13	3	4	4	4	4	2	3	1	1	4	4	?0	3	1	1
14	3	...	4	4	4	1	3	2	1	4	4	?0	3	1	1
15	2	4	4	3	4	1	5	1	1	4	4	?0	2	1	1
16	2	4	4	...	3	2	5	2	1	4	4	?0	2	1	1
17	2	4	4	...	3	2	1	1	1	...	4	4	...	1	2
18	2	4	4	...	3	2	1	1	1	...	4	2	...	1	3
19	2	4	2	4	3	3	1	1	1	...	4	1	...	1	3
20	3	3	2	4	2	4	1	1	1	...	4	?0	...	1	4
21	3	3	3	4	2	2	2	4	?1	1	1	1	4	3	2
22	3	3	2	4	2	2	2	4	?1	1	1	1	4	2	?0
23	2	3	2	4	2	1	1	4	?1	1	1	1	3	1	?0
Midn't	4	3	2	4	2	1	1	4	?1	1	1	1	3	1	?0

* Probably 37°.0. † Highest temperature observed.

June 26th. Thermometer No. 1 broke; mercurial thermometer No. 17 supplied its place. By comparison with the observatory standard, its index error is 1°.0, or its correction —1°.0, which has been applied.

July 1st. The ice, the past two days, has changed remarkably; the water streams from the hills commenced running yesterday, and the warm weather has caused large pools on the surface of the ice in the bay, covering it to the depth of several inches.

July 2d. Thermometer No. 17 broke at 9 A. M. Its place was supplied by No. 16; its correction, from comparison with observatory standard, is —1°.2, and, with Tagliabue's standard, —0°.7. The correction —1°.0 was applied in the table. The water in the streams is still increasing, and the snow disappearing fast from the hills.

July 3d. No observations. On the 3d and 4th, young ice forms under the effect of a clear sky.

July 5th and 7th. The streams from the hills increase.

READINGS OF THE BLACK BULB THERMOMETER, AND CORRESPONDING NOTES ON THE SOLAR LIGHT, OBSERVED AT VAN RENSSELAER HARBOR,

In July, 1854, in Lat. 78° 37′, Long. 70° 53′ W. of Greenwich.

Expressed in degrees of Fahrenheit's scale. At Fern Rock Island and on board the brig.

Hour.	12th.	13th.	14th.	15th.	16th.	22d.	23d.	24th.	25th.	26th.	27th.	28th.	29th.	30th.	31st.
	°	°	°	°	°	°	°	°	°	°	°	°	°	°	°
1h.	+34.0	+37.0	+36.0	+38.0	...	+40.5	+55.0	+45.0	+42.0	...	+36.0	+37.5	...	+37.0	+39.0
2	34.0	38.0	37.5	36.5	...	40.0	53.0	43.0	44.0	...	37.5	39.0	...	37.0	40.0
3	34.0	38.0	35.0	36.0	...	40.5	51.0	43.0	44.0	...	36.2	39.0	...	36.0	41.0
4	37.0	38.0	35.5	38.0	...	41.3	53.0	43.0	45.0	...	35.0	39.0	...	38.0	42.0
5	37.0	37.5	36.0	38.0	+35.5	42.0	54.0	43.5	46.0	+38.0	41.0	?36.5	...	41.0	...
6	39.0	40.0	35.5	39.0	38.2	41.0	57.0	45.0	46.5	39.0	39.0	?37.0	...	46.2	...
7	40.0	40.0	36.6	38.5	39.5	41.0	64.0	45.0	47.0	42.0	43.3	?37.8	...	51.0	...
8	40.0	41.0	39.0	38.0	40.0	42.0	63.0	44.0	47.5	42.0	44.0	41.0	...	58.0	...
9	39.0	41.0	41.0	38.5	39.5	49.0	64.0	48.0	40.0	35.0	47.0	48.0	...	58.0	46.0
10	39.0	41.0	48.5	38.0	39.8	57.0	65.0	49.0	39.0	37.0	46.0	48.0	...	60.0	48.0
11	39.0	41.0	47.5	37.0	40.0	59.0	63.0	55.0	39.0	39.0	45.0	49.0	...	61.0	53.0
Noon	38.0	41.0	49.0	35.5	39.5	59.0	60.0	56.0	39.0	44.0	44.0	50.0	...	59.0	59.0
13	38.0	42.0	50.5	38.0	38.0	60.0	60.0	57.0	58.0	45.0	42.0	52.0	+44.0	57.0	59.0
14	39.0	43.0	52.0	36.0	37.0	59.0	60.0	56.6	59.0	45.3	41.0	54.0	47.0	54.0	59.0
15	41.0	42.0	52.0	36.0	35.0	58.0	62.0	55.0	57.0	44.5	39.0	54.0	46.0	49.0	54.0
16	41.0	43.0	51.0	35.0	+35.0	57.5	62.0	56.0	57.0	44.0	37.0	+50.0	46.0	42.0	42.0
17	40.0	...	50.0	?34.0	...	57.0	61.0	55.0	41.0	?41.0	38.0	...	44.5	43.0	40.0
18	39.0	...	...	36.0	...	56.0	60.0	55.0	39.0	43.0	38.0	...	43.0	46.0	39.0
19	39.0	38.5	...	36.0	...	55.5	59.0	50.0	38.5	43.0	38.0	...	44.0	46.0	38.0
20	+37.0	+37.0	...	36.0	...	56.0	58.0	46.0	38.0	42.0	37.0	...	43.0	47.0	42.0
21	...	...	41.0	38.0	...	55.0	57.5	40.0	39.0	38.5	37.6	...	38.0	47.0	41.0
22	...	...	38.7	36.0	...	56.0	58.0	41.4	38.0	37.0	37.9	...	37.0	43.0	41.0
23	...	...	38.5	35.0	...	57.0	59.0	41.5	37.5	37.0	38.3	...	44.0	41.0	39.0
Midn't	...	...	+37.0	+34.0	...	+57.0	+58.0	+43.0	+36.0	+37.0	+38.2	...	+42.0	+42.0	+36.0

Hour.	12th.	13th.	14th.	15th.	16th.	22d.	23d.	24th.	25th.	26th.	27th.	28th.	29th.	30th.	31st.
1h.	...	4	1	4	...	...	...	4	?0	4	3	...	...	2	1
2	...	4	1	4	...	...	...	4	?0	4	3	...	...	2	1
3	...	4	...	4	...	...	...	3	?0	4	3	...	...	3	1
4	...	4	...	4	...	...	...	3	2	4	3	...	...	3	1
5	4	4	...	4	3	...	...	3	2	*4	3	4	...	2	...
6	4	4	3	4	3	...	...	3	2	*4	2	4	...	1	...
7	4	4	3	4	4	4	1	3	2	*4	2	4	...	1	...
8	4	2	3	4	4	3	1	3	2	*4	1	4	...	1	...
9	4	2	3	4	4	2	1	3	4	4	2	*4	1	1	1
10	4	2	3	4	4	1	1	2	4	4	1	*4	1	1	1
11	4	2	3	4	4	1	1	2	4	4	2	*4	3	1	1
Noon	4	2	3	4	4	1	1	2	3	4	1	*4	3	1	1
13	3	4	2	4	4	1	1	4	1	3	4	*4	2	1	1
14	4	4	1	4	4	1	1	4	2	2	4	*4	2	1	1
15	4	4	2	4	3	1	1	4	2	1	4	*4	2	1	3
16	4	...	3	4	2	1	1	4	1	2	4	2	2	1	4
17	4	...	4	4	4	1	1	4	4	2	4	2	2	1	4
18	4	...	4	4	*4	1	1	4	4	?0	4	2	1	1	4
19	4	4	4	4	*4	1	2	4	4	?0	4	3	1	1	4
20	4	4	4	4	*4	1	3	4	4	?0	4	4	1	1	2
21	?0†	...	4	4	*4	1	3	4	3	3	4	4	2	1	3
22	?0	...	4	4	*4	1	2	4	3	3	4	4	2	1	4
23	?0	...	4	4	*4	1	2	4	2	4	4	4	2	1	4
Midn't	?0	...	4	4	*4	1	2	4	2	4	4	...	1	1	4

* Zeros in the original.

† These and other zeros are inserted by G. Riley, who had been on watch from 8 to 12 since the 5th inst.

July 17th, etc. No observations on the 17th, 18th, 19th, 20th, and 21st, of the black bulb temperatures.

July 28th. The two sun thermometers were taken from the island. At noon, July 29th, these thermometers were suspended on board the brig, 8 feet from deck.

July 31st. Messrs. Sonntag, Ohlsen, and Stevenson returned. They found the sound perfectly open to the southward of the north cape of Bedevilled Reach, and open leads extending to within 6 miles of the brig.

Readings of the Black Bulb Thermometer, and corresponding Notes on the Solar Light, observed at Van Rensselaer Harbor,

In August, 1854, in Lat. 78° 37′, Long. 70° 53′ W. of Greenwich.

Expressed in degrees of Fahrenheit's scale. On board the brig.

Hour.	1st.	2d.	3d.	4th.	5th.	6th.	7th.	8th.	9th.	10th.	11th.	12th.	13th.	16th.	17th.
	°	°	°	°	°	°	°	°	°	°	°	°	°	°	°
1h.	+35.0	+31.0	+35.0	...	+38.0	+45.0	+42.0	+39.0	+39.0	+36.0	+43.0	+33.0	+32.0	+37.0	+33.0
2	35.0	31.5	35.5	...	37.0	43.0	42.0	39.0	42.0	37.0	41.0	36.0	32.5	30.0	32.5
3	35.0	31.0	35.0	...	36.0	39.0	40.0	37.0	43.0	36.0	41.0	37.0	44.0	31.0	35.0
4	36.0	31.0	36.0	...	37.0	43.0	40.5	35.0	47.0	36.3	42.0	38.0	50.0	31.0	39.0
5	36.6	33.0	37.0	+39.0	44.0	37.0	39.0	35.0	48.0	38.0	38.0	39.0	32.0	32.0	39.0
6	37.0	38.0	35.0	40.0	49.0	36.0	47.0	35.5	56.0	39.0	43.0	42.0	33.0	34.0	40.0
7	42.0	43.0	34.0	45.6	50.0	36.5	50.5	39.0	52.0	41.0	46.0	46.0	31.0	38.0	41.0
8	50.0	39.0	36.0	45.0	49.0	40.0	63.0	51.0	53.0	41.0	47.0	41.0	29.0	40.0	42.0
9	63.0	39.0	39.0	...	49.0	48.0	64.0	50.5	55.0	45.0	47.0	36.0	...	42.0	33.0
10	69.0	43.0	39.0	...	49.5	49.5	66.0	49.0	51.0	49.0	50.0	40.0	...	44.0	34.5
11	66.0	45.0	39.0	...	48.0	49.0	62.0	47.0	52.0	52.0	51.0	40.0	...	44.0	36.0
Noon	41.0	48.0	39.0	39.0	49.0	51.0	60.0	46.0	52.5	53.0	55.0	38.0	...	47.0	34.0
13	49.0	43.0	39.0	41.0	53.0	52.0	59.0	47.0	50.0	52.0	55.0	37.0	...	42.0	35.0
14	40.0	44.0	39.0	...	52.0	55.0	59.0	47.0	49.0	51.0	51.0	47.0	...	44.0	37.0
15	39.0	43.0	39.0	...	49.0	56.0	56.0	46.0	48.0	53.0	51.0	48.0	...	55.0	39.0
16	39.0	41.0	39.0	...	41.0	55.0	53.0	45.0	48.0	49.0	49.0	46.0	...	55.0	38.0
17	39.0	41.0	...	...	44.0	53.0	39.0	45.0	46.0	48.0	48.0	43.0	...	54.0	41.0
18	41.0	39.0	...	43.0	44.0	48.0	39.0	42.0	45.5	42.0	47.0	43.0	...	52.0	44.0
19	40.0	51.0	...	...	45.0	...	42.0	39.0	43.0	46.0	46.0	40.0	...	49.0	43.0
20	38.0	49.0	...	...	45.0	...	57.0	38.0	42.0	49.0	45.0	33.0	...	56.0	42.0
21	37.0	39.0	35.0	...	49.0	45.0	49.0	38.3	42.0	39.0	42.0	33.0	...	+42.0	33.0
22	32.0	35.0	35.0	...	48.0	45.0	41.0	36.0	41.0	39.0	42.5	34.0	...	...	33.0
23	31.0	33.5	36.0	...	47.0	44.0	39.0	36.0	39.0	39.0	42.0	34.5	30.0	...	32.0
Midn't	+28.5	+33.0	+37.0	+51.0	+49.0	+42.0	+39.0	+36.0	+37.0	+39.5	+40.5	+35.0	+33.0	...	+32.0

Hour.	1st.	2d.	3d.	4th.	5th.	6th.	7th.	8th.	9th.	10th.	11th.	12th.	13th.	16th.	17th.
1h.	4	3	4	4	2	4	4	2	1	1	1	1	1	1	1
2	4	3	4	4	1	4	...	2	1	1	1	1	1	2	1
3	4	3	4	4	1	4	...	3	1	1	1	1	1	1	1
4	4	3	4	4	1	4	...	3	1	1	1	1	1	1	1
5	4	3	4	3	1	4	1	3	1	1	1	1	1	1	2
6	4	3	4	3	1	2	1	3	1	1	1	1	4	2	2
7	3	2	4	3	1	2	1	3	1	2	1	2	4	2	1
8	2	3	3	2	1	1	1	2	1	2	1	3	4	1	1
9	1	4	4	4	1	1	1	3	1	2	1	3	*4	1	1
10	1	4	4	4	1	1	1	3	1	1	1	2	*4	1	1
11	1	3	4	4	1	1	1	3	1	1	1	1	*4	1	1
Noon	1	2	4	4	1	1	1	4	1	1	1	1	*4	2	2
13	2	2	4	4	1	1	1	3	1	...	1	2	...	4	1
14	4	2	4	4	1	1	1	2	1	...	1	1	...	4	1
15	4	2	4	4	1	1	1	1	1	...	1	1	...	4	1
16	4	3	4	4	1	1	1	1	1	...	1	1	...	4	1
17	4	3	4	4	1	1	2	...	1	...	...	1	*4	1	2
18	4	2	4	4	1	1	2	...	1	1	...	2	*4	1	3
19	4	1	4	4	1	1	2	...	1	1	...	3	*4	1	3
20	4	2	4	4	1	1	1	...	1	1	...	3	*4	1	3
21	4	3	2	4	1	1	1	...	1	1	...	3	*4	2	3
22	4	4	...	4	1	1	1	...	1	2	...	4	4	...	3
23	4	4	...	4	1	1	1	...	1	2	...	2	2	...	3
Midn't	4	4	...	1	1	1	1	...	1	2	...	1	2	...	3

* The original has zeros.

August 14th. At 4 A. M., black bulb +32°.0; solar light 2.

August 15th. At 11 and 12 P. M., black bulb +31°.0 and +30°.0; solar light 3 and 2.

August 17th. The young ice bears a man.

READINGS OF THE BLACK BULB THERMOMETER, AND CORRESPONDING NOTES ON THE SOLAR LIGHT, OBSERVED AT VAN RENSSELAER HARBOR,

In August and September, 1854, in Lat. 78° 37′, Long. 70° 53′ W. of Greenwich.

Expressed in degrees of Fahrenheit's scale. On board the brig.

Hour.	18th.	21st.	23d.	24th.	28th.	29th.	31st.	1st.	4th.	5th.	6th.	7th.	8th.	10th.	11th.
	°	°	°	°	°	°	°	°	°	°	°	°	°	°	°
1h.	+41.0	...	+23.0	+19.0	...	...	...	...	...	...	...	...	...	...	...
2	...	...	...	21.0	...	...	...	...	...	...	...	...	...	...	...
3	...	...	...	29.0	...	...	...	...	...	...	...	...	...	...	...
4	36.0	...	...	31.0	...	...	...	...	...	...	...	...	...	...	...
5	40.0	...	...	23.0	...	+39.0	...	+18.0	...	+ 6.0	...	...	+11.5	...	...
6	41.0	...	...	23.0	...	39.0	...	18.5	...	9.0	...	...	11.0	+13.0	...
7	39.0	+36.0	...	27.0	...	38.0	+34.0	18.0	...	9.5	...	+10.0	16.0	...	+11.0
8	40.0	37.0	24.0	31.0	...	39.0	32.0	23.0	...	11.0	...	11.0	17.0	...	16.0
9	40.0	37.0	24.0	37.0	...	38.0	34.0	23.0	+19.0	16.0	+20.0	13.0	18.0	45.0	20.0
10	41.0	38.0	42.0	36.0	+41.0	37.0	35.0	31.0	21.0	18.0	21.0	17.0	29.0	57.0	23.0
11	42.0	31.5	41.0	34.0	42.0	?	30.0	34.0	28.0	21.0	25.0	24.0	31.0	31.0	23.0
Noon	48.0	41.0	46.0	37.0	40.0	35.0	30.0	...	33.0	20.0	28.0	29.0	19.0	33.0	26.0
13	43.0	38.0	43.0	...	38.0	...	30.0	...	31.0	22.0	33.0	30.0	+15.0	31.0	22.0
14	48.0	36.0	43.0	...	38.0	...	31.0	...	32.0	17.0	30.0	29.0	...	31.0	31.0
15	53.0	38.0	42.0	...	39.0	...	32.0	...	27.5	13.0	29.0	28.0	...	30.0	17.0
16	52.0	+41.0	41.0	...	45.0	...	31.0	...	26.5	+11.5	+26.0	+27.0	...	+27.0	+27.0
17	49.0	...	...	+33.0	36.0	...	30.0	24.0	25.0	...	...	...	...	...	...
18	47.0	...	39.0	...	39.0	...	...	22.0	21.0	...	...	...	...	...	...
19	39.0	...	37.0	...	37.0	...	...	19.0	19.0	...	...	...	...	...	...
20	38.5	...	35.0	...	+33.0	...	...	20.0	+17.0	...	...	...	...	...	...
21	+37.0	...	...	...	...	...	23.0	20.0	...	...	...	...	...	...	...
22	...	...	31.0	...	...	...	21.0	19.0	...	...	...	...	...	...	...
23	...	...	27.0	...	...	...	+20.0	+18.0	...	...	...	...	...	...	...
Midn't	...	...	+27.0	...	...	...	...	...	...	...	...	...	...	...	...

Hour.	18th.	21st.	23d.	24th.	28th.	29th.	31st.	1st.	4th.	5th.	6th.	7th.	8th.	10th.	11th.
1h.	1	*	3	1	...	...	...	...	...	...	...	...	...	...	...
2	...	*	*	1	...	...	5	...	...	...	...	...	...	...	...
3	...	*	*	1	...	1	4	...	...	...	...	...	...	...	...
4	1	*	*	1	...	1	3	...	...	...	...	...	...	...	...
5	1	*	*	1	...	1	?0	1	*	1	...	...	1	...	...
6	1	*	*	1	...	1	?0	1	*	1	...	...	1	1	...
7	1	1	2	1	...	2	1	1	*	1	...	1	1	?0	1
8	1	1	*	1	...	1	3	1	*	1	...	1	1	?0	1
9	1	...	*	2	1	4	2	1	3	1	...	1	1	1	1
10	2	...	1	2	1	4	2	1	3	1	...	1	1	1	1
11	2	...	1	*	1	4	2	1	1	1	...	1	1	1	1
Noon	2	1	1	1	1	4	2	1	1	1	...	1	1	1	1
13	1	1	1	*	1	4	2	...	1	1	...	1	1	1	1
14	1	1	1	*	1	3	2	...	1	1	...	1	3	1	1
15	1	1	1	*	2	4	2	...	1	1	...	1	3	1	1
16	1	1	1	*	2	2	2	...	1	1	...	1	3	1	1
17	1	*	...	4	...	*	2	...	1	1	2	...	3	1	1
18	2	*	2	*	...	*	...	3	1	1	2	...	3	1	1
19	1	*	2	*	...	*	...	...	1	1	2	...	3	1	...
20	1	*	2	*	...	*	...	...	1	1	2	...	1	1	...
21	1	*	1	*	2	*	1	...	...	...	...	...	...	...	...
22	4	*	1	*	2	*	3	...	...	...	...	...	...	...	...
23	4	*	1	*	?2	...	3	...	...	...	...	...	...	...	...
Midn't	4	*	2	*	?2	...	...	...	...	...	...	...	...	...	...

* Zero's in manuscript.

August 19th. The outside bergs no longer move either with tide or current. Black bulb at 9, 10, 11, 12 A. M., 31°, 32°, 36°, 34°; solar light, 4, 4, 3, 4.

August 20th. Black bulb at 3, 4, 5 P. M., 45°, 43°, 31°; solar light, 4, 4, 3.

August 22d. Black bulb at 10, 11, 12 A. M., 35°, 36°, 25°; solar light, 3, 2, 1.

August 24th. By calculation, the lower limb of the sun just grazes the horizon at the northern meridian.

August 25th. Black bulb at 5, 6, 7, 8 A. M., 28°, 28°.5, 28°.5, 30°; solar light, *.

August 25th, 26th, 27th, 30th, and September 2d, 3d, 9th. No observations.

READINGS OF THE BLACK BULB THERMOMETER AND CORRESPONDING NOTES ON THE SOLAR LIGHT—Continued and completed.

Sept. 12. At 6h., 7, 8, 9, 10, 11, 12, 1, 2, 3, 4, 5h.: B. B. +6°, 12, 18, 21, 23, 21, 19, 18, 16, 14, 13, 8°
S. L. 3, . . , . . , 1, 1, 1, 1, 1, 1, 1, 1, 2
Sept. 13. Same hours: B. B. +2°, 7, 20, 33, 31, 31, 33, 34, 28, . . , 19, 16°
S. L. 1, 1, 1, 1, 1, 1, 1, 1, 1, . . , 1, 1
Sept. 14 and 15. No. observations.
Sept. 16. At 8 A. M., 1, 2, 3 P. M.: B. B. +13°, 16, 17, 14°; S. L. 1, 1, 1, 1
Sept. 17. At 1, 2, 4, 5 P. M.: B. B. +19°, 16, 13, 9°; S. L. 1, 1, 1, 2
Sept. 18. No observations.
Sept. 19. At 11 and 12 A. M.: B. B. +11°, 13°; S. L. 1, 1
Sept. 20. At 11 A. M. and 3 and 4 P. M.: B. B. +9°, 45, 5°; S. L. 1, 3, 3
Sept. 21. At 9, 10, 12 A. M.: B. B. +8°, 11, 18°; S. L. 1, 1, 1
Sept. 22. At 12, 1, 2 P. M.: B. B. +20°, 16, 12°; S. L. 1, 2, 3
Sept. 23. At 10, 11, 12 A. M.: B. B. +2°, 6.5, 5°; S. L. 3, 1, 1
Sept. 24, 25, 26. No observations.
Sept. 27. At 10, 11, 12 A. M.: B. B. +13°, 13, 10°; S. L. 1, 1, 2
Sept. 28. At 11 A. M.: B. B. +13°; S. L. 2
Sept. 29, 30, Oct. 1, to 14. No observations of the black bulb thermometer.
Oct. 15. At 11 and 12 A. M.: B. B. —3°, —4°; S. L. 1, 1
The black bulb readings were discontinued on Oct. 18.

Decrease of Temperature with Elevation.—Readings of the temperature at the level of the sea, and at eighty feet elevation on the mast of the brig, were taken during the months of August, September, and October, 1853. These observations were made with the same thermometer at the upper and lower position. The following are the mean differences obtained from twelve observations (bi-hourly) a day for the months August, September, and October, in the two positions: —0°.14, —0°.67, and —0°.30, the minus sign indicating "colder above." We have, therefore, for an elevation of eighty feet, an average change of —0°.37 of temperature during these three months; or the elevation corresponding to a decrease of temperature of 1° Fahr. becomes 210 feet.

Surface Temperature of Sea Water.—The following table contains the mean monthly values, from hourly observations, of the temperature of the surface water in Van Rensselaer Harbor. On the 19th of October, 1854, an order was given to immerge the thermometer four feet below the surface. On the previous day, the water alongside gave at the surface 32°; at three feet deep, 30°.5. After November 27th, the readings remaining constant at +29°, the observations were discontinued.

Year	Month	Temp.	Year	Month	Temp.
1853	September	29°.1	1854	May	28°.9
	October	28.8		June	30.3
	November	28.7		July	32.3
	December	28.7		August	31.8
1854	January	28.7		September	31.3
	February	28.7		October	30.9
	March	28.7		November	29.0
	April	28.8		December	. .

The index error of thermometer is not known; it must be small.

For a preliminary project of the isothermal lines of Baffin's Bay and adjacent islands, constructed for each month of the year, the reader is referred to Appendix No. XIII. of the 2d Vol. of the Narrative.

APPENDIX.

(See note on preceding page 2.)

Extract from Appendix No. XI. 2d volume of the Narrative, p. 405, on the Determination of Temperatures.

* * * * SIR EDWARD PARRY, and more recent Arctic voyagers, have shown that there is a difference, amounting sometimes to two degrees, between the temperatures adjacent to, and at a distance from, the vessel. This was abundantly confirmed by our experience. During the intense cold of our winters, the instruments became very impressible to artificial elevation of temperature. The approach of the observer, the use of the lantern, the neighborhood of articles taken from a heated apartment, &c. &c., were at once perceptible in our records.

Except in naval expeditions, Arctic temperatures, whether Asiatic or American, have been recorded with a limited number of instruments. The results of these must be received with extreme caution; for the differences which alcoholic thermometers exhibit, at temperatures below the freezing point of mercury, are so varying as to require a large number of comparisons, and upon many instruments, to determine their proper correction. It was not uncommon for thermometers which had given us correct and agreeing temperatures as low as —40°, to show at —60° differences of from fifteen to twenty degrees. Such, too, was the case with the well-constructed instruments of Sir James Ross at Leopold Harbor.

To give an example of this, I may refer to the record of six thermometers suspended near each other, as above described, and observed for purposes of comparison at noon February 5th, 1854.

—71°, —63°, —54°, —53°, —50°, and —50°.

All of these, at temperatures above —40°, agreed within 1°.8, and were selected as the most consistent of nearly thirty spirit thermometers.

At 9 A. M. of the same day, eleven similar thermometers gave, under like circumstances, a mean of 68°, the extreme readings being —56°.4 and —80°. For the purpose of obtaining the most probable temperature from these conflicting records, my first impulse was to reject the lowest (coldest) extremes, and take the mean of those which accorded best; but upon advising with our astronomer, Mr. Sonntag, I determined to take the mean of all without rejecting any, the view which he took being simply that those instruments which indicated the extremes in the low scale had never, in temperatures above —40°, shown any anomaly which deprived them of an equal claim to confidence with the rest, and that there was no reason, *à priori*, to consider the results which they gave as less probable than those shown by the others.

In a word, I adopted the views of Professor Airy, as published in the 95th number of the *American Astronomical Journal*. The causes which had produced the errors were mostly unknown, and the quantity to which these errors might amount was entirely so.

Our thermometers were made with great care by Tagliabue, of New York. But, independently of other mechanical sources of error, I am obliged to say that I do not regard the contraction of colored alcohol, at very low temperatures, as sufficiently investigated to enable us to arrive at the causes or the quantity of error. In most of the spirit thermometers, the uniform thickness of the tube was tested before leaving New York; and the freezing of carefully distilled mercury, which I had taken with me for the purpose, gave excellent determinations of absolute temperature.

But it may not be uninteresting to state that the freezing point of this metal varied between —38°.5 and —41°.5, and that its rate of contraction as a solid was so uniform that, in our long and excellent 36 inch standards, it descended after freezing as low as —44°. This result is in accordance with that obtained by Sir Edward Belcher, whose experiments go even further than my own, the mercury having been observed by him to descend as low as 46° below zero.

I may mention the fact, as in some degree confirming the propriety of not excluding an eccentric result from the computation of means, that two or more instruments may agree well together and still differ considerably from the most probable temperatures. This was the case with two long spirit thermometers, which never, even at the lowest temperatures, showed differences amounting to one degree, but which, at —68°, varied 7°.7 from the mean of eleven others. The cause was in this instance easily explained. The two instruments were *fac-similes* of each other; any errors of division of the scale, or from the unequal contraction of the fluid, which was the same in both, and the same in quantity, and probably taken from the same preparation of spirits, were of course common to both. The error induced by the coloring matter of the fluid adhering in small particles to the sides of the tube became very marked at low temperatures. Our routine of daily observation was as follows: Two 36 inch register spirit thermometers were noted hourly, as well as a varying number of instruments of smaller size. For purposes of comparison, the long spirit thermometers and from five to twelve of the others, in selected groups, were generally read at the same time. The difference between the mean of these observations and the reading of any one instrument, gave the correction which was applied to that instrument in order to get the true or most probable temperature. * * * * * *

PART II.

DIRECTION AND FORCE OF THE WIND.

RECORD AND DISCUSSION OF THE DIRECTION AND FORCE OF THE WIND.

THE observations of the direction and force of the wind at Van Rensselaer Harbor, North Greenland, extend over the same period as the other meteorological observations, viz: from September 1st, 1853, to May 1st, 1855. With few exceptions, these observations were made hourly, and their record available for discussion, extends to January 24th, 1855. Those taken after this date will be found recorded (three times a day) in Appendix No. XII. of the second volume of the Narrative of the Expedition.

No self-registering anemometric instrument was used. The direction of the wind is given uncorrected for magnetic variation of the needle, and was noted in reference to eight principal points of the compass. The course of the wind thus given refers to the lower or surface stratum of the atmosphere. The force of the wind has been estimated as near as possible according to a scale extending from 1 to 10; the former number indicating light airs, the latter a hurricane. Zero denotes a calm air. These figures, expressive of the relative force of the wind, are placed in front of the letters indicating the direction, as given by its initial letter, and their relation to the velocity and pressure of the wind is shown in the following table, used in the United States Coast Survey.[1]

DENOMINATION OF WIND.	Estimated No. of force.	Pressure in pounds per square foot.	Velocity in miles per hour.	DENOMINATION OF WIND.	Estimated No. of force.	Pressure in pounds per square foot.	Velocity in miles per hour.
Calm	0	0.000	0	Fresh gale . . .	6	7.9	40
Light air . . .	1	0.005	1	Strong gale . . .	7	12.0	50
Gentle breeze . .	2	0.08	4	Storm	8	18.0	60
Moderate breeze .	3	0.9	13	Tempest . . .	9	31.0	80
Fresh breeze . .	4	2.6	23	Hurricane . . .	10	49.0	100
Strong breeze . .	5	5.1	32				

The relation of the tabular numbers of pressure and velocity is according to Smeaton's table, and is practically the same as that following from D. Bernoulli's formula.[2] It may be questioned whether the upper limit (No. 10) of the above table has been reached among the few observations marked 10 in this latitude;

---

[1] The scale of winds adopted by the Smithsonian Institution does not materially differ from it; see directions on the blank forms furnished to observers. The Coast Survey table will be found p. 277 of the Superintendent's Annual Report of 1856.

[2] See art. Meteorology, in Encyclopædia Britannica, 8th edition.

and, since the force of the wind depends altogether on an estimation, I prefer, in the small number of cases in which the forces 9 and 10 occur, to adopt the numbers 70 and 80 as the corresponding velocity in miles per hour.[1]

In the following hourly abstract of the anemometric observations, the direction is indicated by the initial letter or letters of the compass point, and the force by a number preceding it, according to the scale given above. Any intermediate directions, dividing the compass into 16 points, have been placed alternately in the column of the preceding and following principal direction; thus two successive entries in the log-book of N. N. E., will be found noted in the abstract as N. E. and N. In this manner the mean directions have in all cases been preserved. These intermediate directions are of comparatively rare occurrence. In a few instances, particularly during the first ten days (of September), there is some doubt as to the true meaning of a blank in the log, all other meteorological observations being duly recorded, whether this indicates a calm or an omission of observation. In these cases, I have likewise left a blank in the record, if not otherwise guided by the abstract given in Appendix No. XII. of the Narrative. The first vertical column in the abstract contains the hour of mean local time. Horizontal dashes (- - -) in the body of the abstract indicate "no observation," and two inverted commas (") signify the same force and direction as for the hour immediately preceding. The fall of snow (and rain) is also noted.

---

[1] Mr. Sonntag's views on this subject agree with mine; he thinks the forces rather over-estimated, produced by the greater sensation of cold.

Direction and Force of the Wind observed at Van Rensselaer Harbor,
In September, 1853, in Lat. 78° 37′, Long. 70° 53′ W. of Greenwich.[1]
The directions are magnetic. Variation of compass 108° W.

Hour.	1st.	2d.	3d.	4th.	5th.	6th.	7th.	8th.	9th.	10th.	11th.	12th.	13th.	14th.	15th.
1h.	- - -	3 N.	3 N. W.	- - -	- - -	0	6 S. W.	2 N. W.	0	1 W.	2 W.	2 W.	0	0	1 E.
2	“	“	2 N. W.	“	“	“*	4 S. W.	“	“	“	“	“	“	“	“
3	“	“	1 N. W.	“	“	“*	3 S. W.	“	“	“	- - -	“	“	“	“
4	“	“	“	“	“*	“*	5 S. W.	3 N. E.	“	“	“	“	“	“	“
5	2 N. W.	3 N. W.*	- - -	“	“*	“	4 S. W.	1 N. E.	“	- - -	“	0	“	1 S. E.	2 E.
6	“	3 N.*	“	“	“	“	3 S. W.	“	“	“	“	2 S. E.	“	“	“
7	“	2 N. W.*	“	“	“	“	“	0	“	“	“	0	“	0	“
8	3 N. W.	2 N.	“	“	“	“	4 S. W.	1 N. W.	“	“	“	“	“	“*	“
9	4 N.	2 N. W.	“	“	“	1 S. W.	3 S. W.	0	4 N. W.	“	0	“	“	“*	“
10	“	1 N.	“	“	“	“	“	“	4 N.	“	“	“	“	“*	4 E.
11	“	1 N. W.	“	“	“	2 S. W.	2 S. W.	“	4 N. W.	“	1 W.	“	“	“*	3 E.
Noon	“	1 N.	“	“	“	“	“	“	3 N.	“	0	“	“	“*	2 E.
13	4 N. W.	5 N. W.	“	“	1 N. W.	“*	3 E.*	“	- - -	“	- - -	“	“	“	1 E.
14	“	“	“	“	“	“*	2 E.*	“	“	“	“	“	“	“	“
15	“	“	“	“	“	3 S. W.	“*	“	“	“	“	“	“	“	0
16	“	“	“	“	“	5 S. W.	1 E.	“	“	“	“	“	“	1 S.*	“
17	4 W.	4 N. W.	“	“*	“	6 S. W.	1 N. W.	“	“	“	“	“	“	1 N.*	2 N.
18	“	“	“	“*	0	“	0	“	“	“	“	“	“	“	“
19	“	4 N.	“	“	“	“	“	“	“	“	“	“	“	1 N. E.	“
20	“	3 N. W.	“	“	“	“	“	“	“	“	“	“	“	“	1 N.
21	4 N. W.	2 N.	“	“	“	“	“	“	2 W.	0	0	“	“	“	0
22	“	2 N. W.*	“	“	“	7 S. W.	“	“	2 S. W.	“	“	“	“	1 E.	“
23	“	2 N.	“*	“	“	“	“	“	3 W.	3 W.	“	4 N.	“	“	“
Midn't	3 N. W.	2 N. W.	“*	“	“	“	“	“	3 S.	4 W.	“	3 N.	“	“	“

Hour.	16th.	17th.	18th.	19th.	20th.	21st.	22d.	23d.	24th.	25th.	26th.	27th.	28th.	29th.	30th.
1h.	0	1 N. W.	1 S.	0	0	0	2 S.	3 S.†	0	1 S. W.	0	2 S. E.	2 S. E.	2 N.	0
2	“	“	“	“	“	“	1 S.	4 S.†	“	2 S. W.	“	“	“	“	“
3	“	“	“	1 W.	“	“	“	3 S.†	“	3 S. W.	“	“	3 S. E.	“	“
4	“	“	“	0	“	“	“	2 S.†	“	4 S. W.	“	1 S. E.	2 S. E.	“	“
5	1 N.	“	0	1 N. E.	“	1 S.	1 S. W.	2 S. W.	“	2 S. W.	1 S. W.	2 W.	2 S. W.	“	1 W.
6	“	1 W.	“	2 N. E.*	“	“	1 S.	“	1 S. W.	1 S. W.	“	3 W.	1 S. W.	“	“
7	1 N. E.	“	“	2 E.	“	“	“	“	“	“	“	“	- - -	“	“
8	2 N. E.	“	“	“	“	“	“	“	“	“	“	1 W.	“	“	1 S. W.
9	0	- - -	“	0	“	0	0	“	1 S. E.	1 S.	0	2 E.	1 N. W.‡	“	1 S. E.
10	“	“	“	“	“	“	“	3 S. W.	2 S. E.	“	“	2 N. E.†	“‡	“	“
11	“	“	“	“	“	“	“	2 S. W.	“	2 S.‡	“	1 N. E.†	2 N. W.‡	“	1 E.
Noon	“	“	1 N. W.	“	“	“	“†	1 S. W.	“	1 S.‡	“	“†	2 W.	“	1 N. E.
13	“	0	0	“	“	“	1 S.†	“	1 S. W.	“	“	1 S. E.	3 N.	2 N. W.	“
14	“	“	“	“	“	“	“†	“	“	“	“	“	“	3 N. W.	1 S. E.
15	“	“	“	“	“	“	“†	“	“	“	“	“	“	2 N. W.	“
16	“	“	“	“	“	“	“†	“	“	“	“	“	“	“	0
17	“	1 W.	“	“	“	2 S. W.	3 S. E.†	“*	0	0	1 S. E.	“	2 N.	0	1 S.
18	“	“	“	“	“	3 S. W.	2 S. E.	“*	“	“	“	“	3 N.	“	2 S. W.
19	“	0	“	“	“	“	“	“*	“	“	“	“	“	“	1 S. W.
20	“	“	“	“	“	4 S. W.	3 S. E.	“*	“	“	2 S. E.	3 S.	“‡	1 N.	“
21	“	“	“	“	2 N.	3 S. W.	3 S.	“*	“	1 S. W.	“	- - -	“	0	1 W.
22	“	“	“	“	4 N. W.	“	“	“*	“	“	“	“	2 N.	“	“
23	“	“	“	“	1 N.	“	- - -	“*	“	“	3 S. E.	“	1 S.	“	0
Midn't	“	“	“	“	0	“	3 S. W.	“	“	“	“	“	“	“	1 S.

[1] This longitude resulted from the discussion of the moon culminations.

* Light snow falling.

† Light snow falling occasionally. At 17h., light spiculæ of snow falling, having been preceded for three hours by a misty atmosphere.

‡ Very light snow falling.

Direction and Force of the Wind observed at Van Rensselaer Harbor,

In October, 1853, in Lat. 78° 37′, Long. 70° 53′ W. of Greenwich.

The directions are magnetic. Variation of compass 108° W.

Hour.	1st.	2d.	3d.	4th.	5th.	6th.	7th.	8th.	9th.	10th.	11th.	12th.	13th.	14th.	15th.
1h.	0	2 S. E.	1 E.	4 S.	2 S.	3 S.	1 S. E.	3 N. W.	5 S. E.	1 S.	3 S. E.	0	1 S. W.	0	0
2	"	"*	0	5 S.	"	2 S.	"	4 N. W.	6 S. E.	3 W.	2 S. E.	"‡	2 S. W.	"	"
3	"	"	"	5 S. E.	"	"	2 S. E.	"	"	1 W.	"	"	1 S. W.	"	"
4	"	"	"	5 S.	3 S.	"	3 S. E.	5 N. W.	4 S. E	2 W.	1 S. E.	"	0	"	"
5	"	3 S.	1 S.	"	"	3 S.	2 S. E.	"	5 S. E.	2 S. E.	"	2 S. W.	1 S.	"	"
6	"	"	"	"	3 S. E.	"	"	"	1 S. E.	3 S. W.	"	"	"	1 S. E.	"
7	"	"	"	"	3 S.	"	"	"	"	2 S. E.	"	"	"	"	"
8	"	"	"	"	3 S. E.	"	"	"	"	"†	1 S. W.	1 S. W.	"‡	"	"
9	"	3 N.	1 S. E.	"	"	2 S. E.	"	3 N. W.	"	2 S.	0	1 S.	"‡	2 N. W.	"
10	"	"	"	5 S. E.	"	"	"	2 N. W.	"	"‡	"	0	"‡	1 N. W.	"
11	"	2 N.	"	"	2 S.	"	3 S. E.	2 N.	0	1 S.	"	"	"‡	0	"
Noon	"	"	"	4 S. E.	"	"	3 S.	2 N. W.	"	3 S. E.	1 S. E.	"	"‡	"	"
13	"	"	1 E.	3 S. E.	2 S.	3 S.	2 S.	1 N. W.	1 S. E.	2 S. E.	"	1 S. W.	"‡	"	"
14	"	1 N.	"	"	2 S. E.	3 S. W.*	"	1 N.	"	"	"	1 S.	"‡	"	"
15	"	"	"	"	2 S.	3 E.	"	1 N. W.	"	"	"	"	"	"	"
16	"	"	"	2 S. E.	2 S. E.	"	"	1 N.	"	"	"	1 S. W.	"	"	"
17	"	1 N. E.	"	"	2 S.	2 E.	4 S.	1 N. W.	"	3 S. E.	"	"	2 S. E.	1 S. E.‡	"
18	"	1 E.	"	"	2 S. E.	1 E.	5 S. E.	"	"	"	0	4 S. W.	"	"‡	"
19	"	"	2 S. E.*	3 S. E.	1 S.	"	4 S. E.	"	2 S. E.	"	"	1 S. W.	3 S. E.	"‡	"
20	2 S. E.	"	4 S. E.	"	1 S. E.	"	0	"	3 S. E.	"	"	0	"	"‡	"
21	- - -	"	4 S.	4 S.	4 S.	2 S. E.	4 N. W.	4 N. W.	0	1 S. E.	"	"	2 S. E.	1 S.	"
22	"	"	"	"	"	1 S. E.	0	6 N. W.	"	3 S. E.	"	"	"	"	"
23	"	"	"	"	3 S.	"	"	"	"	"	"	"	4 S. E.	"	"
Midn't	"	"	"	5 S. W.	"	"	"	"	"	"	"	"	1 S. E.	"	"

Hour.	16th.	17th.	18th.	19th.	20th.	21st.	22d.	23d.	24th.	25th.	26th.	27th.	28th.	29th.	30th.	31st.
1h.	0	0	0	1 S. W.	3 S. W.	3 S.	1 S.	1 S.	1 S. E.‡	2 S. E.	0	0	1 S.	0	0	0
2	"	"	"	2 S. W.	2 S. W.	"	"	"	"‡	1 S. E.	"	"	2 S.	"	"	"
3	"	"	"	"	4 S.	1 S.	2 S.	0	"‡	2 S. E.	2 S. E.	"	3 S.	"	"	"
4	"	"‡	"	"	3 S.	2 S.	"	"	"‡	"	0	"	0	"	"	"
5	1 S.	"	"	"	6 S.	1 S.	- - -	"	"‡	"	"	"	"	"	"	"
6	"	"	"	1 S. W.	1 S.	"	"	1 S. E.	"‡	"	"	"	"	"	"	"
7	3 S.	"	"	"	"	"	"	2 S. E.	"‡	2 S.	"	"	"	"	"	"
8	"	"	"	"	"	"	"	"	"	1 S.	"	"	"	"	"	"
9	0	"‡	"	2 S. W.	"	0	2 S.	- - -	2 S.	2 S.	"	"	"	"	"	"
10	"	"‡	"	"	"	"	1 S.	3 S. E.	2 S. W.	"	"	"	"	"	"	"
11	"	1 S. E.‡	"	1 S. W.	2 S.	"	0	1 S. E.	3 S. W.	"	"	"	"	"	"	"
Noon	"	"	"	"	1 S.	"	"	- - -	6 S. W.	1 S.	"	"	"	"	"	"
13	"	1 S.	1 S. E.	"	"	"	1 S.	2 S.	5 S. W.	5 S. E.	1 S. E.	"	2 S.	"	"	1 S. E.
14	"	"	"	"	"	"	0	"	6 S. W.	2 S. E.	"	"	1 S.	"	"	"
15	"	"	"‡	"	- - -	"	"	3 S. E.	"	1 S. E.	2 S. E.	"	0	"	"	"
16	"	"	"‡	"	"	"	"	2 S. E.	5 S. W.	"	"	"	"	"	"	2 S. E.
17	"	"	3 S. E.	2 N. W.	4 S.	"	"	1 S. E.	1 S. W.	1 S.	3 S. E.	"	"	"	"	3 S. E.
18	"	0‡	1 S. E.‡	"	"	"	2 S. E.	"	3 S. W.	"	2 S. E.	"	"	"	"	1 S. E.
19	"	"‡	"‡	"	3 S.	"	1 S. E.	2 S. E.	"	1 S. E.	"	2 S. E.	"	"	"	"
20	"	"‡	"‡	1 N. W.	0	1 S.	"	1 S. E.§	"‡	"	1 S. E.	1 S. E.	"	"	"	"
21	"	"	2 S. E.‡	1 S. W.	"	"	"	"	0‡	0	0	0	"	"	"	0
22	"	"	"‡	3 S. W.	"	0	"	"	"‡	"	"	"	"	"	"	"
23	"	"	0	1 S. W.	"	"	"	"	"‡	"	"	"	"	"	"	"
Midn't	"	"	"	"	"	"	"	"	"‡	"	"	"	"	"	"	"

* Dark and threatening.

† Very light snow falling; wind squally and varying. At 3 o'clock P. M. clouds dispersing.

‡ Snowing.

§ Snowing slightly.

Direction and Force of the Wind observed at Van Rensselaer Harbor,

In November, 1853, in Lat. 78° 37′, Long. 70° 53′ W. of Greenwich.

The directions are magnetic. Variation of compass 108° W.

Hour.	1st.	2d.	3d.	4th.	5th.	6th.	7th.	8th.	9th.	10th.	11th.	12th.	13th.	14th.	15th.
1h.	0	0	0	0	0	0	0	2 N. W.*	1 S. E.	1 S. E.	3 E.	3 S. E.	0	0	0
2	“	“	“	“	1 S. W.	“	“	“*	“	“	“	1 S. E.	“	“	“
3	“	“	“	“	“	“	“	3 N. W.*	“	2 S. E.	1 E.	0	“	“	“
4	“	“	“	“	- - -	“	“	1 N. W.*	2 S. E.	3 S. E.	“	“	“	“	“
5	“	“	“	“	1 W.	“	“	“*	0	2 S.	2 S. E.	“	“	“	1 S. W.
6	“	“	“	“	“	“	“	“*	“	1 S.	1 S. E.	1 S. E.	1 S. W.	“	“
7	“	“	“	“	“	“	“	1 S. E.*	“	“	“	2 S. E.	2 S. W.	“	0
8	“	“	“	“	“	“	“	2 S. E.	“	0	“	5 S.	“	“	“
9	“	“	“	“	0	“	1 E.	0	“	3 S. E.	1 N. W.	6 S.	1 W.	“	1 S. E.
10	“	“	“	“	“	“	0	“	“	“	2 S. E.	5 S.	1 S.	“	0
11	“	“	“	“	“	“	1 E.	“	1 S.	0	“	5 S. E.	1 S. E.	“	“
Noon	“	“	“	“	“	“	0	“	0	1 S. E.	3 S. E.	4 S. W.	“	“	1 S. E.
13	“	“	“	“	1 W.	“	“	“	“	2 S. E.	0	1 S.	0	“	0
14	“	“	“	“	“	“	“	“	“	1 S. E.	“	0	“	“	“
15	“	“	“	“	“	“	2 N. E.	“	“	“	“	“	1 S.	“	1 S. E.
16	“	“	“	“	1 S. W.	“	1 N. E.	“	“	“	“	“	0	“	0
17	“	“	“	“	1 W.	“	“	“	2 S. E.	“	1 S. E.*	2 S. W.	1 S. E.	1 S. E.	1 S. E.
18	“	“	“	“	“	“	“	“	3 S. E.	“	2 S. E.	1 S. W.	0	“	0
19	“	“	“	“	“	“	2 N. E.	“	2 S. E.	2 S. E.	“	“	“	“	“
20	“	“	“	“	“	“	“	“	“	3 S. E.	“	“	“	2 S. E.	1 S. E.
21	“	“	“	“	0	1 S. W.	3 N. W.	“	1 S. E.	0	1 S. E.	1 S. E.	“	0	“
22	“	“	“	“	“	“	“	“	“	“	2 S. E.	2 S. E.	1 S. E.	“	“
23	“	“	“	“	“	0	4 N. W.	“	3 S. E.	“	3 S. E.	3 S. E.	0	“	“
Midn't	“	“	“	“	“	“	3 N.	“	2 S. E.	1 E.	4 S. E.	4 S. E.	“	“	1 S. E.

Hour.	16th.	17th.	18th.	19th.	20th.	21st.	22d.	23d.	24th.	25th.	26th.	27th.	28th.	29th.	30th.
1h.	0	0	0	0	0	2 N. E.	0	0	0	0	0	1 S.	0	0*	1 S. W.*
2	“	“	“	“	“	“	1 S. E.	“	“	“	4 N.	0	2 S.	“*	2 S. E.*
3	“	“	“	1 S.	“	“	“	“	1 S. E.	“	1 N.	1 S.	1 S.	“*	“*
4	“	“	“	0	“	0	0	“	0	“	“	2 S.	“	“*	1 S. E.*
5	“	1 S. E.	2 S.	“	“	2 S.	“	“	“	“	0	1 S. E.	0	1 S. W.*	0*
6	“	2 S. E.	1 S.	“	“	“	“	“	“	“	“	“	“	2 S. W.*	“*
7	1 S. W.	1 S. E.	“	“	“	1 S.	“	“	“	1 S. E.	2 S. E.	0	1 S. E.	1 S. W.*	1 N. W.*
8	2 S. E.	2 S.	“	“	“	“	“	“	“	2 S. E.	1 S. E.	“	0	“*	0
9	0	0	0	“	“	0	“	“	“	“	1 S.	1 S.	3 S. E.†	1 S.*‡	1 S. E.
10	“	“	“	“	“	1 S.	“	“	“	5 S. E.	“	“	“	2 N. W.*	“*
11	“	“	1 E.	“	“	0	“	“	“	6 S. E.	0	“	2 S. E.	“	0*
Noon	“	1 S. E.	0	“	“	“	“	“	“	5 S. E.	“	“	3 S. E.	1 N. W.	1 S. E.*
13	“*	0	“	“	“	“	“	“	“	4 S. E.	1 S. E.	“	“	0	“*
14	“*	“	“	“	“	“	“	“	“	3 S. E.	2 S.	“	“	“	3 S. E.*
15	“*	“	“	“	“	“	“	“	“	2 S. E.	“	2 S.	2 S. E.	“	4 S. W.*
16	“*	“	“	“	“	“	“	“	“	“	“	1 S.	1 S. E.	“	1 S. W.*
17	1 S. E.*	1 S. E.	“	“	2 S.	“	“	“	“	“	1 S. E.	1 S. E.	0	2 S.	1 S. E.*
18	3 S. E.	2 S. E.	“	“	“	“	“	“	“	1 S. E.	0	1 E.	“	1 S.	1 E.*
19	2 S. E.	1 S. E.	“	“	0	“	“	“	“	2 S. E.	“	“	“	0	2 N. W.*
20	4 S. E.	2 S. E.	“	“	1 S.	“	“	“	“	3 S. E.	1 N.	0	“	“	2 S. W.*
21	0	5 S. E.	“	“	0	“	“	“	“	6 S. W.	2 S.	“	“	“	1 N. W.
22	1 S. E.	“	“	“	3 S. E.	“	“	“	“	“	1 S.	1 S.	“*	“	“
23	0	1 S. E.	“	“	1 S. E.	“	“	“	“	5 S. W.	“	“	“*	“	0
Midn't	“	“	“	“	0	“	“	“	“	4 S. W.	0	2 S. E.	“*	1 S. W.	“

* Snowing.

† "After 8 o'clock A. M., the wind, which had been previously from the S'd, set in from due S. E. The thermometer instantly rose 2°.1, and by 6 P. M. gave us the extraordinary temperature of —5°.4. This, when compared with the record of the 24th inst., which gave a minimum of —41°.8, shows a change of 36°.4. This effect is due to the S. E. wind, and is sometimes much more excessive."

‡ "The wind is from the S'd, and the temperature continues rising; by 9 A. M. of to-day it attained its maximum of +1°.0. At this temperature, the deck house snow thawed and became very wet; snow fell freely. This S. wind is very slight, and apparently cannot satisfactorily account for this deviation of temperature, as we have had it constantly from this quarter without such effect. We all suffer much from heat.

DIRECTION AND FORCE OF THE WIND OBSERVED AT VAN RENSSELAER HARBOR,

In December, 1853, in Lat. 78° 37′, Long. 70° 53′ W. of Greenwich.

The directions are magnetic. Variation of compass 108° W.

Hour.	1st.	2d.	3d.	4th.	5th.	6th.	7th.	8th.	9th.	10th.	11th.	12th.	13th.	14th.	15th.
1h.	2 N. E.	2 S. W.	0	2 N. W.	3 S. E.	0	0	0	0	2 S. E.	2 S. E.*	2 S. E.	2 S. E.	0	0
2	1 N. E.	“	1 S.	1 N. W.	4 S. E.	“	“	“	“	“	1 S. E.*	3 S. E.	“	“	“
3	0	1 S. W.	“	“	2 S. E.	1 W.	“	“	“	“	“	0	3 S. E.	“	“
4	“	3 W.	“	“	1 W.	1 S.	“	“	“	1 S. E.	2 S.	“	“	“	“
5	“	1 W.	“	“*	2 W.	0	“	“	“	0	0	“	1 S. E.	“	“
6	“	0	0	2 N. W.*	1 W.	“	“	“	“	“	“	3 N. E.	“	“	“
7	“	“	“	5 N. W.*	3 S. W.	“	“	1 N.	“	1 S. E.	“	“	“	“	“
8	“	“	“	4 N. W.*	3 S.	1 N. W.	“	0	“	“	“	2 N. E.	“	1 S. E.	“
9	“	2 S. E.	2 N. W.	1 N.	1 S.	“	“	“	“	2 S. E.	“	0	0	“	“
10	1 S. E.	1 S. E.	1 N. W.	“	“	0	1 S.	“	“	1 S. E.	1 S.	2 S.	“	“	“
11	0	“	“	0	“	“	“	1 S. E.	“	2 S. E.	2 S. E.	2 S. E.	“	“	“
Noon	“	3 S. E.	“	“	0	“	“	“	“	10 S.†	“	5 E.	“	“	“
13	“	3 S.	0	2 S.	“	“	0	1 S.	2 S. E.	9 S. E.	1 S. E.	7 S. E.	“	“	“
14	“	1 S.	“	4 S. E.	“	“	1 S. E.	0	“	6 S. E.	2 S. E.	4 S. E.	“	“	“
15	“	0	“	3 S. W.	“	“	0	“	“	2 S. E.	3 N. E.	3 S. E.	“	“	“
16	“	“	“	2 S. W.	1 N.	2 S. E.	“	1 S.	1 S. E.	1 S. E.	1 N. E.	6 S. E.	“	“	“
17	1 S.	1 S. E.	“	2 S. E.	0	1 S.	“	0	“	2 S. E.	“	2 S. E.	“	“	“
18	3 S.	1 S.	2 S.	1 S. E.	“	“	“	“	“	4 N. E.	0	3 S. E.	“	“	“
19	6 S.	“	2 S. W.	“	“	0	“	1 S. W.	“	2 E.	“	2 S. E.	“	“	“
20	1 S.	0	3 S. W.	“	“	“	“	“	“	2 S. W.	2 N. E.	1 S. E.	“	“	“
21	“	“	0	“	“	“	“	0	2 S. E.	2 W.	1 N. E.	0	“	“	“
22	0	“	“	2 S. E.	“	“	“	“	1 S. E.	0	0	“	“	“	“
23	1 S. E.	“	“	2 E.	“	“	“	“	3 S. E.	“	“	1 S. E.	“	“	“
Midn't	1 S.	“	“	0	“	“	“	“	1 S. E.	4 N. E.	1 S. E.	3 S. E.	“	“	“

Hour.	16th.	17th.	18th.	19th.	20th.	21st.	22d.	23d.	24th.	25th.	26th.	27th.	28th.	29th.	30th.	31st.
1h.	1 S. E.	0	2 N. E.	1 S.	0	1 S. E.	1 S.W.	1 S. W.	2 S. E.	0	0	0*	8 S. E.	2 S. E.	0	1 S. E.*
2	“	“	2 S. E.	“	“	“	“	1 S.	“	“	“	“*	“	5 S. E.	“	“*
3	“	“	1 N.	2 S.	1 S. E.	“	“	2 S.	6 S. E.	3 S. E.	“	1 W.*	10 S. E.	2 S. E.	“	2 S. E.*
4	“	“	0	1 S.	2 S. E.	0	“	1 S.	7 S.	5 S. E.	“	“*	8 S. E.	2 S.	“	1 S.*
5	0	“	“	0*	1 E.	“	“	2 S. E.	4 S. W.	4 S. E.	2 W.	“*	4 W.*	3 W.*	“	2 W.
6	“	“	“	“*	2 E.	1 N. E.	“	3 S. E.	6 S. W.	2 S.	“	“*	9 S.W.*	4 W.	2 S.	2 N.W.*
7	“	“	“	1 N. W.*	2 S.	1 N. W.	“	“	6 W.	1 S.	“*	“*	8 W.*	3 S.	1 S.	1 N.W.*
8	“	“	“	2 N. W.*	1 S.	“	2 S. E.	1 S. E.	“	“	1 W.*	2 S.*	7 W.	2 W.*	1 S.W.	“*
9	“	“	“	1 N. W.*	1 S. E.	0	1 S. E.	2 S. E.	6 S. E.	0	0*	0*	7 S. W.	1 S.	1 S.	“
10	“	“	“*	2 N. W.*	“	“	“	1 S. E.	6 E.	“	2 E.*	“*	5 S. W.	“	0	“
11	“	“	“*	1 N. W.*	“	“	0	“	“	“	1 S. E.*	“	2 S. W.	“	“	“
Noon	“	“	“*	“*	“	“	“	4 S. E.	5 E.	“	0*	“	3 S.*	“	1 S.	“
13	“	“	“*	“*	“	“	“	3 S. E.	6 E.	“	1 S.*	“	5 S.*	1 S. W.	0	2 W.
14	“	“	“*	0*	“	“	“	2 S. E.	6 S.	“	“*	“	7 S.W.*	“	“	3 N. W.
15	“	“	“	“	0	1 S. E.	“	1 S. E.	“	1 S. W.	0*	“	8 S.*	0	“	2 N. W.
16	“	“	“	1 N. W.	2 S. E.	“	“	0	“	“	“*	“	5 S. E.*	“	“*	1 N. W.
17	2 S. E.	“	1 N. W.	0	0	0	“	“	5 E.	0	“	“	8 S. E.	“	“	0
18	1 S. E.	“	2 N. W.	1 S. E.	“	“	“	“	5 S. E.	“	“	“	“	“	“	1 N. W.
19	“	“	1 N. W.	0	“	“	“	“	4 S. E.	“	“	“	“	“	“	0
20	“	“	“	“	“	“	“	1 S. E.	“	“	“	“	“	“	“	“
21	0	“	0	“	“	1 S. E.	“	0	2 S. W.	“	“*	1 W.	10 S. E.	“	“*	“*
22	“	“	“	“	“	“	“	1 W.	2 S. E.	“	“*	“	9 S. E.	1 S. E.	“*	“*
23	“	“	“	“	“	“	“	“	2 N. W.	“	“*	“	6 S. E.	0	“*	“*
Midn't	“	1 N. E.	“	“	3 S. E.	0	“	0	0	“	“*	“	5 S. E.	“	“*	“*

* Snowing. † “Temperature rising, and wind blowing heavily; very dark and cloudy.”

“Temperature at noon Dec. 8th, —43°.5; wind S. E. and generally calm. Temperature at noon Dec. 9th, —31°.5; wind S. E. or calm. Temperature at noon Dec. 10th, —10°.5; wind S. E. and heavy blow. The connection of the rise of temperature with the wind is embarrassing.”

Dec. 12th. Calm, with squalls at intervals.

Dec. 24. “4 to 8 A. M., overcast, and blowing heavy from S. W. and W. 12 to 4 P. M., thickly overcast, and strong breeze from the S.”

Dec. 28. The twenty-four hours have been characterized by the only heavy gale of wind experienced in Smith's Strait since the closure of our winter harbor. The wind rose to No. 8, blowing in squalls from the S. E., and, after 2 A. M., blew a regular gale (No. 10). Temperature rose from —6°.4 at midnight, to +16°.5 at 5 A. M.; difference nearly 23°.

Direction and Force of the Wind observed at Van Rensselaer Harbor,

In January, 1854, in Lat. 78° 37′, Long. 70° 53′ W. of Greenwich.

The directions are magnetic. Variation of compass 108° W.

Hour.	1st.	2d.	3d.	4th.	5th.	6th.	7th.	8th.	9th.	10th.	11th.	12th.	13th.	14th.	15th.
1h.	0*	0	0*	2 N.*	0	0	0	4 S.	1 S. E.	0	0	0	1 S.	0	0
2	“*	1 S.	“*	“*	“	“	3 S. E.	2 S.	“	1 S. E.	“	“	“	“	“
3	1 S. E.*	“	“*	“*	1 S. E.	“	2 S. E.	1 S.	“	“	“	1 S. E.	“	1 S. E.	“
4	“*	“	“*	“*	“	“	“	“	1 S.	“	“	3 S. E.	“	0	“
5	“*	0	“*	2 W.*	“	2 S. W.	1 S. E.*	“	0	“	“	“	2 S.	“	“
6	“*	“	“*	1 W.	“	1 S. W.	3 W.	“	“	“	“	“	1 S.	“	“
7	“*	“	“*	“	“	2 S. E.	2 W.*	“	“	“	“	“	2 N. E.	“	“
8	2 S. E.*	“	“*	2 S. E.	1 N.	1 S.	3 S.*	“	“	“	“	“	1 N. E.	“	“
9	1 S. E.	“	1 S. E.*	1 S. E.	“	1 N. E.	2 S.	0	“	0	“	“	“	“	“
10	0	“*	2 S. E.*	“	“	“	“	“	“	“	“	“	“	“	“
11	1 S. W.	4 W.	1 S. E.*	“	“	“	1 S.	“	“	“	1 S.	1 S.	2 N. W.	“	“
Noon	2 S. W.	2 W.	2 S. E.*	“	“	“	3 S.	“	“	“	“	1 S. W.	1 N. W.	“	“
13	0	4 S. W.	1 S. E.*	“	“	0	3 S. W.	“	“	“	“	“	0	“	“
14	“	“	4 S. E.	“	“	“	2 S.	“	“	“	“	“	“	“	“
15	“	2 S. W.	1 S.*	1 S.	“	“	“	“	“	“	“	“	“	“	“
16	“	3 S. W.	2 S.*	“	0	“	“	“	“	“	“	“	“	“	“
17	“	0	1 S. E.	0	“	“	0	“	“	“	“	0	“	“	“
18	“	1 S. E.	“	“	“	“	“	“	“	“	“	“	“	“	“
19	“	“	“	“	1 S. E.	“	“	“	“	“	“	“	“	“	“
20	“	0	0	“	0	“	“	“	“	“	“	“	“	“	“
21	“	1 N.	2 S.*	“	“	3 W.	1 S. E.	“	1 S.	“	“	2 S.	“	“	“
22	“	1 N. W.	0*	“	“	“	2 S. E.*	1 W.	“	“	“	“	“	“	“
23	“	1 W.	“*	“	“	2 W.	1 S. E.*	2 W.	0	“	“	2 S. E.	“	“	“
Midn't	“	0	“*	“	“	3 S. W.	4 S. E.*	0	“	“	“	1 S.	“	“	“

Hour.	16th.	17th.	18th.	19th.	20th.	21st.	22d.	23d.	24th.	25th.	26th.	27th.	28th.	29th.	30th.	31st.
1h.	0	1 S.	0	0	2 S. E.	0	1 N. W.	1 E.	0	1 S.	2 N. W.	0	0	0	2 N. W.	1 S.
2	“	“	“	“	1 S. E.	“	1 S. E.	“	“	“	0	“	“	“	“	“
3	“	“	“	“	“	“	2 N. W.	2 S. E.	“	1 S. E.	“	“	1 S. E.	2 S.	1 N. W.	2 S.
4	“	“	“	“	“	“	1 E.	“	“	“	“	“	1 S. W.	“	1 S. W.	1 S.
5	“	1 N. W.	“	“	0	“	2 N. E.	0	1 S.	2 S. E.	“	3 S. W.	0	0	1 S. E.	0
6	“	“	“	“	“	“	1 E.	“	1 W.	“	“	2 S. W.	3 S. E.	“	1 N.	“
7	“	“	“	“	“	“	1 N.	“	“	1 S. W.	“	1 S. W.	1 S. W.	“	“	“
8	“	“	“	“	“	“	“	“	“	“	“	“	0	“	1 N. W.	“
9	“	0	“	“	“	2 S. E.	2 N.	1 S. W.	“	0	“	“	1 W.	“	0	1 S. E.
10	“	“	“	“	“	1 S. E.	“	“	0	“	“	“	0	1 S.	“	1 S.
11	“	“	“	“	“	0	“	1 S.	1 N.	“	“*	0	“	“	“	“
Noon	“	1 S. E.	1 S. E.	“	“	2 S. E.	1 N.	“	1 N. W.	“	2 S. W.	“	“	“	“	“
13	“	0	0	“	“	1 N. W.	“	0	1 S. E.	“	“	1 S. E.	“	“	“	0
14	“	“	“	1 N. W.	“	2 W.	“	1 S. E.	“	“	1 S.	2 S. E.	“	“	“	“
15	“	“	“	“	“	1 W.	0	“	1 N.	“	“	1 S. E.	“	0	“	“
16	“	“	“	1 S. E.	“	1 W.	1 N. E.	“	2 N. W.	“	0	“	“	“	“	“
17	“	“	“	0	1 S. E.	2 S. E.	0	“	0	“	“	0	1 E.	1 S.	“	“
18	“	“	1 S. E.	“	2 S. W.	1 S.	1 S. W.	0	“	“	“	“	0	“	“	“
19	“	“	“	“	1 S. W.	2 S.	1 S.	“	“	“	2 S. E.	“	“	0	2 S. W.	“
20	“	“	“	“	0	- - -	1 S. W.	“	“	“	1 S. E.	“	“	“	1 S.	“
21	“	“	0	2 N.	2 S. E.	1 S. E.	0	“	“	1 S. W.	0	“	“	“	0	“
22	1 S.	1 S. E.	“	1 N.	1 S. E.	- - -	“	“	1 N. W.	“	“	1 W.	2 S. W.	“	2 S. E.	“
23	1 S. W.	“	“	“	“	“	“	“	0	0	“	“	0	“	0	1 E.
Midn't	1 S.	“	“	1 N. E.	“	2 S. E.	“	“	“	“	“	“	“	“	“	0

* Snowing.

January 2d. From 8 to 12 P. M., slight snow and light variable winds.

January 7th. From 4 to 8 A. M., heavy bank of clouds to S. E.

Direction and Force of the Wind observed at Van Rensselaer Harbor,

In February, 1854, in Lat. 78° 37′, Long. 70° 53′ W. of Greenwich.

The directions are magnetic. Variation of compass 108° W.

Hour.	1st.	2d.	3d.	4th.	5th.	6th.	7th.	8th.	9th.	10th.	11th.	12th.	13th.	14th.
1h.	1 S.	0	0	1 S. E.	1 W.	2 S. E.	0	1 S. E.	1 S. E.	0	2 E.	3 S. E.	2 S. E.	1 S. W.
2	"	"	"	0	"	"	"*	"	"	"	3 S.	3 S.	"	2 E.
3	0	"	"	"	0	3 S. E.	"	"	2 E.	"	3 S. E.	4 S.	1 S. E.	2 S. E.
4	"	"	"	"	"	1 S. E.	"	"	1 E.	"	2 S. E.	5 S.	2 S. E.	1 S.
5	"	"	"	1 S. W.	1 N. W.	1 N. W.	2 E.	0	0	1 S. E.	0	6 S.	0	0†
6	"	"	"	0	0	"	"	"	"	2 S. E.	"	3 S.	1 S.	1 E.
7	"	"	"	1 N. W.	"	2 N.	7 S.	1 E.	"	1 S.	"	2 S. E.	2 S.	"
8	"	"	1 N.	"	"	1 N.	8 S.	"	1 S.	2 S. W.	"	"	3 S.	"
9	"	"	0	0	"	2 S. W.	5 S.	3 S. E.	3 S. E.	3 S. W.	2 S. E.	3 S. E.	0	0
10	2 N. W.	"	"	"	"	1 S. W.	6 S.	"	1 S. E.	5 S. W.	1 S. E.	"	"	1 E.
11	"	"	"	"	"	"	8 S. E.	2 S. E.	"	"	0	1 S. E.	"	0
Noon	1 N. W.	"	"	"	1 S.	"	10 S.	3 S. E.	"	6 S. W.	2 S. E.	"	"	"
13	0	"	"	"	0	1 S.	7 S. E.	"	0	"	1 S. E.	2 S.	"	1 E.
14	"	"	"	"	"	0	5 S. E.	2 S. E.	"	"	0	4 S. W.	"	0
15	1 S.	"	"	"	"	"	5 S.	"	"	5 S. W.	"	2 S. W.	"	"
16	"	"	"	"	"	1 S.	4 S.	1 S. E.	"	3 S. W.	"	4 S. W.	"	"
17	0	"	"	"	1 S.	1 S. E.	2 S.	1 E.	1 S. E.	4 E.	2 S. E.	"	1 S. E.	1 S. W.
18	"	"	"	"	"	"	2 S. W.	"	2 S.	"	5 S. E.	5 S. W.	2 S. E.	2 S. W.
19	"	"	"	"	2 S.	"	3 S. W.	1 S. E.	1 S. W.	5 E.	6 S. E.	4 S. W.	1 S. E.	1 S. W.
20	"	"	"	1 S.	1 S.	"	3 S.	1 N.	"	1 S. E.	8 S. E.	"	2 S.	"
21	"	"	"	0	"	0	2 S. E.	0	0	"	2 S. E.	2 S. W.	"	0
22	"	"	"	"	2 S.	"	1 S. E.	"	"	"	3 S. E.	1 S. W.	3 S.	"
23	1 E.	"	"	"	1 S.	"	2 S. E.	3 S. E.	"	2 N.	1 S. E.	2 S. W.†	"	"
Midn't	0	"	"	"	1 E.	"	1 S. E.	"	"	"	"	"	1 S.	"

Hour.	15th.	16th.	17th.	18th.	19th.	20th.	21st.	22d.	23d.	24th.	25th.	26th.	27th.	28th.
1h.	0	10 S.W.†	1 S. E.†	0	1 S.	0	1 W.	0	0	0	3 S. E.	3 S. E.	0	0
2	"	7 S.	"†	"	2 S.	"	0	1 S. E.	"	"	4 S. E.	1 S. E.	"	"
3	1 S. W.†	5 S.	0	1 S.	0	1 N. E.	"	"	"	"	3 S. E.	0	"	"
4	0	4 S.	"	0	"	1 S. E.	"	0	2 S.	"	"	"	"	"
5	"	2 S. W.	"	"	1 E.	"	2 E.	"	"	"	"	1 S. E.	"	2 S. W.†
6	"	1 S. W.	"	2 S. E.	0	"	2 S. E.	"	1 S.	"	"	"	1 S. W.	1 S. W.
7	"	2 S. W.	2 S.	0	1 S.	2 W.	1 S. E.	"	1 W.	"	2 S. E.	0	2 S. W.	"
8	"	"	1 S.	"	0	1 W.	4 S. E.	"	0	"	1 S. E.	1 S. E.	1 S. W.	"
9	1 E.	1 S. W.	0	"	"	2 W.	1 N. W.	"	"	1 S.	0	0	1 N. W.	0
10	2 E.	"	1 S.	"	"	"†	"	"	"	"	"	"	0	1 E.
11	1 S.	"	"	"	"	1 S.	"	"	"	"	"	"	"	1 S. E.
Noon	2 S. W.	1 S. E.	0	"	"	2 S. E.	"	"	"	0	"	"	2 S. E.	"
13	4 S. W.	0	"	"	"	1 S. E.	"	"	"	2 S.	"	"	0	0
14	3 S. W.	"	"	"	"	0	"	"	"	1 S.	"	"	"	"
15	5 S. W.	"	"	1 E.	"	1 S. E.	0	2 S.	"	2 S.	1 S. E.	"	"	"
16	"	2 S. W.	1 W.	0	"	0	"	1 S.	"	1 S.	2 W.	"	"	"
17	3 S. W.	1 S.	0	"	"	"	1 S. E.	0	2 S.	0	0	"	1 S. E.	"
18	5 S. W.	0	"	"	"	"	0	"	1 S.	"	"	1 E.	"	"
19	3 S. W.†	"	1 S. W.	"	"	"	"	"	3 S.	1 S. E.	1 S. E.	0	"	"
20	2 S. W.†	"	2 S. W.	"	"	"	"	"	2 S.	"	"	"	"	"
21	6 S. E.†	"	2 N. W.	1 W.	"	"	2 S. E.	"	0	2 S.	"	"	"	"
22	"†	1 S. E.†	1 S. W.	0	"	"	1 E.	"	1 S.	0	2 S. E.	"	0	"
23	8 E.†	3 S. E.†	0	"	"	"	0	"	2 S.	1 S.	1 S. E.	"	"	"
Midn't	9 E.†	2 S. E.†	"	"	"	"	1 N.	"	1 S. W.	1 S. W.	"	"	"	1 S.

* Between the hours of 2 and 4 A. M., the temperature was elevated 22°.5. The wind then set in from the E'd, hauled to S'd, and blew a gale (No. 10). Temperature rose as high as —20°.5 at noon. These warm changes are very trying to the health, and curious in their relation to the winds.

† Snowing.

February 15th and 16th. Strong wind between 24h. and 1h., blowing a heavy gale (No. 10).

Direction and Force of the Wind observed at Van Rensselaer Harbor,

In March, 1854, in Lat. 78° 37′, Long. 70° 53′ W. of Greenwich.

The directions are magnetic. Variation of compass 108° W.

Hour.	1st.	2d.	3d.	4th.	5th.	6th.	7th.	8th.	9th.	10th.	11th.	12th.	13th.	14th.	15th.
1h.	1 N. E.	1 S.	0	0	2 S.	2 S. W.	0	1 W.	2 S. W.	0	0	0	0	0	0
2	“	“	“	“	“	0	“	“	3 E.	1 W.	“	“	“	“	“
3	0	“	“	“	“	“	“	0	3 S.	0	“	“	“	“	“
4	“	2 S.	“	“	“	“	1 W.	“	5 E.	“	1 W.	“	“	“	“
5	“	0	“	“	“	“	0	“	2 S. E.	“	0	“	“	“	1 S. E.
6	“	“	“	“	“	“	“	“	“	1 S. E.	“	“	“	“	“
7	“	“	“	“	“	“	“	“	“	“	“	“	“	“	“
8	“	“	“	“	0	“	“	“	1 S. E.	0	“	“	“	“	“
9	“	“	1 S.	“	1 S. E.	“	“	“	2 S. E.	“	“	“	“	“	3 S.
10	“	“	“	“	1 S.	“	“	“	“	“	“	“	“	“	“
11	“	“	“	“	2 S. W.	1 W.	“	“	“	“	“	“	“	“	2 S.
Noon	1 S.	1 S.	0	“	1 S. W.	“	“	“	“	“	“	“	“	“	3 S.
13	0	“	1 S.	1 S.	“	“	“	1 W.	“	“	“	“	1 S.	“	“
14	“	2 S.	0	“	0	“	“	“	1 N. W.	“	“	“	0	“	2 S.
15	“	1 S.	“	0	“	1 E.	“	0	“	“	“	“	“	“	0
16	“	“	1 W.	“	“	0	1 S. E.	“	“	“	“	“	“	“	1 W.
17	“	“	0	“	“	“	0	“	0	“	“	“	“	“	2 S. E.
18	“	2 S.	“	“	“	“	“	“	“	“	“	“	“	“	“
19	“	1 S.	“	“	“	“	“	“	“	“	“	“	“	1 S. W.	“
20	“	“	“	“	“	“	“	“	“	“	“	“	“	0	3 S. E.
21	“	“	“	“	“	“	“	“	“	“	“	“	“	“	4 S.
22	“	“	“	“	“	“	“	1 S. E.	“	“	“	“	“	“	“
23	“	“	“	1 S.	“	“	“	0	“	“	“	“	“	“	“
Midn't	“	0	“	2 S.	“	“	“	“	“	“	“	“	“	“	“

Hour.	16th.	17th.	18th.	19th.	20th.	21st.	22d.	23d.	24th.	25th.	26th.	27th.	28th.	29th.	30th.	31st.
1h.	3 S.	0	0	1 N. W.	0	1 S.	1 S. E.	2 S. E.	1 W.*	0	0	1 S.	0	3 S. E.	0	0
2	2 S.	“	“	0	“	“	“	4 S. E.	1 N. W.*	2 S.	“	4 S.	“	“	“	“
3	3 S.	“	“	“	“	“	“	1 S. E.	2 N. W.*	1 S.	“	2 S. E.	“	2 S. E.	“	“
4	1 S.	“	“	“	“	“*	“	“	“*	0	“	1 S. E.	“	“	“	“
5	“	“	“	“	“	0*	0	“	0*	1 S.	“	1 S.	“	1 S. E.	“	“
6	“	“	“	“	“	“*	1 S. E.	1 S.	“*	2 S.	“	2 S. E.	“	2 S. E.	“	1 N.
7	“	“	“	“	“	“*	2 S. E.	“*	1 W.*	1 S.	“	3 S. E.	“	1 S. W.	“	“
8	“	“	“	“	1 S.	“*	3 S. E.	“*	“*	“	“	“	“	0	“	0
9	2 S.	“	“	“	1 S. E.	“	0	0	“*	“	“	1 S. E.	“	“	“	“
10	1 S.	“	“	“	0	“	1 S.*	1 N. W.	“*	“	1 N. W.	“	“	“	“	“
11	“	1 S.	“	“	1 S. E.	1 S. W.*	“*	0	“*	0	“	“	1 S.	“	“	“
Noon	“	1 S. W.	“	2 N. W.	0	“*	“	“	2 W.*	“	“	“	“	“	“	“
13	“	0	“	0	1 S. E.	0	0	1 W.*	“*	“	0	“	0	“	“	“
14	“	“	“	“	2 S. E.	“	1 S.	“*	3 W.*	“	“	“	“	“	“	“
15	“	“	“	“	1 S. E.	“	“	0*	3 N. W.*	“	“	“	1 S. E.	1 S. W.	“	“
16	0	“	“	1 S. E.	1 S. E.	“	“	“*	4 N. W.*	“	“	“	“	“	“	“
17	1 S. W.	“	“	0	0	“	0	“*	“*	“	“	2 S. E.	“	“	“	“
18	“	“	“	“	“	“	“	“*	“*	“	“	“	“	0	“	“
19	“	“	“	“	“	“	“	“*	2 N. W.	“	“	1 S. E.	1 S.	1 S.	“	“
20	“	“	“	“	“	“	2 S.	“*	4 N. W.	“	“	“	2 S.	0	“	“
21	1 N. W.	“	“	1 S.	“	“	2 S. E.	2 W.*	3 N. W.*	“	“	“	0	1 S.	“	2 S.
22	“	“	“	0	“	1 S.	2 S.	“*	2 N. W.*	“	1 S.	“	4 S.	“	1 W.	“
23	0	“	“	“	1 S.	0	0	“*	1 N. W.	“	“	0	“	“	“	3 S.
Midn't	“	“	“	“	“*	“	2 S. E.	“*	0	“	“	1 S. E.	2 S. E.	2 N. W.	“	6 S.

* Snow.

March 9th. Between the hours 1 and 2 A. M., the temperature rose 13°.5.

Direction and Force of the Wind observed at Van Rensselaer Harbor,

In April, 1854, in Lat. 78° 37′, Long. 70° 53′ W. of Greenwich.

The directions are magnetic. Variation of compass 108° W.

Hour.	1st.	2d.	3d.	4th.	5th.	6th.	7th.	8th.	9th.	10th.	11th.	12th.	13th.	14th.	15th.
1h.	6 S. W.	2 S. E.	- - -	2 N.	1 S.*	1 S. W.	1 S.	1 S.	0	1 S.	3 S.	1 S.	3 S.	6 S. W.	3 S. W.
2	4 S. W.	3 S. E.	“	“	“*	3 S. W.	2 S.	“	“	“	1 S.	“	2 S.	7 S. W.	4 S. W.
3	5 S. W.	“	“	“	0*	4 S. W.	3 S.	- - -	1 S. E.	0	“	“	1 S.	6 S. W.	3 S. W.
4	3 S. E.	2 S. E.	“	“	“*	3 S.	“	“	2 S.	“	“	“	3 S.	4 S. W.	1 S. W.
5	3 S.	“	“	2 S. E.	“*	2 S. W.	2 S.	0	0	2 S. W.	0	“	0	5 S. W.	4 S. E.
6	2 S.	3 S. E.	“	1 S. E.	“	1 S. W.	1 S.	“	1 S.	1 S. W.	“	0	“	4 S. W.	2 S. E.
7	3 S.	“	“	“	“	3 S. W.	“	1 S.	0	0	“	“	“	“	3 S. E.
8	2 S.	1 S. E.	“	4 S. E.	“	“	“	1 S. E.	“	“	“	“	“	3 S. W.	4 S. E.
9	3 S.	“	“	1 S. E.	1 S.*	“	0	2 S.	“	2 S.	1 S.	1 S.	“	“	3 S. E.
10	2 S.	“	“	2 S.	“*	2 S. W.	“	1 S.	“	1 S.	“	“	1 S.	“	2 S. E.
11	“	“	“	1 S.	“	“	“	“	“	“	2 N.	1 S. W.	“	4 S. W.	1 S.
Noon	“	“	“	“	“	1 S. W.	“	0	“	1 S. E.	1 N. W.	0	0	3 S. W.	“
13	1 S.	- - -†	0	- - -	2 S. W.	1 S.	1 S.	“	1 S. E.	1 S.	1 N.	“	“	4 S. W.	2 S. E.
14	“	“	“	“	“	“	2 S.	1 S. W.	“	0	0	1 N. W.	“	“	“
15	“	“	“	“	1 S.	“	1 S.	“	“	“	“	“	“	“	1 E.
16	“	“	“	“	“	“	0	1 S.	0	“	“	“	“	“	“
17	0	“	“	2 S. W.	0	“	“	2 S. E.	“	“	1 S.	1 S.	“	3 S. W.	1 S. E.
18	“	“	“	1 S. W.	1 S. W.	0	“	1 S. W.	“	“	“	“	“	2 S. W.	0
19	“	“	“	1 S. E.*	- - -	“	“	0	“	3 S.	“	2 S.	“	1 S. W.	2 S. E.
20	“	“	“	“*	“	“	“	“	“	2 S.	“	“	“	2 S. W.	“
21	“	“	“	“*	1 W.*	“	1 S.	1 S.	1 S.	“	“	1 S. W.	“	4 S. W.	3 S.
22	“	“	“	2 S. E.*	“	“	“	“	“	“	“	1 S.	2 S.	3 S. W.	6 S. W.
23	2 S. E.	“	“	“*	“	1 S. W.	0	2 S. E.	“	3 S.	2 S.	“	“	2 S. W.	10 S. W.
Midn't	“	“	“	“*	“	“	1 S.	1 S. E.	“	“	3 S.	“	“	1 S. W.	10 S.

Hour.	16th.	17th.	18th.	19th.	20th.	21st.	22d.	23d.	24th.	25th.	26th.	27th.	28th.	29th.	30th.
1h.	8 S. W.	0	1 N.	1 N.	1 S. W.	0	3 S. W.	1 N. W.	1 S. E.	2 N. W.	0	1 S.	1 S. W.	1 S. E.	3 S. E.
2	“	“	“	“	“	“	1 S. W.	0	“	1 N. W.	“	“	“	“	1 E.
3	“	“	0	“	0	“	“	1 N. W.	0	0	1 S. E.	“	“	“	0
4	“	“	1 S.	“	“	2 N. W.	0	“*	“	“	“	“	“	“	“
5	7 S. W.	“	“	0	“	1 N. W.	“	1 W.	“	“	“	“	0	0	1 S.
6	4 S. W.	1 S.	“	“	“	0	“	0	“	1 N. W.	“	“	“	“	“
7	2 S. W.	0	0	“	“	“	“	“	“	“	“	0	“	“	“
8	1 S. W.	“	“	“	(8 N. W.‡)	“	“	“	“	“	0	“	“	“	“
9	“	“	1 N.	“	0	“	“	“	“	2 N. W.	“	“	“	“	0
10	“	“	“	“	“	1 N.	“	“	“	“	“	“	“	“	“
11	0	“	“	1 N.	“	1 N. W.	“	“	“	“	“	“	“	“	“
Noon	1 S.	“	“	“	“	“	“	“	“	“	“	“	“	“	1 N. W.
13	1 S. W.	1 N. W.	“	“	“	“	1 S.	1 N. W.	“	“	“	“	“	“	0
14	“	“	“	“	1 N. W.	“	“	“	“	1 N. W.	“	“	“	“	“
15	0	“	“	“	0	“	“	“	“	“	1 S.	“	“	“	“
16	1 S. W.	“	1 N. W.	“	“	“	“	“	“	“	“	“	“	“	“
17	0	“	0	“	“	0	“	0	“	2 S. E.	“	“	“	“	“
18	“	“	“	“	“	“	0	“	“	“	“	“	“	“	“
19	1 S. E.	“	“	“	“	“	“	“	“	0	2 S.	“	“	“	“
20	“	“	“	“*	“	“	“	“	“	“	“	“	“	“	“
21	“	“	“	“*	“	“	“	“	“	- - -	1 S.	“	1 S. E.	1 S. E.	“
22	“	“	1 S.	“*	“	“	“	“	“	“	“	“	2 S. E.	“	“
23	0	“	“	“*	“	“	“	“	“	“	“	“	“	“	“
Midn't	“	“	“	1 S. W.*	“	“	“	“	“	“	“*	“	“	“	“

* Snow.

† No observations, on account of the confusion attendant upon the returning party.

‡ This entry seems to be doubtful. The temperature, beyond a great diurnal variation, is but slightly affected, and the barometer not at all. Since there is no mention made in the notes of any sudden squall, I prefer to omit the entry altogether.

April 1st. Wind continues blowing from the S'd and S. W'd, increasing to a gale.

April 15th. About 9 P. M., the wind shifted to S. W., blowing a gale, with heavy snow drift.

Direction and Force of the Wind observed at Van Rensselaer Harbor,

In May, 1854, in Lat. 78° 37′, Long. 70° 53′ W. of Greenwich.

The directions are magnetic. Variation of compass 108° W.

Hour.	1st.	2d.	3d.	4th.	5th.	6th.	7th.	8th.	9th.	10th.	11th.	12th.	13th.	14th.	15th.
1h.	2 N. W.	1 N. W.*	0	4 S. E.	1 N. W.*	0	1 S. E.	1 S. W.	1 S.	2 S. W.	1 N.	1 N. W.*	1 N. W.	0	1 S. W.
2	"	"*	"	"	"*	"	"	"	2 S.	4 S. W.	"	"	"	"	"
3	"	"*	"	3 S. E.	"*	"	"	2 S. W.	"	3 S. W.	"	"	"	"	"
4	3 S. W.	"*	"	0	"*	"	3 S. E.	3 S.	1 S.	2 S. W.	"	"	"	"	"
5	1 S. E.	"*	1 N.W.*	"	"*	"	5 S. E.	5 S.	0	1 S. W.	1 W.	"	"	"	1 S.
6	0	"*	"*	1 S. E.	"*	"	"	6 S.	"	"	"	"	"	"	1 S. E.
7	1 S. E.	"*	"	"	"*	"	"	4 S.	1 S.	"	1 S. W.	"	"	"	"
8	"	"*	"	"	0*	"	1 S. E.	3 S.	3 S.	"	"*	"	"	"	0
9	2 S.	"*	"	3 S. E.	"*	"	1 S.	"	1 S.	1 S. W.	"*	2 S.	"	"	1 N. W.
10	"	2 N. W.*	"	1 S. E.	"*	"	2 S.	4 S.	1 N. W.	2 N.	"*	1 S.	"	"	"
11	1 N. W.	1 N. W.*	"	1 N. W.	"*	"	4 S.	"	"	3 N.*	1 N.*	1 N. W.	"	"	"
Noon	"	"*	"	"	"*	"	3 S.	3 S.	"	"*	"	"	"	"	"
13	"	2 N. W.*	"	2 N. W.	"*	"	6 S.	"	"	2 N.*	1 S. W.	0	"	"	"
14	"	"*	"	"	"*	"	"	2 S.	"	"*	"	"	"	"	"
15	0	3 N. W.*	"	"	"	"	"	1 S.	"	"*	2 S. W.	"	"	"	"
16	1 N. W.	"*	"	3 N. W.	"	"	7 S.	"	0	1 N.*	"	"	"	"	"
17	"	1 N. W.	"	1 N. W.	"	"	"	"	"	"*	"	"	"	"	"
18	"	"	0	1 S. E.	"	"	4 S.	"	1 N. W.	"*	1 S. W.	"	"	"	"
19	0	"	"	"	"	2 S. E.	2 S.	"	"	"*	"	"	"	"	"
20	"*	"	"	0	"	1 S. E.	4 S.	"	"	"*	2 S. W.	"	"	"	"
21	"*	"	"	"	"	0	3 S.	2 S.	2 S. W.	0*	"	"	"	1 S. W.	"
22	"*	0	"	"	"	2 S. E.*	2 S.	3 S.	4 S. W.	1 N.*	1 S. W.	"	1 W.	"	2 S.
23	"*	"	"	"	"	0	3 S.	1 S.	"	"*	"	"	"	0	1 S.
Midn't	"*	"	"	1 N. W.	"	"	5 S.	2 S.	3 S. W.	"*	"	"	"	1 S. W.	"

Hour.	16th.	17th.	18th.	19th.	20th.	21st.	22d.	23d.	24th.	25th.	26th.	27th.	28th.	29th.	30th.	31st.
1h.	1 S. E.	1 S.	0*	2 S. E.	3 S. W.	1 S. W.	5 S. W.	0	0	0	1 W.*	0*	0*	0	0	0
2	2 S. E.	"	"*	4 S. E.	1 S. W.	"	4 S. W.	"	"	"*	0*	"*	"*	"	"	"
3	1 S. E.	"	"*	1 S. E.	"	"	3 S. W.	"	"	"*	"*	"*	"*	"	"	"
4	1 E.	"	"*	2 S. E.	"	2 S. W.	0	"	"	"*	"*	"*	"*	"	"	"
5	"	"	"*	"	"	3 S. W.	1 S. W.	"	"	1 N.*	1 W.*	"*	"*	1 N.W.*	"	"
6	2 E.	"	"*	1 S. E.	"	2 S. W.	2 S. W.	"	"	"*	"*	"*	"*	"*	"	"
7	1 E.	0	1 N. W.*	0	"	3 S. W.	2 S.	"	"	0*	"	"*	"*	"*	"	"
8	"	"	"*	"	"	2 S. W.	1 S. E.	"	"	"	0	"*	"*	0*	"	"
9	"	1 N. W.	0*	1 S. W.	"	3 S. W.	1 S.	1 N.	"	"	1 N.	"*	"	"	"	"
10	0	"	1 N.*	0	1 N. W.	4 S. W.	"	"	1 N.	"	"	"*	"	"*	"	"
11	"	2 N. W.	"*	"	"	"	0	"	"	"	"	"*	"	"*	2 N.	"
Noon	"	"	"*	"	"	3 S. W.	1 N.	"	"	"*	2 N.	"*	"	"	1 N.	1 N.
13	"	"	"*	"	0	"	"	"	"	"*	1 N.	"*	"	"	"	"
14	2 N. W.	"	"*	"	"	"	2 N.	"	"	"	1 N. W.	"*	"	"	"	0
15	"	"	"*	1 S. W.	"	4 S. W.	3 N.	"	0	"*	"	"*	"*	"	"	"
16	"	"	"*	"	"	"	"	1 N. W.	"	1 N.	"	"*	"	"	0	"
17	1 N. W.	1 N. W.	"*	"	"	"	"	"	1 N.	"	"*	"*	"	"	"	"
18	0	"	"*	3 S. W.	"	"	2 N.	2 N. W.	"	"	"*	"*	"	"	"	"
19	"	"	"*	"	"	"	"	"	"	"	"*	"*	"	"	"	"
20	"	"	"	2 S. W.	1 S. W.	3 S. W.	"	"	0	1 S. W.	"*	"*	"	"	"	"
21	"	0	1 S. W.	"	3 S. W.	4 S. W.	0	0	"	"	"*	"*	"	"	"	"
22	"	"	3 S. W.	"	2 S. W.	"	1 N.	"	"	"	"	"*	"	"	"	"
23	"	"	2 S. W.	3 S. W.	1 S. W.	"	0	"	"	"	"*	"	"	"	"	"
Midn't	"	"	"	"	2 S. W.	3 S. W.	"	"	"	"*	"*	"	"	"	"	"

* Snowing.

May 7th and 8th. Strong breeze and gale from the S'd; ceased at noon of the 8th.

Direction and Force of the Wind observed at Van Rensselaer Harbor,

In June, 1854, in Lat. 78° 37′, Long. 70° 53′ W. of Greenwich.

The directions are magnetic. Variation of compass 108° W.

Hour.	1st.	2d.	3d.	4th.	5th.	6th.	7th.	8th.	9th.	10th.	11th.	12th.	13th.	14th.	15th.
1h.	0	0	1 S. W.	6 N. E.	0	0	4 N. W.	0	0	0	0	0	1 N. W.	2 N. W.	0
2	“	“	“	5 N. E.	“	“	0	“	1 N. W.	“	“	“	“	3 W.	“
3	“	“	“	“	“	“	3 N. W.	“	“	“	3 N. W.	“	0	4 W.	“
4	“	“	0	“	“	“	“	“	0	“	3 N.	“	“	“	“
5	1 W.	1 S. W.	- - -	- - -	“	1 N. W.	“	“	2 N. W.	“	1 N. W.	1 N. W.	1 N. W.	0	“
6	0	2 S. W.	“	“	1 N. W.	“	“	“	“	“	“	“	1 W.	“	“
7	1 W.	1 S. W.	“	“	“	“	“	“	“	“	“	“	1 N. W.	“	“
8	“	2 N. W.	“	“	“	“	“	“	1 N. W.	“	“	“	1 W.	“	“
9	“	“	1 N.	3 N. W.	“	0*	2 N. W.	“	“	“	2 N. W.	2 N. W.	1 N. W.	“	“
10	“	“	“	“	2 N.	“*	0	“	0	“	“	“	2 W.	“	“
11	“	1 N. W.	“	“	2 N. W.	“	“	“	“	“	0	0	2 N. W.	“	“
Noon	0	2 N. W.	“	“	3 N. W.	“	“	“	3 W.	“	“	1 N. W.	0	“	1 N. W.
13	“	1 N. W.	2 N. W.	5 N.	1 N. W.	“	“	“	0	“	“	“	1 N. W.	“	“
14	“	“	3 N. W.	“	0	“	1 N. W.	“	2 N. W.	“	“	“	6 N. W.	“	0
15	“	“	4 N. W.	“	2 N. W.	3 N. W.	“	3 N. W.	0	“	1 N. W.	“	“	1 N. W.	“
16	“	“	“	“	“	2 N.	3 N. W.	“	4 N. W.	“	“	0	“	0	“
17	“	“	“	3 N. W.	3 N.	0	0	“	“	“	“	2 N. W.	“	“	“
18	“	“	“	“	4 N.	1 N. W.*	2 N. W.	“	2 N. W.	“	“	“	5 N. W.	“	“
19	“	“	3 N. W.	“	2 N. W.	2 W.	1 N. W.	2 N. W.	3 N. W.	1 S. W.	2 W.	“	2 N.	“	“
20	“	“	“	2 N. W.	“	2 N. W.	0	“	“	0	1 N. W.	1 N. W.	1 N. W.	“	“
21	“	0	2 N. W.	2 N.	“	“	“	1 N. W.	2 N. W.	1 S. W.	1 W.	2 W.	1 N.	“	“
22	“	“	“	1 W.	“	1 N. W.	“	“	1 N. W.	- - -	0	4 N. W.	1 N. W.	“	“
23	“	“	“	0	1 N. W.	3 N. W.	“	“	0	“	“	3 N. W.	0	“	“
Midn't	“	“	“	“	2 N. W.	2 N. W.	4 S. W.	“	“	“	“	2 N. W.	1 W.	“	“

Hour.	16th.	17th.	18th.	19th.	20th.	21st.	22d.	23d.	24th.	25th.	26th.	27th.	28th.	29th.	30th.
1h.	0	7 S. W.	0	0	0	1 S. W.*	1 S. W.*	4 N. W.*	0	0	0	0	0	- - -	0
2	“	8 S. W.	“	“	“	2 S. W.*	2 S. W.*	1 N. W.	“	“	“	2 N. E.	“	“	“
3	“	7 S. W.	“	“	“	3 S. W.*	1 S. W.*	0	“	“	“	3 N. E.	“	“	“
4	“	5 S. W.	“	“	“	0	“*	2 N. W.	“	“	“	2 N. E.	“	“	1 S. W.
5	“	3 S. W.	“	“	“	“	0*	4 N. W.*	“	“	“	0	“	0	“
6	“	3 S. W.	“	“	“	“	“*	“*	“	“	“	“	“	“	0
7	“	“	“	“	“	“	“*	“*	“	“	“	“	“	“	“
8	“	1 S. W.	“	“	“	“	“*	“*	“	“	“	“	“	“	“
9	“	“	“	“	“	“	“*	1 N. W.	“	“	“	“	“	“	“
10	“	“	“	“	2 N. W.	“	“	“*	“	“	“	“	“	“	“
11	“	2 S. W.	“	“	2 W.	“	“	“*	“	1 N. W.	“	“	“	“	“
Noon	“	“	“	“	0	“	“	“*	“	2 N. W.	“	“	“	“	“
13	“	0	“	“	“	“	“	0*	“	0	“	“	“	“	“
14	“	“	“	“	“	“	“	“	“	“	“	“	“	“	“
15	“	“	“	“	“	“	“	“	- - -	“	“	“	“	“	“
16	“	“	“	“	“	“	1 S. W.	“	“	“	“	“	“	“	“
17	“	“	“	“	“	“	“	“	“	“	“	“	“	“	“
18	“*	“	“	“	“	“	0	“	“	“	“	“	“	“	“
19	1 S.W.*	1 S. W.	“	“	“	“*	2 N. W.	1 W.	1 N. W.	3 N.	“	“	“	“	“
20	0*	“	“	“	“	“	“*	“	1 W.	“	“	“	“	“	1 N.
21	“	0	“	“	“	“	3 N. W.*	“	0	2 N.	“	“	“	“	1 N. W.
22	“	1 W.	“	“	“	“	“*	0	“	1 N. W.	1 N. W.	“	“	“	0
23	“	0	“	“	“	“*	4 N. W.*	“	“	“	0	“	“	“	1 N. W.
Midn't	“	“	“	“	“	“*	- - -*	“	1 N. W.	0	“	“	“	“	0

* Snow.

DIRECTION AND FORCE OF THE WIND OBSERVED AT VAN RENSSELAER HARBOR,

In July, 1854, in Lat. 78° 37′, Long. 70° 53′ W. of Greenwich.

The directions are magnetic. Variation of compass 108° W.

Hour.	1st.	2d.	3d.	4th.	5th.	6th.	7th.	8th.	9th.	10th.	11th.	12th.	13th.	14th.	15th.
1h.	0	- - -	0*	0	0	0	0	0	0	1 N. W.	1 N. W.	0	0	2 S. E.*	0
2	“	“	“*	“	“	“	“	“	“	“	0	1 W.	“	1 S. E.*	“*
3	“	“*	“	“	2 N. W.	1 N. E.	“	“	“	0	“	“	“	0*	“
4	“	“*	“	3 S. W.	0	0	“	“	“	“	“	0	“	“*	“
5	“	S. E.*	“	1 S. W.	“	1 N. W.	“*	“	2 W.	1 N. W.	1 W.	“	“	“*	“
6	“	“*	“	“	“	“	“	“	1 W.	2 N. W.	“	“	“	“	“
7	“	“*	“	1 N.	“	“	“	“	“	1 N. W.	0	“	“	“	“
8	“	S.*	“	0	“	2 N. W.	“	“†	0	“	1 W.	“	“	“	“
9	“	S. E.	1 N.	“	“	“	“	“†	“	0	0	“	“	“	“
10	“	E.	“	“	“	“	“	“†	“	“	“	“	“	“	“
11	“	“	“	“	“	“	“*	“†	“	“	“	“	“	“	“
Noon	“	S. E.	“	“	“	“	“*	“†	“	“	1 N.	“	“	“	“
13	“	S.	0	“	“	“	“*	“	“	“	“	“	“	“	“†
14	“	“	“	“	“	1 N. W.	“*	“	“	“	“	“	“	“	2 N.
15	“	S. W.	“	“	“	2 N. W.	“*	“	“	1 S. W.	1 N. E.	“	“	“	1 N.†
16	“	“	“	“	“	3 N. W.	“*	“	“	1 W.	“	“	“	“	“†
17	“	“	“	“	1 S. W.	2 W.*	“*	“	“	“	1 N. W.	“	- - -	“	0
18	“	“	“	“	“	1 W.*	“*	“	“	“	“	“	“	“	“
19	“	N. W.	“	“	“	“*	“*	“	“	“	2 S. E.	“	0	“	“
20	“	“	“	“	“	1 N. W.	“*	“	“	“	1 E.	“	“	“	“
21	“	- - -	“	“	0	“	“	“	1 W.	0	1 N.	“	- - -	“	“
22	“	“	“	“	“	“	“	“	0	“	“	“	“	“	3 S. W.
23	1 N. W.*	“	“	“	“	“	“	“	“	“	0	“	“	“	“
Midn't	“*	“	“	“	“	“	“	“	“	“	“	“	“	“	“

Hour.	16th.	17th.	18th.	19th.	20th.	21st.	22d.	23d.	24th.	25th.	26th.	27th.	28th.	29th.	30th.	31st.
1h.	- - -	- - -	- - -	- - -	0	0	0	0	0	0	0*	1 N.	0	5 S. W.	0	0
2	“	“	“	“	“	“	“	“	“	“	“*	2 N.†	“	6 S. W.	“	“
3	“	“	“	“	“	“	“	“	“	“	“*	4 N. W.	1 N. W.	4 S. W.	“	“
4	“	“	“	“	“	“	“	“	“	“	“*	3 N. W.	2 S. E.	“	“	“
5	1 N.	0	0	0	1 W.	“*	“	“	“	“	“*	0	2 S. W.	4 W.	1 W.	- - -
6	“	“	“	“	0	“*	“	“	“	“	“	“	3 S. W.*	3 W.	“	“
7	“	1 S.	“	“	“	“*	“	“	“	“	“	“	5 S. W.	0	2 W.	“
8	“	“	“	“	2 N. W.	1 N.*	“	“	“	“	1 S. E.	“	“	“	“	“
9	“	0	“	“	0	“*	“	“	“	“*	1 S.	“	“	“	0	0
10	“	“	“	“	“	1 S.*	“	“	“	“*	1 N.	“	“	“	“	“
11	0	“	“	“	“	“*	“	“	“	“*	1 N. E.	“	6 S. W.	“	“	“
Noon	“	“	“	“	“	“*	“	“	“	“*	“	2 N. W.	6 S.	“	2 N. W.	“
13	“	“	1 E.	“	“	0*	“	“	“	“	2 N.	1 N. W.	6 S. W.	3 N.	3 W.	“†
14	1 N.	1 N.	0	“	2 N. W.	“*	“	“	“	“	3 N. E.	1 W.	6 S.	0	3 N. W.	“
15	5 S.	“	“	“	1 N. W.	“*	“	“	“	“	0	0	8 S. W.	“	2 N. W.	“
16	6 S.	0	1 S.	“	“	“*	“	“	“	“	“	“	“	“	“	“
17	“	“	0	“*	“	“	“	1 W.	“	“	“	“	“	3 N. W.	“	“
18	“	“	“	“*	“	“	“	“	“	“	“	“	“	“	3 N. W.	“
19	“	“	“	“*	“	“	“	“	“	“	“	“	7 S. W.	“	4 N. W.	“
20	“	“	“	“*	“	“	“	“	“	“	“	“	“	0	3 N. W.	“
21	4 S.	- - -	“	“	“	“	“	1 N. W.	“	“	“	“	6 S. W.	“	1 N. W.	“
22	3 S.	“	“	“	“	“	“	“	“	“	“	“	2 S. W.	“	“	“
23	2 S.	“	“	“	0	“	“	“	“	“	“	“	“	“	“	“*
Midn't	0	“	“	“	“	“	“	0	“	“	“*	“	2 S. E.	“	0	“*

* Rain. † Snow.

July 2d. The force of the wind was not noted on this day; estimated force 2.

July 28th. The bergs outside are now in motion.

Direction and Force of the Wind observed at Van Rensselaer Harbor,

In August, 1854, in Lat. 78° 37′, Long. 70° 53′ W. of Greenwich.

The directions are magnetic. Variation of compass 108° W.

Hour.	1st.	2d.	3d.	4th.	5th.	6th.	7th.	8th.	9th.	10th.	11th.	12th.	13th.	14th.	15th.
1h.	0	0	0	1 S. E.	0	0	0	1 N.	0	0	0	0	1 S. E.	0	3 N. W.
2	"	"	1 N. W.	0	"	"	"	1 S. E.	"	"	"	"	"	"	3 W.
3	"	"	1 N.	"	"	"	"	3 N. W.	"	"	"	"	"	"	2 N. W.
4	"	"	1 N. W.	"	"	"	"	1 N. W.	"	"	"	1 S. W.	0	"	0
5	1 W.	"	0	"	1 S. E.	"	"	0	"	"	"	"	1 N. E.	"	"*
6	"	"	"	2 N. E.	1 N.	"	"	"	"	"	"	"	0	1 S. E.	"*
7	1 N. W.	"	1 S. E.	1 N.	"	"	"	"	"	"	"	"	2 N.	"	"*
8	"	"	0	1 S.	0	"	"	"	"	"	"	"	3 N.	0	"*
9	0	"	"	0	"	"	"	"	"	"	"	"	2 N.*	"	"*
10	"	"	"	"	"	"	"	"	"	"	"	"	1 N.	1 N.	"*
11	"	"	"	"	"	"	"	"	"	"	"	0	2 N.	2 S. E.	"*
Noon	"	"	"	"	"	"	"	"	"	"	"	"	1 N.	3 N. W.	"*
13	"	"	"	"	"	"	"	"	"	"	"	"	"	4 W.	"*
14	"	"	"	"	"	"	"	2 S.	"	"	1 W.	"	2 N. W.	2 W.	1 N. W.
15	"	"	"	"	"	"	"	1 S.	"	"	"	"	"	3 W.	0
16	"	"	"	"	"	"	"	"	"	1 S.	"	"	1 N. W.	4 W.	"
17	"	"	"	"	"	"	"	0	"	"	0	"	2 N.	3 N. W.	"
18	"	"	"	"	"	"	"	"	"	"	1 S.	"	1 N.	4 N. W.	"
19	"	"	"	"	"	"	"	"	1 S.	"	"	"	0	3 N. W.	"
20	"	"	"	"	"	"	"	"	"	"	"	"	"	2 N. W.	"
21	"	"	"	"	"	"	"	"	"	0	"	"	"	4 N. W.	"
22	"	"	"	"	"	"	"	"	"	"	"	1 S. E.	"	3 N. W.	"
23	"	"	"	"	"	"	"	"	"	"	"	"	"	4 N. W.	"
Midn't	"	"	"	"	"	"	"	"	"	"	"	"	"*	0	"

Hour.	16th.	17th.	18th.	19th.	20th.	21st.	22d.	23d.	24th.	25th.	26th.	27th.	28th.	29th.	30th.	31st.
1h.	0	0	0	1 N. W.	0	0	0	2 S. E.	0	0	0*	- - -	- - -	2 S. E.	7 S.	5 S.
2	"	"	2 N.	0	"	"	"	1 S. E.	"	"	"	"	"	3 S. E.	"	"
3	"	"	4 N.	"	"*	"	"	0	"	"	"	"	"	"	"	"
4	"	"	2 N.	"	"*	"	"	"	"	"	"	"	"	"	"	"
5	"	"	2 N. W.	1 N.	"*	"	"	1 S. E.	"	"	"	1 S. E.	"	3 E.	1 S.	4 S.
6	"	"	2 W.	"	1 N. W.*	"	"	0	"	"	"	"	"	5 S. E.	"	3 S.
7	"	"	"	0	"*	"	"	"	1 S.	"	"	"	"	6 S. E.	1 E.	"
8	"	"	"	1 E.	"*	1 W.	"	"	"	"	"	"	"	2 S. E.	"	2 S.
9	- - -	2 N.	1 N. W.	1 S. E.	"*	0	"	"	0	"	"	1 S.	"	4 S. E.	1 S. E.	2 S. E.
10	"	"	"	0	3 N. W.*	"	"	"	"	"	"	"	"	3 S. E.	2 S. E.	"
11	"	"	"	1 E.	1 N. W.	"	"	"	"	"	"	"	"	4 S. E.	5 S. E.	2 S.
Noon	"	"	"	"	2 W.	"	"	"	"	"	"	"	"	"	"	"
13	0	3 N. W.	2 N. W.	1 S. E.	"	"	"	"	"	"	"	"	"	5 S. E.	- - -	"
14	"	2 N. W.	2 N. E.	0	"	"	"	"	"	"	"	"	"	6 S.	"	0
15	"	"	0	"	2 N. W.	"	"	"	1 S.	"	1 S. E.	"	"	"	"	"
16	"	3 N. W.	"	"	3 N. W.	"	"	"	"	"	"	"	"	"	"	"
17	"	1 N. W.	2 N. W.	"	1 N. W.	"	"	"	"	"	"	0	"	"	"	"
18	"	0	3 N. W.	"	"	"	"	"	1 S. E.*	"	"	"	"	"	"	- - -
19	"	1 S. E.	"	1 E.	"	1 S.	"	"	2 S. E.	"	"	"	"	"	"	"
20	"	"	4 N. W.	"	"	"	"	"	"	"	- - -	"	"	"	"	"
21	"	"	3 N. W.	2 E.*	"	"	"	"	1 S. E.	2 S. W.	"	"	"	6 S. E.	3 S. E.	0
22	"	0	"	"*	0	"	"*	"	3 N. W.	1 S. W.	"	"	"	"	"	"
23	"	1 S. E.	4 N. W.	1 N.*	"	0	"	"	1 N. W.	2 S. W.	"	"	"	"	4 S. E.	"
Midn't	"	0	"	0	"	"	"	"	1 S. E.	0	"	"	"	6 S.	4 S.	"

* Snow.

Direction and Force of the Wind observed at Van Rensselaer Harbor,

In September, 1854, in Lat. 78° 37′, Long. 70° 53′ W. of Greenwich.

The directions are magnetic. Variation of compass 108° W.

Hour.	1st.	2d.	3d.	4th.	5th.	6th.	7th.	8th.	9th.	10th.	11th.	12th.	13th.	14th.	15th.
1h.	0	- - -	0*	0	0	0	0	0	0	0	0	0	0	1 S. W.	0*
2	"	"	"*	"	"	"	"	"	"	"	"	"	"	"	"*
3	"	0	"*	"	"	"	"	"	"	"	"	"	"	0	"*
4	"	"*	"*	"	"	"	"	"	"	"	"	"	"	"	"*
5	"	"*	"	"	1 S.	"	"	"	"	"	"	"	1 N. W.	"	"*
6	"	"*	"	"	2 S.	"	"	"	"	"	"	"	0	"	"*
7	"	"*	"	"	0	"	"	"	"	"	"	"	"	"	- - -
8	"	"*	"	"	"	"	"	"	"	"	"	"	"	"	"
9	"	"*	"	"	"	"	"	"	"	"	"	"	"	"	0*
10	"	"*	"	"	"	"	"	"	"	"	"	"	"	"	2 N. E.*
11	"	"*	"	"	"	"	"	"	"	- - -	"	"	"	2 S. W.	1 N. E.*
Noon	"	"*	"	"	"	"	"	"	"	"	"	"	"	"	2 N.*
13	"	"*	"	"	"	"	"	"	- - -	0	"	"	"	3 S. W.	0
14	"	"	"	"	"	"	"	"	"	"	"	"	"	2 S. W.	"
15	"	"	"	"	"	"	"	"	"	"	"	"	"	1 S. W.	"
16	"	"	1 S.	"	"	"	"	"	"	"	"	"	"	"	"
17	"	"	1 S. E.	"	"	"	- - -	"	0	- - -	"	"	"	"	1 S.
18	"	"	1 N.	"	"	"	"	"	"	0	"	"	"	"	"
19	"	"	0	"	"	"	"	"	"	"	"	"	"	0	"
20	"	"	"	"	"	"	"	"	"	"	"	"	3 S.	"	"
21	"	"	"	"	1 S.	"	0	"	"	"	"	"	5 S.	1 S. W.	"
22	"	"	"	"	"	"	"	"	"	"	"	"	"	"	"
23	"	"	"	"	"	"	"	"	"	"	"	"	2 S.	1 S.	"
Midn't	"	"	"	"	"	"	"	"	1 S. W.	"	"	"	1 S.	"	"

Hour.	16th.	17th.	18th.	19th.	20th.	21st.	22d.	23d.	24th.	25th.	26th.	27th.	28th.	29th.	30th.
1h.	0	0	0	0	0	2 W.	2 N. W.	1 S.	0	0*	0	0	3 S.	3 S.	10 S. W.
2	"	"	2 S. E.	"	"	1 W.	3 N. W.	0	2 S. E.	"*	1 S. W.	"	1 S.	4 S.	9 S.
3	"	"	"	"	"	0	0	"	1 W.	"*	2 S. W.	"	"	5 S.	8 S. W.
4	"	"	3 E.	"	"	"	1 N. W.	"	0	"*	"	2 S.	"	"	9 S. W.
5	"	"	3 S. E.	"	"	"	3 S. E.	"	1 W.	"*	"	1 S.	2 S. W.	3 S.	7 S. W.
6	"	"	5 E.	"	"	"	"	"	0	"*	4 S. W.	1 S. W.	3 S. W.	2 S.	"
7	"	1 S. W.	4 S. E.	"	"	"	2 E.	"	2 S. W.	"*	3 S. W.	3 S. W.	"	5 S.	"
8	"	0	3 S. E.	1 S. E.	"	"	2 S. E.	"	1 S. W.	"*	4 S.*	4 S. W.	2 S. W.	"	5 S. W.
9	"	"	2 S. E.	2 S. E.	"	"	1 S. E.	"	"	"	3 S.	"	3 S. W.	4 S. W.*	7 S. W.
10	"	"	0	1 S. E.	"	"	"	"	1 E.	"	"*	5 S. W.	4 S. W.	5 S. W.*	"
11	"	"	"	"	"	1 W.	2 S. E.	"	0	"	2 S. W.*	3 S. W.	"	"*	"
Noon	"	"	"	"	- - -	0	4 S. E.	"	"	"	1 S. W.*	4 S. W.	2 S. W.	3 S. W.*	7 S.
13	"	"	"	"	"	"	3 S. E.	"	"	"	1 S.	5 S. W.	"	2 S. W.*	6 S. W.
14	"	"	"	"	"	"	2 S. E.	"	"	"	0	4 S. W.	"	"	5 S. W.
15	"	"	"	0	0	"	0	"	2 S. E.	"	"	4 S.	3 S. W.	2 S.	7 S. W.
16	"	"	"	"	"	"	"	"	1 S. E.*	1 W.	"	5 S.	2 S. W.	"	"
17	"	"	"	"	"	"	"	"	1 E.*	0	"	4 S. W.	3 S. W.	"	5 S. W.
18	"	"	"	2 S. E.	"	"	"	"	0*	"*	"	5 S. W.	2 S. W.	3 S.	"
19	"	1 N. E.	"	"	"	"	"	"	"*	"*	"	"	"	"	3 S. W.
20	"	"	"	0	"	"	"	1 S. W.	"	2 S.*	"	"	1 S. W.	4 S.	5 S.
21	"	"	2 S. E.	"	"	"	"	- - -	"*	3 S.*	"	"	4 S. E.	"	3 S. E.
22	"	"	"	"	"	"	"	"	"*	4 S.*	"*	"	5 S.	5 S.	"
23	"	"	"	"	"	"	"	"	"*	3 S.*	2 S. E.*	3 S.	6 S.	5 S. E.	"
Midn't	"	"	"	"	"	2 N. W.	"	"	"*	2 S.*	"*	"	5 S.	5 S.	"

* Snow.

Sept. 30th. From 12 to 2 A. M., heavy drift and wind squall.

Direction and Force of the Wind observed at Van Rensselaer Harbor,

In October, 1854, in Lat. 78° 37′, Long. 70° 53′ W. of Greenwich.

The directions are magnetic. Variation of compass 108° W.

Hour.	1st.	2d.	3d.	4th.	5th.	6th.	7th.	8th.	9th.	10th.	11th.	12th.	13th.	14th.	15th.
1h.	2 S.	2 S. W.	6 S. W.	3 N. E.	0	2 N. E.	2 N. W.	0*	3 S. W.	0	1 W.	0	2 W.	4 W.	9 S. E.
2	“	5 S. W.	1 S.	2 N. E.	“	“	“	“*	“	“	2 S. W.	“	“	“	8 S.
3	0	6 S. W.	0	3 S. W.	“	2 N. W.*	2 N.	“	“	“	1 S. W.	“	0	3 N. W.	“
4	“	1 S. W.	“	“	“	“*	1 N.	“	“	“	“	“	“	“	6 S.
5	2 S. W.	4 S. W.	“	“	2 S.	2 W.*	0	“	2 W.	“	0	“	2 S. W.*	2 N. W.	4 S. W.
6	1 S. W.	3 S. W.	1 S. W.	“	1 S. W.	2 N. W.*	“	“	3 S. W.	“	“	“	“*	“	4 S.
7	1 S.	1 N.	0	“	1 S.	“*	3 S. W.	2 S.*	1 S.	“	“	1 S. W.	3 S. W.	1 N. W.*	4 S. W.
8	“	“	“	4 S. W.	0	“*	“	1 S.*	7 S.	“	“	“	2 S. W.	“*	4 S.
9	“	3 W.	“	3 S. W.	“	0*	4 S. W.	“	3 S. W.	“	“	“	3 S. W.	2 W.*	3 S. W.
10	“	4 S. W.	2 S. W.	0	“	“*	5 S. W.	“	1 S. W.	“	“	“	4 S. W.	“*	3 S.
11	“	5 S.	“	1 S. W.	“	“	“	“	0	“	“	1 S. E.	“	3 N. W.	1 S.
Noon	0	“	2 S.	2 S. W.	“	“	5 S.	“	“	“	“	“	“	“	0
13	“	2 S.	0	“	1 S.	“	4 S.	1 S. W.	“	“	“	0	“	“	2 S. W.
14	“	3 S. W.	2 S. W.	“	0	“	4 S. W.	“	“	“	“	“	“	2 N. W.	2 S.
15	“	3 S.	3 S. W.	0	“	“	3 S. W.	“	“*	“	“	“	3 S. W.	2 S.	3 S. W.
16	“	“	“*	“	“	“	1 S. W.	“	“	“	“	“	2 S. W.	1 S.	2 S. W.
17	“	2 S. W.	1 S. W.	1 N. W.	“	“	“	2 S.	“	“	“	“	3 S. W.	“	“
18	“	3 S. W.	“	0	“	“	“	1 S.	“	“	“	1 S. W.	1 S. W.	“	“
19	“	1 S. W.	0	1 N. W.	“	“	2 S. W.	“	“	“	1 W.	“	0	“	3 S. W.
20	“	“	“	“	“	“	2 S.	2 S.*	“	“	“	“*	“	“	“
21	“	5 S. W.	3 S. W.	2 N. W.	“	2 N. W.	3 S.W.*	“	“	“	2 W.	0*	2 N. W.	“	5 S. W.
22	“	6 S. W.	“	0	“	“	1S.W.*	1 S.	“	“	“	“*	2 W.	“	“
23	4 S. W.	6 S.	4 S. W.	2 S. W.	3N.W.*	3 N. W.*	“*	“	“	“	3 W.	“	“	3 S.	6 S.
Midn't	3 S. W.	“	“	“	3 W.*	“*	0*	“	“	“	2 S. W.	“	“	5 S.	“

Hour.	16th.	17th.	18th.	19th.	20th.	21st.	22d.	23d.	24th.	25th.	26th.	27th.	28th.	29th.	30th.	31st.
1h.	5 W.	0	0	1 S. E.	0	0	- - -	- - -	1 N.	1 S.	- - -	0	1 S.	0	1 S. W.	- - -
2	6 S. W.	“	“	0	“	“	“	“	“	“	“	1 S. E.	“	“	1 S.	“
3	4 W.	“	“	“	“	“	0	0	0	0	1 S. W.	0	“	“	3 S. W.	“
4	6 W.	“	“	“	“	“	“	“	“	“	“	“	“	1 S.	“	“
5	4 W.	“	“	“*	“	“	1 S. E.	“	“	“	- - -	“	0	“	2 S. W.	1 S.W.*
6	“	“	“	“	“	“	“	“	“	“	“	“	1 S.	“	“	0*
7	0	1 S.	“	“	“	“	0	“	“	1 S. W.	0	“	0	0	0	“*
8	1 E.	“	“	“	“	“	“	“	“	2 S. W.	“	“	“	“	“	“*
9	1 S.	“	“	“*	“	“	“	“	“	1 S. W.	“	“	“	“	“	“
10	2 S.	0	“	“	“	“	“	“	1 S. E.	“	“	“	“	1 S. E.	1 S. W.	“
11	2 S. W.	“	“	“	“	“	“	“	“	0	“	“	2 S.	“	“	- - -
Noon	0	“	“	“	“	“	“	“	“	“	1 N. E.	“	“	“	“	“
13	“	“	“	“	“	“	“	“	0	“	1 S. E.	“	1 S. E.	1 S.	“	“
14	“	“	“	“	“	“	“	“	“	“	“	“	1 S.	“	“	“
15	“	“	“	“	“	“	1 S. E.	“	“	“	0	“	1 S. E.	- - -	“	1 S.
16	“	“	“	“	“	“	“	“	“	“	“	“	1 E.	“	“	“
17	“	“	“	“	“	“	0	“	“	1 S. E.	“	“	“	“	“	0
18	“	“	“	“	“	“	“	“	1 S. E.	“	“	“	“	“	“	“
19	“	“	“	“	“	“	“	“	“	“	“	1 S. W.	0	“	0	“
20	“	“	“	“	“	“	“	“	“	“	“	“	“	“	“	“
21	“	“	“	“*	“	“	“	“	“	2 S. E.	“	“	“	“	“	“
22	“	“	“	“*	“	“	“	“	0	“	“	“	“	“	“	“
23	“	1 S. W.	“	2 S. W.	“	“	“	“	“	“	“	1 S.	“	0	“	“
Midn't	“	2 S. W.	“	1 S. W.	“	“	“	“	“	1 S. E.	“	“	“	“	“	“

* Snow.

October 15th. From 12 to 2 A. M., the wind blowing a heavy gale (9) from the S. S. E.

DIRECTION AND FORCE OF THE WIND OBSERVED AT VAN RENSSELAER HARBOR,
In November, 1854, in Lat. 78° 37′, Long. 70° 53′ W. of Greenwich.
The directions are magnetic. Variation of compass 108° W.

Hour.	1st.	2d.	3d.	4th.	5th.	6th.	7th.	8th.	9th.	10th.	11th.	12th.	13th.	14th.	15th.
1h.	0	0	0	- - -	- - -	- - -	- - -	- - -	- - -	- - -	0	0	0	0	0
2	"	"	"	"	"	"	"	"	"	"	"	"	"	"	"
3	"	"	"	"	"	"	"	"	"	"	"	1 N.	"	"	"
4	1 S.	"	"	"	"	"	"	"	"	"	"	0	"	"	"
5	0	"	"	"	"	"	"	"	"	"	3 N.	"	"	1 S. W.	"
6	"	"	1 W.	"	"	"	"	"	"	"	2 N.	"	"	"	"
7	1 S.	"	"	"	"	"	"	"	"	"	1 N.	"	"	2 S. W.	"
8	2 S.	"	0	"	"	"	"	"	"	"	"	"	"	1 S. W.	"
9	4 S.	"	"	"	"	"	"	"	"	"	0	"	"	0	"
10	3 S.	"	"	"	"	"	"	"	"	"	"	"	"	"	"
11	"	"	"	"	"	"	"	"	"	"	"	"	"	"	"
Noon	"	"	"	"	"	"	"	"	"	"	"	"	"	"	"
13	"	"	"	"	"	"	"	"	"	"	"	"	"	"	"
14	"	"	"	"	"	"	"	"	"	"	"	"	"	"	"
15	"	"	"	"	"	"	"	"	"	"	"	"	"	"	"
16	0	"	"	"	"	"	"	"	"	"	"	"	"	"	"
17	"	"	"	"	"	"	"	"	"	"	- - -	1 N.	"	"	"
18	"	"	"	"	"	"	"	"	"	"	"	"	"	"	"
19	"	"	"	"	"	"	"	"	"	"	0	0	"	"	"
20	1 S.	"	"	"	"	"	"	"	"	"	"	"	"	"	"
21	"	"	"	"	"	"	"	"	"	"	"	"	"	"	"
22	0	"	"	"	"	"	"	"	"	"	"	"	"	"	"
23	1 W.	"	"	"	"	"	"	"	"	"	"	"	"	"	"
Midn't	0	"	"	"	"	"	"	"	"	"	"	"	"	"	"

Hour.	16th.	17th.	18th.	19th.	20th.	21st.	22d.	23d.	24th.	25th.	26th.	27th.	28th.	29th.	30th.
1h.	0	0	2 S. E.	0*	7 S. W.	0	0	0	0	0	2 N. E.	1 S.	0	1 N. W.	0
2	"	"	0	"*	8 S. W.	"	"	"	"	"	"	"	1 S. E.	0	"
3	1 N.	"	1 S. E.	3 S. W.*	7 S. W.	"	"	"	"*	"	2 S.	"	1 N. E.	3 S. W.	"
4	"	"	1 W.	2 S. W.*	8 S. W.	"	"	"	"*	"	3 S. E.	1 S. W.	2 N. W.	2 S. W.	"
5	0	"	- - -	1 S. W.*	"	1 S. W.	"*	"	"*	"	3 S.	0	"	1 E.	"
6	"	"	"	1 S. W.*	9 S. W.	0	"*	"	"*	1 S.	4 S.	"	2 S. W.	2 E.	"
7	"	"	0	0*	"	"	"*	"	1 W.	"	5 S.	"	0	0	"
8	"	"	"	"*	8 S. W.	"	"*	"	3 W.	2 S.	3 S.	"	"	"	1 N. W.
9	"	"	1 S. E.	"	9 S. W.	"	1 W.*	"	2 S.	3 S. W.	0	1 W.	1 S. E.	"	0
10	"	"	3 S. E.	"	"	"	"*	"	1 S.	4 S. W.	"	"	"	"	"
11	"	"	0	"	0	1 S.	0*	1 N. E.	2 S.	5 S.	"	0*	0	"	"
Noon	"	"	1 E.	"	"	0	"*	0	0	4 S.	"	"*	"	"	"
13	"	"	5 S. E.	2 S. E.	1 S.	1 S. E.	"*	2 N. E.	"	3 E.	"	1 S.	2 S. W.	"	"
14	"	"	1 S. E.	3 S.	2 S.	0	"*	"	"	"	"	0	0	"	1 N. W.
15	"	"	1 S.	1 N. W.	0	"	"*	2 S. W.	"	0	"	"	"	"	0
16	"	"	3 S.	2 N. W.	"	1 N.	"*	3 S. W.	"	"	"*	"	"	"	"
17	1 N. W.	"	0	1 S. W.	"	0	"	2 S. W.	"	"	"	"	"	"	"
18	"	"	"	3 S. W.	"	"	"	"	1 N.	"	"	"	"	"	"
19	0	"	"	2 S. W.	"	"	"	"*	0*	"	"	"	"	"	"
20	"	"	"	3 S. W.	"	"	"	"*	"	"*	1 S.	"	"	"	"
21	"	"	"	2 S. E.	3 S.	"	"	0*	"	"	2 S.	"	"	"	"
22	"	"	1 E.	0	"	"	"	"	"	"	"	"	"	"	"
23	"	"	"	4 S.	"	1 W.	1 N.	2 S. W.*	1 S. W.*	2 S. W.	3 S.	"	"	1 S.	"
Midn't	"	"	"	5 S.	2 S.	"	"	1 S. W.	"*	"	"	"	1 E.	"	"

* Snowing.

Direction and Force of the Wind observed at Van Rensselaer Harbor,

In December, 1854, in Lat. 78° 37′, Long. 70° 53′ W. of Greenwich.

The directions are magnetic. Variation of compass 108° W.

Hour.	1st.	2d.	3d.	4th.	5th.	6th.	7th.	8th.	9th.	10th.	11th.	12th.	13th.	14th.	15th.
1h.	0	0	0	0	0	0	---	---	---	---	---	---	---	0	0
2	"	"	"	"	"	"	"	"	"	"	"	"	0	1 W.	"
3	"	"	1 S. W.	"	"	"	0	"	0	"	3 S. W.	0	"	0	"
4	"	1 S. E.	2 S. W.	"	"	"	"	"	"	"	2 S. W.	"	1 W.	"	"
5	"	"	"	1 W.	3 S. E.	"	"	0	---	"	0	1 S. W.	0	1 E.	"
6	2 W.*	"	3 S. W.	"	1 S. W.	"	"	"	"	"	"	1 W.	"	0	"
7	"	"	5 S. W.	0	0	"	1 S.	"	0	1 N.	"	"	"	"	"
8	1 W.	"	1 S. W.	"	"	"	"	"	"	"	"	1 S. W.	"	"	"
9	0	"	"	"	"	"	3 S. W.	1 W.	1 W.	2 N.	2 S. E.	"	"	"	"
10	"	1 N.	"	"	"	"	4 S. W.	0	1 S.	"	3 S. E.	1 S.	"	"	"
11	"	0	3 S.	"	"	"	0	"	"	"	0	3 S.	"	"	"
Noon	"	"	1 S.	"	"	"	"	"	2 S.	"	"	5 S. W.	"	"	"
13	"	"	2 S. W.	"	"	"	"	"	0	0	"	0	"	"	"
14	"	1 N.	3 S. W.	"	"	"	"	"	"	"	"	"	"	"	"
15	"	0	2 S. W.	"	"	"	1 W.	"	"	"	1 S. E.	2 S.	"	"	"
16	"	"	4 S. W.	"	"	"	1 S.	"	"	"	0	0	"	"	"
17	"	"	6 S. W.	"	"	"	0	"	"	"	"	"	"	"	"
18	"	"	4 S. W.	"	"	"	"	"	"	3 S. E.	"	"	"	"	1 W.
19	"	"	3 S. W.	"	"	"	"	"	"	1 S.	"	"	"	"	0
20	"	"	0	"	"	"	"	"	1 S.	"	"	"	"	"	"
21	"	"	"	"	"	"	---	"	0	4 S.	"	4 W.	"	"	---
22	2 N. W.	"	"	"*	"	"	"	"	"	5 S.	"	0	"	"	"
23	4 N. W.	1 S.	1 S. W.	"	"	"	"	"	---	---	---	---	"	"	"
Midn't	0	0	"	"	"	"	"	"	"	"	"	"	"	"	"

Hour.	16th.	17th.	18th.	19th.	20th.	21st.	22d.	23d.	24th.	25th.	26th.	27th.	28th.	29th.	30th.	31st.
1h.	0	0	0	6 S. E.	5 S. W.	1 S.	0	0	---	0	0	0	0	0	3 S.	0
2	"	"	"	1 N.	4 S.	2 S.	"	"	0	---	"	"	1 W.	"	2 S. W.	"
3	"	"	"	0	2 S. W.	0	"	---	"	0	3 E.	"	0	2 S. E.	0	"
4	"	1 W.	"	"	1 S.	"*	"	0	"	"	1 N. E.	"	"	0	"	"
5	"	0	"	2 S. E.	2 S. E.	"*	"	"	"	"	0	"	"	"	"	"
6	"	1 E.	"	1 S. E.	0	"*	"	"	"	"	"	"	"	"	"	"
7	"	"	"	"	"	"*	"	"	"	"	"	"	"	"	"	5 S. W.
8	"	"	"	"	"	"*	"	"	"	2 S. W.	"	"	"	"	"	4 S.
9	"	"	"	0	"	"*	"	"	"	3 S. W.	"	"	"	3 E.	"	5 S. W.
10	"	"	1 S.	"	"	"	"	"	"	4 S. W.	"	"	"	4 E.	"	7 S.
11	"	"	0	1 N.	"	2 S.	"	"	"	3 S. W.	"	"	"	"	"	4 S. W.
Noon	"	1 S.	"	"	"	3 S. W.	"	"	"	0	"	"	"	5 S. E.	"	7 S.
13	"	0	"	"	"	0	"	"	"	"	"	"	"	4 S. E.	"	0
14	"	"	"	"	"	3 S. E.	"	"	"	2 S.	"	"	"	2 S. E.	"	"
15	"	"	9 S. E.	"	"	5 S. E.	"	"	2 S. W.	1 S.	"	"	3 S.	"	"	"
16	"	"	"	"	"	3 S. E.	"	1 S. E.	"	1 S. W.	"	"	5 S. W.	3 S.	"	"
17	"	"	8 S. E.	"	1 E.	2 S. E.	"	"	1 W.	"	"	"	6 S.	1 S.	"	4 S.
18	"	"	"	"	"	"	"	"	1 N.	2 S. W.	"	"	3 S. W.	0	"	3 S.
19	"	"	7 S. E.	"	0	3 S. E.	"	0	0	1 S. W.	"	"	2 S.	"	"	1 S.
20	"	"	5 S. E.	"	"	0	"	"	"	0	"	"	4 S. W.	"	"	0
21	"	"	3 S. E.	---	"	---	"	---	"	"	"	"	0	3 S.	"	2 S.
22	1 E.	"	1 S. E.	"	"	5 S. E.	"	0	"	"	"	"	"	4 S. W.	"	1 S. W.
23	0	"	0	"	"	4 S. E.	"	"	"	"	"	"	"	5 S.	"	2 S.
Midn't	"	"	"	"	"	0	"	"	"	"	"	"	"	2 S. W.	"	0

* Snow.

Direction and Force of the Wind observed at Van Rensselaer Harbor,

In January, 1855, in Lat. 78° 37′, Long. 70° 53′ W. of Greenwich.

The directions are magnetic. Variation of compass 108° W.

Hour.	1st.	2d.	3d.	4th.	5th.	6th.	7th.	8th.	9th.	10th.	11th.	12th.	13th.	14th.	15th.
1h.	2 W.	0	0	0	- - -	- - -	- - -	0	1 S. E.	1 S.	0	0	0*	1 S. W.	0
2	1 W.	"	"	"	0	"	"	"	"	- - -	"	"	"*	"	"
3	"	"	"	"	"	2 S. E.	1 S. W.	"	0	0	"	"	"*	2 S. W.	"
4	0	"	1 W.	"	"	"	"	"	"	"	"	"	"*	"	"
5	"	"	0	"	"	1 S. E.	"	"	"	"	"	"	"*	1 S. W.	"
6	"	"	"	"	"	0	"	"	"	"	"	"	"*	0	"
7	"	"	"	"	"	"	"	"	"	"	"	"	"*	"	"
8	"	"	"	"	"	"	"	"	"	"	1 S. W.	"	2 S. W.*	"	2 W.
9	"	"	"	"	"	2 N. W.	"	"	"	"	1 S.	1 S. E.	"*	1 S. W.	1 W.
10	"	"	"	"	"	1 N. W.	"	"	"	"	2 S. W.	2 S. E.	4 S. W.*	"	2 S. W.
11	"	"	"	"	"	2 N. W.	"	"	"	"	2 S.	"	7 S. W.*	"	"
Noon	"	"	"	"	"	3 N. W.	"	"	"	"	4 S. W.	1 S. E.	6 S. W.	"	3 S. W.
13	"	"	"	"	1 W.	2 N. W.	"	"	"	"	3 S.	0	5 S. W.	"	4 S. W.
14	"	"	"	"	"	"	"	1 W.	"	"	1 S. W.	"	"	0	3 S. W.
15	"	"	1 N.	"	1 N. W.	0	"	0	"	1 E.	0	"	2 S. W.	"	0
16	"	"	2 N. W.	"	0	"	"	"	"	0	"	"	0	"	2 S.
17	"	"	0	1 S.	"	"	"	"	"	"	"	"	"	"	3 S. W.
18	"	"	"	2 S. W.	"	"	"	"	"	"	"	"	"	"	3 S.
19	"	"	"	0	"	"	"	"	"	"	"	"	2 S. E.	"	2 S. W.
20	"	"	"	"	1 S.	"	"	"	1 S.	"	"	"	1 S. E.	"	0
21	"	"	"	"	1 S. E.	1 var.	"	"	0	"	"	"	3 S. E.	- - -	- - -
22	"	"	"	"	3 S. E.	- - -	"	"	"	1 var.	"	"	9 S. E.	"	"
23	"	"	"	"	2 S. E.	1 S. W.	"	"	2 S.	"	"	1 var.	10 S. E.	"	"
Midn't	"	"	"	1 S. W.	1 S. E.	"	"	1 N.	1 W.	"	"	2 N. W.*	9 S. E.	"	"

Hour.	16th.	17th.	18th.	19th.	20th.	21st.	22d.	23d.	24th.	25th.	26th.	27th.	28th.	29th.	30th.	31st.
1h.	0	0	0	8 S. W.	2 S. W.	1 W.	2 S. W.	0	0*							
2	"	"	1 W.	7 S. W.	1 W.	0	"	"	"*							
3	"	"	2 S. W.	6 S.	1 S. E.	"	0	1 S. E.	"*							
4	"	"	1 S. W.	6 S. W.	"	1 S.	"	"	"*							
5	"	"	- - -	- - -	- - -	- - -	- - -	- - -	"*							
6	"	1 S. W.	"	"	"	"	"	"	"*							
7	2 N. W.	0	3 S. E.	5 S. W.	"	"	"	"	"*							
8	1 N. W.	"	2 S. E.	6 S. W.	"	"	"	"	"*							
9	1 N.	1 W.	"	3 S.	1 S. E.	2 S.	0	1 S. E.	1 S. E.*							
10	"	2 W.	"	2 S.	"	3 S.	"	"	"*							
11	"	4 S. W.	1 S. E.	"	"	"	"	"	"*							
Noon	"	5 S. W.	"	1 S.	"	"	"	"	"*							
13	- - -	- - -	- - -	- - -	- - -	- - -	- - -	"	0*							
14	"	"	"	"	"	"	"	"	"*							
15	"	"	"	"	"	"	"	"	"*							
16	"	"	"	"	"	"	"	"	"*							
17	"	"	7 S. W.	1 S. W.	2 S. W.	2 S. W.	0	"	- - -							
18	"	"	8 S. W.	"	"	2 W.	"	"	"							
19	1 N.	"	5 S. W.	- - -	- - -	- - -	- - -	- - -	"							
20	"	"	2 S. W.	"	"	"	"	"	"							
21	0*	0	- - -	"	"	"	"	1 S. E.	"							
22	"	"*	"	1 S. E.	"	"	"	"	"							
23	"	"	"	"	"	"	"	"*	"							
Midn't	- - -	"	"	5 S. E.	"	"	"	"	"							

* Snow.

January 17th. From 10h. to 12h., blowing hard from S. W., with thick snow drift.

The immediate bearing of the wind on the temperature, the weight and moisture of the atmosphere, and upon the climate in general, as well as its practical relation to navigation, renders this meteorological element of equal importance with any of the others, though it has, perhaps, received comparatively less attention.

Method of Reduction.—In the following discussion, we have to consider the average direction and force, as well as the quantity of air blown over the place of observation.

In regard to the mean direction and velocity of the wind for any given period—a day, month, or year—the customary formula of Lambert has been so far modified as to include the velocity, and not to depend on the relative frequency of the winds alone.

Let $\theta_1\ \theta_2\ \theta_3\ \ldots\ldots$ be the angles which the directions of the wind make with the meridian, reckoned round the compass, according to astronomical usage, from the south, westwards to 360°, or in a direction indicated by the law of rotation; and $v_1\ v_2\ v_3\ \ldots\ldots$ its respective velocities, which may be supposed expressed in miles per hour; and let the observations be made at equal intervals of time, say hourly. By adding up all velocity-numbers referring to the same wind during a given period, and representing these quantities, or the number of miles of air transferred bodily over the place in each direction, by $s_1\ s_2\ s_3\ \ldots\ldots$, then the quantity of air passed over the place of observation by winds *from* the southward is expressed by

$$R_s = s_1 \cos\theta_1 + s_2 \cos\theta_2 + s_3 \cos\theta_3 + \ldots\ldots$$

And for winds *from* the westward

$$R_w = s_1 \sin\theta_1 + s_2 \sin\theta_2 + s_3 \sin\theta_3 + \ldots\ldots$$

The resulting quantity R, and the angle ϕ it forms with the meridian, is found by the expressions

$$R = \sqrt{R_s^2 + R_w^2}, \text{ and } \tan\phi = \frac{R_w}{R_s}.$$

The general formulæ, in the case of eight principal directions θ, assume the convenient form

$$R_s = (S—N) + (SW—NE)\sqrt{\tfrac{1}{2}} — (NW—SE)\sqrt{\tfrac{1}{2}}$$
$$R_w = (W—E) + (SW—NE)\sqrt{\tfrac{1}{2}} + (NW—SE)\sqrt{\tfrac{1}{2}}$$

Where the letters S, SW, W, etc., stand for the sum of all velocities during the given period, or for the quantity of air moved in the directions S, SW, W, etc., respectively; R_s stands for the total quantity of air transported *to* the northward, and R_w for the same transferred *to* the eastward. These formulæ, for practical working, may be put in the following shape:—

Put $S—N = a$ $\qquad$ $SW—NE = c$
$\qquad W—E = b$ $\qquad$ $NW—SE = d$

Then

$$R_s = R\cos\phi = a + 0.707\ (c—d)$$
$$R_w = R\sin\phi = b + 0.707\ (c+d).$$

Since R_s, R_w, R, represents the quantity of air passed over during the given period in the direction 0, 90°, ϕ, respectively, we must, in order to find the mean velocity in any resulting direction, divide by n, or the number of observations during that period; we then have

$$V_s = \frac{R_s}{n}, \quad V_w = \frac{R_w}{n}, \quad \text{and } V = \frac{R}{n}.$$

A particle of air which has left the place of observation at the commencement of the period—of a day, for instance—will be found at its close in a direction $180 + \phi$, and at a distance of R miles, equal to a movement with an average velocity of $\frac{R}{n}$; the length of the path described by the particle can be found by the summation of all the v's (for each hour) during the period.

The above development supposes that all particles of the air surrounding the station equally participate in the general motion, or that all particles describe equal and parallel paths.

To admit nothing arbitrary in the reduction, no attempt has been made to interpolate values in those instances where occasional omissions occur in the hourly abstract.

The great variability in the direction and force of the aerial motion renders the taking of mean values for short intervals unnecessary, and we can at once proceed to the mean monthly values.

For the convenience of reference, and in illustration of the method of reduction, one of the monthly abstracts of the sum of the velocity numbers of each wind is here inserted. Similar abstracts were made for each of the seventeen months during which the observations continued.

Abstract of the Quantity of Wind in each of the Eight Principal Directions, observed at Van Rensselaer Harbor, In September, 1858.

Magnetic Direction.	1st.	2d.	3d.	4th.	5th.	6th.	7th.	8th.	9th.	10th.	11th.	12th.	13th.	14th.	15th.	
S.	0	0	0	---	0	0	0	0	13	0	0	0	0	1	0	...
N.	92	102	0	---	0	0	0	0	36	0	0	36	0	2	13	...
W.	92	0	0	---	0	0	0	0	17	40	9	16	0	0	0	...
E.	0	0	0	---	0	0	22	0	0	0	0	0	0	3	66	...
S. W.	0	0	0	---	0	413	214	0	4	0	0	0	0	0	0	...
N. E.	0	0	0	---	0	0	0	15	0	0	0	0	0	3	0	...
N. W.	199	217	19	---	5	0	1	13	46	0	0	0	0	0	0	...
S. E.	0	0	0	---	0	0	0	0	0	0	0	4	0	2	0	...
Sum & check	383	319	19	---	5	413	237	28	116	40	9	56	0	11	79	...
Magnetic Direction.	16th.	17th.	18th.	19th.	20th.	21st.	22d.	23d.	24th.	25th.	26th.	27th.	28th.	29th.	30th.	Sums.
S.	0	0	4	0	0	4	40	53	0	11	0	13	2	0	2	143
N.	2	0	0	0	5	0	0	0	0	0	0	0	112	49	0	449
W.	0	5	0	1	0	0	0	0	0	0	0	31	4	0	5	220
E.	0	0	0	8	0	0	0	0	0	0	0	4	0	0	1	104
S. W.	0	0	0	0	0	105	14	50	7	52	4	0	5	0	7	875
N. E.	5	0	0	5	0	0	0	0	0	0	0	6	0	0	2	36
N. W.	0	5	1	0	23	0	0	0	0	0	0	0	6	25	0	560
S. E.	0	0	0	0	0	0	34	0	13	0	41	20	25	0	4	143
Sum & check	7	10	5	14	28	109	88	103	20	63	45	74	154	74	21	2530

Resulting Monthly Direction of the Wind.—The resulting monthly direction ϕ of the wind is obtained by adding up the velocity-numbers for each wind separately, from the hourly observations taken during the month, irrespective of omissions. The numbers thus obtained are then treated in accordance with the preceding formulæ. For the month of September, 1853, for instance, we would have—

Σ S. $= 143$	Hence $c = +839$	$R_s = -11$
Σ N. $= 449$	$d = +417$	$R_w = +995$
Σ W. $= 220$	$c - d = +422$	$R = 995$
Σ E. $= 104$	$c + d = +1256$	$\phi = 89° 22'$
Σ S. W. $= 875$	$0.7\ (c - d) = +295$	equivalent to a
Σ N. E. $= 36$	$0.7\ (c + d) = +879$	west wind.
Σ N. W. $= 560$	$a = -306$	
Σ S. E. $= 143$	$C = +116$	

To convert the resulting ϕ from the magnetic into the true direction, apply the magnetic declination, viz: 108° 12′ west.[1]

In like manner, the mean direction of the wind for each month has been made out. The following table exhibits the sum of the velocity-numbers for each wind, as well as the resulting direction of the winds for each month of observation:—

Direction.	1853.				1854.				
	September.	October.	November.	December.	January.	February.	March.	April.	May.
S.	143	1069	197	532	176	735	464	463	668
N.	449	47	39	5	52	16	2	48	164
W.	220	18	12	290	100	23	61	5	9
E.	104	47	35	233	6	254	46	3	9
S. W.	875	413	219	348	158	733	26	1187	730
N. E.	36	1	54	107	17	1	2	0	0
N. W.	560	408	90	132	38	25	154	68	251
S. E.	143	1102	763	1718	326	838	243	300	249
Magnetic ϕ	89°	353°	333°	334°	359°	351°	357°	25°	27°
True ϕ	341	245	225	226	251	243	249	277	279

Direction.	1854.							1855.
	June.	July.	August.	September.	October.	November.	December.	January.
S.	0	381	776	897	726	436	437	123
N.	229	50	89	5	9	28	27	8
W.	108	88	106	9	273	24	45	28
E.	0	10	28	51	4	36	82	1
S. W.	308	832	16	1505	1297	888	572	792
N. E.	157	18	9	11	26	18	1	0
N. W.	1163	261	397	23	165	18	27	44
S. E.	0	38	527	296	109	77	661	365
Magnetic ϕ	132°	47°	359°	21°	37°	27°	356°	22°
True ϕ	24	299	251	273	289	279	248	274

To obtain the resulting direction of the wind in each month, each season, and for the whole year, we first take the mean of the values R_s and R_w respectively, for the same months in the different years and find—

[1] See my discussion of Dr. Kane's magnetical observations, in Vol. X. of the Smithsonian Contributions to Knowledge, 1858, p. 25.

Month.	R_s.	R_w.	Mag. φ.	True φ.	Month.	R_s.	R_w.	Mag. φ.	True φ.
September	+1059	+904	40°	292°	March	+ 541	— 30	357°	249°
October	+1682	+486	17	269	April	+1408	+ 670	25	277
November	+ 901	+ 89	6	258	May	+1014	+ 512	27	279
December	+1530	—482	342	234	June	— 937	+1027	132	24
January	+ 659	+174	15	267	July	+ 745	+ 805	47	299
February	+1800	—288	351	243	August	+ 783	— 8	359	251

By means of ΣR_s and ΣR_w for the respective periods, we find the following mean directions:—

	Magnetic φ.	True φ.	True direction.
Winter (December, January, February)	351°	243°	E. 27° N.
Spring (March, April, May)	21	273	E. 3 S.
Summer (June, July, August)	72	324	E. 54 S.
Autumn (September, October, November)	22	274	E. 4 S.
Year	19	271	E. 1 S.

From the above results we see that, in general, the mean *true* direction of the wind is from the eastward, varying in the several months to the northward and southward of it. There is but one exception, namely: in the month of June, the wind veers round to the westward of south. In spring and autumn, the resulting *true* direction is almost exactly east, as well as for the whole year; in winter it is E. N. E., and in summer S. E. by S.

Average Velocity in the Mean Direction of the Wind.—The average velocity in the mean direction of the wind—or, in other words, the mean velocity of the resulting wind—which is necessarily smaller than the mean velocity of the several winds on account of the neutralization by opposing winds, is found by dividing the quantity R by the actual number of observations (exclusive of calms). Thus, for September, 1853, we found $R = 995$, n the number of hours of observations $= 348$, hence $V = 2.9$ miles per hour. In similar manner, V has been found for each month of the year. In the table below, the quantities opposite the months from September to January inclusive, are mean values derived from the years 1853 and 1854, and 1854 and 1855.

Table of the Mean Velocity of the Resulting Wind.

Month.	R	n	V	Month.	R	n	V
September . . .	1637	278	5.9	March	541	262	2.1
October	1892	377	5.0	April	1559	385	4.0
November . . .	1016	213	4.8	May	1136	441	2.6
December . . .	1633	213	7.7	June	1390	257	5.4
January	694	256	2.7	July	1097	200	5.5
February . . .	1823	332	5.5	August	783	244	3.2
Average V for the whole year . . . . 4.5 miles per hour.							

Having found the resulting direction of the wind and its mean velocity in this direction, we proceed to determine the mean velocity of each wind.

Mean Velocity of the Winds.—The average velocity with which each of the eight winds passes over the place of observation in each month and for the whole year, is found by dividing the sum of their velocity-numbers in the period by their respective number of entries in the table; thus, for the month of September, 1853, we have:—

Direction (Magnetic).	Sum of velocities.	Number of entries.	Mean velocity.	Direction (Magnetic).	Sum of velocities.	Number of entries.	Mean velocity.
S.	143	40	3.6	N. E.	36	15	2.4
S. W.	875	88	10.0	E.	104	25	4.2
W.	220	35	6.3	S. E.	143	38	3.8
N. W.	560	55	10.2				
N.	440	52	8.6	Sums and mean .	2530	348	7.3

In the following table of the mean velocity of the winds, the values for September, October, November, December, and January are mean values. As in the above example, the weighted means are given in the table.

Magnetic Direction.	Jan.	Feb.	March.	April.	May.	June.	July.	Aug.	Sept.	Oct.	Nov.	Dec.
	Miles.	Miles.	Miles.	Miles.	Miles.	Miles.	Miles.	Miles.	Miles.	Miles.	Miles.	Miles.
S.	2.9	9.4	4.3	3.3	10.9	- - -	18.1	12.1	10.1	8.2	6.3	9.1
S. W.	8.2	11.3	1.5	14.6	7.1	8.7	23.1	1.6	14.2	9.2	15.6	11.5
W.	3.2	2.1	2.0	1.0	1.0	4.3	2.9	6.3	5.6	10.4	1.5	7.0
N. W.	2.7	1.5	6.4	1.5	1.6	6.8	4.1	7.2	9.7	10.4	4.2	3.6
N.	1.7	2.3	1.0	1.3	2.2	11.4	1.7	3.6	8.4	3.3	2.6	2.0
N. E.	1.6	1.0	1.0	- - -	- - -	22.4	4.5	3.0	2.0	4.5	4.8	7.2
E.	1.0	8.5	11.5	1.0	1.5	- - -	2.5	2.8	5.1	2.1	3.5	13.1
S. E.	4.3	6.7	3.3	4.1	6.9	- - -	2.9	8.8	5.7	5.5	5.8	11.1
Weighted mean . .	4.4	7.9	3.8	5.4	4.7	7.6	8.4	8.0	9.6	7.6	6.9	9.5

The winds, therefore, blow with their greatest strength in the months of September and December, and with their least strength in the months of March and May; in the former the mean velocity is 9.6, and in the latter case 4.2 miles per hour. In the following table is exhibited the mean velocity of each wind separately:—

Magnetic direction.	Mean velocity in miles per hour.
S.	7.4
S. W.	11.2
W.	4.1
N. W.	4.8
N.	3.5
N. E.	6.2
E.	6.0
S. E.	6.3

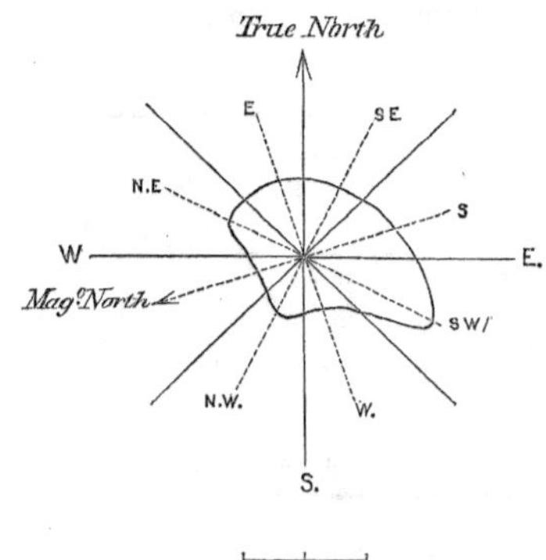

Of all winds, the S. W. (magnetic) blows with the greatest force, and the north wind with the least. The relation of the velocity of the wind to its direction is further illustrated by the annexed diagram.

Quantity and Relative Frequency of the Winds.—The sum of the velocity-numbers, or the number of miles travelled over by the air in any direction for any given period, may be called the quantity (q) of the wind which has been transferred over the place of observation during that time. It will not be necessary to take into account the variations in the density of the air, and the number given below refers, therefore, to an average density. The velocity-numbers for each wind and month have been given in a preceding table; they require, however, a correction, in order to find q, for the occasional omissions in the observations. Thus, in September, 1853, no observations were recorded during 109 hours, and we may assume that during this time the several winds (inclusive of calms) occurred, or would have occurred in quantity and with a frequency directly proportional to their numbers found from the 720 — 109 remaining hours of the month. After adding this proportional number for each wind and month, and after taking mean values for the same months, the following table of the quantity of wind (q) has been made out.

Magnetic Direction.	Jan.	Feb.	March.	April.	May.	June.	July.	Aug.	Sept.	Oct.	Nov.	Dec.	Yr. mls.
S.	187	735	464	488	668	0	402	830	545	918	385	497	6119
S. W.	713	733	26	1250	730	317	877	17	1291	880	693	477	8004
W.	72	23	61	5	9	111	93	113	134	150	22	169	962
N. W.	54	25	154	71	251	1197	275	425	342	293	57	81	3225
N.	33	16	2	51	164	236	53	95	267	28	38	17	1000
N. E.	9	1	2	0	0	162	19	10	27	14	39	54	337
E.	4	254	46	3	9	0	11	30	88	26	41	160	672
S. E.	455	838	243	316	249	0	40	564	236	616	433	1210	5200
Sums	1527	2625	998	2184	2080	2023	1770	2084	2930	2925	1708	2665	25519

The following table gives the number of hours during which each wind blew, or the relative frequency of each wind for every month.

Magnetic Direction.	Jan.	Feb.	March.	April.	May.	June.	July.	Aug.	Sept.	Oct.	Nov.	Dec.	Yr. hrs.
S.	58	78	108	146	61	0	22	68	56	112	57	55	821
S. W.	81	65	17	85	103	36	38	11	93	95	42	42	708
W.	24	11	31	5	9	26	32	18	24	15	14	24	233
N. W. . . .	19	16	24	50	152	175	67	59	34	28	14	22	660
N.	20	7	2	40	74	21	31	27	32	8	16	9	287
N. E.	5	1	2	0	0	7	4	3	12	3	9	7	53
E.	3	30	4	3	6	0	4	11	16	12	12	12	113
S. E.	97	124	74	76	36	0	14	64	43	111	75	108	822
Calm	437	340	482	315	303	455	532	483	410	360	481	465	5063
Check sum . .	744	672	744	720	744	720	744	744	720	744	720	744	8760

The preceding tabular results have been laid down graphically on the accompanying diagrams. The two rectangular diagrams show the quantity of each wind for each month; the first for the directions S., S. W., W., and N. W., the second for the directions N., N. E., E., and S. E. The circular diagram exhibits the quantity of each wind for the whole year, as indicated by a full line according to the scale at the foot of the diagram. It likewise shows, by a dotted line, the relative frequency of each wind during the year (on a ten times larger scale).

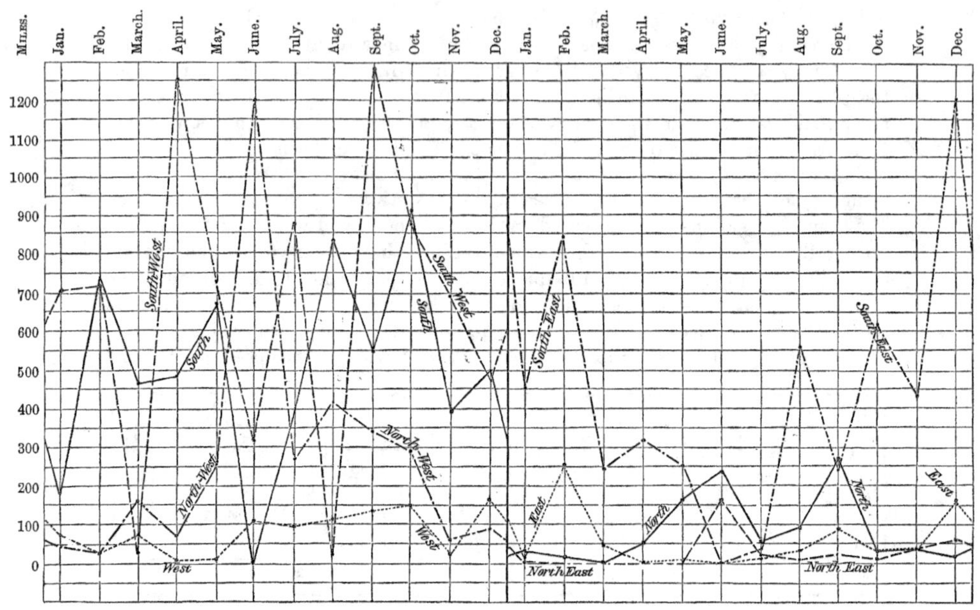
Miles.
Jan.
Feb.
March.
April.
May.
June.
July.
Aug.
Sept.
Oct.
Nov.
Dec.
Jan.
Feb.
March.
April.
May.
June.
July.
Aug.
Sept.
Oct.
Nov.
Dec.
1200
1100
1000
900
800
700
600
500
400
300
200
100
0
South-West
South
North-West
West
South-West
South
North-West
West
South-East
East
North East
North
South-East
North
East
North East

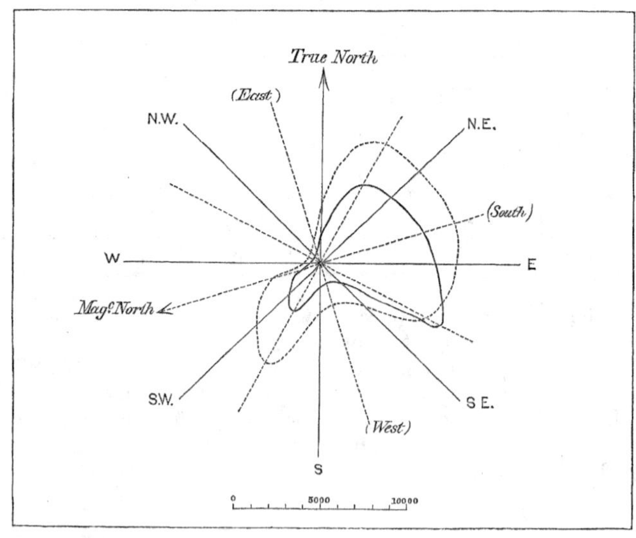
True North
(East)
N.W.
N.E.
(South)
W
E
Magc North
S.W.
S E.
(West)
S
0
5000
10000

The greatest quantity of air moved over the place during the year comes from a quarter bounded by the true directions S. E. by E. and N. N. E.; the prevailing wind also comes from this quarter. With the exception of true S. W. by S. winds, there is comparatively hardly any wind from the remaining directions; the quadrant between (true) west and north is particularly defective in this respect.

The calms greatly predominate, there being during the year more hours of calm (5063) than hours of wind from any direction (3697)—a circumstance quite characteristic of the locality.

Average Duration of the Winds.—The number of consecutive hours during which any one wind blew is given in the table below. It contains average values made out from all observations during the seventeen months. The number of consecutive hours during which, on the average, calms lasted, is likewise given.

Magnetic direction.	Mean duration.	Magnetic direction.	Mean duration.
S.	$2^{h}.8$	N. E.	$2^{h}.1$
S. W.	3.4	E.	2.1
W.	2.0	S. E.	3.3
N. W.	3.4		
N.	2.7	Calm	7.8

Rotation of Winds.—Owing to the great number of calms, and partly, also, to the generally small quantity and velocity of the winds between the (true) S. and (true) N. W. directions, Dove's laws of rotation cannot well be verified in this locality. There is, however, a tendency of the magnetic S., S. E., and E. (E. N. E., N. N. E., and N. N. W., true) winds to shift, in accordance with the law, in the proportion of three cases for to one case against it, or with a relative probability of three-fourths in favor of the law.

Note on the Occurrence of Gales.—Between September 1st, 1853, and January 24th, 1855, there were recorded thirteen gales (with a force of 7 and above, and a duration of not less than two hours). The date, direction, and duration of these gales is shown in the following table.

Date.		General (mag.) direction.	Duration.	Date.		General (mag.) direction.	Duration.
1853	Dec. 10	S. E.	$2^{h.}$	1854	Sept. 30	S. W.	$16^{h.}$
	Dec. 28	S. E.	22		Oct. 15	S. E.	3
1854	Feb. 7	S. E.	3		Nov. 20	S. W.	10
	Feb. 15–16	S.	4		Dec. 18	S. E.	5
	April 15–16	S. W.	7	1855	Jan. 13	S. E.	3
	June 17	S. W.	3		Jan. 18–19	S. W.	4
	July 28	S. W.	6				

These gales do not appear to be confined to any particular season of the year. On the average they last seven hours, and in summer they have a tendency to blow from the S. W. (true E. S. E.), and in winter from the S. E. (true N. N. E.). These two directions are the only ones from which gales were observed.

Thermometric and Barometric Wind Rose.—The investigation of the connection of the temperature and weight of the atmosphere with the direction of the wind, will be found in the discussion of the observations for temperature and barometric pressure, parts I and III of this paper.

Relation of the Direction of the Wind to the Amount of Snow (or Rain).—The dependence of the fall of snow (or rain) on the direction of the wind, is shown in the following table, which contains the aggregate number of hours during which snow (or rain) fell for any direction of the wind and during calms.

Direction (mag.)	Hours.	Direction (mag.)	Hours.
S.	52	N. E.	6
S. W.	71	E.	10
W.	43	S. E.	75
N. W.	110	Calm	328
N.	45		
		Total	740
			in 17 months.

The snowy (or rainy) quarter is between N. N. E. (true) and E. S. E. (true), or from the direction of the Spitzbergen Sea, and also from the direction S. S. W. (true), or from the upper Baffin Bay. During almost half the time, it snowed during calms. From the directions W. N. W. (true) and N. N. W. (true), there was hardly any precipitation.

PART III.

ATMOSPHERIC PRESSURE.

RECORD AND DISCUSSION OF THE ATMOSPHERIC PRESSURE.

THE barometric observations at Van Rensselaer Harbor, North Greenland, were made hourly, and commence June 8th, 1853. The record now available, however, commences with June 27th, 1853, and extends to January 24th, 1855. The mean daily values subsequent to this date, up to April 22d, 1855, inclusive, together with the corresponding mean temperature, are to be found in Appendix No. XII. second volume of the Narrative of the Expedition. It is proposed to discuss here the observations taken between September 1st, 1853, when the brig entered her winter quarters in Van Rensselaer Bay, and January 24th, 1855, at which date the log-book on hand terminates.

Instruments.—The expedition was provided with a mercurial barometer and two aneroids. The mercurial marine barometer was made for Dr. Kane by Mr. Tagliabue, of New York. Its length was thirty-three and a half inches; it had a brass scale seven inches in length, and a glass cistern with an adjusting point for the surface of the mercury. In its adjustment, the correction for capillarity was included.[1] The readings are expressed in English inches. The aneroids have the numbers 4796 and 1400. Of these, the first one was read daily (and hourly) from the commencement of the record (June 27th, 1853) till its conclusion (January 24th, 1855). That aneroid 4796 (and not 1400) was thus used, I infer from a note in Mr. Sonntag's report dated Godhavn, September 12th, 1855, and in which he refers to the comparisons between this aneroid and the mercurial barometer, for the purpose of deducing the corrections to the former. These comparisons, as found recorded in the volume containing meteorological constants, commence with September 30th, 1853, and end on January 9th, 1854—65 in number.

The readings of the mercurial barometer commence October 24th, 1853, and terminate with January 24th, 1855. The preference has been given to these readings. The indications of the aneroid were only used for the time between September 1st and October 24th, 1853; its readings are also valuable as corroborating those of the mercurial barometer.

The aneroid was kept on deck till September 19th, 1853, 9 A. M., when the temperature was so low that the attached thermometer failed to record. The instrument was then taken into the cabin; its position there was six feet lower than on deck.

In his reduction of a part of the above 65 comparisons between the mercurial

---

[1] The above information of the construction of the instrument was received from the maker. Scale and cistern were connected by brass.

and aneroid barometers, the reduction of the former to the temperature 32° is applied by Mr. Sonntag, astronomer to the expedition, for the case of a brass connection between the cistern and scale. Table No. XVII. Series C, p. 63, in Guyot's Meteorological and Physical Tables, edition of 1858, prepared for the Smithsonian Institution, answers this case, and has been adopted by me for the temperature reductions. This reduction, in general, is not very great, as may be seen on p. 425, Appendix No. XII. of the second volume of the Narrative, where the mean readings of the attached thermometer, for the year 1854, is given as +40°.3.

Reduction of the Aneroid to the Mercurial Barometer.—A number of comparisons of the two instruments, for the purpose of reducing the readings of the first to their equivalent values by the second instrument, were made, as stated above. The differences in the indications of the mercurial and aneroid barometers, or $M-A$, may be supposed to be proportional to the variations in pressure and temperature, and may be represented by the equation

$$B = A + c + m\,(A - \text{mean pressure}) + n\,(T - \text{mean temperature}),$$

c being an index error. The quantities c, m, n, are to be determined from the following comparisons. In the absence of any better information, the attached thermometers were supposed free of index error. The comparisons were made by Mr. Sonntag.

TABLE OF COMPARISONS OF ANEROID BAROMETER NO. 4796 WITH TAGLIABUE'S MERCURIAL BAROMETER.

No.	Date.	Hour.	Mercurial barometer.	Att'd ther.	Aneroid barometer.	Att'd ther.	Mer'l bar. referred to same temp.	No.	Date.	Hour.	Mercurial barometer.	Att'd ther.	Aneroid barometer.	Att'd ther.	Mer'l bar. referred to same temp.
	1853		Inch.	°	Inch.	°	Inch.		1853		Inch.	°	Inch.	°	Inch.
1	Sept. 30	21	29.962	21.3	30.00	65	30.080	35	Nov. 30	21	29.730	39.0	29.67	77	29.832
2	Oct. 1	2	29.925	23.8	29.93	72	30.055	36	Dec. 3	21.5	29.833	35.0	29.76	80	29.952
3	" 1	12	29.790	11.0	29.84	62	29.927	37	" 4	21.5	29.640	37.0	29.58	75	29.740
4	" 1	23	29.653	21.7	29.66	70	29.780	38	" 5	21.5	29.448	36.5	29.39	80	29.562
5	" 2	12	29.440	15.9	29.46	70	29.582	39	" 6	21.5	29.660	32.0	29.625	76	29.776
6	" 2	22	29.165	22.0	29.19	76	29.305	40	" 7	21.5	29.725	31.4	29.68	76	29.843
7	" 3	3	29.122	34.2	29.18	64	29.199	41	" 8	21.5	29.686	27.0	29.66	74	29.811
8	" 3	12	29.140	26.8	29.22	65	29.240	42	" 9	21.5	29.850	36.2	29.78	75	29.953
9	" 3	23	29.308	29.0	29.35	64	29.400	43	" 10	21.5	29.870	41.5	29.80	74	29.956
10	" 24	20.5	29.765	49.2	29.70	77	29.839	44	" 11	21.5	29.952	37.0	29.90	77	30.059
11	" 25	20.5	30.165	48.9	30.05	78	30.244	45	" 13	21.5	30.022	37.0	29.93	81	30.140
12	" 26	21	29.960	41.4	29.87	76	30.051	46	" 14	21.5	29.898	33.2	29.81	83	30.030
13	" 27	21	29.800	33.0	29.74	75	29.911	47	" 15	21.5	29.860	34.7	29.79	82	29.985
14	Nov. 4	21	29.732	36.0	29.67	75	29.835	48	" 16	21.5	29.802	37.2	29.73	79	29.912
15	" 5	21	29.610	34.6	29.53	78	29.723	49	" 18	21.5	30.000	40.2	29.89	80	30.106
16	" 6	21	29.825	42.3	29.73	78	29.922	50	" 20	21.5	30.105	39.2	30.00	79	30.211
17	" 7	21	29.966	37.2	29.87	78	30.075	51	" 21	21.5	29.475	40.0	29.43	75	29.567
18	" 8	21	29.916	34.2	29.84	76	30.026	52	" 22	21.5	29.760	42.0	29.70	79	29.858
19	" 9	21	29.230	32.9	29.20	77	29.345	53	" 23	21.5	30.188	40.5	30.07	82	30.301
20	" 10	21	29.330	38.5	29.26	79	29.436	54	" 24	21.5	30.230	35.2	30.135	80	30.350
21	" 11	21	29.555	41.6	29.475	76	29.645	55	" 25	21.5	30.270	40.0	30.175	77	30.369
22	" 12	21	30.130	39.2	30.05	76	30.228	56	" 26	21.5	29.425	46.0	29.35	78	29.508
23	" 13	21	30.213	34.8	30.14	72	30.309	57	" 31	21.5	29.610	41.0	29.56	78	29.707
24	" 15	21	29.895	29.0	29.82	74	30.016		1854						
25	" 17	21	29.750	30.2	29.70	76	29.872	58	Jan. 1	21.5	29.600	43.0	29.55	79	29.695
26	" 18	21	29.735	32.8	29.675	77	29.853	59	" 3	21.5	29.300	37.0	29.27	76	29.400
27	" 20	21	29.720	29.2	29.67	74	29.838	60	" 4	22.5	29.510	36.5	29.47	77	29.617
28	" 21	22	29.777	24.8	29.73	76	29.912	61	" 5	21.5	29.515	45.0	29.46	75	29.593
29	" 22	21	29.922	34.5	29.84	80	30.044	62	" 6	21.5	29.790	42.6	29.70	78	29.882
30	" 24	22	29.616	33.7	29.57	77	29.730	63	" 7	21.5	29.760	47.3	29.68	74	29.831
31	" 25	21	29.605	35.2	29.55	75	29.709	64	" 8	21.5	29.925	37.0	29.90	70	30.013
32	" 27	21	29.210	41.0	29.175	84	29.321	65	" 9	21.5	29.700	43.0	29.65	74	29.781
33	" 28	21	29.375	42.4	29.32	79	29.470								
34	" 29	22	29.665	41.3	29.59	75	29.753		Means	...	...	...	29.672	75.78	29.831

The constant c is, therefore, + 0.159 inches, at a mean temperature 75°.78 and a mean barometric pressure 29.831. To deduce the coefficients m and n, the correction c has first been applied to the aneroid readings. The following differences were then formed: $B - (A + c)$, $(A + c) - 29.831$, and $T - 75°.8$. We then have the 65 conditional equations :—

1. $-0.079 = +0.328\,m - 10.8\,n$
2. $-0.034 = +0.258\,m - 3.8\,n$
3. $-0.072 = +0.168\,m - 13.8\,n$
4. $-0.039 = -0.012\,m - 5.8\,n$

etc. etc.

Their solution furnishes m and n. Making first the coefficient of n as great as possible, by addition and change of sign of the equation when necessary, we find

$$203.4\,n + 0.846\,m = +1.374$$

$$\text{or,} \quad n = +0.00675 - 0.004\,m,$$

and, in like manner, m results from the equation—

$$12.56\,m + 40\,n = +1.190$$

$$m = +0.072, \qquad \text{and } n = +0.0065$$

Hence the formula for reduction—

$$B = A + \overset{\text{Inch.}}{0.159} + 0.072\,(A - \overset{\text{Inch.}}{29.672}) + 0.0065\,(T - 75°.8).$$

To show the result by the formula in extreme cases, the following eight comparisons are here inserted.

No.			Inch.		Inch.	Difference.
No. 3	Lowest temp.	Computed reading B =	29.92,	same observed (M) =	29.93	—0.01
" 9		"	29.41,	"	29.40	+0.01
" 32	Highest temp.	"	29.35,	"	29.32	+0.03
" 46		"	30.03,	"	30.03	0.00
" 23	Greatest pressure	"	30.31,	"	30.31	0.00
" 54		"	30.35,	"	30.35	0.00
" 6	Least pressure	"	29.33,	"	29.31	+0.02
" 7		"	29.23,	"	29.20	+0.03

These differences prove a sufficient approximation in the terms of the above expression, and likewise leave no doubt that the indications of the aneroid may generally be relied on to nearly within one-hundredth of an inch.

To facilitate the reduction, the following table of corrections has been calculated according to the above formula:—

	TEMPERATURE.									
BAROMETER.	15°	20°	25°	30°	40°	45°	50°	52°.5	55°.0	57°.5
29.0	—0.28	—0.25	—0.22	—0.19	—0.12	—0.09	—0.06	—0.04	—0.02	—0.01
29.5	—0.25	—0.22	—0.18	—0.15	—0.09	—0.05	—0.02	0.00	+0.01	+0.03
30.0	—0.21	—0.18	—0.15	—0.12	—0.05	—0.02	+0.01	+0.03	+0.05	+0.07
BAROMETER.	60°.0	62°.5	65°.0	67°.5	70°.0	72°.5	75°.0	77°.5	80°.0	
29.0	+0.01	+0.03	+0.04	+0.05	+0.07	+0.09	+0.11	+0.13	+0.14	...
29.5	+0.04	+0.06	+0.08	+0.09	+0.11	+0.13	+0.14	+0.16	+0.17	...
30.0	+0.08	+0.09	+0.11	+0.13	+0.15	+0.16	+0.18	+0.19	+0.21	...

The hourly record of the barometer and attached thermometer readings is given for mean local time, English inches and degrees of Fahrenheit, and for an average elevation of the cistern of the barometer above the mean level of the sea of five feet.

For the months of September and October, 1853, the barometric and thermometric means are not directly comparable with the corresponding figures in Appendix No. XI. of the Narrative (2d vol.) for this reason: In the Appendix the uncorrected aneroid readings are given, while the present abstract contains the corrected or referred readings according to the preceding investigation. After October 23d, the readings of the mercurial barometer take the place of the aneroid readings.

A star (*) attached to any date in the following record indicates that a corresponding remark will be found in the notes appended to the abstract.

Occasional omissions in the hourly record of either barometer or thermometer readings, as seen by the blanks in the table, have in all cases been supplied by simple interpolations before the means (hourly or daily) were taken, in order to give the result independent of these omissions.

Hourly Abstract of the Readings of the Barometer and Attached Thermometer at Van Rensselaer Harbor, In September, 1853, in Lat. 78° 37′, Long. 70° 53′ W. of Greenwich.

Aneroid Barometer in cabin. 29 inches +. Readings in English inches and degrees of Fahrenheit.

Day.	1h.		2h.		3h.		4h.		5h.		6h.		7h.		8h.		9h.		10h.		11h.		Noon.		13h.	
	Inch.	°	Inch.	°	Inch.	°	Inch.	°	Inch.	°	Inch.	°	Inch.	°	Inch.	°	Inch.	°	Inch.	°	Inch.	°	Inch.	°	Inch.	°
1st	.80	68	.79	64	.80	68	.81	69	.78	63	.76	63	.76	74	.74	74	.73	73	.71	70	.72	72	.70	71	.69	66
2d	.67	67	.69	69	.69	69	.68	68	.70	75	.70	73	.69	72	.67	68	.68	70	.66	68	.66	68	.67	67	.69	66
3d	.71	68	.72	68	.72	68	.74	70	.71	66	.71	64	.72	64	.72	64	.74	65	.74	64	.75	66	.77	72	.76	70
4th	.83	68	.81	66	.83	68	.80	64	.81	66	.80	64	.84	68	.86	73	.84	72	.83	70	.82	67	.81	60	.87	71
5th	.89	66	.90	66	.88	63	.93	70	.87	72	.84	65	.86	65	.85	64	.85	64	.85	68	.83	70	.83	70	.78	65
6th	.81	65	.86	66	.88	68	.86	66	.83	62	.86	64	.86	64	.86	62	.86	66	.85	65	.85	63	.85	63	.85	66
7th	.55	68	.53	69	.57	71	.46	71	.38	67	.39	70	.34	69	.31	66	.28	65	.30	68	.35	72	.34	72	.26	75
8th	.25	70	.23	71	.24	68	.22	65	.23	63	.25	71	.24	69	.25	68	.27	67	.27	68	.27	68	.27	68	.25	64
9th	.32	66	.22	60	.30	52	.32	52	.33	54	.33	54	.33	52	.35	59	.36	62	.38	64	.37	64	.36	64	.37	66
10th	.38	60	.38	60	.41	62	.40	61	.43	65	.43	65	.43	62	.46	64	.47	68	.46	67	.45	66	.45	66	.50	66
*11th	.49	62	.49	63	.49	63	.49	63	.47	54	.48	62	.50	64	.50	65	.52	67	.53	68	.53	66	.50	65	.50	65
12th	.57	63	.59	62	.59	63	.64	63	.67	60	.67	63	.65	61	.68	64	.68	63	.70	66	.70	65	.71	68	.71	68
13th	.49	65	.53	67	.49	66	.52	63	.52	66	.54	67	.53	63	.57	62	.57	62	.56	61	.57	62	.57	62	.54	64
*14th	.52	60	.53	62	.51	60	.55	68	.55	69	.54	67	.55	68	.52	67	.49	63	.54	67	.53	66	.53	69	.51	66
15th	.35	20	.41	21	.42	22	.40	22	.36	17	.37	18	.38	18	.38	18	.43	24	.41	23	.42	24	.41	24	.41	26
16th	.40	13	.43	13	.43	13	.44	13	.42	13	.45	14	.47	15	.49	16	.51	18	.52	18	.52	19	.50	19	.50	19
17th	.67	26	.67	26	.67	26	.70	29	.71	23	.63	18	.66	24	.65	21	.70	29	...	...	...	...	...	...	.73	29
18th	.72	13	.73	14	.73	13	.74	14	.72	11	.72	12	.74	14	.75	18	.79	22	.81	26	.81	27	.83	34	.81	29
*19th	.73	22	.73	22	.74	23	.73	22	.65	10	.65	11	.64	(9)	.64	(9)	.66	12	.86	60	.88	62	.89	65	.89	65
20th	.94	69	...	...	.94	69	.90	58	.91	61	.91	61	.92	62	.93	60	.91	60	.91	59	.89	60	.88	60	.80	42
21st	.83	61	.83	59	.85	56	.83	54	.84	55	.84	54	.84	54	.87	62	.87	62	.89	64	.86	60	.85	56	.83	54
22d	.86	55	.85	54	.87	58	.87	57	.87	56	.90	56	.90	56	.90	56	.90	54	.88	51	.86	48	.87	50	.88	50
23d	.88	48	.89	48	.90	50	.91	52	.93	55	.90	50	.87	44	.86	42	.86	43	.87	45	.88	46	.88	46	.87	43
24th	.92	61	.90	56	.89	54	.88	52	.89	58	.88	58	.88	58	.87	58	.89	62	.87	60	.87	58	.87	61	.85	60
25th	0.91	(59)	0.93	58	0.96	57	0.99	56	1.01	54	1.05	52	1.05	52	1.05	52	1.07	54	1.10	58	1.10	58	1.11	64	1.12	64
26th	1.13	63	1.11	61	1.09	57	1.12	58	1.13	54	1.13	53	1.13	55	1.15	60	1.10	56	1.12	57	1.08	56	1.08	60	1.06	57
27th	0.99	62	0.99	62	1.02	64	0.98	60	0.97	58	0.91	55	0.91	58	0.89	58	0.99	57	1.00	58	0.99	58	0.99	58	0.96	56
28th	1.02	58	1.02	58	1.01	57	1.02	60	1.04	58	1.03	58	1.04	60	1.02	58	...	...	1.07	70	1.05	67	1.07	68	1.01	60
29th	1.01	66	1.01	66	1.04	70	1.06	74	1.03	70	1.05	70	1.04	68	1.01	65	0.99	64	0.99	64	0.99	62	0.98	60	0.98	(59)
30th	1.07	65	1.02	60	1.02	60	1.03	61	1.05	62	1.07	60	1.04	54	...	...	1.06	56	1.06	56	1.04	54	1.03	53	1.05	55
Means	.724	55.9	.724	54.8	.733	55.3	.734	56.5	.727	53.9	.726	53.7	.727	53.9	.728	54.4	.737	55.2	.748	58.7	.745	58.4	.744	59.1	.734	56.9
B. at 32°	29.651		29.654		29.663		29.660		29.660		29.659		29.660		29.660		29.667		29.669		29.667		29.663		29.659	

Day.	14h.		15h.		16h.		17h.		18h.		19h.		20h.		21h.		22h.		23h.		Midn't.		Means.		B. 32°.
	Inch.	°	Inch.	°	Inch.	°	Inch.	°	Inch.	°	Inch.	°	Inch.	°	Inch.	°	Inch.	°	Inch.	°	Inch.	°	Inch.	°	Inch.
1st	.70	68	.74	73	.65	68	.67	67	.66	66	.65	64	.66	66	.66	66	.64	65	.66	67	.67	68	.715	68.0	.610
2d	.63	60	.63	60	.67	65	.67	66	.67	65	.66	64	.66	64	.67	63	.69	69	.70	66	.68	64	.674	66.9	.571
3d	.75	69	.76	70	.79	73	.79	73	.79	71	.81	70	.82	70	.82	70	.82	70	.81	68	.82	68	.762	68.4	.656
4th	.87	74	.88	75	.86	70	.86	68	.88	67	.87	65	.88	66	.87	63	.87	66	.88	66	.90	68	.849	67.7	.745
5th	.78	63	.78	61	.79	60	.86	70	.83	67	.86	69	.85	68	.82	67	.79	63	.81	65	.80	64	.839	66.0	.739
6th	.79	65	.81	62	.79	61	.72	62	.83	76	...	...	.72	70	.67	72	.63	74	.59	70	.55	68	.791	66.4	.690
7th	.25	70	.24	68	.17	68	.23	68	.28	69	.24	66	.29	64	.27	67	.26	67	.25	68	.30	74	.327	68.8	.221
8th	.25	68	.25	64	.27	66	.28	64	.35	66	.27	67	.29	65	.30	66	.31	64	.29	62	.29	62	.266	66.4	.167
9th	.38	68	.39	70	.38	68	.41	68	.43	68	.42	67	.42	67	.43	66	.41	64	.41	64	.41	64	.368	63.5	.278
10th	.50	66	.51	70	.51	70	.50	64	.53	66	.53	66	.51	68	.49	66	.49	65	.49	64	.50	63	.467	65.0	.371
*11th	.49	67	.49	65	.49	68	.50	70	.50	70	.51	72	...	...	.53	68	.53	66	.53	63	.57	64	.505	65.3	.409
12th	.71	68	.71	68	.70	66	.67	64	.67	65	.65	66	.65	66	.63	65	.61	65	.58	67	.56	65	.654	64.8	.558
13th	.58	64	.59	68	.57	64	.57	62	.54	61	.54	61	.54	61	.57	65	.58	67	.55	66	.54	66	.549	64.0	.455
*14th	.51	64	.35	25	.36	26	.40	28	.38	26	.37	25	.37	26	.34	19	.31	16	.31	16	.33	18	.454	47.5	.404
15th	.42	27	.43	29	.41	26	.40	25	.38	22	.38	21	.37	20	.39	20	.40	18	.44	18	.38	17	.398	21.7	.416
16th	.54	26	.59	29	.59	29	.62	30	.62	27	.63	30	.63	30	.63	31	.60	25	.64	24	.66	23	.503	21.1	.523
17th	.73	29	.73	29	.73	29	.71	22	.71	22	.73	23	.72	21	.72	20	.71	19	.73	19	.70	17	.700	24.6	.710
18th	.81	32	.79	27	.79	27	.76	23	.74	21	.73	20	.74	21	.71	18	.68	14	.68	14	.68	14	.750	19.9	.773
*19th	.88	63	.91	69	.91	68	.91	66	.92	67	.87	63	.87	61	.86	58	.86	59	.86	59	.86	60	.808	45.4	.763
20th	.80	42	.84	42	.78	38	.78	38	.79	39	.82	51	.81	53	.90	60	.93	68	.84	61	.84	61	.871	56.2	.797
21st	.82	53	.89	65	.87	63	.88	63	.85	59	.85	59	.83	56	.84	56	.84	56	.84	54	.84	56	.849	58.0	.771
22d	.88	48	.88	48	.98	60	.92	50	.92	50	.91	50	.90	50	.90	53	.91	56	.91	56	.89	48	.892	52.9	.826
23d	.88	46	.89	47	.92	53	.92	53	.94	56	.97	61	.98	62	.97	62	.99	66	.99	68	.95	66	.913	52.2	.850
24th	.85	62	.84	60	.85	60	.89	60	.89	60	.89	60	.89	59	.90	60	.94	65	.94	65	.90	60	.885	59.5	.802
25th	1.14	66	1.14	66	1.12	64	1.10	60	1.11	58	1.12	58	1.12	59	1.13	60	1.15	64	1.15	66	1.14	64	1.077	59.3	.994
26th	1.05	53	1.06	54	1.10	58	1.10	58	1.07	58	1.06	56	...	62	1.03	60	1.04	64	1.00	64	1.01	66	1.082	58.3	1.002
27th	0.96	54	0.97	56	0.99	57	0.99	56	0.99	54	0.97	52	0.99	55	1.01	58	1.01	58	1.02	58	1.03	60	.980	57.6	.903
28th	1.02	60	1.01	60	1.02	60	1.00	56	1.01	58	0.99	58	1.00	58	0.98	58	0.99	60	0.98	60	0.97	60	1.017	60.9	.930
29th	0.97	(58)	0.97	(57)	0.97	(56)	0.97	55	0.96	56	0.98	55	1.01	58	1.03	58	1.03	60	1.09	68	1.09	68	1.010	62.8	.919
30th	1.05	55	1.05	55	1.03	53	...	...	1.11	54	1.12	56	1.11	56	1.09	54	1.13	58	1.13	58	1.13	58	1.067	56.8	.992
Means	.733	56.9	.732	56.4	.735	56.4	.738	55.5	.745	55.5	.739	55.0	.739	55.2	.738	55.6	.738	56.4	.737	56.1	.733	55.8	.735	55.9	
B. at 32°	29.658		29.658		29.661		29.666		29.674		29.669		29.668		29.667		29.665		29.664		29.660		29.662		

HOURLY ABSTRACT OF THE READINGS OF THE BAROMETER AND ATTACHED THERMOMETER AT VAN RENSSELAER HARBOR,
In October, 1853, in Lat. 78° 37′, Long. 70° 53′ W. of Greenwich.
Aneroid in cabin, Mercurial Barometer in house on deck. 29 inches +. Readings in English inches and degrees of Fahr.

Day.	1h.		2h.		3h.		4h.		5h.		6h.		7h.		8h.		9h.		10h.		11h.		Noon.		13h.	
	Inch.	°	Inch.	°	Inch.	°	Inch.	°	Inch.	°	Inch.	°	Inch.	°	Inch.	°	Inch.	°	Inch.	°	Inch.	°	Inch.	°	Inch.	°
1st	1.12	58	1.13	60	1.14	62	1.17	66	1.08	56	1.09	56	1.10	60	1.13	66	1.11	65	1.10	64	1.10	70	1.11	74	...	...
2d	.93	62	.93	62	.93	62	.90	64	.88	(64)	.88	(64)	.87	(64)	.87	(64)	.81	65	.82	72	.78	70	.78	70	.78	70
3d	.56	80	.55	78	.52	73	.49	68	.34	60	.35	60	.32	60	.32	(60)	.32	60	.34	62	.40	64	.37	64	.36	65
4th	.29	68	.29	68	.31	70	.36	64	.36	(64)	.40	(64)	.45	(64)	.45	(64)	.41	64	.39	62	.39	62	.40	64	.45	69
5th	.51	64	.52	66	.53	67	.53	67	.53	68	.53	68	.53	68	.53	69	.53	69	.54	70	.53	69	.54	69	.53	64
6th	.52	62	.52	63	.52	62	.55	68	.54	64	.57	66	.54	66	.54	66	.58	75	.58	75	.61	78	.62	81	.62	78
7th	.75	76	.76	74	.79	74	.81	74	.75	65	.79	73	.83	70	.85	75	.81	68	.86	70	.88	70	.91	74	.93	70
8th	.89	74	.86	74	.82	75	.83	77	.79	(70)	.73	63	.74	64	.73	64	.84	75	.83	73	.82	69	.81	68	.86	60
9th	1.23	68	1.25	68	1.25	65	1.25	63	1.26	64	1.30	68	1.34	69	1.39	78	1.36	71	1.36	72	1.37	74	1.37	74	1.37	74
10th	1.35	78	1.29	74	1.26	72	1.23	70	1.24	70	1.28	74	1.30	76	1.32	78	1.25	70	1.27	73	1.29	74	1.29	74	1.30	72
11th	1.57	70	1.58	70	1.58	69	1.58	69	1.59	70	1.61	72	1.61	71	1.57	70	1.59	71	1.57	70	1.57	68	1.54	65	1.52	67
12th	1.39	70	1.38	73	1.38	78	1.39	80	1.38	76	1.37	76	1.38	74	1.37	70	1.35	68	1.33	64	1.36	63	1.37	64	...	...
13th	1.21	70	1.20	70	1.18	67	1.10	64	1.07	64	1.07	64	1.08	68	1.03	64	1.03	64	1.02	64	.99	60	.99	70	.99	70
14th	.85	65	.93	80	.93	80	.86	78	.87	76	.87	76	.85	71	.89	74	.86	72	.87	72	.86	70	.87	70	.86	70
15th	.81	70	.78	70	.75	64	.77	72	.79	74	.78	72	.77	72	.77	72	.75	72	.75	74	.74	72	.74	72	.75	76
16th	.90	70	.91	70	.93	74	.96	75	.97	76	.97	74	.96	72	.96	68	.96	68	.97	66	.97	63	.98	62	.98	64
17th	.97	67	.97	67	.98	68	1.00	68	1.01	70	.99	68	.97	64	.99	66	.97	65	.97	65	.96	64	.96	64	.98	66
18th	1.01	68	1.01	71	1.01	73	1.02	74	.98	70	.98	70	.98	70	.98	70	.95	66	...	...	...	...	...	...	...	...
19th	.94	72	.94	72	.93	71	.92	70	.92	70	.89	68	.89	68	.90	68	.90	68	.92	70	.92	70	.91	70	.90	71
20th	.87	69	.88	68	.89	70	.88	69	.88	68	.90	(69)	.89	(69)	.89	(70)	.90	71	.88	69	.89	73	.86	74	.87	74
21st	.85	76	.86	73	.89	72	.89	72	.90	(72)	.91	(72)	.91	(72)	.91	(72)	.91	73	.88	70	.97	66	.99	69	1.00	70
22d	1.07	73	1.06	72	1.08	68	1.11	82	1.09	76	1.09	74	1.16	72	1.17	72	1.18	72	1.16	68	1.18	68	1.17	69	1.20	72
23d	1.20	72	1.20	73	1.20	73	1.19	71	1.18	70	1.19	76	1.19	76	1.12	72	1.09	72	1.09	72	1.07	74	1.08	76	1.03	69
24th	.70	39	.70	44	.60	39	.60	35	.60	40	.61	41	.64	43	.64	45	.77	43	.76	44	.76	42	.76	41	.76	41
25th	.73	47	.73	44	.72	45	.70	46	.65	47	.65	47	.70	43	.75	44	.76	47	.74	43	.74	45	.74	45	.91	78
26th	1.10	47	1.10	50	1.10	49	1.10	45	1.10	45	1.12	45	1.12	47	1.12	47	1.20	45	1.15	45	1.16	45	1.16	45	1.17	49
27th	1.05	40	1.05	40	1.05	35	1.05	33	1.00	37	1.00	38	1.00	39	1.00	40	.96	41	.95	42	.94	41	.94	40	.95	48
28th	.80	33	.80	34	.80	31	.80	27	.80	28	.78	34	.75	36	.72	37	.80	37	.84	36	.84	35	.84	38	.83	47
29th	.84	35	.84	34	.84	25	.82	31	.78	36	.78	35	.76	37	.76	37	.76	34	.78	32	.78	32	.78	33	.76	36
30th	.67	32	.66	32	.60	34	.65	29	.68	35	.63	31	.63	33	.63	33	.60	34	.60	33	.60	33	.60	33	.60	32
31st	.64	35	.65	35	.64	34	.64	33	.65	35	.64	34	.65	32	.66	33	.63	32	.64	33	.65	34	.65	38	.70	30
Means	.914	62.2	.914	62.2	.908	61.3	.908	61.4	.892	60.6	.895	61.0	.900	61.0	.902	61.5	.901	61.1	.901	61.0	.906	60.8	.906	61.9	.916	63.1
B. at 32°	29.823		29.823		29.820		29.820		29.807		29.809		29.813		29.814		29.814		29.814		29.820		29.816		29.823	

Day.	14h.		15h.		16h.		17h.		18h.		19h.		20h.		21h.		22h.		23h.		Midn't.		Means.		B. 32°.
	Inch.	°	Inch.	°	Inch.	°	Inch.	°	Inch.	°	Inch.	°	Inch.	°	Inch.	°	Inch.	°	Inch.	°	Inch.	°	Inch.	°	Inch.
1st	1.09	(72)	1.08	(72)	1.06	(72)	1.07	72	1.02	68	1.01	65	.98	60	.97	60	.93	60	.90	60	.90	60	1.062	64.6	.965
2d	.77	70	.74	(68)	.73	(66)	.70	64	.70	64	.70	61	.67	62	.62	60	.62	(65)	.57	(65)	.50	70	.770	65.3	.674
3d	.24	65	.23	66	.20	(65)	.21	64	.22	62	.23	64	.24	64	.24	64	.26	66	.26	66	.26	66	.326	65.3	.231
4th	.44	69	.42	68	.42	69	.44	66	.46	62	.46	61	.48	61	.51	66	.51	66	.51	65	.51	66	.421	65.2	.326
5th	.55	65	.55	64	.55	64	.57	64	.51	63	.53	63	.53	63	.53	64	.54	66	.54	66	.55	67	.535	66.1	.436
6th	.56	70	.62	70	.61	68	.61	68	.61	68	.62	68	.62	68	.62	(67)	.65	(66)	.66	64	.68	63	.590	68.5	.484
7th	.94	70	.94	70	.92	71	.94	73	.96	75	.94	73	.94	73	.90	66	.91	72	.88	70	.86	70	.869	71.5	.756
8th	.87	62	.89	66	.86	61	.94	65	1.02	69	1.09	73	1.18	75	1.12	64	1.12	63	1.14	62	1.15	61	.914	67.8	.809
9th	1.35	70	1.34	74	1.33	73	1.32	72	1.31	72	1.30	70	1.26	64	1.29	(66)	1.30	(69)	1.31	(72)	1.33	(75)	1.314	70.2	1.202
10th	1.31	70	1.36	71	1.39	68	1.39	(68)	1.40	(69)	1.42	(69)	1.43	(70)	1.43	70	1.40	68	1.38	64	1.39	66	1.332	71.2	1.217
11th	1.51	66	1.50	64	1.48	62	1.48	64	1.43	66	1.42	64	1.42	64	1.40	66	1.39	64	1.39	65	1.40	66	1.512	67.2	1.406
12th	1.34	64	1.33	64	1.34	66	1.33	66	1.32	68	1.32	70	1.30	69	1.23	64	1.26	72	1.25	72	1.22	70	1.335	69.4	1.224
13th	.98	70	.95	68	.95	70	.94	69	.92	67	.93	68	.93	68	.90	70	.85	73	.86	70	.86	68	1.001	67.5	.896
14th	.86	70	.84	70	.84	68	.83	68	.82	67	.79	65	.78	64	.78	64	.77	64	.74	66	.80	76	.842	70.7	.730
15th	.76	70	.77	70	.77	70	.79	72	.80	71	.80	70	.81	70	.81	70	.81	70	.87	70	...	(70)	.784	71.0	.671
16th	.99	66	.98	64	1.00	67	1.02	68	1.02	68	1.01	67	1.01	72	1.03	74	1.05	76	1.01	72	1.01	74	.981	69.6	.871
17th	.96	64	.96	64	.98	64	.98	64	.98	64	.98	63	.99	64	1.01	66	1.02	68	1.02	68	1.00	66	.983	65.7	.883
18th	.99	70	.93	70	.93	70	.93	70	.91	67	.89	64	.91	66	.89	64	.91	66	.89	71	.88	70	.952	68.9	.843
19th	.86	70	.87	71	.86	70	...	...	.89	76	.87	74	.89	72	.88	70	.88	70	.86	70	.85	70	.895	70.5	.784
20th	.87	70	.86	70	.86	76	.84	71	.86	74	.86	73	.86	74	.86	74	.84	70	.83	70	.83	70	.869	71.0	.756
21st	1.00	70	1.01	71	1.00	70	1.00	69	.93	70	.95	68	.98	69	1.04	70	1.06	70	1.06	70	1.06	70	.957	70.7	.845
22d	1.20	72	1.19	71	1.19	71	1.22	72	1.23	72	1.22	69	1.22	69	1.22	70	1.22	72	1.21	(72)	1.20	(72)	1.168	71.7	1.051
23d	.99	68	.99	69	1.01	69	1.02	72	1.01	69	1.00	68	1.02	72	.99	76	.97	74	.95	72	.94	72	1.072	72.0	.955
24th	.76	46	.75	46	.74	43	.72	45	.75	47	.75	45	.75	46	.74	47	.74	43	.75	45	.73	45	.712	43.1	.674
25th	.91	78	.91	76	.98	82	.91	43	.92	44	.97	51	1.00	52	1.02	54	1.03	51	1.05	58	1.06	54	.845	52.6	.780
26th	1.16	49	1.15	47	1.10	44	1.10	41	1.11	42	1.09	41	1.09	40	1.12	(40)	1.10	(40)	1.09	(40)	1.08	(40)	1.120	44.5	1.077
27th	.95	48	.94	44	.94	49	.95	48	.90	47	.93	40	.93	38	.81	33	.79	34	.76	35	.76	35	.942	40.2	.911
28th	.85	47	.84	47	.85	36	.82	36	.82	37	.82	40	.82	37	.81	37	.81	38	.81	36	.81	38	.811	36.7	.789
29th	.75	33	.75	36	.76	31	.76	35	.75	36	.76	35	.72	36	.72	36	.72	37	.71	38	.70	37	.766	34.5	.751
30th	.60	34	.61	34	.61	36	.62	34	.62	35	.61	35	.61	35	.61	38	.62	37	.62	37	.62	36	.621	34.0	.606
31st	.72	32	.72	29	.73	29	.73	37	.74	32	.74	32	.74	33	.74	33	.75	33	.76	32	.76	33	.690	33.0	.678
Means	.907	62.6	.904	62.3	.903	62.2	.905	61.0	.901	61.0	.904	61.1	.907	60.3	.898	60.0	.898	60.7	.892	60.7	.890	61.1	.903	61.3	
B. at 32°	29.816		29.813		29.813		29.819		29.815		29.817		29.822		29.814		29.814		29.806		29.803		29.815		

Hourly Abstract of the Readings of the Barometer and Attached Thermometer at Van Rensselaer Harbor, In November, 1853, in Lat. 78° 37′, Long. 70° 53′ W. of Greenwich.

Mercurial Barometer in house on deck. 29 inches +. Readings in English inches and degrees of Fahrenheit.

Day.	1h.		2h.		3h.		4h.		5h.		6h.		7h.		8h.		9h.		10h.		11h.		Noon.		13h.	
	Inch.	°	Inch.	°	Inch.	°	Inch.	°	Inch.	°	Inch.	°	Inch.	°	Inch.	°	Inch.	°	Inch.	°	Inch.	°	Inch.	°	Inch.	°
1st	.75	25	.75	23	.75	24	.75	26	.73	30	.74	30	.74	31	.74	32	.78	33	.78	34	.79	35	.79	34	.78	25
2d	.85	29	.85	28	.85	29	.85	29	.85	28	.85	31	.85	36	.85	37	.85	35	.85	32	.85	32	.85	29	.85	35
3d	.81	34	.82	30	.81	29	.81	28	.70	25	.80	25	.78	26	.78	25	.75	33	.75	24	.73	19	.72	23	.73	31
4th	.70	35	.71	32	.75	30	.75	28	.73	30	.72	28	.70	25	.70	26	.72	30	.74	34	.73	33	.75	36	.74	32
5th	.78	37	.78	35	.76	31	.76	32	.75	33	.75	30	.74	32	.78	35	.75	37	.74	37	.74	38	.74	40	.74	40
6th	.70	35	.69	35	.68	35	.68	35	.67	34	.65	33	.63	34	.62	33	.62	34	.62	34	.62	36	.57	34	.58	32
7th	.72	37	.75	37	.77	39	.77	39	.79	38	.79	40	.80	40	.82	41	.85	40	.78	39	.79	33	.75	35	.84	37
8th	.87	35	.87	35	.88	33	.88	34	.88	39	.90	39	.93	39	.90	37	.95	37	.95	37	1.00	39	1.02	37	1.02	38
9th	1.08	39	1.06	32	1.05	33	1.04	31	1.05	33	1.05	33	1.02	35	1.01	35	.92	34	.88	35	.84	34	.82	35	.75	35
10th	.24	35	.23	34	.20	33	.20	30	.15	32	.16	32	.20	31	.20	32	.23	34	.25	33	.30	34	.35	35	.40	34
11th	.59	34	.60	33	.55	32	.55	34	.50	34	.48	35	.44	34	.38	35	.35	30	.35	35	.35	38	.29	32	.22	38
12th	.23	28	.25	25	.30	24	.35	25	.41	32	.45	34	.47	34	.48	(36)	.54	38	.54	41	.52	38	.55	39	.60	38
13th	1.03	33	1.03	29	1.07	30	1.07	30	1.09	34	1.09	32	1.10	35	1.12	37	1.15	38	1.14	38	1.14	40	1.15	37	1.20	35
14th	1.22	29	1.22	31	1.22	32	1.22	32	1.22	33	1.22	32	1.20	33	1.20	33	1.21	35	1.20	35	1.23	34	1.22	35	1.23	33
15th	1.17	31	1.17	29	1.17	27	1.17	22	1.12	23	1.12	24	1.13	24	1.10	24	1.10	38	1.12	37	1.11	37	1.10	31	1.10	30
16th	1.00	24	1.00	24	1.00	25	1.01	26	.96	26	.93	23	.90	23	.85	23	.87	30	.86	27	.85	28	.85	29	.85	31
17th	.75	24	.75	28	.78	29	.78	26	.80	33	.82	31	.84	32	.84	32	.84	31	.86	30	.85	31	.87	32	.88	35
18th	.85	34	.85	36	.85	27	.85	27	.80	27	.80	27	.81	26	.76	27	.79	30	.75	30	.75	32	.75	31	.75	34
19th	.75	33	.74	34	.74	33	.74	33	.72	32	.74	34	.74	31	.73	34	.70	32	.77	33	.77	33	.77	32	.75	39
20th	.68	34	.68	33	.68	39	.68	37	.68	32	.69	31	.68	30	.65	30	.65	31	.62	31	.62	31	.64	30	.64	39
21st	.73	30	.73	28	.72	29	.72	30	.71	29	.71	27	.72	27	.72	28	.71	30	.71	32	.71	36	.71	32	.75	39
22d	.75	33	.75	30	.75	29	.75	26	.75	21	.75	20	.75	18	.75	22	.75	27	.77	30	.78	29	.80	32	.83	24
23d	.90	33	.90	33	.90	35	.90	34	.90	31	.90	31	.90	29	.90	31	.90	34	.92	34	.93	31	.93	31	.93	30
24th	.95	30	.95	29	.95	29	.95	32	.95	29	.95	30	.95	30	.95	30	.95	33	.95	34	.95	32	.95	33	.99	35
25th	.97	35	.90	34	.85	35	.78	32	.77	31	.75	32	.72	35	.69	35	.65	30	.60	32	.57	34	.56	37	.54	37
26th	.58	33	.59	33	.61	35	.61	36	.60	36	.60	32	.60	33	.60	32	.60	35	.60	35	.60	39	.60	40	.60	40
27th	.46	35	.44	35	.43	34	.41	33	.39	32	.35	32	.33	34	.29	37	.26	37	.26	37	.26	36	.25	37	.20	35
28th	.20	38	.20	37	.20	35	.20	36	.21	38	.24	37	.24	36	.22	38	.22	42	.22	41	.21	41	.20	40	.20	40
29th	.18	39	.20	38	.23	38	.25	39	.25	41	.20	39	.25	39	.30	40	.36	43	.41	41	.41	41	.42	41	.45	43
30th	.55	37	.60	35	.61	35	.61	35	.62	37	.62	37	.64	38	.65	45	.65	46	.65	37	.65	38	.65	40	.65	40
Means	.735	32.9	.735	31.8	.737	31.6	.736	31.2	.725	31.8	.727	31.4	.727	32.0	.719	32.7	.722	34.6	.721	34.3	.722	34.3	.721	34.3	.726	35.1
B. at 32°	29.713		29.726		29.729		29.728		29.717		29.719		29.718		29.708		29.706		29.705		29.706		29.705		29.709	

Day.	14h.		15h.		16h.		17h.		18h.		19h.		20h.		21h.		22h.		23h.		Midn't.		Means.		B. 32°.
	Inch.	°	Inch.	°	Inch.	°	Inch.	°	Inch.	°	Inch.	°	Inch.	°	Inch.	°	Inch.	°	Inch.	°	Inch.	°	Inch.	°	Inch.
1st	.80	23	.80	24	.80	26	.82	34	.84	34	.84	35	.85	33	.85	33	.84	33	.84	34	.84	34	.791	30.2	.787
2d	.85	27	.85	35	.86	33	.85	33	.86	32	.84	33	.85	32	.85	34	.89	34	.83	32	.82	33	.850	32.0	.841
3d	.68	30	.69	32	.70	38	.72	41	.72	37	.72	35	.72	35	.72	34	.72	34	.74	34	.70	29	.742	30.4	.737
4th	.74	30	.75	31	.75	30	.75	34	.75	36	.79	36	.78	36	.78	32	.78	37	.78	38	.79	37	.745	32.3	.735
5th	.72	41	.74	40	.74	39	.75	37	.75	39	.75	42	.75	40	.75	38	.75	37	.73	37	.70	37	.747	36.8	.725
6th	.59	33	.61	42	.68	40	.64	35	.63	36	.63	33	.64	37	.68	36	.69	38	.70	38	.72	38	.648	35.4	.630
7th	.84	37	.85	40	.85	38	.68	40	.69	37	.70	43	.72	35	.87	35	.87	37	.86	33	.86	36	.792	37.7	.767
8th	1.01	37	1.02	38	1.05	38	1.05	40	1.06	43	1.07	43	1.07	45	1.07	35	1.07	35	1.07	35	1.07	33	.986	37.5	.961
9th	.70	35	.65	38	.59	38	.50	37	.44	35	.40	40	.32	39	.30	36	.30	36	.26	34	.22	30	.719	35.1	.702
10th	.43	33	.43	34	.50	37	.59	30	.51	36	.58	36	.56	40	.58	37	.60	38	.60	36	.60	38	.379	34.3	.364
11th	.19	37	.15	36	.12	35	.11	39	.08	35	.07	35	.07	36	.10	35	.19	29	.12	38	.17	29	.292	34.5	.278
12th	.65	37	.70	40	.81	43	.83	42	.84	40	.88	41	.90	34	.95	32	.95	37	.96	39	.99	37	.631	35.6	.613
13th	1.22	36	1.22	36	1.22	34	1.22	38	1.23	39	1.22	37	1.22	37	1.20	36	1.19	34	1.21	37	1.20	35	1.155	35.3	1.137
14th	1.23	34	1.23	34	1.28	36	1.23	34	1.23	33	1.22	36	1.21	35	1.20	30	1.16	30	1.15	33	1.16	32	1.213	33.1	1.201
15th	1.10	32	1.10	35	1.10	31	1.11	36	1.09	30	1.07	28	1.06	29	1.05	28	1.05	29	1.02	26	1.03	25	1.102	29.4	1.100
16th	.85	34	.84	36	.83	41	.82	37	.80	36	.78	34	.78	33	.75	28	.75	31	.75	31	.75	27	.860	29.4	.857
17th	.88	30	.89	32	.89	33	.90	33	.90	32	.90	30	.90	29	.88	27	.85	31	.87	31	.85	28	.849	30.4	.845
18th	.75	34	.75	31	.75	33	.75	34	.75	35	.74	35	.73	35	.75	34	.75	33	.80	34	.76	33	.777	31.6	.768
19th	.75	36	.75	37	.75	36	.75	35	.73	36	.74	37	.73	38	.70	37	.70	37	.70	37	.71	39	.736	34.9	.718
20th	.65	39	.65	36	.65	37	.69	36	.70	36	.70	38	.70	39	.70	37	.70	37	.70	32	.70	33	.672	34.5	.656
21st	.75	38	.75	39	.75	31	.75	33	.75	36	.75	33	.75	33	.75	34	.75	30	.75	30	.75	31	.733	31.9	.724
22d	.84	23	.85	29	.85	32	.85	35	.85	35	.85	35	.85	39	.88	38	.90	34	.92	35	.92	37	.812	29.7	.809
23d	.93	29	.93	30	.93	33	.93	36	.93	33	.93	33	.93	36	.95	33	.95	34	.95	39	.95	29	.922	32.6	.912
24th	1.00	36	1.00	37	1.00	37	1.00	34	1.00	38	.99	39	.99	32	.99	31	.99	32	.98	32	.97	34	.971	32.8	.960
25th	.53	37	.53	40	.53	33	.51	35	.52	31	.55	32	.55	40	.56	30	.56	34	.57	35	.59	36	.640	34.2	.625
26th	.62	40	.60	38	.59	38	.59	37	.56	34	.52	31	.50	35	.50	37	.47	35	.47	36	.47	36	.570	35.7	.550
27th	.20	36	.20	35	.20	34	.20	40	.20	39	.20	34	.20	40	.20	43	.20	39	.20	37	.20	37	.272	36.2	.261
28th	.18	40	.16	40	.16	41	.14	39	.11	40	.10	43	.10	43	.12	41	.12	42	.15	42	.17	41	.178	39.6	.158
29th	.46	43	.49	41	.51	44	.52	41	.52	41	.55	41	.57	43	.57	40	.58	36	.58	36	.58	36	.410	40.2	.380
30th	.65	38	.65	38	.65	42	.70	40	.72	40	.74	43	.73	41	.72	42	.72	42	.72	41	.72	40	.661	39.5	.631
Means	.726	34.5	.728	35.8	.736	36.0	.732	36.5	.725	36.1	.727	36.4	.724	36.6	.732	34.8	.735	34.8	.733	35.1	.732	34.0	.728	34.1	
B. at 32°	29.710		29.709		29.716		29.711		29.705		29.706		29.703		29.715		29.718		29.716		29.717		29.713		

HOURLY ABSTRACT OF THE READINGS OF THE BAROMETER AND ATTACHED THERMOMETER AT VAN RENSSELAER HARBOR,
In December, 1853, in Lat. 78° 37′, Long. 70° 53′ W. of Greenwich.
Mercurial Barometer in house on deck. 29 inches +. Readings in English inches and degrees of Fahrenheit.

Day.	1h.		2h.		3h.		4h.		5h.		6h.		7h.		8h.		9h.		10h.		11h.		Noon.		13h.	
	Inch.	°	Inch.	°	Inch.	°	Inch.	°	Inch.	°	Inch	°	Inch.	°	Inch.	°	Inch.	°	Inch.	°	Inch.	°	Inch.	°	Inch.	°
1st	.73	37	.73	37	.73	35	.73	36	.75	35	.75	35	.75	36	.74	37	.74	40	.71	39	.70	37	.66	37	.65	39
2d	.47	35	.47	34	.47	35	.47	33	.48	31	.48	33	.49	33	.49	34	.50	35	.50	33	.50	40	.52	43	.53	43
3d	.60	35	.60	37	.60	37	.60	37	.59	38	.60	39	.60	35	.60	34	.61	37	.63	35	.63	36	.64	37	.64	39
4th	.70	35	.71	37	.71	35	.72	32	.75	40	.75	43	.75	38	.75	38	.75	33	.75	35	.77	35	.80	37	.84	38
5th	.83	37	.80	34	.80	34	.80	34	.80	30	.80	35	.71	35	.78	33	.65	37	.64	37	.60	37	.59	38	.57	35
6th	.48	38	.48	38	.48	36	.46	34	.46	35	.45	35	.45	35	.45	39	.45	34	.45	36	.45	34	.42	35	.43	34
7th	.57	34	.57	35	.57	35	.60	35	.59	30	.59	27	.60	28	.62	25	.66	31	.68	31	.69	25	.69	26	.68	28
8th	.75	29	.75	33	.75	32	.75	32	.75	34	.72	27	.72	24	.71	29	.72	31	.72	32	.72	30	.72	32	.73	33
9th	.65	28	.65	25	.65	24	.65	23	.67	27	.67	22	.67	25	.65	25	.70	29	.69	25	.69	24	.70	27	.69	25
10th	.76	37	.80	36	.81	37	.82	36	.80	35	.80	36	.82	37	.82	37	.83	36	.83	37	.85	35	.85	36	.85	34
11th	.95	40	.95	38	.95	40	.95	35	.94	34	.90	32	.90	32	.85	36	.85	36	.87	40	.85	35	.84	37	.82	37
12th	.88	36	.88	34	.87	33	.87	31	.90	36	.94	32	.94	29	.95	32	.95	35	.97	39	1.00	35	1.00	32	1.00	34
13th	1.03	34	1.03	31	1.03	31	1.03	33	1.04	31	1.03	33	1.03	32	1.03	33	1.03	34	1.03	34	1.02	33	1.02	34	1.01	36
14th	1.03	37	1.03	37	1.03	37	1.03	37	1.02	32	1.02	38	1.02	36	1.02	45	1.02	36	1.02	35	1.02	35	1.02	36	1.02	36
15th	1.03	36	1.03	36	1.03	32	1.03	33	.97	28	.97	32	.95	32	.93	32	.91	34	.90	35	.87	34	.86	31	.86	29
16th	.86	31	.86	24	.86	22	.86	25	.85	23	.85	24	.85	27	.85	41	.85	34	.85	33	.85	32	.85	33	.86	33
17th	.80	38	.80	37	.80	38	.80	37	.80	35	.80	32	.81	32	.80	36	.80	39	.80	35	.80	36	.80	35	.81	37
18th	.86	33	.86	31	.87	31	.91	32	.93	33	.94	34	.97	36	1.00	36	1.00	35	1.00	35	1.02	35	1.04	36	1.03	36
19th	1.12	33	1.12	35	1.12	33	1.12	35	1.12	36	1.12	36	1.10	38	1.08	39	1.00	43	.97	39	.95	39	.94	40	.92	42
20th	.55	35	.50	35	.50	38	.50	38	.46	38	.46	39	.44	39	.42	43	.45	32	.43	32	.40	37	.47	33	.41	40
21st	.80	35	.83	34	.87	33	.90	34	.96	37	1.02	40	1.04	37	1.09	38	1.10	39	1.10	38	1.10	36	1.10	36	1.10	40
22d	.80	36	.75	35	.73	34	.70	34	.65	34	.57	34	.57	33	.50	36	.50	40	.49	38	.47	39	.43	44	.39	45
23d	.55	38	.60	42	.60	38	.60	40	.65	39	.67	40	.70	40	.74	44	.74	41	.76	41	.76	39	.76	37	.77	40
24th	.85	42	.90	42	.95	41	.97	43	.97	42	1.03	41	1.07	41	1.11	42	1.11	41	1.20	40	1.20	35	1.20	36	1.23	37
25th	1.40	39	1.40	39	1.40	39	1.40	41	1.37	41	1.32	42	1.28	36	1.25	36	1.25	36	1.24	36	1.23	39	1.23	31	1.17	41
26th	1.25	35	1.25	37	1.25	36	1.25	35	1.27	35	1.27	36	1.27	36	1.27	37	1.27	41	1.27	43	1.27	40	1.27	41	1.19	39
27th	.86	39	.84	36	.80	37	.75	38	.65	39	.60	37	.55	40	.50	40	.49	44	.40	46	.40	45	.40	40	.25	40
28th	.15	45	.20	42	.25	42	.28	39	.30	37	.32	31	.40	33	.45	37	.45	43	.45	37	.54	39	.56	39	.57	26
29th	1.30	45	1.33	43	1.35	44	1.35	45	1.37	44	1.39	44	1.40	43	1.44	43	1.45	40	1.45	40	1.45	41	1.45	40	1.48	41
30th	1.45	36	1.40	35	1.40	35	1.40	33	1.40	35	1.40	36	1.36	36	1.34	37	1.34	35	1.34	35	1.34	33	1.34	31	1.26	35
31st	1.15	39	1.15	40	1.15	40	1.15	41	1.10	41	1.10	40	1.08	40	1.07	43	1.07	39	1.05	40	1.00	42	.97	41	.90	41
Means	.845	36.4	.847	35.8	.851	35.3	.853	35.2	.850	35.0	.849	35.0	.848	34.6	.848	36.7	.846	36.8	.845	36.5	.843	35.9	.843	35.8	.828	36.5
B. at 32°	29.824		29.827		29.832		29.835		29.833		29.832		29.832		29.826		29.824		29.824		29.823		29.824		29.807	

Day.	14h.		15h.		16h.		17h.		18h.		19h.		20h.		21h.		22h.		23h.		Midn't.		Means.		B. 32°.
	Inch.	°	Inch.	°	Inch.	°	Inch.	°	Inch.	°	Inch.	°	Inch.	°	Inch	°	Inch.	°	Inch.	°	Inch.	°	Inch.	°	Inch.
1st	.65	39	.60	41	.60	43	.60	40	.60	40	.58	43	.58	39	.58	37	.56	36	.50	34	.50	36	.655	37.8	.631
2d	.52	38	.52	38	.55	42	.60	40	.60	40	.60	42	.61	42	.60	45	.61	41	.59	39	.59	40	.532	37.9	.508
3d	.64	38	.64	37	.64	39	.70	40	.73	43	.73	48	.73	48	.70	37	.70	35	.70	35	.71	35	.648	38.0	.623
4th	.84	38	.85	40	.85	41	.90	37	.90	37	.90	41	.90	36	.89	35	.88	35	.85	36	.85	36	.807	37.0	.785
5th	.55	37	.55	40	.55	40	.55	35	.53	35	.53	36	.53	37	.52	38	.52	38	.53	37	.54	38	.636	36.1	.616
6th	.43	34	.43	34	.43	37	.42	34	.45	34	.46	35	.46	31	.48	31	.49	38	.52	29	.52	30	.458	34.6	.442
7th	.70	30	.70	35	.72	34	.75	33	.75	33	.75	33	.75	33	.78	34	.75	33	.75	32	.75	30	.677	31.2	.670
8th	.74	34	.74	33	.75	34	.70	32	.70	32	.68	31	.68	31	.67	31	.66	31	.66	36	.66	31	.715	31.4	.707
9th	.70	25	.70	26	.70	28	.75	33	.75	34	.75	38	.75	36	.75	34	.75	32	.75	34	.75	36	.700	28.6	.700
10th	.85	36	.87	40	.87	41	.92	40	.92	39	.92	39	.92	41	.94	40	.94	40	.94	42	.94	41	.861	37.8	.837
11th	.82	36	.82	37	.82	36	.83	38	.82	34	.82	36	.82	37	.83	37	.84	35	.85	36	.85	35	.864	36.2	.844
12th	1.00	35	1.00	34	1.00	36	1.03	36	1.04	35	1.04	35	1.04	32	1.04	33	1.04	25	1.04	26	1.04	34	.978	33.3	.965
13th	1.01	36	1.01	38	1.00	40	1.00	36	1.00	32	1.00	37	1.00	37	1.00	35	1.00	36	1.01	35	1.01	37	1.017	34.5	1.001
14th	1.02	36	1.03	33	1.03	35	1.03	37	1.02	34	1.02	38	1.00	30	.99	27	.98	28	.97	30	.97	32	1.015	33.9	1.000
15th	.86	26	.86	37	.85	32	.85	36	.85	34	.85	29	.85	30	.86	37	.86	36	.85	34	.85	35	.905	32.9	.893
16th	.87	35	.87	30	.86	39	.84	39	.84	31	.84	34	.82	32	.80	33	.80	33	.80	36	.80	37	.843	31.7	.834
17th	.81	38	.82	31	.82	27	.83	29	.83	30	.83	31	.83	32	.83	30	.83	23	.84	30	.84	32	.814	33.3	.802
18th	1.03	35	1.03	38	1.05	38	1.10	31	1.10	39	1.10	39	1.10	41	1.12	37	1.12	36	1.12	34	1.12	33	1.017	35.2	.999
19th	.90	46	.90	45	.88	42	.85	38	.82	39	.80	44	.74	35	.62	41	.62	39	.62	42	.62	49	.919	39.5	.889
20th	.41	39	.45	38	.46	40	.55	43	.57	45	.60	42	.65	37	.75	35	.80	32	.80	34	.82	34	.535	37.4	.512
21st	1.05	39	1.10	39	1.10	41	1.06	37	1.04	36	1.02	43	1.00	40	.95	40	.90	35	.80	34	.75	33	.991	37.2	.968
22d	.36	42	.36	44	.36	44	.35	41	.36	37	.40	42	.41	35	.42	43	.45	36	.47	38	.50	40	.500	38.5	.473
23d	.80	38	.80	39	.80	44	.82	41	.82	40	.82	42	.82	42	.85	41	.86	40	.86	41	.87	44	.751	40.4	.720
24th	1.25	34	1.27	27	1.31	39	1.34	35	1.35	35	1.35	36	1.35	34	1.33	39	1.33	35	1.35	35	1.35	37	1.182	37.8	1.156
25th	1.17	37	1.19	36	1.17	42	1.19	39	1.19	37	1.18	35	1.18	34	1.20	35	1.20	40	1.23	34	1.25	35	1.254	37.5	1.229
26th	1.14	38	1.13	40	1.12	43	1.06	40	1.05	42	1.02	43	1.00	41	.95	40	.95	39	.90	37	.87	34	1.148	38.7	1.120
27th	.21	42	.20	43	.17	44	.14	43	.09	40	.08	40	.06	47	.05	45	.10	49	.15	47	.15	46	.370	42.0	.334
28th	.67	40	.74	27	.81	32	.90	31	.94	35	1.00	40	1.05	30	1.12	37	1.15	36	1.20	40	1.27	40	.657	36.6	.636
29th	1.48	36	1.49	38	1.51	35	1.50	31	1.50	30	1.50	35	1.49	37	1.50	36	1.50	38	1.48	38	1.45	36	1.442	39.3	1.413
30th	1.25	35	1.25	36	1.25	39	1.22	38	1.21	40	1.20	42	1.17	40	1.17	38	1.17	39	1.15	41	1.15	39	1.290	36.6	1.268
31st	.85	39	.84	39	.82	40	.77	39	.73	41	.75	36	.75	36	.72	(37)	.72	(39)	.67	(39)	.65	(41)	.925	39.7	.894
Means	.825	36.5	.831	36.5	.834	38.3	.844	36.8	.842	36.5	.843	38.2	.840	36.5	.839	36.7	.841	35.7	.837	36.0	.838	36.6	.842	36.2	
B. at 32°	29.804		29.810		29.808		29.822		29.821		29.817		29.819		29.818		29.822		29.817		29.817		29.821		

HOURLY ABSTRACT OF THE READINGS OF THE BAROMETER AND ATTACHED THERMOMETER AT VAN RENSSELAER HARBOR,
In January, 1854, in Lat. 78° 37′, Long. 70° 53′ W. of Greenwich.

Mercurial Barometer in house on deck. 29 inches +. Readings in English inches and degrees of Fahrenheit.

Day.	1h.		2h.		3h.		4h.		5h.		6h.		7h.		8h.		9h.		10h.		11h.		Noon.		13h.	
	Inch.	°	Inch.	°	Inch.	°	Inch.	°	Inch.	°	Inch.	°	Inch.	°	Inch.	°	Inch.	°	Inch.	°	Inch.	°	Inch.	°	Inch.	°
1st	.65	42	.65	43	.65	43	.65	42	.64	42	.64	40	.64	40	.64	40	.63	39	.61	41	.61	42	.61	43	.60	40
2d	.56	40	.55	42	.55	43	.55	42	.55	41	.55	41	.55	44	.55	43	.61	43	.60	42	.60	41	.60	40	.64	37
3d	.70	38	.70	40	.68	39	.65	40	.62	43	.60	43	.56	45	.56	52	.56	48	.52	42	.50	39	.48	35	.43	37
4th	.35	36	.35	38	.35	39	.35	39	.35	40	.35	40	.34	40	.30	42	.30	39	.30	38	.30	35	.30	35	.30	39
5th	.40	36	.40	36	.42	37	.42	37	.44	37	.44	37	.46	37	.47	37	.48	37	.51	36	.52	34	.52	35	.50	36
6th	.45	42	.45	43	.45	43	.45	44	.41	40	.45	41	.47	39	.48	46	.49	42	.51	43	.52	46	.55	46	.57	36
7th	.74	43	.74	43	.74	43	.74	43	.74	43	.74	43	.74	44	.76	44	.76	42	.79	41	.79	37	.80	33	.73	39
8th	.80	40	.80	43	.80	43	.80	43	.80	45	.81	44	.81	48	.81	47	.77	46	.77	43	.75	42	.75	41	.75	42
9th	.90	40	.90	39	.90	40	.90	40	.90	39	.90	39	.92	39	.92	39	.94	36	.94	43	.93	42	.93	47	.95	50
10th	.75	39	.72	41	.72	40	.72	39	.72	36	.72	43	.72	50	.72	47	.70	41	.70	43	.70	37	.70	45	.70	65
11th	.63	39	.63	39	.62	37	.61	38	.60	35	.61	34	.55	40	.50	40	.56	37	.56	41	.55	41	.55	46	.55	35
12th	.45	50	.45	38	.47	37	.50	34	.50	32	.50	26	.50	25	.50	29	.50	37	.50	36	.50	36	.50	31	.51	37
13th	.69	39	.68	32	.68	36	.68	37	.70	35	.70	28	.70	30	.70	35	.70	39	.70	39	.70	40	.67	38	.69	35
14th	.53	26	.52	26	.52	28	.52	29	.55	28	.55	26	.53	24	.53	26	.53	28	.53	28	.53	29	.53	29	.51	29
15th	.40	23	.40	21	.40	21	.35	17	.35	22	.35	17	.34	10	.34	13	.28	13	.28	20	.26	14	.33	17	.37	15
16th	.50	13	.50	12	.50	9	.50	9	.50	17	.53	14	.53	14	.55	16	.55	12	.55	4	.55	12	.55	16	.55	13
17th	.60	10	.60	7	.60	19	.60	14	.60	20	.61	16	.60	11	.51	14	.57	9	.56	6	.56	11	.55	17	.55	15
18th	.56	19	.58	14	.56	15	.58	24	.56	14	.58	10	.58	11	.60	13	.60	21	.60	18	.60	21	.60	13	.62	13
19th	.57	12	.57	9	.57	10	.58	(9)	.57	9	.57	7	.57	8	.57	7	.57	15	.57	15	.57	19	.57	20	.57	18
20th	.70	8	.70	9	.70	8	.70	10	.69	17	.69	13	.69	9	.69	10	.69	18	.67	13	.65	12	.64	14	.64	10
21st	.45	12	.45	11	.45	12	.45	19	.34	13	.34	15	.34	21	.34	26	.34	27	.34	26	.34	27	.27	29	.26	22
22d	.25	27	.27	27	.27	29	.27	27	.27	21	.27	28	.27	21	.27	25	.27	28	.27	29	.27	30	.27	30	.28	29
*23d	.10	16	.10	15	.08	14	.05	19	.05	15	.05	14	.05	19	.05	25	*.97	26	*.92	24	*.87	22	*.86	22	*.86	24
*24th	*.95	30	*.95	25	*.95	28	*.95	30	*.95	31	*.97	29	*.97	29	*.97	27	*.97	28	*.97	29	*.95	23	*.95	27	.00	26
*25th	*.98	26	*.97	19	*.95	22	*.95	28	*.95	28	*.95	29	*.95	30	*.95	34	*.95	39	*.95	30	*.95	26	*.95	24	*.92	25
26th	.00	33	.00	32	.00	31	.00	31	.09	30	.06	30	.06	28	.08	27	.08	27	.08	20	.10	23	.10	27	.15	30
27th	.21	32	.21	31	.21	31	.21	34	.21	30	.21	29	.21	30	.20	31	.18	32	.18	26	.18	27	.18	30	.19	30
28th	.21	24	.21	22	.21	24	.21	26	.22	27	.22	25	.22	22	.22	28	.25	27	.25	26	.25	22	.25	19	.25	22
29th	.30	23	.30	19	.30	19	.30	17	.32	18	.32	20	.32	20	.32	23	.40	23	.35	17	.35	21	.37	22	.38	22
30th	.50	25	.49	23	.49	23	.49	22	.49	16	.50	14	.50	15	.50	16	.50	21	.50	20	.50	21	.50	19	.50	21
31st	.50	27	.50	22	.50	20	.50	19	.50	21	.50	24	.50	20	.50	21	.57	27	.57	26	.55	24	.57	25	.57	24
Means	.464	29.4	.463	27.8	.461	28.5	.459	29.1	.459	28.5	.460	27.7	.458	27.8	.455	29.8	.460	30.5	.456	29.2	.452	28.9	.452	29.5	.452	29.5
B. at 32°	29.461		29.465		29.461		29.457		29.459		29.462		29.460		29.452		29.454		29.454		29.451		29.450		29.450	

Day.	14h.		15h.		16h.		17h.		18h.		19h.		20h.		21h.		22h.		23h.		Midn't.		Means.		B. 32°.
	Inch.	°	Inch.	°	Inch.	°	Inch.	°	Inch.	°	Inch.	°	Inch.	°	Inch.	°	Inch.	°	Inch.	°	Inch.	°	Inch.	°	Inch.
1st	.60	39	.60	39	.60	42	.60	40	.60	41	.60	42	.60	39	.60	39	.60	40	.57	40	.55	39	.614	40.7	.582
2d	.70	39	.70	42	.72	40	.71	35	.74	39	.74	42	.74	42	.72	38	.70	39	.68	39	.69	39	.637	40.5	.605
3d	.43	34	.42	41	.42	37	.41	37	.41	42	.40	41	.40	39	.40	41	.41	38	.32	39	.35	39	.497	40.4	.465
4th	.30	40	.30	37	.30	37	.31	38	.32	38	.33	41	.34	39	.38	37	.39	36	.39	35	.39	36	.333	38.1	.307
5th	.50	39	.50	46	.50	49	.49	45	.49	45	.49	45	.46	44	.49	42	.49	42	.49	42	.44	42	.472	39.7	.443
6th	.57	46	.62	44	.62	47	.62	44	.63	43	.65	48	.66	46	.67	45	.68	45	.70	42	.75	43	.561	43.5	.521
7th	.73	39	.73	39	.73	39	.73	40	.75	40	.77	43	.80	45	.80	44	.80	41	.80	44	.80	43	.760	41.5	.726
8th	.75	46	.75	46	.75	40	.76	39	.77	41	.80	41	.82	40	.82	36	.82	37	.83	36	.85	37	.789	41.9	.753
9th	.95	50	.93	50	.90	46	.90	44	.90	41	.92	42	.90	40	.80	36	.77	36	.77	39	.77	40	.893	41.5	.858
10th	.72	68	.72	69	.73	68	.74	43	.74	44	.74	44	.74	45	.69	39	.69	39	.69	39	.69	39	.716	46.0	.670
11th	.55	35	.55	36	.55	41	.51	40	.51	43	.50	36	.46	37	.48	38	.50	37	.50	37	.50	38	.547	38.3	.521
12th	.55	38	.56	36	.56	33	.56	34	.60	33	.60	34	.63	36	.65	38	.65	38	.65	39	.65	39	.543	35.2	.525
13th	.70	36	.69	37	.70	40	.68	36	.65	30	.60	30	.56	28	.56	28	.56	27	.56	28	.57	26	.659	33.7	.645
14th	.51	21	.51	17	.51	21	.50	21	.48	23	.48	19	.45	21	.45	19	.45	15	.45	15	.43	20	.504	23.7	.517
15th	.37	20	.37	17	.37	16	.35	15	.35	15	.40	9	.40	12	.45	20	.45	13	.45	15	.49	14	.371	16.2	.403
16th	.55	19	.54	16	.54	12	.60	19	.60	18	.60	20	.60	18	.61	18	.62	22	.62	20	.62	11	.557	14.7	.594
17th	.55	18	.55	17	.55	16	.55	19	.55	13	.55	26	.55	25	.59	27	.59	26	.56	19	.56	24	.569	16.5	.601
18th	.62	21	.62	18	.62	19	.64	20	.65	21	.65	20	.62	19	.60	14	.60	14	.59	11	.59	11	.601	16.4	.633
19th	.56	20	.60	19	.60	19	.65	20	.65	21	.65	21	.65	22	.69	24	.69	15	.69	13	.69	12	.606	15.2	.641
20th	.64	18	.64	17	.64	21	.55	19	.55	25	.53	20	.49	16	.50	22	.50	18	.50	15	.50	13	.620	14.8	.657
21st	.22	24	.19	25	.19	29	.20	26	.20	25	.20	25	.20	23	.20	26	.20	27	.19	27	.19	20	.287	22.4	.303
22d	.28	34	.28	31	.26	28	.26	34	.26	32	.26	30	.26	25	.25	29	.25	26	.25	28	.25	22	.265	27.9	.267
*23d	*.86	31	*.86	30	*.86	28	*.86	27	*.86	29	*.86	30	*.86	26	*.89	30	*.92	33	*.94	30	*.94	26	*.947	23.9	*.959
*24th	.00	32	.00	29	.00	24	.00	30	.00	30	.00	32	.00	30	.00	29	.00	30	.00	30	.00	24	*.979	28.4	*.979
*25th	*.94	25	*.94	31	*.95	32	*.94	31	*.93	32	*.95	33	*.95	33	*.95	30	.00	28	.00	30	.00	30	*.955	28.9	*.954
26th	.16	29	.17	32	.17	30	.20	37	.21	31	.20	32	.20	30	.20	30	.20	37	.20	31	.20	31	.121	30.0	.117
27th	.19	30	.19	32	.19	33	.20	27	.20	31	.20	31	.20	32	.21	31	.21	31	.22	31	.22	31	.200	30.5	.194
28th	.25	23	.25	23	.25	21	.25	23	.25	24	.25	29	.25	23	.30	25	.30	24	.31	24	.31	21	.247	23.9	.259
29th	.38	24	.40	30	.44	30	.45	24	.45	30	.45	28	.50	27	.50	29	.50	27	.50	26	.50	32	.392	23.8	.404
30th	.50	21	.50	21	.50	21	.50	24	.50	23	.51	25	.51	23	.51	24	.50	26	.50	27	.50	26	.500	21.5	.518
31st	.60	25	.60	27	.60	25	.60	26	.60	31	.60	31	.60	31	.58	31	.55	25	.55	27	.55	27	.553	25.2	.561
Means	.459	31.7	.461	32.1	.462	31.7	.462	30.9	.465	31.4	.467	31.9	.465	30.8	.469	30.9	.471	30.1	.467	29.6	.469	28.9	.461	29.8	
B. at 32°	29.451		29.451		29.454		29.455		29.457		29.459		29.459		29.462		29.467		29.464		29.468		29.458		

HOURLY ABSTRACT OF THE READINGS OF THE BAROMETER AND ATTACHED THERMOMETER AT VAN RENSSELAER HARBOR, In February, 1854, in Lat. 78° 37′, Long. 70° 53′ W. of Greenwich.

Mercurial Barometer in house on deck. 29 inches +. Readings in English inches and degrees of Fahrenheit.

Day.	1h.		2h.		3h.		4h.		5h.		6h.		7h.		8h.		9h.		10h.		11h.		Noon.		13h.	
	Inch.	°	Inch.	°	Inch.	°	Inch.	°	Inch.	°	Inch.	°	Inch.	°	Inch.	°	Inch.	°	Inch.	°	Inch.	°	Inch.	°	Inch.	°
1st	.55	27	.55	22	.50	21	.50	20	.50	21	.50	20	.50	20	.50	22	.51	26	.51	17	.49	18	.45	25	.50	25
2d	.62	28	.62	29	.62	23	.62	21	.65	20	.65	17	.65	20	.65	22	.72	25	.72	24	.72	26	.72	25	.70	24
3d	.52	26	.48	26	.46	21	.43	20	.43	21	.41	21	.39	20	.38	24	.38	25	.40	19	.40	18	.40	18	.40	23
4th	.60	25	.60	25	.62	24	.62	24	.67	16	.67	15	.67	21	.69	21	.70	27	.70	20	.70	15	.68	16	.68	20
5th	.52	16	.50	16	.50	15	.47	11	.40	6	.38	5	.35	5	.33	15	.34	16	.30	16	.30	14	.25	17	.25	15
6th	.30	15	.30	17	.30	16	.30	10	.40	9	.43	8	.43	4	.50	19	.50	18	.50	18	.51	12	.52	15	.55	20
7th	.65	18	.66	17	.66	16	.66	14	.66	18	.67	19	.67	21	.68	20	.80	21	.80	22	.80	22	.80	15	.90	17
8th	1.22	26	1.22	25	1.22	24	1.22	24	1.40	17	1.40	25	1.40	24	1.40	26	1.40	20	1.40	9	1.35	9	1.30	13	1.22	14
9th	.60	24	.60	24	.60	27	.60	26	.67	16	.65	8	.60	6	.60	16	.60	18	.60	18	.60	20	.60	25	.60	16
10th	.45	17	.45	14	.43	16	.47	18	.60	24	.55	16	.60	15	.65	15	.65	12	.68	4	.75	10	.78	12	.79	16
11th	.88	21	.88	20	.86	20	.86	17	.85	16	.83	18	.80	18	.80	23	.80	24	.80	22	.80	20	.80	22	.77	24
12th	1.03	22	1.04	20	1.07	19	1.08	21	1.10	19	1.15	20	1.20	24	1.20	24	1.20	23	1.20	23	1.25	27	1.25	29	1.23	26
13th	1.15	22	1.15	21	1.10	20	1.10	18	1.05	22	1.03	23	1.00	23	.96	21	.90	21	.90	21	.90	21	.88	26	.90	35
14th	.94	21	.94	18	.94	17	.95	16	.93	24	.95	20	.97	20	.97	24	.95	20	.95	23	.90	24	.85	24	.85	27
15th	.40	27	.40	28	.35	27	.35	26	.40	25	.46	21	.46	23	.46	24	.35	24	.35	24	.40	25	.40	26	.46	28
16th	.86	22	.88	22	.88	19	.88	19	.90	20	.90	31	.94	29	.95	30	.99	29	.99	29	.99	29	.99	27	.99	33
17th	1.01	35	1.02	33	1.04	32	1.04	33	1.00	31	1.02	33	1.02	31	1.04	32	1.03	32	1.02	36	1.02	36	1.00	35	.85	31
*18th	.39	32	.30	29	.25	30	.20	27	.15	26	.13	27	.10	28	.05	29	.02	33	.00	31	*.95	30	*.93	31	*.93	37
*19th	*.90	34	*.90	35	*.91	33	*.91	33	*.91	32	*.91	31	*.91	31	*.92	35	*.88	35	*.86	33	*.84	30	*.90	28	*.90	29
20th	.14	34	.14	30	.14	31	.17	33	.20	34	.22	33	.25	33	.27	30	.25	30	.27	30	.27	29	.30	29	.30	29
21st	.25	30	.23	28	.21	29	.18	30	.15	29	.12	27	.10	28	.10	30	.11	31	.15	33	.16	33	.25	31	.25	31
22d	.32	31	.35	33	.35	35	.35	32	.35	31	.35	30	.40	30	.40	31	.41	32	.44	25	.45	28	.48	28	.48	31
23d	.62	32	.63	30	.63	28	.63	27	.63	25	.63	23	.64	23	.66	24	.62	23	.65	25	.65	26	.68	31	.68	32
24th	.82	27	.83	27	.85	28	.86	28	.86	27	.86	28	.90	28	.95	30	1.05	33	1.05	33	1.05	27	1.06	28	1.10	29
25th	1.23	23	1.21	21	1.21	21	1.21	23	1.15	24	1.16	25	1.17	26	1.15	29	1.08	26	1.08	28	1.06	28	1.05	33	1.00	31
26th	.50	17	.49	19	.45	18	.45	18	.44	18	.42	20	.42	20	.38	20	.40	20	.40	20	.35	24	.35	22	.34	23
27th	.50	23	.50	23	.55	24	.55	25	.57	25	.57	26	.60	23	.60	28	.60	28	.62	21	.60	18	.60	23	.60	23
28th	.60	18	.60	18	.60	16	.60	20	.60	19	.60	18	.60	20	.60	23	.60	27	.60	25	.60	22	.58	24	.60	25
Means	.627	24.7	.624	24.0	.618	23.2	.616	22.6	.629	22.0	.629	21.7	.634	21.9	.637	24.5	.637	25.0	.641	23.2	.638	22.9	.637	24.2	.636	25.5
B. at 32°	29.637		29.636		29.632		29.632		29.646		29.647		29.651		29.647		29.646		29.655		29.653		29.648		29.644	

Day.	14h.		15h.		16h.		17h.		18h.		19h.		20h.		21h.		22h.		23h.		Midn't.		Means.		B. 32°.
	Inch.	°	Inch.	°	Inch.	°	Inch.	°	Inch.	°	Inch.	°	Inch.	°	Inch.	°	Inch.	°	Inch.	°	Inch.	°	Inch.	°	Inch.
1st	.50	26	.50	25	.52	22	.51	24	.51	26	.51	30	.51	27	.61	26	.60	29	.62	30	.62	27	.524	24.0	.536
2d	.70	23	.71	24	.70	27	.70	28	.70	28	.70	25	.67	25	.66	26	.66	26	.66	27	.66	24	.674	24.5	.684
3d	.40	24	.45	23	.45	22	.48	24	.50	27	.54	26	.57	26	.60	27	.60	27	.60	25	.60	23	.469	23.2	.483
4th	.68	17	.65	12	.63	12	.62	14	.62	16	.62	20	.63	21	.60	16	.60	19	.60	20	.55	19	.642	19.0	.667
5th	.25	16	.23	15	.24	13	.24	20	.24	20	.26	27	.28	24	.28	15	.28	14	.32	11	.33	15	.327	14.9	.363
6th	.56	17	.57	21	.58	20	.63	20	.65	24	.65	25	.65	24	.65	24	.65	27	.68	7	.70	8	.521	16.6	.553
7th	.90	16	1.15	16	1.05	21	1.07	21	1.12	27	1.15	28	1.16	27	1.23	25	1.23	23	1.25	22	1.30	22	.917	20.3	.938
8th	1.22	14	1.22	18	1.22	17	1.16	16	1.11	20	1.09	23	1.06	21	1.00	24	1.00	19	.95	17	.90	18	1.212	19.3	1.236
9th	.60	14	.60	22	.60	20	.58	19	.54	19	.54	19	.48	19	.46	17	.46	22	.45	20	.43	18	.569	18.9	.595
10th	.80	24	.82	30	.93	18	.91	31	.91	32	.91	30	.91	25	.95	23	.95	25	.95	22	.93	20	.742	19.5	.766
11th	.77	22	.80	24	.80	24	.85	25	.87	24	.90	23	.90	21	.95	22	.95	26	1.00	24	1.00	23	.855	21.8	.874
12th	1.27	28	1.30	30	1.30	28	1.33	29	1.33	27	1.33	27	1.28	22	1.28	21	1.26	24	1.24	25	1.20	28	1.213	24.4	1.223
13th	.90	36	.90	25	.90	24	.90	24	.95	30	.95	35	.95	32	.95	32	.95	25	.95	22	.95	22	.970	25.0	.979
14th	.80	26	.78	31	.73	28	.73	28	.73	30	.73	31	.73	31	.60	28	.58	30	.50	30	.50	30	.812	25.1	.821
15th	.53	24	.59	30	.60	30	.68	30	.70	28	.75	32	.75	30	.76	32	.76	30	.80	25	.80	26	.540	26.9	.544
16th	.97	34	.97	38	.99	35	.99	33	1.00	40	1.00	42	1.00	37	1.00	35	1.00	35	1.01	35	1.01	37	.962	30.8	.956
17th	.87	32	.84	32	.80	28	.75	23	.70	26	.68	28	.65	31	.60	31	.56	33	.50	32	.45	33	.855	31.6	.847
*18th	*.93	37	*.93	37	*.93	45	*.98	38	*.95	31	*.95	31	*.95	29	*.94	38	*.94	38	*.92	35	*.91	34	.030	32.6	.018
*19th	*.95	30	.00	34	.00	36	.03	38	.05	38	.05	38	.05	36	.06	36	.10	30	.11	35	.12	35	*.965	33.5	*.952
20th	.25	34	.25	35	.25	33	.27	33	.27	29	.27	35	.27	33	.25	32	.25	32	.25	32	.25	31	.240	31.8	.232
21st	.25	31	.25	31	.25	32	.29	32	.29	31	.29	28	.27	27	.27	29	.27	28	.27	34	.30	33	.219	30.2	.214
22d	.48	32	.51	34	.52	32	.55	34	.55	35	.56	32	.56	28	.55	30	.55	32	.60	32	.60	32	.465	31.3	.457
23d	.68	33	.70	32	.70	32	.70	28	.74	27	.74	28	.75	29	.76	28	.77	28	.77	26	.80	24	.686	27.7	.688
24th	1.10	27	1.10	25	1.10	26	1.15	25	1.15	27	1.19	28	1.23	31	1.24	32	1.24	31	1.24	30	1.24	29	1.051	28.5	1.051
25th	1.00	30	.95	32	.92	30	.90	24	.84	20	.89	20	.70	19	.65	15	.61	14	.57	18	.54	14	.972	23.9	.984
26th	.34	21	.34	22	.34	22	.40	26	.40	27	.40	26	.43	26	.43	23	.45	23	.48	20	.48	21	.412	21.5	.430
27th	.60	23	.60	24	.60	25	.60	20	.65	25	.65	26	.65	23	.65	22	.62	21	.61	21	.60	21	.595	23.4	.608
28th	.63	26	.65	25	.62	25	.60	18	.59	19	.55	20	.55	22	.56	24	.58	24	.58	22	.58	23	.595	21.8	.613
Means	.640	25.6	.656	26.7	.655	26.0	.664	25.9	.666	26.9	.673	28.0	.664	26.6	.662	26.2	.660	26.2	.660	25.0	.655	24.6	.644	24.7	
B. at 32°	29.648		29.661		29.662		29.671		29.671		29.674		29.669		29.668		29.666		29.669		29.666		29.654		

Hourly Abstract of the Readings of the Barometer and Attached Thermometer at Van Rensselaer Harbor,
In March, 1854, in Lat. 78° 37′, Long. 70° 53′ W. of Greenwich.

Mercurial Barometer in house on deck. 29 inches +. Readings in English inches and degrees of Fahrenheit.

Day.	1h.		2h.		3h.		4h.		5h.		6h.		7h.		8h.		9h.		10h.		11h.		Noon.		13h.	
	Inch.	°	Inch.	°	Inch.	°	Inch.	°	Inch.	°	Inch.	°	Inch.	°	Inch.	°	Inch.	°	Inch.	°	Inch.	°	Inch.	°	Inch.	°
1st	.56	21	.55	20	.55	21	.56	20	.55	20	.55	20	.55	20	.50	20	.50	22	.50	20	.50	22	.46	20	.46	23
2d	.56	20	.56	18	.60	18	.61	19	.65	18	.65	17	.70	12	.70	15	.70	21	.70	17	.72	19	.74	22	.75	26
3d	.92	16	.94	14	.95	14	.97	15	.99	14	1.00	15	1.05	16	1.10	18	1.15	20	1.16	17	1.17	20	1.20	22	1.20	1
4th	1.25	13	1.35	12	1.35	14	1.36	12	1.38	13	1.38	13	1.40	14	1.40	16	1.45	23	1.45	23	1.45	15	1.45	15	1.43	13
5th	1.27	15	1.26	17	1.24	19	1.24	17	1.24	15	1.20	18	1.20	20	1.20	21	1.15	24	1.15	24	1.12	23	1.10	22	1.07	25
6th	1.00	15	.95	11	.95	11	.95	12	.95	13	.95	13	.95	14	.95	15	.95	24	.95	16	.93	14	.92	13	.90	11
7th	.80	21	.80	20	.80	21	.76	20	.75	17	.75	17	.72	11	.72	13	.72	12	.70	16	.72	19	.67	20	.65	19
8th	.60	10	.60	7	.60	8	.60	8	.60	7	.60	6	.60	8	.60	9	.64	11	.65	12	.66	21	.68	16	.68	15
9th	.72	19	.72	5	.72	4	.72	3	.72	10	.72	17	.72	10	.72	15	.74	20	.77	19	.77	19	.80	19	.80	18
10th	.84	7	.84	4	.84	2	.84	0	.84	2	.84	4	.84	0	.85	11	.87	8	.87	11	.87	10	.87	10	.85	8
11th	.80	11	.80	10	.80	9	.80	8	.80	7	.80	5	.80	7	.80	9	.78	12	.80	14	.80	13	.80	13	.80	16
12th	.70	3	.71	1	.71	0	.71	0	.71	3	.72	3	.72	5	.72	6	.74	9	.71	8	.65	13	.62	15	.62	7
13th	.53	2	.52	1	.52	0	.52	0	.52	0	.52	0	.52	2	.53	6	.54	12	.54	10	.54	10	.54	11	.52	18
14th	.50	8	.50	6	.50	4	.50	4	.50	-14	.48	-14	.45	5	.45	15	.45	12	.45	12	.42	14	.42	14	.41	14
15th	.41	7	.41	6	.41	2	.41	0	.40	- 1	.41	4	.42	7	.43	11	.45	10	.47	20	.47	21	.47	21	.50	21
16th	.65	11	.69	15	.69	13	.70	11	.72	12	.72	14	.76	16	.80	17	.82	21	.84	22	.84	17	.84	16	.85	20
17th	.96	11	.96	10	.96	11	.96	10	1.00	9	1.00	10	1.05	12	1.06	16	1.06	16	1.06	18	1.06	19	1.10	16	1.10	23
18th	1.10	4	1.07	2	1.07	2	1.07	1	1.07	2	1.07	3	.90	9	.90	12	.90	14	.90	14	.85	14	.85	13	.73	13
19th	.55	27	.55	25	.55	25	.55	24	.55	24	.57	22	.60	22	.62	21	.63	21	.65	23	.70	27	.80	24	.82	27
20th	1.11	22	1.12	22	1.10	24	1.07	20	1.06	19	1.08	15	1.08	16	1.05	18	1.05	20	1.02	19	.98	23	.90	23	.87	25
21st	.52	15	.52	16	.52	17	.66	18	.60	19	.60	18	.60	20	.60	21	.72	31	.72	30	.74	29	.74	27	.70	26
22d	.46	22	.46	21	.46	23	.46	24	.47	20	.49	20	.54	19	.56	24	.62	30	.69	31	.69	27	.69	27	.72	25
23d	.88	20	.88	19	.85	17	.85	17	.85	17	.85	19	.84	17	.83	17	.80	23	.80	18	.76	13	.81	18	.83	21
24th	.85	17	.82	15	.82	13	.82	14	.82	14	.82	13	.82	11	.80	20	.82	22	.82	21	.85	16	.86	14	.86	13
25th	.95	11	.97	8	.97	6	.97	6	.97	5	.97	7	.97	6	.97	10	1.00	12	1.02	12	1.04	16	1.05	23	1.09	23
26th	1.06	11	1.06	12	1.06	10	1.06	11	1.06	7	1.06	6	1.05	6	1.05	10	1.05	16	1.05	10	1.05	12	1.03	16	1.02	12
27th	.85	11	.85	11	.85	5	.85	4	.85	-3	.82	-10	.82	-12	.80	-8	.80	0	.80	7	.80	12	.80	15	.79	13
28th	.48	2	.45	0	.43	0	.42	0	.41	1	.40	3	.40	9	.40	15	.40	18	.40	20	.38	16	.38	18	.37	18
29th	.22	10	.20	8	.20	0	.20	-10	.18	9	.18	9	.16	1	.16	7	.16	8	.16	10	.16	11	.16	12	.16	15
30th	.30	2	.35	0	.38	0	.42	- 3	.44	3	.47	1	.50	5	.51	9	.54	10	.55	14	.56	14	.56	15	.60	18
31st	.64	12	.61	10	.60	7	.58	6	.58	6	.53	8	.50	7	.55	9	.55	12	.53	14	.51	17	.50	15	.50	3
Means	.743	12.8	.744	11.2	.744	10.3	.748	9.4	.750	9.3	.748	9.5	.750	10.2	.753	13.5	.766	16.6	.770	16.8	.766	17.3	.768	17.6	.763	17.1
B. at 32°	29.784		29.789		29.792		29.798		29.800		39.798		29.798		29.793		29.798		29.802		29.796		29.798		29.794	

Day.	14h.		15h.		16h.		17h.		18h.		19h.		20h.		21h.		22h.		23h.		Midn't.		Means.		B. 32°.
	Inch.	°	Inch.	°	Inch.	°	Inch.	°	Inch.	°	Inch.	°	Inch.	°	Inch.	°	Inch.	°	Inch.	°	Inch.	°	Inch.	°	Inch.
1st	.49	25	.49	25	.49	26	.50	26	.50	26	.52	25	.55	25	.52	22	.52	21	.55	21	.55	19	.519	22.1	.536
2d	.75	22	.76	23	.77	22	.78	20	.80	20	.80	21	.80	22	.89	23	.90	22	.90	20	.90	20	.737	19.9	.760
3d	1.18	6	1.21	19	1.23	8	1.23	9	1.25	10	1.25	10	1.30	10	1.32	13	1.34	14	1.34	14	1.35	12	1.158	13.6	1.197
4th	1.45	16	1.44	10	1.42	9	1.42	8	1.40	16	1.40	21	1.40	21	1.40	19	1.40	18	1.35	17	1.32	18	1.396	15.4	1.430
5th	1.07	25	1.07	24	1.05	20	1.05	17	1.05	19	1.05	20	1.05	21	1.05	20	1.05	20	1.03	16	1.00	16	1.123	19.9	1.146
6th	.90	9	.90	12	.90	12	.90	12	.90	13	.90	13	.90	14	.86	12	.86	12	.85	19	.84	18	.917	13.7	.957
7th	.65	19	.65	21	.65	22	.65	20	.65	20	.65	19	.65	12	.65	11	.64	9	.63	7	.62	12	.694	16.6	.726
8th	.68	17	.68	18	.68	15	.70	15	.70	11	.70	14	.70	14	.72	14	.72	13	.72	12	.73	10	.660	12.1	.705
9th	.80	18	.80	18	.80	19	.80	17	.80	17	.82	17	.83	15	.85	11	.85	15	.85	12	.85	10	.779	14.5	.816
10th	.85	9	.83	10	.83	10	.83	9	.83	9	.83	8	.83	10	.83	10	.83	10	.83	10	.83	9	.842	7.5	.897
11th	.80	16	.81	16	.81	16	.82	15	.82	14	.82	12	.82	10	.80	10	.80	7	.74	7	.70	3	.797	10.8	.844
12th	.65	17	.65	12	.65	14	.65	4	.65	6	.65	8	.65	8	.64	10	.55	3	.55	2	.53	2	.661	6.6	.720
13th	.55	15	.55	13	.55	15	.56	14	.56	10	.56	11	.56	10	.55	10	.55	10	.53	10	.52	10	.537	8.3	.590
14th	.41	16	.41	17	.41	16	.41	16	.41	14	.41	17	.41	15	.40	14	.40	13	.40	13	.40	10	.438	10.0	.487
15th	.50	17	.57	26	.57	23	.56	23	.56	21	.56	21	.56	18	.55	24	.55	17	.55	19	.55	14	.489	14.7	.526
16th	.85	19	.90	24	.90	23	.90	22	.90	21	.90	21	.90	20	.90	26	.92	20	.90	16	.92	14	.825	18.0	.853
17th	1.10	10	1.10	20	1.10	22	1.10	16	1.10	12	1.10	9	1.10	8	1.12	21	1.14	20	1.13	7	1.11	5	1.064	13.8	1.103
18th	.70	23	.70	23	.65	21	.65	20	.65	18	.64	18	.64	22	.60	22	.57	25	.57	23	.55	27	.808	14.4	.845
19th	.86	22	1.05	20	.95	23	.98	26	.99	26	1.05	23	1.07	26	1.09	24	1.10	20	1.10	20	1.10	22	.812	23.5	.825
20th	.85	25	.80	23	.75	20	.70	21	.66	21	.65	20	.64	19	.57	16	.57	15	.54	15	.53	12	.865	19.7	.889
21st	.70	32	.68	30	.65	30	.63	22	.62	20	.60	20	.58	18	.57	27	.51	31	.49	26	.47	25	.614	23.7	.627
22d	.70	27	.79	29	.80	23	.82	24	.84	22	.85	25	.85	23	.85	25	.85	25	.85	27	.86	22	.682	24.4	.692
23d	.83	22	.83	25	.83	24	.85	27	.85	30	.85	29	.85	28	.85	26	.86	21	.86	20	.86	13	.839	20.9	.860
24th	.86	14	.89	14	.90	14	.93	18	.94	17	.94	18	.95	18	.96	19	.96	17	.96	14	.96	12	.876	15.7	.909
25th	1.09	29	1.10	29	1.10	19	1.09	13	1.07	18	1.07	17	1.07	14	1.07	16	1.07	17	1.07	16	1.07	17	1.034	14.6	1.071
26th	1.02	14	1.00	14	1.00	15	.97	10	.97	12	.95	10	.95	10	.95	12	.90	7	.90	5	.90	2	1.007	10.4	1.055
27th	.78	16	.77	10	.77	12	.71	10	.67	4	.65	12	.64	9	.63	14	.57	10	.50	5	.50	3	.744	6.3	.804
28th	.37	19	.38	16	.38	14	.37	15	.37	11	.37	13	.37	13	.36	9	.30	2	.28	3	.24	-1	.379	9.7	.429
29th	.15	14	.15	14	.19	16	.21	15	.24	12	.24	10	.27	11	.30	12	.36	9	.30	9	.30	4	.209	9.0	.260
30th	.63	19	.65	16	.65	12	.65	9	.65	12	.69	5	.69	6	.65	14	.67	14	.67	14	.65	15	.560	9.2	.611
31st	.50	-1	.48	7	.45	6	.45	8	.45	9	.45	7	.48	12	.48	13	.48	11	.48	10	.50	20	.516	9.5	.567
Means	.765	17.8	.777	18.6	.770	17.5	.770	16.2	.769	15.8	.772	16.0	.776	15.5	.774	16.7	.767	15.1	.755	13.8	.749	12.7	.761	14.5	
B. at 32°	29.794		29.803		29.800		29.802		29.803		29.805		29.810		29.806		29.803		29.794		29.791		29.798		

HOURLY ABSTRACT OF THE READINGS OF THE BAROMETER AND ATTACHED THERMOMETER AT VAN RENSSELAER HARBOR, In April, 1854, in Lat. 78° 37′, Long. 70° 53′ W. of Greenwich.

Mercurial Barometer in house on deck. 29 inches +. Readings in English inches and degrees of Fahrenheit.

Day.	1h.		2h.		3h.		4h.		5h.		6h.		7h.		8h.		9h.		10h.		11h.		Noon.		13h.	
	Inch.	°	Inch.	°	Inch.	°	Inch.	°	Inch.	°	Inch.	°	Inch.	°	Inch.	°	Inch.	°	Inch.	°	Inch.	°	Inch.	°	Inch.	°
1st	.58	−2	.60	−7	.63	1	.68	1	.70	1	.69	3	.70	4	.72	7	.75	8	.75	6	.78	10	.80	10	.83	10
2d	.83	17	.83	6	.83	6	.83	8	.83	5	.85	1	.84	10	.83	16	.83	16	.83	18	.80	17	.80	17	.80	21
3d	...	...	...	...	...	...	...	...	...	...	...	...	...	...	...	...	...	...	...	...	...	...	...	...	.27	25
4th	...	...	...	...	...	...	...	...	.33	23	.33	23	.33	21	.33	17	.33	21	.33	27	.35	26	.35	26	.34	27
5th	.35	26	.33	26	.35	28	.33	28	.35	28	.35	29	.35	27	.35	31	.37	31	.37	31	.37	30	.37	33	.37	27
6th	.52	23	.63	24	.65	25	.68	26	.70	22	.71	20	.75	21	.79	25	.84	26	.86	27	.90	24	.94	26	.93	26
7th	1.15	23	1.15	21	1.15	18	1.15	15	1.20	19	1.20	20	1.20	25	1.18	22	1.26	27	1.33	29	1.33	29	1.33	29	1.21	27
8th	1.15	30	1.16	32	1.15	33	1.15	33	1.12	28	1.12	18	1.12	17	1.10	16	1.10	16	1.10	14	1.10	13	1.10	23	1.10	22
9th	1.10	22	1.10	22	1.10	22	1.08	21	1.04	21	1.07	22	1.06	20	1.05	25	1.05	31	1.05	30	1.05	31	1.05	34	.98	37
10th	1.15	31	1.15	31	1.15	31	1.15	31	1.15	27	1.15	26	1.15	23	1.21	30	1.25	36	1.25	34	1.25	34	1.24	23	1.25	23
11th	1.33	27	1.33	30	1.33	33	1.32	27	1.20	13	1.18	15	1.18	16	1.15	18	1.13	22	1.13	23	1.13	23	1.10	30	1.08	30
12th	.85	27	.85	23	.84	24	.84	20	.87	18	.89	17	.96	19	.96	23	.98	34	.98	37	.98	36	1.00	32	1.00	35
13th	1.04	30	1.04	34	1.03	35	1.03	34	1.03	24	1.02	24	1.00	28	1.00	30	1.00	31	.95	31	.95	31	.94	34	.95	33
14th	.80	25	.80	23	.80	21	.80	23	.80	24	.84	30	.84	29	.84	29	.84	23	.85	35	.88	38	.90	38	.90	39
15th	1.00	24	1.00	24	1.02	21	1.03	20	1.04	18	1.04	18	1.03	23	1.05	35	1.05	29	1.05	31	1.05	33	1.05	33	1.05	34
16th	.90	25	.90	25	.90	24	.93	25	.95	24	.98	31	1.03	35	1.06	38	1.10	39	1.10	39	1.10	40	1.10	42	1.13	39
17th	1.24	31	1.24	29	1.23	26	1.21	25	1.21	26	1.21	28	1.20	34	1.20	34	1.20	35	1.20	36	1.18	37	1.18	38	1.18	39
18th	1.14	32	1.14	26	1.14	25	1.14	23	1.15	19	1.15	24	1.16	19	1.20	35	1.20	31	1.23	31	1.22	34	1.25	35	1.25	40
19th	1.30	33	1.34	30	1.34	32	1.34	20	1.31	18	1.31	19	1.31	23	1.31	31	1.31	32	1.30	33	1.30	35	1.30	36	1.30	37
20th	1.30	26	1.30	24	1.30	24	1.30	20	1.35	20	1.34	19	1.36	21	1.35	23	1.36	36	1.36	34	1.36	34	1.35	35	1.35	35
21st	1.24	25	1.16	23	1.16	22	1.16	21	1.15	20	1.14	24	1.12	32	1.12	31	1.12	34	1.12	33	1.08	33	1.05	33	1.06	37
22d	.95	25	.95	22	.95	21	.95	23	.95	22	.95	22	.95	28	.95	29	.95	36	.95	36	.95	38	.95	38	.93	38
23d	.90	28	.90	29	.90	25	.90	25	.90	28	.90	28	.92	29	.94	30	.95	36	.97	37	.97	40	.97	40	.98	46
24th	.98	28	.96	25	.95	27	.92	26	.92	25	.92	29	.92	34	.90	32	.90	39	.90	38	.90	40	.88	43	.90	39
25th	.97	30	.97	28	.97	27	.97	25	.97	27	.97	29	.97	30	.97	30	1.00	32	1.00	34	1.00	36	1.00	37	1.00	39
26th	.95	26	.95	25	.95	24	.96	24	.96	27	.97	30	1.01	33	1.03	37	1.05	38	1.12	37	1.15	40	1.20	39	1.20	38
27th	1.28	37	1.28	37	1.31	28	1.29	30	1.25	33	1.25	35	1.25	35	1.25	33	1.15	36	1.15	40	1.12	40	1.09	40	1.09	40
28th	1.07	35	1.05	34	1.07	35	1.07	37	1.09	36	1.10	32	1.12	35	1.15	36	1.19	37	1.17	38	1.17	40	1.20	43	1.20	42
29th	1.03	34	1.03	36	1.00	37	1.00	36	.98	32	.95	32	.95	35	.93	33	.90	37	.92	39	.90	40	.90	38	.87	38
30th	.90	33	.90	32	.90	30	.90	32	.90	32	.90	31	.95	31	.97	32	.99	37	.99	38	.99	39	1.01	40	1.00	43
Means	.962	26.4	.963	25.3	.964	25.0	.964	24.2	.962	22.8	.964	23.5	.971	25.4	.976	28.1	.984	30.4	.989	31.4	.988	32.2	.990	33.0	.983	33.5
B. at 32°	29.968		29.971		29.973		29.975		29.978		29.977		29.979		29.977		29.979		29.981		29.978		29.978		29.970	

Day.	14h.		15h.		16h.		17h.		18h.		19h.		20h.		21h.		22h.		23h.		Midn't.		Means.		B. 32°.
	Inch.	°	Inch.	°	Inch.	°	Inch.	°	Inch.	°	Inch.	°	Inch.	°	Inch.	°	Inch.	°	Inch.	°	Inch.	°	Inch.	°	Inch.
1st	.82	10	.85	11	.90	11	.90	12	.90	14	.90	15	.92	17	.92	17	.92	15	.92	15	.92	11	.795	8.3	.848
2d	.73	20	.72	19	.71	22	.70	22	.69	25	.64	23	.65	24	...	...	...	...	...	...	...	...	.748	17.0	.779
3d	.28	25	.29	25	.31	23	.33	26	.35	27	.36	25	.39	27	.40	25	.36	25	.34	26	.33	17	.379	24.8	.388
4th	.38	25	.36	25	.38	27	.39	37	.39	38	.37	34	.38	34	.38	34	.36	35	.36	30	.33	30	.351	26.6	.356
5th	.37	28	.37	28	.40	29	.42	27	.44	29	.45	27	.47	28	.47	25	.51	27	.51	26	.50	20	.397	27.9	.398
6th	.93	27	.98	28	1.00	29	1.08	29	1.08	27	1.10	27	1.11	30	1.10	27	1.14	23	1.14	20	1.16	21	.905	25.1	.914
7th	1.18	25	1.15	25	1.15	26	1.16	23	1.16	22	1.16	21	1.16	24	1.16	23	1.16	24	1.16	25	1.16	27	1.192	23.7	1.205
8th	1.10	22	1.10	22	1.10	23	1.10	23	1.10	27	1.10	31	1.10	33	1.13	31	1.13	27	1.10	22	1.09	23	1.113	24.1	1.125
9th	1.00	36	1.04	34	1.05	33	1.07	33	1.09	29	1.10	27	1.10	32	1.15	35	1.15	36	1.15	33	1.18	30	1.077	29.0	1.076
10th	1.25	24	1.26	25	1.28	26	1.29	27	1.30	33	1.30	30	1.30	34	1.30	...	1.32	...	1.32	...	1.32	...	1.239	29.1	1.238
11th	1.08	37	1.05	35	1.03	32	1.00	30	1.00	30	1.00	29	1.00	30	1.00	30	.93	32	.90	35	.83	35	1.100	27.6	1.103
12th	1.02	36	1.04	37	1.05	36	1.03	34	1.04	35	1.04	30	1.04	28	1.02	29	1.00	28	1.03	29	1.03	29	.972	29.4	.969
13th	.95	34	.93	35	.90	36	.90	33	.88	33	.86	33	.86	34	.80	31	.80	32	.80	33	.80	32	.936	31.9	.927
14th	.90	37	.90	35	.93	27	.95	35	.96	33	.98	39	.98	35	.98	33	.98	32	1.00	33	1.00	35	.894	31.3	.886
15th	1.05	33	1.05	35	1.05	36	1.07	36	1.09	36	1.09	38	1.07	36	1.05	35	1.03	32	1.00	31	1.00	32	1.042	30.1	1.038
16th	1.13	40	1.13	40	1.15	39	1.10	42	1.12	44	1.22	41	1.23	39	1.22	33	1.23	34	1.25	32	1.25	31	1.092	35.0	1.075
17th	1.18	38	1.15	38	1.15	38	1.12	31	1.12	35	1.12	35	1.12	38	1.12	35	1.12	33	1.12	32	1.14	31	1.172	33.4	1.158
18th	1.25	37	1.28	35	1.28	33	1.32	34	1.34	32	1.35	34	1.35	34	1.32	35	1.30	35	1.30	32	1.30	34	1.240	31.2	1.233
19th	1.30	36	1.30	36	1.30	34	1.30	35	1.30	32	1.30	32	1.30	30	1.30	29	1.30	27	1.30	24	1.30	24	1.307	29.9	1.303
20th	1.35	34	1.35	34	1.32	33	1.30	33	1.30	33	1.30	32	1.30	34	1.25	33	1.25	34	1.18	35	1.18	35	1.311	30.0	1.307
21st	1.05	37	1.05	38	1.05	37	1.00	35	1.00	39	1.00	36	1.00	27	1.00	35	1.00	30	1.00	28	1.00	24	1.076	30.6	1.070
22d	.93	37	.93	37	.90	38	.90	35	.90	39	.90	37	.90	38	.88	36	.88	34	.88	33	.90	31	.926	32.2	.916
23d	.97	43	.97	40	.98	37	1.02	39	1.02	41	1.02	43	1.02	41	1.00	40	1.00	36	1.00	31	.95	29	.960	35.0	.943
24th	.90	37	.90	38	.90	37	.92	37	.93	35	.95	35	.95	35	.95	33	.95	32	.96	32	.96	30	.926	33.6	.912
25th	1.00	40	1.00	39	1.00	38	1.00	37	1.00	38	.96	38	.96	38	...	...	...	...	...	...	...	...	.979	33.5	.965
26th	1.20	35	1.20	37	1.20	37	1.22	39	1.25	36	1.25	37	1.25	36	1.25	37	1.28	36	1.25	36	1.25	36	1.129	34.2	1.113
27th	1.09	38	1.09	37	1.05	38	1.02	39	1.05	39	1.05	40	1.06	39	1.07	39	1.07	39	1.07	35	1.07	35	1.144	36.8	1.122
28th	1.19	41	1.19	39	1.18	37	1.14	35	1.14	36	1.14	38	1.14	38	1.14	37	1.10	38	1.07	38	1.04	34	1.130	37.1	1.108
29th	.84	40	.84	38	.84	37	.80	37	.80	37	.82	36	.83	36	.85	35	.85	33	.87	34	.90	34	.900	36.0	.880
30th	1.00	41	1.05	40	1.05	38	1.03	38	1.03	39	1.03	39	1.03	38	1.03	37	1.03	36	1.03	34	1.03	35	.985	36.0	.965
Means	.981	33.1	.984	32.8	.986	32.2	.986	32.4	.992	33.1	.995	32.7	.999	32.9	.994	32.0	.991	31.1	.985	30.0	.981	28.9	.981	29.7	
B. at 32°	29.969		29.973		29.976		29.976		29.980		29.983		29.987		29.985		29.984		29.981		29.980		29.977		

Hourly Abstract of the Readings of the Barometer and Attached Thermometer at Van Rensselaer Harbor,
In May, 1854, in Lat. 78° 37′, Long. 70° 53′ W. of Greenwich.

Mercurial Barometer in house on deck. 29 inches +. Readings in English inches and degrees of Fahrenheit.

Day.	1h.		2h.		3h.		4h.		5h.		6h.		7h.		8h.		9h.		10h.		11h.		Noon.		13h.	
	Inch.	°	Inch.	°	Inch.	°	Inch.	°	Inch.	°	Inch.	°	Inch.	°	Inch.	°	Inch.	°	Inch.	°	Inch.	°	Inch.	°	Inch.	°
1st	1.00	36	1.00	37	1.00	36	1.00	35	1.00	38	1.00	37	1.00	37	1.00	41	1.00	34	1.00	35	1.00	36	.95	34	.95	37
2d	.95	34	.92	28	.90	33	.90	51	.90	52	.90	57	.90	58	.90	48	.90	37	.90	35	.90	35	.90	35	.90	30
3d	.90	34	.90	38	.90	35	.90	38	.87	41	.87	55	.87	61	.87	55	.87	57	.85	58	.80	62	.75	60	.72	61
4th	.46	35	.46	28	.44	30	.42	44	.41	51	.41	58	.41	57	.41	58	.40	56	.40	56	.40	57	.34	52	.29	50
5th	.27	30	.27	30	.30	31	.30	54	.30	56	.32	56	.34	57	.37	55	.37	54	.40	42	.45	40	.46	37	.48	38
6th	.65	30	.65	30	.65	29	.65	30	.69	37	.75	57	.76	56	.76	57	.76	46	.76	46	.76	45	.75	44	.73	46
7th	.75	40	.77	48	.77	54	.78	56	.80	61	.80	64	.82	66	.85	68	.96	54	.97	52	1.00	50	1.00	50	1.00	47
8th	1.20	46	1.20	44	1.24	45	1.24	47	1.25	47	1.25	48	1.28	56	1.28	57	1.30	60	1.30	61	1.30	61	1.30	62	1.30	64
9th	1.33	50	1.33	52	1.33	49	1.33	51	1.35	55	1.33	56	1.30	55	1.27	55	1.27	62	1.25	61	1.23	59	1.23	60	1.20	57
10th	.87	57	.85	56	.85	57	.85	59	.85	59	.85	57	.85	58	.85	59	.84	60	.85	56	.85	58	.85	57	.85	58
11th	.78	61	.78	62	.75	62	.75	58	.75	58	.75	57	.75	57	.75	56	.76	57	.76	56	.72	58	.70	61	.70	60
12th	.71	48	.72	49	.74	50	.75	46	.79	47	.80	50	.80	51	.80	53	.85	56	.86	55	.87	53	.88	58	.90	59
13th	1.02	57	1.02	57	1.03	56	1.03	56	1.02	54	1.02	54	1.04	56	1.04	56	1.06	56	1.06	58	1.06	56	1.07	60	1.07	61
14th	.87	52	.87	54	.87	52	.87	57	.87	50	.87	52	.87	48	.87	51	.87	53	.87	52	.86	52	.84	51	.85	55
15th	.92	52	.92	54	.92	53	.92	56	.92	57	.92	56	.92	55	.92	54	.92	49	.92	47	.92	48	.93	46	.93	42
16th	.97	46	.97	45	.99	47	.99	46	1.00	45	1.02	49	1.04	48	1.06	46	1.07	47	1.07	45	1.07	42	1.07	39	1.07	43
17th	1.06	51	1.06	50	1.06	48	1.05	49	1.05	51	1.03	52	1.03	52	1.00	53	.96	54	.96	56	.96	52	.95	53	.95	55
18th	1.07	61	1.07	60	1.07	52	1.07	48	1.07	51	1.06	51	1.05	52	1.04	54	1.03	56	1.02	57	1.02	50	1.00	50	.98	54
19th	1.05	49	1.05	51	1.05	52	1.05	50	1.03	45	1.03	45	1.05	54	1.05	52	1.05	54	1.08	55	1.10	56	1.15	56	1.17	55
20th	1.24	46	1.24	47	1.24	47	1.24	46	1.24	45	1.24	45	1.24	45	1.23	45	1.25	46	1.25	48	1.25	52	1.25	53	1.27	55
21st	1.35	55	1.35	48	1.35	50	1.35	52	1.35	45	1.35	50	1.37	55	1.40	57	1.42	52	1.42	51	1.43	52	1.45	54	1.47	54
22d	1.50	55	1.50	54	1.50	56	1.52	54	1.52	53	1.52	56	1.52	57	1.52	58	1.50	55	1.45	54	1.45	57	1.45	58	1.40	54
23d	1.23	54	1.23	52	1.23	51	1.23	50	1.20	59	1.20	60	1.18	60	1.17	57	1.15	56	1.15	55	1.15	54	1.14	56	1.14	57
24th	1.17	54	1.17	53	1.17	54	1.17	54	1.17	55	1.17	59	1.17	55	1.15	57	1.14	54	1.11	54	1.10	56	1.10	54	1.10	57
25th	.98	57	.98	58	.95	55	.95	55	.95	52	.95	55	.95	57	.95	57	.93	56	.93	54	.90	55	.90	57	.90	52
26th	.93	52	.93	54	.93	55	.95	54	.95	53	.95	55	.95	58	1.00	57	1.00	59	1.00	57	1.00	55	1.00	56	1.00	57
27th	1.00	54	1.00	55	1.00	57	1.00	53	1.03	57	1.03	55	1.03	56	1.03	54	1.02	54	1.02	56	1.02	54	1.02	55	1.04	54
28th	1.10	56	1.10	54	1.12	53	1.12	54	1.08	55	1.08	54	1.08	56	1.08	55	1.08	57	1.07	58	1.07	58	1.07	59	1.08	56
29th	1.15	57	1.15	55	1.15	56	1.15	58	1.15	55	1.16	56	1.17	56	1.18	57	1.18	56	1.18	58	1.17	59	1.17	60	1.16	60
30th	1.15	56	1.16	57	1.16	57	1.15	55	1.18	53	1.18	53	1.20	54	1.25	55	1.25	57	1.26	56	1.26	58	1.26	60	1.26	60
31st	1.17	48	1.17	47	1.17	49	1.15	48	1.11	50	1.11	47	1.11	48	1.11	49	1.10	48	1.09	51	1.08	53	1.06	52	1.05	54
Means	.994	48.8	.993	48.6	.995	48.7	.995	50.5	.995	51.2	.997	53.4	1.002	54.5	1.005	54.4	1.008	53.3	1.007	52.6	1.005	52.7	.999	52.9	.997	53.0
B. at 32°	29.939		29.939		29.941		29.936		29.934		29.930		29.932		29.935		29.941		29.942		29.940		29.933		29.931	

Day.	14h.		15h.		16h.		17h.		18h.		19h.		20h.		21h.		22h.		23h.		Midn't.		Means.		B. 32°.
	Inch.	°	Inch.	°	Inch.	°	Inch.	°	Inch.	°	Inch.	°	Inch.	°	Inch.	°	Inch.	°	Inch.	°	Inch.	°	Inch.	°	Inch.
1st	.97	39	.97	37	.97	38	.97	42	.97	48	.97	48	.97	48	.97	47	.97	47	.97	40	.97	40	.982	39.5	.953
2d	.92	26	.95	26	.95	36	.96	47	.97	56	.97	58	.97	57	.97	54	.97	47	.97	45	.97	40	.931	42.7	.893
3d	.70	53	.65	41	.65	40	.65	44	.62	47	.62	51	.61	54	.60	56	.60	50	.60	46	.60	41	.749	49.1	.695
4th	.28	54	.27	49	.26	47	.26	49	.25	53	.27	50	.27	46	.27	36	.27	38	.27	36	.27	35	.341	46.9	.292
5th	.50	38	.52	37	.54	44	.59	48	.60	60	.62	57	.63	51	.65	40	.64	40	.65	37	.65	36	.467	44.5	.424
6th	.71	48	.71	49	.73	52	.76	57	.76	55	.76	49	.76	43	.76	38	.75	36	.75	33	.75	34	.730	43.6	.690
7th	1.01	44	1.01	46	1.02	48	1.08	49	1.16	55	1.20	56	1.19	57	1.19	54	1.19	54	1.19	50	1.19	51	.987	53.1	.921
8th	1.30	60	1.33	57	1.33	54	1.33	57	1.33	60	1.33	61	1.33	57	1.33	53	1.33	50	1.33	47	1.33	45	1.293	54.1	1.224
9th	1.17	60	1.13	61	1.12	62	1.10	60	1.07	57	1.05	55	1.00	56	.96	56	.90	56	.90	56	.87	55	1.167	56.5	1.091
10th	.85	57	.85	60	.85	59	.83	56	.83	57	.83	58	.83	56	.83	57	.83	60	.80	58	.81	57	.842	57.7	.765
11th	.70	58	.70	56	.70	52	.70	51	.70	56	.70	60	.70	62	.70	60	.70	55	.70	51	.72	47	.726	56.9	.651
12th	.96	63	.97	61	1.00	61	1.00	64	1.00	57	1.00	56	1.00	53	1.02	55	1.02	56	1.02	54	1.02	51	.895	54.4	.827
13th	1.05	60	1.00	57	.98	61	.96	62	.95	60	.90	56	.90	54	.90	52	.90	51	.88	46	.88	52	.993	56.2	.919
14th	.85	54	.84	55	.84	55	.85	56	.87	58	.89	57	.91	57	.91	55	.91	55	.92	55	.94	55	.874	53.8	.807
15th	.94	43	.94	41	.94	40	.95	40	.95	41	.95	42	.95	41	.95	42	.95	40	.95	40	.95	35	.933	46.4	.885
16th	1.07	49	1.07	52	1.07	55	1.08	57	1.08	56	1.10	55	1.10	54	1.10	53	1.10	50	1.09	52	1.08	51	1.055	48.8	1.001
17th	.95	56	.95	54	.95	56	.95	54	.95	52	.96	56	.96	54	.97	56	.99	57	1.00	55	1.02	58	.990	53.5	.923
18th	.98	53	.98	52	.98	51	.98	50	.98	53	.98	52	.98	51	1.00	51	1.04	52	1.04	51	1.05	51	1.022	52.6	.957
19th	1.18	56	1.20	54	1.20	53	1.20	52	1.20	55	1.20	54	1.20	52	1.21	50	1.23	47	1.24	45	1.25	46	1.134	51.6	1.072
20th	1.27	57	1.27	56	1.27	55	1.27	57	1.27	54	1.28	52	1.28	52	1.30	...	1.32	...	1.32	...	1.34	...	1.265	50.8	1.205
21st	1.47	50	1.47	52	1.48	47	1.50	45	1.50	44	1.50	46	1.50	44	1.50	45	1.50	42	1.52	43	1.52	41	1.438	48.9	1.383
22d	1.40	52	1.38	55	1.37	53	1.37	52	1.37	54	1.37	52	1.36	51	1.32	53	1.30	52	1.25	55	1.23	54	1.420	54.3	1.350
23d	1.14	56	1.14	54	1.14	52	1.14	50	1.14	54	1.14	53	1.14	54	1.16	53	1.16	52	1.16	57	1.17	55	1.168	54.6	1.098
24th	1.10	58	1.10	56	1.10	55	1.10	56	1.09	55	1.08	57	1.06	56	1.06	...	1.05	...	1.03	...	1.00	...	1.111	55.6	1.039
25th	.90	56	.90	56	.90	55	.90	57	.90	55	.90	53	.92	54	.92	56	.92	57	.92	58	.92	56	.926	55.5	.854
26th	1.00	57	1.00	57	1.00	55	1.00	56	1.00	54	1.00	54	.99	55	.99	56	1.00	54	1.00	53	1.00	52	.982	55.2	.910
27th	1.05	54	1.05	56	1.05	57	1.07	55	1.07	57	1.07	56	1.07	56	1.07	55	1.07	57	1.10	56	1.10	54	1.042	55.3	.970
28th	1.08	55	1.10	57	1.10	54	1.10	54	1.10	56	1.10	54	1.10	52	1.10	53	1.10	52	1.10	53	1.10	52	1.092	54.9	1.034
29th	1.15	59	1.15	58	1.14	57	1.12	59	1.12	58	1.12	57	1.15	56	1.15	57	1.15	59	1.15	58	1.15	58	1.153	57.5	1.076
30th	1.26	57	1.25	56	1.25	53	1.25	56	1.25	56	1.24	57	1.20	...	1.20	...	1.18	...	1.18	...	1.18	...	1.215	55.4	1.142
31st	1.05	55	1.05	57	1.05	57	1.00	57	1.00	56	1.00	55	1.00	57	1.00	58	1.00	57	1.02	53	1.02	54	1.069	52.5	1.005
Means	.999	52.8	.997	52.1	.998	52.1	1.001	53.2	1.001	54.5	1.003	54.1	1.001	53.1	1.002	52.1	1.001	51.2	1.001	49.8	1.002	48.9	1.000	52.0	
B. at 32°	29.934		29.934		29.935		29.935		29.931		29.935		29.935		29.939		29.941		29.943		29.947		29.937		

HOURLY ABSTRACT OF THE READINGS OF THE BAROMETER AND ATTACHED THERMOMETER AT VAN RENSSELAER HARBOR,
In June, 1854, in Lat. 78° 37′, Long. 70° 53′ W. of Greenwich.
Mercurial Barometer in house on deck. 29 inches +. Readings in English inches and degrees of Fahrenheit.

Day.	1h.		2h.		3h.		4h.		5h.		6h.		7h.		8h.		9h.		10h.		11h.		Noon.		13h.	
	Inch.	°	Inch.	°	Inch.	°	Inch.	°	Inch.	°	Inch.	°	Inch.	°	Inch.	°	Inch.	°	Inch.	°	Inch.	°	Inch.	°	Inch.	°
1st	.98	47	.98	48	.97	48	.95	46	.95	47	.95	46	.95	47	.95	48	.95	49	.95	49	.90	51	.90	52	.88	53
2d	.82	54	.82	52	.82	55	.82	56	.84	57	.85	57	.85	54	.85	50	.85	52	.85	54	.85	58	.85	56	.84	57
3d	1.25	54	1.25	54	1.25	53	1.25	54	...	...	...	...	...	...	...	...	.94	54	.95	53	.97	56	.97	58	.98	57
4th	1.00	62	1.00	60	1.00	62	.92	63	...	...	...	...	...	...	...	...	1.00	62	1.00	64	1.00	60	1.00	60	.93	51
5th	1.00	50	1.00	52	1.00	47	1.00	47	1.00	48	1.00	48	.98	50	.98	49	.98	47	.98	45	.97	47	.95	46	.94	56
6th	.78	50	.75	46	.75	46	.73	47	.80	54	.78	54	.80	54	.80	55	.80	54	.76	54	.73	50	.72	53	.72	53
7th	.69	(45)	.69	44	.69	46	.69	48	.68	49	.68	50	.67	52	.65	53	.62	53	.62	53	.63	60	.63	73	.56	56
8th	.65	56	.56	46	.59	52	.71	53	.70	53	.73	60	.77	68	.79	56	.80	53	.80	50	.81	54	.83	46	.83	46
9th	.85	52	.86	48	.87	50	.87	52	.87	52	.87	53	.87	53	.86	53	.86	55	.83	51	.83	54	.80	63	.80	64
10th	.60	53	.60	54	.59	52	.59	48	.60	47	.60	54	.60	57	.60	58	.61	58	.62	57	.65	54	.68	54	.68	54
11th	.70	52	.70	54	.70	55	.70	56	.70	52	.70	50	.71	53	.71	53	.65	53	.65	54	.69	50	.69	54	.70	52
12th	.68	56	.68	56	.68	54	.67	54	.66	54	.67	(54)	.67	(54)	.66	(54)	.62	54	.63	54	.64	56	.64	54	.63	58
13th	.64	56	.64	58	.64	56	.64	58	.67	54	.68	51	.68	53	.68	55	.63	54	.63	54	.64	56	.64	56	.64	54
14th	.58	56	.58	54	.58	53	.58	53	.58	54	.58	55	.58	56	.57	60	.55	...	.56	...	.57	...	.60	...	.60	...
15th	.66	60	.65	60	.65	60	.66	60	.70	56	.70	55	.70	54	.70	53	.67	56	.67	58	.70	54	.70	54	.70	56
16th	.63	56	.62	58	.61	58	.61	58	.60	56	.60	55	.60	56	.58	56	.50	58	.49	58	.50	53	.51	52	.53	54
17th	.60	56	.62	54	.63	56	.65	54	.68	49	.70	53	.70	54	.71	55	.72	56	.72	58	.76	56	.79	54	.78	56
18th	.90	56	.97	54	.99	53	.99	52	.90	56	.90	56	.90	56	.94	59	.92	57	.93	58	.94	58	.94	58	.94	58
19th	.95	56	.95	58	.95	60	.95	60	.96	58	.97	57	.97	58	.97	59	.97	58	.98	60	1.02	58	1.03	58	1.03	60
20th	.96	62	.96	64	.92	64	.90	63	.90	58	.90	59	.86	59	.84	55	.80	56	.78	56	.78	56	.77	58	.76	56
21st	.71	56	.73	58	.73	58	.85	58	.80	58	.80	58	.80	57	.79	56	.80	56	.78	56	.78	56	.90	55	.90	54
*22d	.87	58	.87	58	.83	58	.80	58	.85	63	.80	44	.85	47	.85	45	.85	42	.84	39	.86	40	.86	40	.85	37
*23d	.85	34	.83	36	.82	38	.81	38	.76	34	.77	34	.77	34	.77	34	.75	32	.75	34	.75	34	.75	34	.75	36
24th	.75	56	.78	56	.77	56	.77	56	.73	65	.74	65	.76	66	.85	58	.77	56	.77	59	.77	60	.76	58	.75	56
25th	.80	57	.80	56	.80	56	.80	56	.85	60	.85	61	.85	61	.87	58	.86	57	.88	58	.88	59	.88	59	.87	58
26th	.75	58	.75	64	.75	60	.74	60	.72	58	.72	56	.72	57	.72	56	.70	58	.70	57	.70	57	.70	54	.72	58
27th	.76	60	.76	58	.76	57	.76	55	.78	56	.78	54	.78	55	.78	54	.78	54	.78	54	.78	56	.79	53	.80	52
28th	.57	58	.57	56	.57	56	.57	55	.56	55	.56	55	.56	56	.57	57	.59	58	.59	58	.62	56	.62	54	.63	54
29th	.73	55	.73	56	.74	55	.74	57	.75	42	.75	42	.76	44	.76	46	.78	48	.78	48	.78	52	.78	52	.80	51
30th	.84	58	.84	58	.84	52	.85	51	.85	58	.84	58	.85	58	.85	58	.85	55	.85	55	.87	54	.89	53	.90	50
Means	.785	54.6	.785	54.3	.783	54.2	.786	54.2	.786	54.0	.785	53.7	.787	54.6	.788	54.0	.772	53.8	.771	53.9	.779	54.2	.786	54.4	.781	53.9
B. at 32°	29.716		29.717		29.715		29.718		29.720		29.718		29.719		29.721		29.705		29.704		29.712		29.718		29.714	

Day.	14h.		15h.		16h.		17h.		18h.		19h.		20h.		21h.		22h.		23h.		Midn't.		Means.		B. 32°.
	Inch.	°	Inch.	°	Inch.	°	Inch.	°	Inch.	°	Inch.	°	Inch.	°	Inch.	°	Inch.	°	Inch.	°	Inch.	°	Inch.	°	Inch.
1st	.87	55	.86	57	.86	56	.85	55	.85	56	.83	57	.82	57	.84	56	.84	58	.82	56	.82	54	.897	52.0	.834
2d	.84	55	.84	54	.84	52	.83	54	.84	56	.85	56	.85	55	.88	54	.88	53	.90	54	.90	56	.848	54.6	.778
3d	.98	56	.99	55	.99	56	1.00	57	1.00	57	1.00	55	1.00	53	1.00	52	1.00	53	1.00	54	1.00	53	1.047	54.6	.977
4th	.95	50	.94	50	.95	53	1.00	69	1.00	69	1.00	64	1.00	64	1.00	63	1.00	64	1.00	65	1.00	65	.982	61.3	.894
5th	.93	50	.92	51	.91	53	.90	52	.91	52	.88	...	.87	...	.87	...	.87	...	.87	...	.88	...	.941	49.8	.882
6th	.72	45	.73	50	.73	50	.73	52	.73	53	.73	...	.73	...	.74	...	.78	...	.78	...	.75	...	.753	50.6	.693
7th	.59	52	.60	59	.55	57	.55	57	.56	56	.66	...	.65	...	.63	...	.64	...	.65	...	.65	...	.634	54.1	.566
8th	.87	53	.87	52	.87	53	.87	53	.87	53	.87	...	.86	...	.81	...	.86	...	.80	...	.78	...	.787	53.0	.722
9th	.75	64	.74	56	.74	55	.74	54	.73	53	.85	...	.83	...	.81	...	.82	...	.82	...	.85	...	.822	54.2	.754
10th	.66	54	.66	52	.67	52	.67	52	.67	52	.72	56	.73	57	.64	52	.65	52	.64	52	.65	52	.641	53.5	.575
11th	.70	54	.70	53	.70	52	.69	56	.69	55	.67	56	.68	55	.67	56	.67	54	.65	56	.64	54	.686	53.7	.620
12th	.62	52	.63	55	.63	56	.63	57	.63	54	.61	57	.62	56	.64	54	.65	48	.64	48	.64	54	.644	54.3	.576
13th	.64	54	.64	54	.64	54	.64	53	.64	53	.60	54	.61	54	.62	54	.62	56	.59	56	.59	54	.637	54.6	.568
14th	.60	...	.60	...	.60	...	.61	...	.60	...	.60	...	.60	...	.61	...	.61	...	.61	...	.62	...	.590	58.4	.511
15th	.70	54	.73	56	.73	54	.73	54	.73	54	.66	56	.64	58	.65	58	.64	56	.65	58	.64	58	.682	56.3	.608
16th	.53	54	.53	56	.53	56	.53	56	.53	56	.53	58	.52	56	.54	56	.54	56	.56	56	.56	56	.553	56.0	.480
17th	.79	58	.79	56	.79	54	.79	54	.79	54	.79	56	.79	56	.80	58	.78	56	.79	56	.79	56	.740	55.2	.669
18th	.94	56	.94	58	.95	57	.94	56	.94	56	.94	46	.94	44	.99	45	.94	59	.94	60	.94	60	.940	55.3	.869
19th	1.03	60	1.02	60	1.01	60	1.00	60	1.00	60	1.00	58	.97	58	.96	58	.97	58	1.02	58	1.02	58	.987	58.7	.908
20th	.75	54	.70	54	.67	53	.65	52	.65	48	.65	58	.66	53	.66	55	.65	59	.67	59	.70	59	.772	57.1	.696
21st	.90	53	.90	52	.90	48	.90	46	.90	54	.90	56	.92	54	.93	51	.94	50	.94	49	.93	45	.851	53.9	.793
*22d	.85	54	.84	42	.84	42	.83	41	.83	40	.89	34	.87	36	.86	38	.86	34	.88	32	.88	32	.850	43.9	.809
*23d	.75	45	.75	44	.75	44	.75	46	.75	53	.74	57	.74	57	.74	56	.74	54	.76	54	.78	52	.766	42.2	.730
24th	.75	54	.75	52	.75	52	.76	50	.77	54	.83	56	.83	56	.84	56	.84	55	.83	56	.82	56	.781	56.8	.707
25th	.87	55	.87	55	.87	56	.88	57	.86	57	.83	56	.84	53	.86	54	.83	55	.86	54	.86	55	.851	56.8	.777
26th	.71	56	.71	54	.71	54	.71	53	.71	52	.70	58	.69	58	.70	58	.70	58	.69	58	.69	58	.713	57.1	.637
27th	(.80)	(52)	.80	50	.79	53	.75	54	.73	54	.70	58	.70	58	.69	56	.67	56	.66	56	.65	58	.751	55.1	.681
28th	.64	53	.65	52	.65	52	.65	52	.65	54	.70	55	.70	56	.70	56	.72	56	.72	54	.72	53	.628	55.0	.558
29th	.80	50	.80	52	.80	52	.80	54	.80	53	.80	55	.80	57	.80	57	.80	56	.80	57	.80	57	.778	52.0	.716
30th	.91	53	.92	52	.92	52	.93	52	.94	52	.94	48	.94	47	.94	46	.94	45	.94	43	.94	43	.891	52.1	.829
Means	.781	53.8	.781	53.4	.778	53.3	.777	53.9	.777	54.3	.782	54.9	.780	54.4	.781	54.1	.782	54.1	.783	54.0	.783	53.8	.781	54.1	
B. at 32°	29.714		29.714		29.711		29.709		29.708		29.712		29.710		29.712		29.713		29.715		29.716		29.714		

HOURLY ABSTRACT OF THE READINGS OF THE BAROMETER AND ATTACHED THERMOMETER AT VAN RENSSELAER HARBOR,
In July, 1854, in Lat. 78° 37′, Long. 70° 53′ W. of Greenwich.
Mercurial Barometer on deck. 29 inches +. Readings in English inches and degrees of Fahrenheit.

Day.	1h.		2h.		3h.		4h.		5h.		6h.		7h.		8h.		9h.		10h.		11h.		Noon.		13h.	
	Inch.	°	Inch.	°	Inch.	°	Inch.	°	Inch.	°	Inch.	°	Inch.	°	Inch.	°	Inch.	°	Inch.	°	Inch.	°	Inch.	°	Inch.	°
1st	.94	43	.94	43	.94	44	.94	42	.94	44	.94	46	.94	46	.95	45	.95	48	.97	48	.97	48	.97	50	.94	52
2d	.94	43	.94	44	.94	42	.95	44	.93	48	.93	48	.91	49	.90	49	.90	50	.90	50	.90	51	.90	52	.90	53
3d	.89	43	.86	42	.85	43	.84	42	.84	43	.85	44	.85	46	.84	46	.83	46	.83	48	.82	49	.82	51	.84	52
4th	.90	47	.90	48	.89	47	.88	48	.90	53	.90	55	.90	48	.90	56	.90	56	.90	56	.90	55	.90	56	.91	57
5th	.83	52	.82	52	.81	47	.80	47	.80	46	.80	46	.80	49	.80	52	.78	50	.78	51	.78	51	.78	51	.78	60
6th	.77	52	.78	51	.78	57	.78	57	.79	48	.79	49	.79	48	.79	49	.78	49	.78	48	.78	47	.77	46	.77	45
7th	.81	40	.82	41	.82	41	.82	42	.82	40	.82	41	.82	44	.82	45	.81	45	.81	44	.81	44	.81	44	.80	45
8th	.83	42	.83	47	.83	45	.83	41	.83	41	.83	42	.84	43	.84	44	.84	44	.84	44	.83	45	.83	45	.83	45
9th	.78	39	.78	40	.78	38	.79	38	.79	40	.78	40	.78	42	.78	43	.78	44	.78	44	.78	45	.78	49	.77	52
10th	.71	41	.71	41	.70	41	.70	40	.70	42	.70	44	.70	45	.70	46	.70	47	.68	45	.68	49	.67	49	.65	50
11th	.66	42	.65	42	.68	42	.65	42	.65	42	.64	44	.64	45	.64	47	.60	49	.60	49	.60	50	.60	50	.56	57
12th	.64	46	.64	47	.64	46	.64	46	.64	47	.64	48	.64	47	.65	49	.65	47	.65	47	.65	45	.65	43	.65	46
13th	.65	42	.65	43	.65	43	.67	44	.67	45	.67	45	.67	46	.70	48	.70	47	.71	47	.73	45	.73	46	.75	47
14th	.81	40	.81	41	.78	40	.78	41	.78	40	.78	41	.78	43	.78	44	.79	44	.80	47	.79	49	.79	51	.79	51
15th	.66	43	.66	44	.65	44	.65	44	.62	43	.63	41	.63	43	.63	44	.63	45	.63	42	.63	42	.63	43	.64	41
16th	...	...	...	...	...	...	...	...	.50	40	.50	42	.52	41	.52	42	.52	42	.53	42	.53	43	.53	42	.54	42
17th	...	...	...	...	...	...	...	...	.72	46	.73	45	.75	44	.75	45	.76	46	.76	46	.77	48	.77	49	.77	50
18th	...	...	...	...	...	...	...	...	.75	45	.75	43	.75	44	.78	42	.78	42	.78	41	.77	41	.77	41	.77	42
19th	...	...	...	...	...	...	...	...	.80	42	.80	42	.81	44	.82	45	.82	46	.82	47	.85	49	.90	50	.90	50
20th	.98	45	.99	43	1.00	40	1.00	41	1.00	40	1.00	41	1.00	43	1.00	44	1.01	46	1.01	48	1.02	48	1.03	50	1.02	52
21st	.98	42	.98	42	.98	41	.98	41	.95	41	.95	42	.94	43	.94	43	.90	44	.95	44	.95	43	.95	43	.81	44
22d	.79	43	.78	43	.78	44	.79	44	.79	43	.79	44	.81	42	.81	43	.81	45	.81	47	.81	49	.81	54	.81	55
23d	.80	46	.79	45	.79	43	.78	42	.78	45	.78	46	.78	47	.78	48	.78	50	.78	53	.77	53	.77	54	.79	57
24th	.87	44	.86	43	.86	50	.86	48	.86	50	.86	52	.87	42	.87	42	.87	46	.87	48	.89	50	.89	50	.89	49
25th	.80	45	.80	45	.78	44	.78	44	.75	45	.75	45	.75	48	.75	48	.76	49	.77	50	.79	51	.78	52	.78	53
26th	.85	43	.85	42	.85	41	.84	42	.82	40	.82	40	.82	42	.83	42	.83	40	.85	42	.90	43	.90	43	.90	44
27th	.90	42	.92	45	.92	41	.93	40	.92	40	.91	39	.91	38	.90	37	.90	46	.90	46	.88	47	.84	48	.82	49
28th	.54	42	.52	41	.50	42	.46	42	.43	41	.45	42	.48	42	.50	43	.53	44	.54	45	.55	45	.55	45	.58	46
29th	.90	45	.90	43	.90	42	.90	41	.90	38	.90	39	.90	40	.90	47	.90	47	.90	47	.90	47	.90	47	.87	46
30th	.67	38	.65	36	.64	36	.63	34	.63	36	.63	38	.65	40	.65	42	.64	44	.62	49	.61	50	.62	52	.62	54
*31st	.67	37	.66	36	.65	35	.63	36	...	...	...	...	...	...	...	...	.69	42	.70	44	.75	49	.77	52	.77	56
Means	.789	43.1	.786	43.3	.781	42.9	.778	42.8	.772	42.9	.773	43.6	.778	44.0	.781	45.2	.779	46.1	.782	46.7	.787	47.5	.790	48.3	.781	49.7
B. at 32°	29.750		29.746		29.743		29.741		29.734		29.733		29.737		29.736		29.733		29.734		29.739		29.737		29.725	

Day.	14h.		15h.		16h.		17h.		18h.		19h.		20h.		21h.		22h.		23h.		Midn't.		Means.		B. 32.°
	Inch.	°	Inch.	°	Inch	°	Inch.	°	Inch.	°	Inch.	°	Inch.	°	Inch.	°	Inch.	°	Inch.	°	Inch.	°	Inch.	°	Inch.
1st	.94	54	.95	56	.95	59	.95	46	.95	47	.96	46	.96	46	.94	44	.94	45	.94	44	.94	44	.948	47.1	.898
2d	.90	51	.90	49	.90	52	.90	46	.90	46	.90	47	.90	46	.91	47	.91	45	.90	46	.90	45	.912	47.7	.860
3d	.84	52	.84	59	.84	62	.84	57	.84	56	.85	58	.85	57	.87	56	.87	52	.89	55	.90	49	.850	50.3	.792
4th	.91	60	.93	64	.93	59	.92	57	.91	56	.91	57	.91	57	.91	59	.89	59	.85	62	.83	60	.899	55.5	.827
5th	.76	63	.76	65	.77	67	.78	58	.78	61	.78	62	.78	63	.77	58	.77	60	.77	58	.77	54	.785	55.1	.714
6th	.80	46	.80	46	.80	45	.80	43	.80	43	.80	42	.80	42	.80	42	.80	40	.80	48	.80	40	.789	46.8	.740
7th	.80	44	.80	44	.80	43	.80	42	.80	44	.81	44	.81	42	.81	42	.83	41	.83	45	.83	48	.813	43.1	.774
8th	.82	44	.82	44	.82	44	.82	43	.81	44	.81	44	.81	44	.80	44	.80	41	.80	40	.80	39	.822	43.3	.783
9th	.77	51	.77	51	.77	50	.77	51	.77	51	.76	51	.76	52	.75	52	.75	50	.74	46	.71	44	.770	46.0	.724
10th	.65	51	.65	56	.64	60	.64	57	.64	57	.63	55	.62	53	.61	51	.61	52	.61	49	.56	45	.661	48.6	.608
11th	.56	60	.59	62	.64	56	.64	57	.64	58	.64	58	.64	56	.65	49	.65	48	.65	45	.65	44	.630	49.7	.573
12th	.65	46	.65	46	.65	47	.65	46	.65	45	.65	45	.65	44	.65	43	.68	41	.65	43	.65	43	.648	45.5	.603
13th	.75	49	.75	50	.75	50	...	...	...	...	.77	45	.77	45	...	...	...	...	...	...	...	...	.725	45.5	.680
14th	.79	52	.79	55	.79	55	.78	40	.79	54	.79	53	.78	57	.73	47	.71	44	.69	43	.67	43	.774	46.5	.726
15th	.64	41	.64	40	.64	40	.65	42	.65	41	.65	43	.65	42	.65	42	.65	42	.65	41	.65	41	.642	42.2	.605
16th	.54	41	.55	42	.63	44	.60	42	.60	43	.63	42	.65	41	.66	41	.67	42	.68	42	.69	42	.580	41.6	.545
17th	.77	49	.77	46	.77	45	.77	45	.77	45	.77	44	.76	43	...	...	...	...	...	...	...	...	.751	45.4	.706
18th	.77	42	.77	41	.79	42	.81	43	.82	45	.83	44	.84	44	.84	43	.84	43	.84	42	.83	42	.787	43.0	.749
19th	.90	47	.92	51	.93	50	.94	49	.94	48	.94	47	.93	47	.94	45	.96	44	.94	43	.92	43	.877	45.7	.831
20th	1.03	53	1.02	54	1.02	55	1.02	56	1.03	56	1.00	55	1.00	55	1.00	54	1.00	53	1.00	51	1.00	51	1.007	48.9	.953
21st	.81	44	.82	44	.82	45	.82	48	.82	47	.82	49	.82	50	.82	45	.82	46	.82	47	.80	47	.885	44.4	.842
22d	.81	56	.81	55	.80	53	.80	52	.80	53	.80	53	.80	52	.90	44	.95	44	.95	43	.95	43	.823	47.7	.773
23d	.79	57	.78	56	.77	55	.77	55	.75	53	.75	52	.75	51	.73	50	.73	52	.72	51	.73	51	.768	50.5	.709
24th	.85	48	.85	48	.85	48	.80	47	.80	49	.80	49	.80	46	.76	44	.78	44	.78	43	.78	42	.840	46.8	.791
25th	.78	53	.78	53	.78	61	.78	52	.77	50	.77	49	.77	47	.78	47	.75	44	.73	44	.72	43	.769	48.4	.716
26th	.90	43	.90	44	.90	44	.92	49	.92	49	.92	47	.92	46	.93	44	.93	44	.93	44	.93	44	.882	43.4	.842
27th	.80	52	.80	53	.80	55	.80	49	.76	48	.73	47	.69	47	.65	45	.60	44	.58	43	.56	44	.809	45.2	.764
28th	.64	47	.66	46	.70	47	.72	47	.75	46	.78	45	.81	44	.90	44	.90	43	.90	43	.90	42	.637	43.9	.596
29th	.86	45	.86	45	.86	45	.82	44	.80	44	.78	44	.75	44	.72	44	.72	41	.72	43	.69	39	.844	43.6	.804
30th	.62	60	.63	64	.63	60	.63	57	.63	52	.63	49	.63	49	.63	49	.63	46	.63	41	.63	41	.632	46.5	.584
*31st	.73	55	.75	58	.77	57	.78	49	.77	49	.78	47	.78	47	.77	46	.76	45	.75	43	.75	40	.721	44.9	.677
Means	.780	50.2	.784	51.2	.791	51.5	.790	48.9	.788	49.2	.788	48.8	.787	48.4	.788	46.7	.788	45.9	.784	45.7	.777	44.5	.783	46.5	
B. at 32°	29.723		29.724		29.730		29.736		29.733		29.735		29.734		29.740		29.742		29.739		29.734		29.736		

Hourly Abstract of the Readings of the Barometer and Attached Thermometer at Van Rensselaer Harbor,
In August, 1854, in Lat. 78° 37′, Long. 70° 53′ W. of Greenwich.
Mercurial Barometer on deck. 29 inches +. Readings in English inches and degrees of Fahrenheit.

Day.	1h.		2h.		3h.		4h.		5h.		6h.		7h.		8h.		9h.		10h.		11h.		Noon.		13h.	
	Inch.	°	Inch.	°	Inch.	°	Inch.	°	Inch.	°	Inch.	°	Inch.	°	Inch.	°	Inch.	°	Inch.	°	Inch.	°	Inch.	°	Inch.	°
1st	.75	42	.75	42	.74	42	.73	42	.74	41	.72	40	.70	45	.70	46	.67	48	.65	52	.63	50	.63	51	.64	52
2d	.54	37	.54	38	.54	37	.54	38	.54	37	.56	39	.56	42	.57	43	.58	43	.58	43	.60	45	.60	47	.60	45
3d	.60	40	.62	41	.62	42	.65	43	.66	42	.68	42	.69	42	.69	40	.70	39	.70	40	.71	41	.71	42	.75	42
4th	.80	39	.80	39	.80	38	.80	37	.80	37	.80	38	.80	40	.82	43	.82	45	.83	44	.83	44	.85	43	.86	44
5th	.90	40	.90	41	.90	39	.90	38	.90	39	.90	40	.90	41	.90	42	.90	44	.90	46	.90	49	.90	51	.90	50
6th	.85	41	.85	40	.83	39	.83	37	.83	38	.83	37	.83	41	.83	42	.83	45	.82	47	.82	52	.82	52	.82	54
7th	.81	39	.81	37	.80	35	.80	33	.80	36	.80	38	.80	40	.80	42	.80	47	.80	49	.80	51	.80	53	.80	57
8th	.85	40	.85	40	.86	41	.87	40	.87	40	.88	42	.89	44	.91	45	.92	47	.95	49	.95	49	.96	49	.96	47
9th	1.08	45	1.08	43	1.08	41	1.08	41	1.08	39	1.08	40	1.08	41	1.08	43	1.09	44	1.09	45	1.09	45	1.09	45	1.07	43
10th	.98	39	.97	40	.96	41	.96	40	.95	41	.95	40	.95	39	.95	40	.95	41	.95	44	.95	45	.95	47	.94	48
11th	.93	41	.95	40	.95	38	.95	38	.94	39	.94	37	.94	38	.94	39	.94	39	.94	40	.94	46	.94	45	.92	43
12th	.82	40	.82	39	.82	37	.82	37	.82	36	.82	37	.82	38	.81	38	.80	39	.79	40	.78	41	.78	42	.77	44
13th	.77	38	.76	41	.75	36	.74	36	.74	36	.73	36	.73	36	.70	35	.66	35	.65	35	.64	36	.63	36	.62	36
14th	.38	36	.37	34	.35	34	.34	35	.33	35	.32	36	.31	35	.31	35	.31	35	.30	35	.30	36	.30	36	.30	35
15th	.45	34	.46	33	.50	33	.51	33	.64	34	.65	35	.66	36	.67	37	.68	38	.69	39	.71	38	.72	38	.72	39
16th	.76	28	.76	29	.76	28	.76	28	.76	29	.76	31	.76	35	.76	36	.75	38	.75	40	.75	41	.74	43	.74	50
17th	.65	33	.65	32	.64	33	.64	34	.65	36	.66	36	.67	37	.67	36	.67	37	.70	37	.72	39	.70	40	.70	41
18th	.74	34	.74	32	.74	32	.74	31	.74	35	.74	36	.74	38	.74	38	.74	39	.73	38	.73	39	.73	40	.72	41
19th	.70	39	.71	31	.70	32	.70	32	.69	32	.69	32	.69	32	.69	33	.69	32	.69	34	.68	36	.68	37	.67	35
20th	.63	36	.63	37	.63	36	.63	36	.64	34	.64	35	.64	35	.64	35	.64	35	.65	36	.65	35	.65	35	.65	36
21st	.70	32	.70	32	.70	33	.70	32	.70	34	.70	33	.70	34	.70	36	.70	36	.70	37	.70	36	.70	36	.70	36
22d	.72	30	.72	29	.72	25	.72	26	.74	27	.75	28	.75	30	.75	31	.76	32	.76	32	.78	32	.75	34	.77	32
23d	.65	30	.65	28	.64	27	.64	25	.63	26	.60	24	.59	25	.58	24	.56	30	.55	31	.57	34	.57	38	.57	39
24th	.61	28	.61	27	.61	28	.60	28	.73	24	.73	25	.73	28	.73	37	.74	36	.74	37	.74	35	.74	38	.74	36
25th	.74	29	.75	29	.75	30	.75	31	.75	28	.75	29	.76	30	.76	31	.76	32	.75	32	.75	33	.74	34	.74	33
26th	.60	30	.60	29	.60	29	.60	28	.59	26	.58	25	.57	24	.57	27	.65	27	.65	30	.65	30	.65	30	.66	30
*27th	...	...	...	...	...	...	...	...	.65	30	.65	31	.65	30	.65	30	.83	...	.84	...	.84	...	.85	...	.86	...
28th	...	...	...	...	...	...	...	...	...	...	...	...	...	...	...	...	.68	33	.68	34	.68	35	.67	33	.67	36
29th	.70	25	.71	29	.71	29	.71	30	.71	29	.71	30	.72	32	.72	33	.71	34	.71	33	.71	32	.71	32	.70	33
30th	.52	33	.50	33	.47	32	.44	32	.42	32	.41	31	.39	31	.34	30	.30	31	.29	31	.29	32	.29	33	...	...
31st	.30	30	.32	28	.33	27	.34	28	.36	28	.37	30	.38	32	.39	31	.39	32	.39	33	.38	33	.38	33	.38	33
Means	.705	35.2	.706	34.6	.704	34.1	.704	33.9	.712	34.0	.712	34.4	.712	35.6	.711	36.5	.717	37.5	.717	38.5	.718	39.4	.717	40.1	.717	40.5
B. at 32°	29.687		29.690		29.689		29.689		29.697		29.696		29.694		29.690		29.694		29.690		29.689		29.687		29.685	

Day.	14h.		15h.		16h.		17h.		18h.		19h.		20h.		21h.		22h.		23h.		Midn't.		Means.		B. 32°.
	Inch.	°	Inch.	°	Inch.	°	Inch.	°	Inch.	°	Inch.	°	Inch.	°	Inch.	°	Inch.	°	Inch.	°	Inch.	°	Inch.	°	Inch.
1st	.64	53	.63	52	.61	51	.60	50	.59	48	.57	47	.56	47	.55	45	.55	44	.55	42	.55	39	.644	46.3	.597
2d	.60	45	.60	45	.60	45	.61	41	.60	52	.60	49	.60	45	.61	49	.61	48	.61	45	.61	43	.583	43.4	.544
3d	.78	42	.80	41	.80	40	.80	41	.80	42	.80	42	.80	41	.80	42	.80	41	.80	40	.80	38	.732	41.1	.698
4th	.87	43	.88	42	.89	47	.88	45	.88	45	.89	45	.89	43	.90	41	.90	41	.90	40	.90	40	.850	41.7	.815
5th	.90	51	.90	(50)	.90	(50)	.90	50	.90	48	.90	48	.90	47	.90	47	.87	45	.85	44	.85	43	.895	45.1	.851
6th	.82	59	.82	60	.82	54	.83	55	.83	54	.83	52	.82	50	.81	50	.81	49	.81	45	.80	46	.825	47.4	.775
7th	.82	54	.83	59	.85	62	.84	54	.84	54	.84	53	.85	53	.85	51	.85	47	.85	39	.85	41	.820	46.8	.772
8th	.96	48	.96	48	.96	49	.97	44	.97	50	.98	51	1.01	51	1.02	51	1.02	51	1.06	52	1.07	43	.946	46.3	.899
9th	1.06	42	1.03	42	1.04	45	1.02	46	1.02	45	1.00	44	.98	44	.98	43	.98	42	.98	41	.98	41	1.047	42.9	1.009
10th	.94	47	.94	49	.94	52	.94	50	.95	50	.95	53	.95	54	.98	37	.95	39	.95	40	.95	41	.952	44.0	.910
11th	.92	43	.91	45	.91	44	.90	43	.90	40	.88	41	.87	42	.84	42	.84	43	.84	42	.84	42	.911	41.2	.877
12th	.77	47	.77	50	.77	51	.77	49	.77	48	.77	47	.77	46	.77	44	.78	43	.77	42	.77	41	.790	42.3	.753
13th	.58	36	.57	36	.54	36	.54	36	.54	35	.51	35	.49	34	.47	34	.45	34	.41	35	.39	34	.609	35.7	.590
14th	.30	36	.30	36	.31	36	.33	35	.34	35	.35	34	.37	36	.38	34	.40	35	.40	35	.40	35	.337	35.2	.319
15th	.72	39	.73	39	.74	39	.75	39	.76	38	.77	37	.77	35	.79	35	.79	34	.79	34	.79	34	.686	36.2	.666
16th	.73	49	.72	48	.72	49	.70	51	.68	48	.67	46	.67	45	.67	41	.67	39	.65	34	.65	31	.723	39.0	.695
17th	.70	41	.70	43	.70	39	.73	34	.73	33	.73	32	.73	32	.73	35	.74	36	.74	34	.74	32	.695	35.9	.675
18th	.72	44	.72	48	.72	46	.72	45	.72	45	.73	43	.72	43	.71	43	.70	37	.70	35	.70	33	.726	39.0	.698
19th	.65	34	.64	34	.64	34	.64	38	.63	39	.62	38	.62	38	.62	37	.62	37	.63	36	.64	32	.664	34.7	.647
20th	.66	37	.65	38	.67	37	.68	38	.69	37	.70	35	.70	32	.70	30	.70	31	.70	31	.70	31	.661	34.9	.643
21st	.70	35	.70	35	.71	36	.74	36	.73	35	.73	33	.72	33	.72	33	.72	33	.71	33	.70	31	.707	34.2	.692
22d	.76	34	.75	34	.75	34	.75	33	.75	32	.75	32	.75	32	.72	31	.70	31	.67	30	.65	29	.737	30.8	.730
23d	.57	40	.56	41	.56	40	(.57)	(41)	.58	42	.62	34	.63	25	.65	25	.65	25	.65	26	.65	26	.604	31.1	.597
24th	.74	37	.74	38	.74	37	.73	36	.74	36	.74	34	.75	34	.75	33	.76	32	.79	32	.74	32	.720	32.8	.709
25th	.74	33	.74	35	.74	34	.74	34	.70	34	.68	32	.65	32	.65	32	.65	33	.64	32	.60	32	.720	31.8	.712
26th	.67	32	.65	31	.64	31	.62	33	.62	34	.61	35	...	...	...	...	...	...	...	...	...	...	.621	30.1	.617
*27th	.86	...	.85	...	.85	...	.86	...	.86	...	.86	...	.84	...	.84	...	.86	...	.86	...	.86	...	.783	30.8	.777
28th	.67	37	.68	35	.68	35	.67	36	.67	31	.66	34	.66	34	.67	35	.67	37	.68	38	.66	36	.675	34.2	.660
29th	.70	34	.70	34	.70	34	.70	35	.70	34	.70	34	.69	34	.68	33	.68	33	.67	32	.65	32	.700	32.1	.691
30th	...	...	...	...	...	...	...	...	...	...	...	...	...	...	.23	34	.25	33	.30	32	.30	32	.323	32.5	.313
31st	.40	34	.42	34	.43	33	.45	32	...	...	...	...	...	...	.50	26	.50	24	.50	24	.50	23	.410	29.8	.407
Means	.717	41.0	.715	41.5	.715	41.5	.717	40.8	.716	40.6	.715	39.8	.713	39.0	.713	38.0	.713	37.5	.713	36.4	.707	35.4	.713	37.7	
B. at 32°	29.684		29.681		29.681		29.685		29.684		29.685		29.685		29.688		29.690		29.692		29.689		29.689		

HOURLY ABSTRACT OF THE READINGS OF THE BAROMETER AND ATTACHED THERMOMETER AT VAN RENSSELAER HARBOR, In September, 1854, in Lat. 78° 37′, Long. 70° 53′ W. of Greenwich.

Mercurial Barometer on deck. 29 inches +. Readings in English inches and degrees of Fahrenheit.

Day.	1h.		2h.		3h.		4h.		5h.		6h.		7h.		8h.		9h.		10h.		11h.		Noon.		13h.	
	Inch.	°	Inch.	°	Inch.	°	Inch.	°	Inch.	°	Inch.	°	Inch.	°	Inch.	°	Inch.	°	Inch.	°	Inch.	°	Inch.	°	Inch.	°
1st	.51	23	.51	20	.51	20	.51	20	.53	20	.53	21	.52	20	.51	27	.51	27	.51	32	.51	34	.51	25	.51	22
2d	...	...	...	...	.34	20	.34	20	.34	22	.33	23	.33	25	.33	25	.33	25	.33	26	.33	27	.33	28	.33	28
3d	.33	18	.34	19	.34	20	.34	18	.34	18	.34	19	.34	19	.34	20	.34	21	.39	21	.43	23	.47	23	.48	19
*4th	.53	10	.56	8	.56	9	.56	9	.57	9	.59	13	1.02	17	1.04	20	1.05	23	1.06	24	1.09	30	1.12	32	1.15	28
5th	1.16	9	1.16	10	1.16	9	1.16	9	1.12	9	1.11	10	1.09	12	1.07	12	1.06	14	1.06	19	1.05	20	1.05	22	1.01	20
6th	.91	10	.92	11	.93	11	.92	11	.92	12	.92	13	.92	19	.92	21	.93	22	.92	23	.93	23	.94	29	.95	23
7th	.94	14	.94	13	.93	12	.92	12	.91	12	.90	12	.89	12	.88	12	.88	13	.88	14	.86	19	.85	21	.83	21
8th	.84	10	.86	10	.86	11	.87	11	.88	11	.88	12	.88	14	.87	14	.87	19	.86	18	.86	17	.85	16	.85	17
9th	.92	10	.92	10	.92	11	.92	11	.93	(12)	.94	(13)	.94	(14)	.94	(15)	.94	16	.94	17	.95	17	.95	18	.95	19
*10th	.75	13	.77	12	.76	12	.75	12	.77	12	.77	14	.77	15	.77	16	.80	23	.80	26	.80	25	.78	25	.75	27
*11th	...	...	...	...	.75	10	.74	8	.75	9	.75	9	.72	11	.72	12	.70	14	.70	15	.74	18	.75	23	.76	22
12th	.86	46	.87	46	.88	45	.88	43	.89	41	.89	41	.90	42	.90	45	.90	49	.90	49	.92	47	.95	45	.97	41
13th	.92	34	.92	34	.92	33	.92	33	.90	33	.90	37	.90	35	.90	47	.90	45	.90	45	.90	46	.90	54	.90	35
*14th	.75	42	.74	39	.72	37	.70	38	.70	38	.70	40	.69	48	.68	52	.67	49	.64	45	.60	41	.60	42	.57	42
15th	.48	47	.47	45	.45	44	.45	42	.44	43	.44	45	...	...	...	...	.43	48	.43	49	.43	49	.43	43	.43	40
16th	.55	56	.53	51	.45	47	.46	46	.45	45	.47	45	.46	42	.46	44	.63	64	.70	66	.74	64	.78	60	.80	50
17th	.62	49	.62	49	.62	50	.64	48	.65	46	.65	45	.65	45	.65	58	.69	57	.72	57	.86	57	.86	56	.85	56
18th	.68	56	.69	54	.85	61	.80	60	.78	54	.78	51	.78	48	.77	46	.75	43	.80	42	.80	56	.80	58	.80	49
19th	.85	50	.85	47	.86	46	.86	45	.86	42	.85	41	.84	45	.82	58	.75	56	.75	54	.75	56	.75	54	.75	58
20th	.73	54	.73	48	.72	46	.73	45	.75	44	.75	43	.80	59	.80	64	.80	66	.80	62	.82	56	...	...	...	...
21st	.85	53	.84	54	.83	54	.81	55	.80	56	.80	55	.78	56	.75	64	.74	67	.72	68	.70	66	.63	66	.60	59
22d	.25	55	.22	48	.21	47	.19	48	.17	50	.13	51	.10	56	.10	64	.10	58	.10	50	.10	50	.10	67	.12	69
23d	.33	53	.33	55	.34	56	.37	53	.37	53	.37	50	.37	50	.37	53	.37	54	.37	53	.35	54	.31	49	.31	57
24th	.20	51	.20	49	.20	48	.20	48	.20	48	.20	52	.20	58	.20	64	.25	79	.27	68	.27	69	.31	67	.28	67
25th	.22	53	.22	54	.21	56	.20	56	.20	55	.20	57	.20	59	.20	64	.29	65	.18	61	.18	62	.18	63	.19	64
26th	.35	59	.37	57	.40	55	.40	53	.42	54	.45	55	.49	63	.53	65	.54	64	.54	65	.56	65	.55	65	.53	55
27th	.70	56	.73	56	.75	56	.77	55	.80	55	.80	54	.80	56	.83	63	.84	68	.86	62	.86	62	.86	60	.86	60
28th	.83	50	.83	52	.83	52	.83	54	.83	48	.83	47	.85	61	.85	64	.85	60	.83	57	.79	55	.75	54	.71	44
29th	.69	64	.69	57	.69	56	.69	56	.70	56	.70	53	.75	71	.75	73	.71	69	.64	61	.69	63	.72	65	.74	64
*30th	.85	48	.85	50	.83	44	.83	42	.83	42	.84	43	.84	50	.86	53	.90	54	.90	52	.90	65	.90	55	.89	55
Means	.657	37.5	.659	36.3	.661	35.9	.659	35.4	.660	35.0	.660	35.5	.675	38.9	.675	42.7	.684	44.3	.683	43.4	.692	44.5	.694	44.6	.690	42.1
B. at 32°	29.634		29.638		29.641		29.641		29.643		29.642		29.647		29.638		29.641		29.643		29.647		29.651		29.654	

Day.	14h.		15h.		16h.		17h.		18h.		19h.		20h.		21h.		22h.		23h.		Midn't.		Means.		B. 32°.
	Inch.	°	Inch.	°	Inch	°	Inch.	°	Inch.	°	Inch.	°	Inch.	°	Inch.	°	Inch.	°	Inch.	°	Inch.	°	Inch.	°	Inch.
1st	.51	23	.51	25	.50	25	.45	25	.45	26	.45	27	.45	26	.43	26	.42	24	.40	23	.40	23	.485	24.3	.495
2d	.33	26	.33	24	.33	23	.33	22	.33	23	.33	24	.33	24	.33	23	.33	23	.33	22	.33	21	.335	23.6	.348
3d	.49	20	.49	19	.49	21	.49	21	.49	20	.49	20	.49	19	.50	17	.50	17	.52	11	.53	11	.429	18.9	.454
*4th	1.17	29	1.18	27	1.21	27	1.21	26	1.22	22	1.22	22	1.23	22	1.20	18	1.20	15	1.20	11	1.20	13	1.006	19.3	1.031
5th	1.00	20	.99	15	.97	13	.94	12	.94	12	.93	12	.91	11	.90	14	.90	13	.90	13	.90	12	1.023	13.4	1.063
6th	.95	22	.95	22	.95	22	.96	20	.96	21	.96	23	.97	24	.97	22	.96	20	.96	17	.95	14	.940	19.0	.966
7th	.80	22	.78	18	.77	17	...	...	...	...	...	...	...	...	.75	10	.75	10	.75	9	.75	10	.834	14.0	.872
8th	.85	16	.85	17	.85	15	.85	15	.85	14	.85	13	.87	13	.90	16	.90	14	.90	11	.90	11	.867	14.0	.905
9th	.95	20	.95	20	.95	20	.94	20	.94	20	.94	19	.92	19	.85	17	.85	17	.87	16	.87	14	.925	16.0	.959
*10th	.75	26	.75	25	.76	24	.75	20	.74	(18)	.73	(16)	.72	(14)	.70	12	.70	11	...	...	...	...	.753	17.4	.783
*11th	.76	22	.77	21	.79	25	.79	13	.79	10	.81	39	.84	44	.88	49	.88	51	.86	58	.86	57	.774	23.3	.787
12th	.95	42	.81	39	.80	41	.80	46	.80	49	.83	45	.84	48	.90	46	.90	44	.91	43	.92	42	.882	44.4	.839
13th	.90	38	.90	40	.90	44	.90	46	.90	46	.90	45	.87	46	.85	48	.83	46	.79	52	.79	49	.888	42.1	.851
*14th	.57	41	.52	48	.52	50	.52	50	.52	51	.56	55	.56	56	.54	58	.54	57	.54	55	.54	50	.612	46.8	.564
15th	.43	40	.43	37	.43	38	.43	39	.43	48	.42	47	.43	47	.45	58	.45	60	.45	59	.46	56	.440	46.5	.393
16th	.80	47	.82	62	.87	67	.86	74	.86	75	.81	72	.72	69	.65	64	.65	64	.62	62	.62	57	.657	58.0	.579
17th	.85	56	.85	57	.85	56	.85	58	.87	60	.87	64	.86	62	.86	63	.86	63	.82	62	.82	63	.768	55.7	.696
18th	.80	47	.80	46	.83	47	.86	58	.86	64	.86	58	.85	58	.85	58	.85	58	.85	56	.85	51	.806	53.3	.740
19th	.75	60	.75	62	.75	64	.75	65	.75	62	.75	61	.75	57	.75	55	.75	57	.74	60	.74	56	.782	54.6	.714
20th	...	...	.85	47	.86	56	.87	69	.90	69	.90	67	.90	60	.90	56	.88	58	.86	57	.85	54	.821	55.5	.749
21st	.59	55	.55	54	.55	65	.55	68	.59	68	.55	57	.51	55	.40	52	.40	50	.37	56	.28	48	.633	58.4	.554
22d	.14	60	.15	58	.16	54	.17	55	.19	57	.28	68	.30	65	.32	55	.32	53	.30	57	.30	61	.188	56.5	.115
23d	.31	63	.33	56	.32	57	.32	61	.30	74	.30	68	.30	63	...	...	...	...	...	...	...	...	.323	56.7	.250
24th	.28	67	.29	63	.30	62	.31	61	.30	64	.30	63	.30	62	.30	65	.27	64	.23	63	.19	67	.252	61.2	.167
25th	.20	69	.20	70	.21	57	.20	54	.25	66	.30	70	.32	63	.33	57	.33	57	.33	57	.33	56	.236	60.2	.153
26th	.52	57	.50	67	.50	67	.53	75	.54	76	.57	72	.65	70	.65	67	.65	66	.66	65	.66	64	.523	63.4	.431
27th	.86	60	.85	58	.85	59	.86	60	.87	68	.87	65	.87	64	.95	57	.95	56	.86	54	.86	51	.838	59.0	.758
28th	.71	43	.71	54	.71	63	.71	65	.72	69	.73	72	.73	67	.73	65	.73	65	.74	54	.74	55	.774	57.1	.698
29th	.74	63	.75	63	.75	67	.75	70	.75	70	.75	68	.75	62	.82	55	.82	56	.82	57	.82	55	.737	62.2	.647
*30th	.90	61	.90	57	.90	55	.90	54	.90	55	.90	58	.70	58	.90	52	.90	54	.90	55	.90	53	.880	52.8	.815
Means	.690	42.1	.684	42.4	.688	43.4	.687	44.6	.693	46.4	.697	46.7	.697	45.3	.695	43.9	.691	43.4	.681	42.7	.677	41.2	.680	41.6	
B. at 32°	29.654		29.647		29.649		29.644		29.645		29.649		29.652		29.654		29.651		29.644		29.643		29.645		

HOURLY ABSTRACT OF THE READINGS OF THE BAROMETER AND ATTACHED THERMOMETER AT VAN RENSSELAER HARBOR,
In October, 1854, in Lat. 78° 37′, Long. 70° 53′ W. of Greenwich.
Mercurial Barometer in cabin. 29 inches +. Readings in English inches and degrees of Fahrenheit.

Day.	1h.		2h.		3h.		4h.		5h.		6h.		7h.		8h.		9h.		10h.		11h.		Noon.		13h.	
	Inch.	°	Inch.	°	Inch.	°	Inch.	°	Inch.	°	Inch.	°	Inch.	°	Inch.	°	Inch.	°	Inch.	°	Inch.	°	Inch.	°	Inch.	°
1st	.90	51	.90	50	.90	49	.90	48	.90	48	.90	50	.90	55	.90	55	.95	57	.90	56	.95	59	.95	53	.93	54
*2d	.93	49	.93	47	.92	46	.92	46	.92	45	.92	44	.92	45	.92	48	.93	63	.93	57	.92	50	.92	50	.93	52
3d	1.00	44	1.00	44	1.00	44	1.00	43	1.00	54	1.03	56	1.03	56	1.03	58	1.00	58	1.00	54	1.03	51	1.02	55	1.02	53
4th	.95	51	.95	48	.95	48	.95	47	.95	46	.95	45	.95	44	.95	57	1.00	57	1.00	55	1.00	55	1.00	54	1.00	56
5th	1.15	46	1.15	46	1.15	50	1.15	49	1.15	49	1.15	49	1.15	54	1.15	59	1.15	59	1.15	58	1.14	57	1.11	59	1.10	58
6th	.86	65	.83	61	.79	58	.76	58	.73	58	.70	56	.65	58	.64	62	.63	66	.60	63	.58	64	.57	63	.54	63
7th	.50	59	.50	59	.50	59	.50	56	.50	55	.50	55	.50	65	.50	64	.44	60	.44	59	.42	59	.38	63	.38	65
8th	.20	64	.20	60	.20	58	.18	52	.15	57	.15	58	.17	59	.15	65	.15	67	.15	66	.15	65	.15	63	.15	56
9th	.30	58	.30	58	.32	58	.33	59	.34	49	.35	52	.35	51	.35	58	.37	62	.40	64	.42	55	.43	53	.45	54
10th	.58	47	.58	48	.58	48	.58	47	.60	46	.60	45	.64	45	.65	46	.65	54	.65	50	.65	53	.65	56	.68	53
11th	.72	45	.70	43	.70	43	.70	46	.65	47	.65	48	.65	49	.65	49	.65	51	.65	50	.54	55	.53	53	.48	55
12th	.23	49	.23	48	.23	45	.23	44	.23	37	.23	37	.21	43	.21	57	.22	56	.22	54	.20	55	.20	58	.20	54
13th	.06	43	.05	41	.03	40	.03	39	.03	38	.03	37	.02	37	.02	36	.10	48	.10	49	.15	54	.16	53	.17	52
14th	.15	52	.17	49	.19	47	.18	45	.17	45	.16	47	.15	48	.15	49	.15	56	.14	58	.13	57	.10	56	.09	58
15th	.00	57	.04	51	.10	46	.14	44	.20	43	.25	51	.30	59	.31	62	.35	60	.41	61	.50	61	.54	62	.55	65
16th	.84	55	.86	49	.85	51	.88	48	.90	56	.90	48	.92	51	.95	52	.97	58	.97	58	1.00	56	1.00	52	1.00	55
17th	.92	52	.89	50	.85	48	.87	47	.87	45	.87	45	.87	50	.87	48	.86	47	.85	49	.84	50	.84	54	.90	55
18th	.60	50	.57	47	.55	45	.54	46	.50	44	.50	44	.50	45	.50	50	.48	50	.48	49	.48	50	.48	59	.48	57
19th	.74	52	.76	52	.80	50	.80	48	.82	50	.83	52	.82	52	.81	57	.80	53	.80	53	.80	52	.82	51	.84	50
20th	.74	50	.74	48	.71	47	.69	46	.67	45	.65	46	.62	45	.62	51	.60	52	.59	50	.57	52	.57	52	.55	53
21st	.55	52	...	(50)	.56	48	.56	50	.57	45	.57	42	.58	39	.60	43	.60	52	.65	53	.66	48	.64	49	.63	50
*22d	...	...	...	...	.76	45	.79	46	.84	45	.84	44	.83	47	.84	49	.84	49	.84	48	.84	48	.86	50	.86	49
23d	...	...	...	...	1.02	52	1.02	50	1.00	51	1.05	52	1.05	52	1.05	53	1.04	53	1.05	53	1.05	52	1.04	49	1.04	49
24th	1.00	46	1.00	45	.96	46	.95	47	.96	45	.96	44	.97	44	.97	47	.97	47	.97	49	.97	51	1.00	52	1.00	52
25th	1.05	48	1.05	48	1.05	47	1.05	44	1.05	44	1.05	44	1.05	37	1.05	42	1.05	55	1.04	53	1.01	49	1.01	52	1.07	50
26th	1.20	46	1.20	45	1.17	45	1.17	45	1.15	39	1.14	37	1.12	43	1.12	46	1.11	51	1.11	53	1.13	52	1.14	51	1.12	51
27th	1.09	48	1.05	46	1.05	45	1.05	48	1.05	56	1.05	44	1.05	43	1.05	52	1.05	49	1.05	48	1.05	46	1.05	46	1.05	50
28th	.95	46	.94	48	.95	44	.95	40	.99	37	.99	36	.96	40	.94	45	.95	46	.94	48	.93	48	.93	45	.90	44
29th	.85	46	.85	44	.85	43	.85	43	.85	44	.85	41	.85	42	.85	46	.84	47	.85	44	.83	46	.83	45	.84	46
30th	.95	52	.97	52	.97	51	.97	48	.98	46	.99	46	.99	45	.99	48	.99	46	1.03	44	1.07	46	1.06	44	1.06	43
31st	1.12	42	1.12	41	1.15	45	1.12	44	1.10	37	1.09	33	1.08	34	1.07	35	1.04	32	1.03	25	1.03	21	1.00	31	1.00	44
Means	.738	50.7	.737	49.0	.736	48.1	.736	47.2	.736	46.6	.739	46.1	.737	47.6	.737	51.3	.740	53.6	.742	52.6	.743	52.2	.741	52.7	.742	53.1
B. at 32°	29.680		29.683		29.684		29.686		29.688		29.693		29.686		29.677		29.674		29.679		29.680		29.677		29.677	

Day.	14h.		15h.		16h.		17h.		18h.		19h.		20h.		21h.		22h.		23h.		Midn't.		Means.		B. 32°.
	Inch.	°	Inch.	°	Inch.	°	Inch.	°	Inch.	°	Inch.	°	Inch.	°	Inch.	°	Inch.	°	Inch.	°	Inch.	°	Inch.	°	Inch.
1st	.93	55	.93	60	.93	57	.93	52	.93	53	.93	55	.93	56	.90	57	.93	56	.93	53	.93	50	.920	53.7	.853
*2d	.95	48	.95	47	.95	47	.95	55	.99	59	1.02	50	1.04	60	1.04	55	1.04	50	1.04	49	1.04	45	.959	50.3	.900
3d	1.00	50	.99	50	.99	50	.99	59	.99	61	.98	61	.98	59	.98	57	.98	55	.97	53	.97	52	.999	53.2	.932
4th	1.00	56	1.00	57	1.00	55	1.08	52	1.08	60	1.10	64	1.15	64	1.15	62	1.15	59	1.14	59	1.14	57	1.025	54.5	.955
5th	1.10	59	1.10	59	1.09	58	1.09	62	1.06	64	1.04	62	1.00	59	.96	59	.95	62	.95	66	.90	65	1.087	57.0	1.011
6th	.52	62	.52	68	.54	67	.54	64	.54	67	.53	66	.53	68	.52	62	.52	63	.51	62	.51	60	.611	62.7	.519
7th	.36	64	.34	64	.34	65	.33	67	.30	67	.31	67	.28	66	.28	63	.28	64	.27	64	.27	64	.392	62.2	.303
8th	.15	58	.15	59	.20	60	.22	64	.23	63	.27	63	.27	64	.27	62	.27	63	.27	64	.27	61	.197	61.3	.110
9th	.46	55	.51	52	.51	51	.52	52	.55	60	.57	59	.58	52	.57	52	.57	49	.59	49	.58	50	.447	54.7	.378
10th	.68	46	.67	43	.69	44	.69	49	.75	55	.75	56	.76	57	.75	48	.75	49	.75	47	.74	45	.670	49.0	.616
11th	.44	44	.40	42	.40	49	.40	52	.40	55	.38	60	.35	58	.35	58	.33	63	.33	57	.31	54	.515	51.1	.455
12th	.15	52	.13	46	.13	48	.13	53	.12	56	.12	56	.10	52	.10	49	.10	50	.10	46	.08	45	.171	49.6	.115
13th	.17	51	.20	48	.20	53	.25	62	.27	65	.29	62	.31	60	.32	52	.30	55	.30	55	.30	52	.161	49.2	.107
14th	.09	56	.06	54	.06	52	.05	55	.05	59	.05	59	.05	60	.04	59	.02	59	.00	59	.00	59	.100	54.1	.034
15th	.60	59	.65	61	.66	59	.70	60	.75	61	.77	61	.77	62	.79	61	.80	59	.83	59	.83	58	.493	57.6	.417
16th	1.00	51	1.00	51	1.01	50	1.00	50	1.00	55	1.00	58	1.00	54	1.00	52	.99	52	.98	52	.96	52	.958	52.8	.893
17th	.90	55	.81	44	.80	43	.80	53	.80	58	.75	58	.73	56	.69	53	.67	51	.64	50	.63	50	.813	50.5	.755
18th	.50	49	.50	45	.54	43	.60	51	.62	55	.65	54	.65	52	.67	53	.68	53	.70	53	.72	53	.562	49.9	.505
19th	.84	51	.82	48	.82	50	.80	51	.80	52	.82	56	.80	52	.79	52	.78	53	.75	53	.76	53	.801	51.8	.739
20th	.53	51	.53	53	.52	52	.55	51	.55	53	.55	57	.55	57	.55	55	.55	55	.55	54	.55	53	.596	51.2	.536
21st	.63	51	.67	42	.68	43	.68	44	.71	47	.74	50	.74	52	.75	52	.75	53	.75	53	.77	50	.650	48.3	.597
*22d	.86	51	.86	53	.95	48	.95	51	.97	52	.98	53	.98	54	.99	55	.99	56	.99	56	.99	59	.882	50.1	.825
23d	1.04	51	1.05	52	1.05	53	1.05	50	1.05	50	1.05	50	1.04	51	1.03	52	1.02	51	1.00	47	1.00	46	1.033	51.3	.973
24th	1.01	53	1.03	52	1.03	50	1.00	52	1.02	57	1.04	60	1.04	56	1.05	51	1.05	52	1.05	55	1.06	54	1.002	50.3	.943
25th	1.07	58	1.11	43	1.12	47	1.16	56	1.17	58	1.20	64	1.20	63	1.20	56	1.20	56	1.21	55	1.21	54	1.101	51.0	1.041
26th	1.12	47	1.10	45	1.09	49	1.10	50	1.10	52	1.10	55	1.09	54	1.10	56	1.10	53	1.10	50	1.10	50	1.124	48.5	1.070
27th	1.05	46	1.05	48	1.05	50	1.04	52	1.02	51	1.02	47	1.02	46	1.02	46	1.02	45	1.02	48	1.02	48	1.042	47.8	.991
28th	.90	44	.88	43	.88	47	.88	47	.88	47	.86	47	.86	46	.86	46	.85	46	.85	46	.85	45	.911	44.6	.868
29th	.84	44	.84	46	.84	46	.84	46	.84	48	.84	45	.84	45	.85	45	.85	45	.86	44	.86	49	.845	45.0	.801
30th	1.07	41	1.08	42	1.08	45	1.08	46	1.10	48	1.11	44	1.11	41	1.11	43	1.11	43	1.11	43	1.11	43	1.045	45.4	1.000
31st	1.00	50	1.00	44	1.00	46	1.00	40	1.00	42	1.00	43	1.00	42	1.00	39	1.00	41	1.00	47	1.00	46	1.040	39.3	1.011
Means	.741	51.9	.740	50.4	.747	50.9	.755	53.2	.763	55.8	.768	56.2	.766	55.4	.764	53.6	.761	53.6	.759	53.2	.757	52.3	.747	51.5	
B. at 32°	29.679		29.682		29.688		29.689		29.691		29.694		29.694		29.698		29.695		29.693		29.694		29.686		

HOURLY ABSTRACT OF THE READINGS OF THE BAROMETER AND ATTACHED THERMOMETER AT VAN RENSSELAER HARBOR, In November, 1854, in Lat. 78° 37′, Long. 70° 53′ W. of Greenwich.

Mercurial Barometer in cabin. 29 inches +. Readings in English inches and degrees of Fahrenheit.

Day.	1h.		2h.		3h.		4h.		5h.		6h.		7h.		8h.		9h.		10h.		11h.		Noon.		13h.	
	Inch.	°	Inch.	°	Inch.	°	Inch.	°	Inch.	°	Inch.	°	Inch.	°	Inch.	°	Inch.	°	Inch.	°	Inch.	°	Inch.	°	Inch.	°
1st	1.00	45	1.00	45	1.00	45	1.00	45	1.00	43	1.00	42	1.01	43	1.01	45	1.01	46	1.01	47	1.02	44	1.02	40	1.03	44
2d	1.04	43	1.02	43	1.02	43	1.00	44	.98	44	.95	42	.92	41	.92	47	.89	47	.87	46	.83	45	.81	43	.80	45
3d	.80	42	.80	40	.82	40	.83	41	.84	38	.87	38	.87	39	.87	40	.90	49	.91	48	.90	41	.92	42	.92	41
*4th																										
5th																										
6th																										
7th																										
8th																										
9th																										
10th																										
11th	.90	60	.94	58	.90	56	.89	51	.78	46	.75	47	.70	47	.70	52	.70	52	.65	52	.62	53	.61	52	.60	58
12th	.60	58	.60	57	.60	55	.60	55	.60	53	.62	55	.65	58	.65	59	.73	59	.74	60	.74	57	.74	59	.75	56
13th	.80	58	.80	60	.80	54	.80	54	.80	54	.80	54	.80	59	.80	58	.71	62	.71	61	.74	55	.74	53	.75	50
14th	.70	54	.70	54	.70	53	.73	53	.75	54	.75	54	.76	56	.78	58	.84	57	.84	54	.84	51	.84	50	.79	51
15th	1.02	54	.99	56	1.03	51	1.03	53	1.02	56	1.02	56	1.02	55	1.02	51	.94	53	.99	50	1.00	49	1.00	47	1.00	50
16th	.95	61	.95	62	.95	52	.95	54	.95	57	.95	56	.96	59	.99	58	1.00	58	1.05	57	.99	51	.99	53	1.00	58
17th	1.00	57	1.00	56	1.10	49	1.10	48	1.10	50	1.10	51	1.10	52	1.10	53	1.10	58	1.09	57	1.09	54	1.09	53	1.00	58
18th	1.00	38	1.00	36	1.11	33	1.11	32	...	...	...	...	1.21	41	1.25	42	1.34	51	1.35	51	1.34	48	1.35	48	1.33	56
19th	1.20	62	1.17	60	1.15	43	1.08	41	1.09	40	1.05	35	1.00	48	1.00	50	1.00	53	1.00	54	1.00	52	1.00	56	1.00	58
20th	1.08	48	1.09	45	1.10	42	1.10	40	1.12	46	1.12	45	1.25	55	1.25	58	1.35	60	1.33	56	1.33	51	1.33	52	1.34	61
21st	1.43	46	1.43	43	1.42	42	1.41	41	1.37	39	1.35	35	1.31	42	1.31	49	1.31	43	1.29	48	1.23	47	1.18	48	1.15	52
22d	.76	49	.65	43	.64	41	.63	41	.60	40	.59	40	.55	42	.60	43	.56	45	.55	53	.53	49	.53	53	.53	60
23d	.55	46	.57	45	.60	44	.60	43	.60	42	.60	40	.60	41	.60	49	.55	51	.59	52	.64	47	.64	52	.67	56
24th	.67	52	.64	50	.64	48	.64	47	.60	45	.60	44	.60	51	.60	58	.61	60	.61	57	.59	54	.59	58	.59	59
25th	.70	47	.69	44	.73	49	.75	48	.75	47	.75	47	.75	45	.80	56	.81	63	.84	60	.84	60	.85	61	.87	62
26th	.85	52	.88	52	.89	45	.89	48	.87	46	.87	44	.87	41	.88	46	.89	60	.90	61	.90	56	.90	53	.80	52
27th	.87	56	.87	56	.83	45	.80	44	.77	44	.74	40	.74	49	.74	56	.73	58	.68	52	.66	51	.65	54	.62	54
28th	.20	50	.17	48	.13	46	.12	45	.10	42	.05	40	.05	45	.05	48	.05	56	.09	51	.09	54	.10	57	.10	57
29th	.50	47	.51	45	.53	44	.58	43	.58	42	.59	37	.65	40	.67	41	.70	52	.73	53	.72	52	.75	52	.76	50
30th	.90	53	.95	52	.94	51	.95	49	.95	46	.95	45	.98	49	.92	51	.95	55	.96	53	.97	51	.97	52	.97	53
Means	.849	51.2	.844	50.0	.853	46.6	.852	46.1	.842	45.6	.836	44.6	.841	47.7	.848	50.8	.855	54.3	.860	53.6	.853	51.0	.852	51.7	.842	54.0
B. at 32°	29.789		29.786		29.805		29.805		29.797		29.793		29.790		29.790		29.787		29.793		29.793		29.790		29.774	

Day.	14h.		15h.		16h.		17h.		18h.		19h.		20h.		21h.		22h.		23h.		Midn't.		Means.		B. 32°.
	Inch	°	Inch.	°	Inch.	°	Inch.	°	Inch.	°	Inch.	°	Inch.	°	Inch.	°	Inch	°	Inch.	°	Inch.	°	Inch.	°	Inch.
1st	1.03	46	1.05	51	1.05	51	1.05	52	1.06	53	1.06	50	1.07	48	1.05	47	1.05	46	1.06	45	1.06	45	1.029	46.2	.981
2d	.80	46	.80	48	.80	48	.80	49	.80	48	.80	45	.80	46	.80	45	.80	43	.80	44	.80	44	.869	45.8	.823
3d	.92	44	.92	47	.92	47	.93	49	.90	49	.89	52	.85	51	.85	50	.85	51	.71	50	.70	45	.862	44.7	.819
*4th																									
5th																									
6th																									
7th																									
8th																									
9th																									
10th																									
11th	.60	57	.48	57	.41	57	.55	56	.52	57	.53	55	.55	56	.55	55	.55	55	.56	58	.56	57	.650	54.3	.582
12th	.75	58	.75	60	.75	61	.76	59	.76	58	.76	57	.76	55	.77	55	.76	54	.76	56	.76	59	.707	57.2	.631
13th	.73	54	.71	59	.71	59	.71	59	.71	57	.72	58	.70	56	.70	54	.70	55	.70	56	.70	57	.743	56.5	.669
14th	.77	50	.75	43	.75	52	.84	54	.96	55	.97	51	.98	51	.99	53	1.00	52	1.00	46	1.00	52	.834	52.4	.771
15th	1.00	51	.97	51	.96	52	.95	54	.95	55	1.00	51	1.00	52	.96	53	.95	52	.95	56	.94	57	.988	52.7	.924
16th	1.00	59	1.00	50	1.03	52	1.03	48	1.05	44	1.05	49	1.09	52	1.07	51	1.08	48	1.09	47	1.09	47	1.011	53.4	.944
17th	.98	61	1.08	57	1.11	61	1.12	58	1.11	58	1.10	51	1.10	50	1.11	52	1.11	49	1.11	44	1.11	40	1.084	53.2	1.018
18th	1.35	54	1.40	55	1.40	56	1.37	52	1.35	52	1.35	52	1.31	53	1.28	52	1.27	53	1.27	52	1.25	50	1.262	47.1	1.212
19th	1.00	60	1.00	59	1.00	59	1.03	63	1.04	62	1.04	64	1.05	60	1.04	56	1.06	52	1.06	50	1.07	48	1.047	53.5	.980
20th	1.35	63	1.39	60	1.45	64	1.49	62	1.50	66	1.50	61	1.45	57	1.45	54	1.45	51	1.45	49	1.44	46	1.321	53.8	1.253
21st	1.12	52	1.11	51	1.09	52	1.05	60	1.00	60	.95	57	.99	50	.85	51	.82	49	.75	47	.74	45	1.152	47.9	1.100
22d	.53	60	.53	58	.52	61	.52	59	.52	58	.52	55	.52	58	.52	56	.55	53	.56	51	.55	49	.565	50.7	.506
23d	.63	58	.68	58	.70	61	.85	59	.86	61	.74	60	.74	60	.72	57	.72	55	.72	54	.72	52	.662	51.8	.600
24th	.58	59	.60	62	.62	63	.65	64	.65	59	.65	62	.65	63	.68	60	.70	58	.71	55	.71	53	.632	55.9	.559
25th	.89	66	.89	63	.89	66	.92	56	.92	62	.90	62	.90	61	.90	59	.90	59	.90	56	.90	55	.835	56.4	.761
26th	.81	54	.78	54	.92	60	.92	59	.91	59	.90	60	.90	55	.91	53	.91	52	.90	50	.89	49	.881	52.5	.718
27th	.63	58	.58	65	.51	58	.51	58	.51	58	.43	57	.40	58	.35	59	.33	57	.25	55	.23	52	.601	53.9	.534
28th	.17	58	.20	59	.25	61	.26	57	.30	58	.30	60	.35	59	.36	56	.40	54	.42	51	.46	49	.199	52.5	.136
29th	.77	50	.85	54	.88	56	.88	54	.87	52	.91	56	.91	56	.93	56	.93	54	.94	55	.94	58	.753	50.0	.696
30th	.98	50	.99	54	1.00	50	1.00	55	1.00	54	1.00	58	1.00	58	1.00	55	.98	54	.99	52	1.00	52	.971	52.2	.908
Means	.843	55.1	.848	55.4	.857	56.8	.878	56.3	.880	56.3	.873	55.8	.873	55.0	.863	53.9	.864	52.4	.855	51.3	.853	50.5	.855	51.9	
B. at 32°	29.772		29.776		29.782		29.804		29.806		29.801		29.802		29.796		29.801		29.794		29.794		29.792		

HOURLY ABSTRACT OF THE READINGS OF THE BAROMETER AND ATTACHED THERMOMETER AT VAN RENSSELAER HARBOR,
In December, 1854, in Lat. 78° 37′, Long. 70° 53′ W. of Greenwich.
Mercurial Barometer in cabin. 29 inches +. Readings in English inches and degrees of Fahrenheit.

Day.	1h.		2h.		3h.		4h.		5h.		6h.		7h.		8h.		9h.		10h.		11h.		Noon.		13h.	
	Inch.	°	Inch.	°	Inch.	°	Inch.	°	Inch.	°	Inch.	°	Inch.	°	Inch.	°	Inch.	°	Inch.	°	Inch.	°	Inch.	°	Inch.	°
1st	1.02	50	.95	48	.90	40	.90	39	.90	37	.91	31	.90	33	.90	37	.90	50	.97	60	.85	44	.85	43	.79	40
2d	.71	36	.71	35	.70	35	.70	34	.70	34	.70	33	.70	37	.69	42	.77	52	.80	50	.82	49	.84	43	.87	43
3d	.68	48	.70	44	.70	44	.69	42	.68	40	.68	39	.69	48	.70	58	.70	56	.70	54	.70	53	.70	51	.71	55
4th	.85	45	.85	44	.85	44	.85	42	.85	39	.86	35	.86	43	.86	51	.89	52	.89	53	.88	48	.88	50	.90	50
5th	.99	30	.99	28	1.00	26	1.05	25	1.12	25	1.12	24	1.11	40	1.12	47	1.14	46	1.15	46	1.16	45	1.15	50	1.12	47
6th	1.15	36	1.14	32	1.15	36	1.13	39	1.10	43	1.07	44	1.05	45	1.02	46	.96	48	.90	44	.88	46	.80	50	.75	54
7th	...	...	...	...	.40	42	.40	41	.40	43	.40	48	.41	51	.41	49	.41	49	.40	50	.40	49	.39	45	.39	43
8th	...	...	...	...	...	...	...	...	...	45	...	48	.70	59	.70	59	.75	60	.77	59	.82	60	.83	55	.85	53
9th	...	...	...	...	...	45	...	44	...	...	...	...	.75	42	.72	48	.67	59	.65	55	.60	43	.56	48	.50	50
*10th	...	...	...	...	.00	40	.00	43	...	...	...	...	*.94	48	*.96	49	*.97	58	*.98	57	*.99	57	*.99	57	.01	56
11th	...	...	...	...	.35	44	.39	44	.41	43	.45	42	.49	48	.50	48	.52	48	.53	42	.54	49	.53	49	.55	48
12th	...	...	...	...	.50	48	.45	48	.43	49	.41	50	.40	51	.36	51	.36	52	.35	52	.35	52	.36	50	.40	50
13th	...	...	.50	49	.50	50	.47	52	.43	53	.39	57	.35	58	.35	59	.35	57	.37	58	.40	56	.45	58	.47	56
14th	.70	48	.70	53	.70	54	.70	56	.70	60	.70	62	.71	64	.75	65	.78	60	.80	55	.80	47	.83	50	.83	51
15th	.84	56	.83	57	.81	57	.76	56	.72	52	.70	49	.70	50	.67	52	.65	54	.62	54	.58	49	.54	49	.54	51
16th	.71	50	.71	51	.76	49	.78	48	.80	46	.80	46	.80	45	.80	48	.81	50	.81	50	.81	51	.81	50	.85	50
17th	1.00	52	1.02	49	1.02	45	1.03	46	1.00	46	.99	45	.97	53	.96	53	.96	48	.96	49	.95	50	.93	51	.88	55
18th	.45	42	.45	40	.45	40	.45	37	.44	36	.44	36	.45	57	.47	56	.48	51	.50	52	.57	55	.62	57	.68	60
19th	.80	46	.80	45	.80	44	.80	44	.80	43	.80	43	.82	48	.83	52	.85	57	.85	57	.85	58	.86	61	.87	63
*20th	.73	46	.73	44	.73	41	.70	40	.68	39	.63	43	.57	48	.55	53	.50	58	.46	54	.41	51	.36	52	.32	55
21st	.21	45	.23	44	.24	43	.30	41	.35	39	.41	38	.47	52	.47	54	.50	65	.55	60	.57	60	.58	59	.59	60
22d	.76	44	.76	45	.76	45	.77	46	.77	44	.78	42	.78	55	.81	60	.85	62	.85	58	.88	57	.85	57	.85	59
23d	.86	45	.86	45	...	...	.87	43	.87	42	.85	42	.82	42	.80	60	.80	46	.80	41	.80	40	.80	40	.83	44
24th	...	...	.80	32	.80	32	.80	31	.80	31	.83	30	.85	32	.85	36	.85	40	.87	45	.87	42	.88	41	.91	37
25th	1.05	45	...	...	1.00	46	.98	39	.97	37	.95	35	.96	35	.95	46	.95	54	.92	55	.92	57	.92	59	.92	60
26th	1.02	48	1.02	45	1.02	44	1.02	40	1.02	37	1.02	35	1.02	34	1.02	48	1.02	49	1.03	43	1.05	41	1.07	41	1.05	44
27th	.93	45	.91	42	.87	40	.85	38	.83	39	.80	45	.79	50	.75	58	.73	54	.70	48	.65	46	.63	44	.61	48
28th	.41	40	.41	39	.40	39	.40	37	.47	39	.52	44	.56	48	.57	50	.59	54	.59	53	.59	54	.58	54	.58	55
29th	.55	53	.56	50	.56	47	.56	51	.56	53	.56	54	.57	55	.58	54	.58	56	.61	54	.65	52	.64	57	.65	59
30th	.97	45	1.02	44	1.05	43	1.07	43	1.07	42	1.05	40	1.03	48	1.05	50	1.05	51	1.03	53	1.01	55	1.00	57	1.00	56
31st	.82	61	.82	60	.82	54	.87	52	.92	50	.98	51	1.00	51	1.01	54	1.03	58	1.05	59	1.11	59	1.14	63	1.16	64
Means	.720	46.0	.724	44.7	.715	43.5	.716	42.8	.717	42.4	.717	42.6	.717	47.4	.715	51.4	.722	53.4	.725	52.3	.725	50.8	.722	51.3	.724	52.1
B. at 32°	29.674		29.681		29.675		29.679		29.680		29.680		29.667		29.655		29.656		29.662		29.666		29.662		29.662	

Day.	14h.		15h.		16h.		17h.		18h.		19h.		20h.		21h.		22h.		23h.		Midn't.		Means.		B. 32°.
	Inch.	°	Inch.	°	Inch.	°	Inch.	°	Inch.	°	Inch.	°	Inch.	°	Inch.	°	Inch.	°	Inch.	°	Inch.	°	Inch.	°	Inch.
1st	.79	40	.80	47	.80	48	.76	44	.75	43	.73	...	.72	...	.70	52	.70	...	.70	42	.71	...	.829	43.7	.789
2d	.87	48	.89	55	.89	54	.89	52	.90	51	.86	48	.83	45	.81	46	.78	45	.75	50	.75	49	.789	44.4	.746
3d	.74	55	.81	57	.81	53	.83	53	.85	53	.85	54	.85	55	.84	52	.84	46	.84	48	.85	48	.756	50.2	.698
4th	.91	51	.93	50	.95	49	.95	55	.95	56	.97	59	.97	57	.96	49	.96	45	.96	42	.97	29	.906	47.4	.855
5th	1.12	52	1.11	54	1.10	52	1.21	51	1.21	52	1.22	57	1.21	56	1.21	49	1.21	45	1.20	42	1.19	38	1.134	42.8	1.096
6th	.73	58	.71	55	.70	54	.65	53	.64	54	.60	53	.57	49	.50	45	.48	41	.44	52	.45	53	.815	47.1	.765
7th	.40	46	.40	49	.41	48	.42	52	.42	53	.42	52	.45	50	...	...	...	...	...	...	...	...	.425	47.9	.374
8th	.88	51	.88	50	.87	47	.90	46	.92	45	.91	45	.92	45	.92	46	.92	49	.92	50	.92	51	.799	50.3	.741
9th	.48	54	...	...	...	...	.34	50	.31	46	.26	45	.25	46	.17	47	.12	48	...	...	...	...	.512	47.9	.460
*10th	.04	58	.05	62	.10	63	.14	59	.16	58	.18	56	.22	55	.22	52	.25	49	...	...	...	...	.074	52.0	.012
11th	.58	51	.60	54	.60	52	.63	51	.64	53	.64	53	.64	51	.64	47	.64	49	...	...	...	...	.532	48.1	.480
12th	.40	51	.42	50	.46	47	.47	48	.49	53	.50	56	.50	54	.50	49	.49	50	...	...	...	...	.446	50.3	.388
13th	.49	59	.50	58	.55	58	.56	59	.59	59	.60	61	.63	60	.47	64	.54	50	.59	52	.64	45	.487	55.7	.415
14th	.85	51	.89	50	.90	54	.92	55	.93	53	.92	53	.91	52	.91	52	.91	51	.88	50	.86	49	.816	54.0	.749
15th	.53	52	.53	53	.56	51	.56	51	.58	52	.60	53	.64	53	...	...	...	...	...	...	...	...	.652	52.3	.589
16th	.87	53	.90	55	.91	54	.91	53	.91	54	.94	45	.95	48	.97	50	.99	51	.99	52	1.00	50	.858	50.0	.801
17th	.86	56	.85	57	.80	57	.80	55	.82	56	.82	59	.82	50	.82	50	.82	51	.80	50	.80	48	.903	51.3	.843
18th	.71	62	.75	64	.73	62	.74	59	.74	58	.74	48	.75	44	.75	42	.75	41	...	...	...	...	.611	49.4	.557
19th	.89	63	.90	59	.90	60	.88	65	.87	66	.85	65	.82	68	...	...	...	...	...	...	...	...	.830	55.4	.758
*20th	.29	61	.25	63	.24	62	.23	59	.22	58	.19	63	.19	60	.18	56	.18	53	.18	50	.20	46	.405	52.3	.341
21st	.62	61	.64	62	.67	64	.69	62	.70	61	.75	65	.75	60	...	...	.75	48	.75	48	.76	49	.554	53.9	.488
22d	.86	62	.87	65	.89	64	.90	60	.90	58	.87	50	.86	44	.83	48	.84	50	.86	46	.87	45	.834	52.7	.770
23d	.87	52	.80	45	.80	58	.80	59	.80	54	.80	58	.80	55	...	...	.80	46	.80	44	.80	40	.820	47.3	.770
24th	.94	31	.99	48	1.00	49	1.02	54	1.02	53	1.03	54	1.07	55	1.11	49	1.16	50	1.12	46	1.07	42	.935	41.5	.900
25th	.92	65	.92	68	.92	65	.92	60	.93	58	.91	56	.90	50	.87	50	.87	50	.90	50	1.05	45	.942	51.2	.882
26th	1.03	47	.98	51	1.00	53	1.03	55	1.05	54	1.04	53	1.03	48	1.00	45	1.00	45	1.00	43	1.00	40	1.022	45.1	.978
27th	.60	54	.60	57	.58	59	.54	57	.52	57	.50	55	.48	53	.47	50	.45	45	.45	42	.41	42	.652	48.7	.600
28th	.59	57	.60	60	.60	62	.60	63	.60	63	.60	60	.57	58	.55	55	.55	54	.54	55	.55	55	.542	52.0	.480
29th	.68	62	.70	63	.70	61	.75	62	.78	64	.79	65	.87	60	.95	55	.95	53	.94	50	.95	48	.695	55.7	.623
30th	1.00	54	.89	51	.85	53	.83	56	.84	57	.84	58	.84	57	.84	61	.83	62	.82	62	.81	63	.949	52.5	.885
31st	1.21	63	1.27	60	1.31	61	1.33	64	1.39	64	1.40	66	1.41	63	1.42	65	1.42	65	1.45	62	1.45	59	1.158	59.5	1.075
Means	.734	54.2	.737	55.6	.741	55.6	.748	55.6	.756	55.4	.753	55.2	.755	53.2	.745	51.4	.746	49.6	.745	48.6	.752	47.0	.732	50.1	
B. at 32°	29.666		29.665		29.669		29.676		29.685		29.682		29.689		29.685		29.690		29.692		29.703		29.675		

HOURLY ABSTRACT OF THE READINGS OF THE BAROMETER AND ATTACHED THERMOMETER AT VAN RENSSELAER HARBOR,
In January, 1855, in Lat. 78° 37′, Long. 70° 53′ W. of Greenwich.
Mercurial Barometer in cabin. 29 inches +. Readings in English inches and degrees of Fahrenheit.

Day.	1h.		2h.		3h.		4h.		5h.		6h.		7h.		8h.		9h.		10h.		11h.		Noon.		13h.	
	Inch.	°	Inch.	°	Inch.	°	Inch.	°	Inch.	°	Inch.	°	Inch.	°	Inch.	°	Inch.	°	Inch.	°	Inch	°	Inch.	°	Inch.	°
1st	1.45	55	1.45	53	1.45	51	1.45	50	1.45	49	1.45	49	1.45	48	1.45	57	1.45	60	1.45	62	1.45	65	1.45	63	1.45	62
2d	1.19	45	1.12	41	1.10	39	1.12	39	1.13	40	1.15	42	1.16	53	1.15	58	1.15	57	1.14	57	1.13	59	1.15	58	1.15	58
3d	1.25	46	1.24	43	1.22	40	1.21	38	1.20	39	1.19	42	1.19	45	1.16	47	1.15	49	1.15	56	1.15	58	1.14	59	1.14	58
4th	.92	48	.91	45	.89	43	.89	42	.87	41	.85	42	.85	56	.85	58	.79	57	.78	57	.78	55	.75	58	.75	59
5th	...	...	.74	40	.77	39	.79	38	.79	37	.80	37	.83	39	.86	44	.88	52	.89	50	.90	53	.93	54	.95	58
6th	...	...	...	...	1.05	38	1.05	35	1.09	33	1.17	32	1.19	36	1.22	47	1.28	51	1.30	50	1.32	52	1.43	54	1.43	55
7th	...	...	...	...	1.45	20	1.44	30	1.44	...	1.45	...	1.45	...	1.49	...	1.53	...	1.54	...	1.54	...	1.54	...	1.54	...
8th	1.44	...	1.43	46	1.40	...	1.38	...	1.34	...	1.31	...	1.27	...	1.22	...	1.18	...	1.16	...	1.14	...	1.12	...	1.09	...
9th	.75	51	.75	50	.78	43	.75	42	.75	41	.74	41	.74	40	.80	46	.78	42	.76	41	.75	44	.74	46	.74	48
10th	.80	46	...	...	.80	...	.78	...	.79	32	.80	32	.80	46	.80	50	.80	...	.80	...	.80	...	.80	...	.80	49
11th	1.00	...	1.00	...	.98	...	.99	...	1.01	37	1.06	40	1.08	44	1.08	50	1.09	...	1.10	...	1.12	...	1.13	...	1.14	...
12th	1.20	...	1.20	...	1.14	...	1.12	...	1.10	...	1.09	...	1.08	...	1.06	...	1.04	...	.99	...	.96	...	.94	...	.92	42
13th	.65	...	.65	...	.61	...	.61	...	.61	45	.60	45	.54	46	.54	46	.61	...	.62	...	.63	...	.63	...	.63	48
14th	.98	...	.97	...	.95	...	.96	...	.96	42	.95	42	.94	43	.95	44	.96	...	.95	...	.93	...	.91	...	.90	49
15th	.70	...	.72	...	.70	...	.68	...	.67	41	.66	40	.66	40	.66	42	.69	...	.70	...	.72	...	.74	...	.75	53
16th	.90	...	.91	...	.90	...	.90	...	.90	37	.89	38	.88	40	.86	45	.85	...	.85	...	.86	...	.86	...	...	...
17th	.90	...	.90	...	.89	...	.89	...	.89	41	.89	42	.90	49	.91	50	.93	...	.94	...	.95	...	.96	...	...	...
18th	.90	...	.91	...	1.23	...	1.22	...	...	...	...	...	1.19	49	1.17	50	1.15	...	1.14	...	1.14	...	1.15	...	...	...
19th	1.33	...	1.34	...	1.30	...	1.32	...	...	...	...	...	1.36	46	1.37	48	1.40	...	1.40	...	1.40	...	1.40	...	...	...
*20th	1.67	...	1.67	...	1.69	...	1.70	...	...	...	...	...	...	...	...	...	1.81	...	1.82	...	1.84	...	1.85	...	...	...
*21st	2.02	...	2.02	...	2.02	...	2.02	...	...	...	...	...	...	...	...	...	1.98	...	1.96	...	1.94	...	1.94	...	...	...
*22d	1.75	...	1.72	...	1.70	...	1.69	...	...	...	...	...	...	...	...	...	1.66	...	1.66	...	1.66	...	1.65	...	...	...
*23d	1.58	...	1.58	...	1.55	...	1.52	...	...	...	...	...	...	...	...	...	1.52	...	1.51	...	1.50	...	1.51	...	1.52	...
*24th	1.33	...	1.35	...	1.24	...	1.25	...	1.19	...	1.18	...	1.18	48	1.18	50	1.18	...	1.17	..	1.17	...	1.17	...	1.16	...
25th	...	...	...	...	...	...	...	...	...	...	...	...	...	...	...	...	...	...	...	...	...	...	...	...	...	...
26th	...	...	...	...	...	...	...	...	...	...	...	...	...	...	...	...	...	...	...	...	...	...	...	...	...	...
27th	...	...	...	...	...	...	...	...	...	...	...	...	...	...	...	...	...	...	...	...	...	...	...	...	...	...
28th	...	...	...	...	...	...	...	...	...	...	...	...	...	...	...	...	...	...	...	...	...	...	...	...	...	...
29th	...	...	...	...	...	...	...	...	...	...	...	...	...	...	...	...	...	...	...	...	...	...	...	...	...	...
30th	...	...	...	...	...	...	...	...	...	...	...	...	...	...	...	...	...	...	...	...	...	...	...	...	...	...
31st	...	...	...	...	...	...	...	...	...	...	...	...	...	...	...	...	...	...	...	...	...	...	...	...	...	...
Means	1.173	46.4	1.166	44.8	1.159	43.4	1.155	42.8	1.152	42.4	1.155	42.9	1.153	45.5	1.155	48.0	1 161	48.8	1.157	49.0	1.157	49.9	1.162	50.4	1.164	50.9
B. at 32°	30.125		30.123		30.119		30.117		30.115		30.117		30.108		30.103		30.107		30.102		30.100		30.103		30.104	
*	30.101		30.099		30.095		30.093		30.091		30.093		30.084		30.079		30.083		30.078		30.076		30.079		30.080	

Day.	14h.		15h.		16h.		17h.		18h.		19h.		20h.		21h.		22h.		23h.		Midn't.		Means.		B. 32.°
	Inch.	°	Inch.	°	Inch.	°	Inch.	°	Inch.	°	Inch.	°	Inch.	°	Inch.	°	Inch.	°	Inch.	°	Inch.	°	Inch.	°	Inch.
1st	1.45	63	1.41	63	1.38	61	1.35	60	1.32	59	1.28	57	1.25	54	1.20	50	1.23	50	1.20	48	1.18	48	1.379	55.7	1.306
2d	1.16	59	1.19	60	1.20	61	1.20	61	1.21	60	1.22	58	1.23	57	1.24	55	1.24	54	1.24	54	1.25	48	1.176	53.0	1.109
3d	1.10	57	1.09	59	1.07	61	1.06	65	1.05	64	1.05	64	1.04	63	1.04	62	1.03	59	1.00	53	.94	51	1.119	53.2	1.051
4th	.75	60	.75	61	.75	60	.74	58	.74	58	.75	56	.75	53	.75	48	.75	52	.75	50	.76	50	.797	52.8	.732
5th	.95	60	.95	61	.86	62	.98	60	.99	58	1.05	55	1.12	52	1.23	50	1.26	45	1.29	46	1.32	48	.953	49.3	.898
6th	1.44	57	1.46	56	1.46	57	1.47	58	1.50	...	1.45	51	1.47	50	1.48	48	...	...	1.48	38	1.45	31	1.335	46.3	1.286
7th	1.54	...	1.53	...	1.53	...	1.53	...	1.53	...	1.52	...	1.50	...	1.47	48	1.47	50	1.47	50	1.45	50	1.495	38.4	1.468
8th	1.05	...	1.00	...	.98	...	.97	51	.95	55	.90	59	.88	56	.85	...	.82	50	.84	40	.80	50	1.105	49.9	1.046
9th	.76	49	.77	50	.79	50	.80	...	.80	...	.80	50	.80	52	.80	50	.80	50	.80	...	.80	46	.773	46.7	.724
10th	.80	50	.80	52	.80	51	.80	52	.80	51	.80	50	.80	48	...	...	.98	50	.98	...	.99	...	.825	46.5	.777
11th	1.16	...	1.18	...	1.19	...	1.20	...	1.20	...	1.23	...	1.24	...	1.20	48	1.20	46	1.20	...	1.20	49	1.124	46.6	1.076
12th	.90	43	.86	42	.82	44	.71	45	.70	46	.69	48	.69	46	.80	48	.70	48	.65	49	.65	...	.917	45.6	.872
13th	.65	50	.67	51	.70	49	.73	49	.77	50	.79	48	.83	51	.87	50	.91	44	.91	40	.92	40	.695	46.8	.647
14th	.90	50	.91	50	.93	49	.94	49	.94	50	.95	48	.95	47	...	...	...	...	...	...	...	...	.922	45.7	.876
15th	.75	54	.77	52	.79	50	.80	49	.81	50	.83	51	.83	49	...	...	...	...	...	...	...	...	.753	46.3	.706
16th	...	...	...	...	...	...	...	...	...	...	.85	50	.85	51	.84	54	.86	52	.87	50	...	...	.868	46.0	.822
17th	...	...	...	...	...	...	...	...	...	...	...	...	...	...	1.20	50	1.20	46	1.19	56	1.16	50	1.017	48.5	.964
18th	...	...	...	...	...	...	1.15	...	1.14	...	1.18	47	1.20	48	...	...	...	...	...	...	...	...	1.163	48.7	1.109
19th	...	...	...	...	...	...	1.61	...	1.63	...	...	...	...	...	...	...	1.66	58	1.69	54	1.67	48	1.480	51.6	1.418
*20th	...	...	...	...	...	...	1.96	...	1.96	...	...	...	...	...	...	...	...	...	...	...	...	...	1.856	48.4	1.803
*21st	...	...	...	...	...	...	1.90	...	1.89	...	...	...	...	...	...	...	...	...	...	...	...	...	1.927	51.0	1.867
*22d	...	...	...	...	...	...	1.63	...	1.62	...	...	...	...	...	...	...	...	...	...	...	...	...	1.647	50.1	1.589
*23d	1.52	...	1.52	...	1.52	...	1.51	...	1.51	...	...	...	...	...	1.50	...	1.50	...	1.48	...	1.47	...	1.517	50.8	1.458
*24th	1.16	...	1.15	...	1.14	...	...	...	...	...	...	...	...	...	...	...	...	...	...	...	...	...	1.155	49.0	1.100
25th	...	...	...	...	...	...	...	...	...	...	...	...	...	...	...	...	...	...	...	...	...	...*	1.148	49.1	1.092
26th	...	...	...	...	...	...	...	...	...	...	...	...	...	...	...	...	...	...	...	...	...	...	1.445	50.7	1.386
27th	...	...	...	...	...	...	...	...	...	...	...	...	...	...	...	...	...	...	...	...	...	...	1.499	52.5	1.434
28th	...	...	...	...	...	...	...	...	...	...	...	...	...	...	...	...	...	...	...	...	...	...	1.482	52.3	1.417
29th	...	...	...	...	...	...	...	...	...	...	...	...	...	...	...	...	...	...	...	...	...	...	.964	52.8	.899
30th	...	...	...	...	...	...	...	...	...	...	...	...	...	...	...	...	...	...	...	...	...	...	.592	51.3	.531
31st	...	...	...	...	...	...	...	...	...	...	...	...	...	...	...	...	...	...	...	...	...	...	.360	49.1	.305
Means	1.166	51.6	1.168	51.9	1.167	51.9	1.172	51.9	1.173	51.9	1.175	51.4	1.177	50.8	1.185	50.4	1.186	49.0	1.182	47.9	1.174	47.4	1.166	48.6	
B. at 32°	30.104		30.106		30.105		30.110		30.111		30.114		30.118		30.127		30.131		30.130		30.124		30.113		
*	30.080		30.082		30.081		30.086		30.087		30.090		30.094		30.103		30.107		30.106		30.100		30.089		

NOTES TO PRECEDING ABSTRACTS.

September, 1853. During the whole month, the readings were taken from the aneroid barometer. They were converted by means of a table to the corresponding readings of the mercurial barometer.

11th. The dates before the 11th, were changed from nautical into civil reckoning.

14th. At 3 P. M., the aneroid barometer was removed from the cabin to the deck; a change of six feet of greater elevation.

19th. At 9 A. M., the barometer was brought from deck to cabin (six feet lower). During the hours 7 and 8 A. M., it became colder than the scale could register.

14th–19th. A correction of +0.006 inch has been applied to the barometer readings, to refer them to the level of the cabin.

October, 1853. 24th. From this day, the readings of the mercurial barometer are given. The position was in house on deck.

25th. Readings at 1, 2, 3, and 4 P. M., supplied from the aneroid in cabin.

January, 1854. 23d. The star prefixed to the hours between 9 A. M. and midnight, indicates that the decimals belong to 28 inches.

24th and 25th. The star indicates 28 inches as above.

February, 1854. 18th and 19th. The star in the place of the units indicates that the decimals belong to 28 inches.

June, 1854. 22d and 23d. The deck house was removed; the mercurial barometer, however, remained on deck.

July, 1854. 31st. Between 1 A. M. and 2 P. M., the readings of the aneroid appear to have been inadvertently inserted in the column for the mercurial barometer. In the abstract the readings were accordingly exchanged.

August, 1854. 27th. The readings of the two barometers between the hours 5 A. M. and 12 P. M. appear to have been accidentally exchanged, as indicated by the temperature readings. After 9 A. M. the aneroid was read, and its indications were changed to those of the mercurial barometer.

September, 1854. 4th. The sudden rise of the barometer between 6 and 7 A. M. is indicated by both instruments. There is apparently no cause for this singular change, so far as is shown by the remaining meteorological observations at these hours.

10th and 11th. Barometer not read during four hours, on account of the darkness.

14th. The readings at 7 and 8 P. M. were changed from 29.65 to 29.56; a correction confirmed by the aneroid readings.

30th. The barometer stand removed to the most forward stanchion of the cabin. Height above the water-line, one foot six inches.

October, 1854. 2d. The original record has the readings 30.2, 30.4, etc., for the hours 19 P. M., etc. It should evidently read 30.02, 30.04, etc., as given in the preceding abstract, and as confirmed by the aneroid readings. Similar mistakes in the displacement of a decimal have occurred in two or three other cases.

22d. Mercurial barometer in cabin against stanchions amidships. Height of cistern, six feet.

November, 1854. 4th to 10th. No record for this interval.

December, 1854. 10th. The star in front of the figures indicates that the decimal places refer to 28 inches.

20th. The mercurial and aneroid barometers were removed to-day; the mercurial barometer being placed six inches lower than before, and the aneroid placed two feet below it.

January, 1855. 20th, 21st, 22d, 23d, and 24th. The temperature readings for these days have been taken from page 422 of the second volume of the Narrative.

25th, 26th, 27th, 28th, 29th, 30th, and 31st. The barometer and temperature readings have been taken from the same page of the Narrative.

The last horizontal column of the reduced barometer readings is derived from the preceding column by subtracting 0.024 inch, so as to allow for the introduction of the means of the last seven days.

February, March, and April, 1855. For these months the original record could not be found. The daily and monthly means of the atmospheric pressure (and corresponding temperature), will be found in Appendix No. XII. of the second volume of the Narrative.

Diurnal Variation of the Atmospheric Pressure.—The following table exhibits the diurnal change of the barometric pressure, for each month of the year and for the whole year, as made out from the preceding abstract. For the months between September and January (inclusive), the mean from the two sets is given.

ABSTRACT OF THE MEAN HOURLY READINGS OF THE (REDUCED) BAROMETER AT THE LEVEL OF THE SEA, FROM OBSERVATIONS AT VAN RENSSELAER HARBOR, BETWEEN SEPT. 1853 AND JAN. 1855.

Atmospheric Pressure in English inches.

Hour.	Sept. 1853–54.	Oct. 1853–54.	Nov. 1853–54.	Dec. 1853–54.	Jan. 1854–55.	Feb. 1854.	March. 1854.	April. 1854.	May. 1854.	June. 1854.	July. 1854.	Aug. 1854.	Means.
1h.	29.642	29.751	29.751	29.749	29.781	29.637	29.784	29.968	29.939	29.716	29.750	29.687	29.763
2	.646	.753	.756	.754	.782	.636	.789	.971	.939	.717	.746	.690	.765
3	.652	.752	.767	.753	.778	.632	.792	.973	.941	.715	.743	.689	.766
4	.650	.753	.766	.757	.775	.632	.798	.975	.936	.718	.741	.689	.766
5	.652	.748	.757	.756	.775	.646	.800	.978	.934	.720	.734	.697	.766
6	.650	.751	.756	.756	.777	.647	.798	.977	.930	.718	.733	.696	.766
7	.653	.750	.754	.750	.772	.651	.798	.979	.932	.719	.737	.694	.766
8	.649	.745	.749	.741	.766	.647	.793	.977	.935	.721	.736	.690	.762
9	.654	.744	.747	.740	.768	.646	.798	.979	.941	.705	.733	.694	.762
10	.656	.746	.749	.743	.766	.655	.802	.981	.942	.704	.734	.690	.764
11	.657	.750	.750	.745	.764	.653	.796	.978	.940	.712	.739	.689	.764
Noon	.657	.746	.748	.743	.765	.648	.798	.978	.933	.718	.737	.687	.763
13	.656	.750	.742	.735	.765	.644	.794	.970	.931	.714	.725	.685	.759
14	.656	.747	.741	.735	.766	.648	.794	.969	.934	.714	.723	.684	.759
15	.652	.747	.742	.738	.766	.661	.803	.973	.934	.714	.724	.681	.761
16	.655	.750	.748	.739	.767	.662	.800	.976	.935	.711	.730	.681	.763
17	.655	.754	.747	.748	.770	.671	.802	.976	.935	.709	.736	.685	.765
18	.660	.753	.755	.753	.772	.671	.803	.980	.931	.708	.733	.684	.767
19	.659	.755	.753	.750	.774	.674	.805	.983	.935	.712	.735	.685	.768
20	.660	.758	.752	.754	.777	.669	.810	.987	.935	.710	.734	.685	.769
21	.660	.756	.755	.752	.782	.668	.806	.985	.939	.712	.740	.688	.770
22	.658	.754	.760	.756	.787	.666	.803	.984	.941	.713	.742	.690	.771
23	.654	.750	.756	.755	.785	.669	.794	.981	.943	.715	.739	.692	.769
Midn't	29.651	29.749	29.755	29.760	29.784	29.666	29.791	29.980	29.947	29.716	29.734	29.689	29.768
Means	29.653	29.750	29.753	29.748	29.773	29.654	29.793	29.977	29.937	29.714	29.736	29.689	29.765

Owing to the small amplitude, the comparatively short period of observation, and the magnitude of the occasional disturbances, the law of the diurnal variation is apparently subject to considerable fluctuations; and it has, therefore, only been attempted to express the figures in the last vertical column, or the mean variation, analytically. Using Bessel's formula, the variation can be expressed by the formula:—

$$\underset{\text{Inches.}}{29.765} + \underset{\text{Inch.}}{0.0034} \, sin \, (\theta + 290^\circ) + \underset{\text{Inch.}}{0.0022} \, sin \, (2\,\theta + 204^\circ);$$

the terms containing $3\,\theta$, etc., becoming too small to have any real value. The angle θ counts from noon, and is expressed in degrees at the rate of 15° an hour.

The annexed diagram exhibits the observed (by dots) and the computed (by a fine line) diurnal variation. Its principal feature is the afternoon inflection, with a

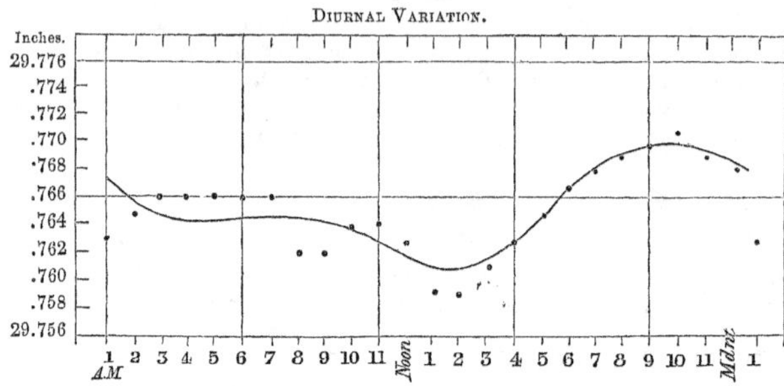

maximum pressure at about 10 P. M. The principal minimum is reached at 1 P. M. The 10 P. M. maximum is in strict conformity with the general law deduced from observations in the northern hemisphere. The 1 P. M. minimum seems to occur about three hours earlier than indicated by more southern stations. Kaemtz takes as amplitude of the diurnal variation, the difference between the mean of the maxima and the mean of the minima. Other meteorologists take the maximum difference. According to this latter view, we have the diurnal amplitude 29.7701 — 29.7604 = 0.0097 inches. The diurnal fluctuation here considered is the change in the gross pressure of the atmosphere, there being no means on hand for separating the pressure of dry air from the pressure of aqueous vapor.[1]

In connection with this subject, it may be stated that the latitude of Van Rensselaer Harbor is about 14° higher north, than the latitude (64°) in which the mean height of the barometer is a minimum (at the level of the sea).

Annual Fluctuation of the Atmospheric Pressure.—The following is an abstract of the monthly means of the barometer readings (reduced to 32°). The values for February, March, and April, 1855, were taken from the second volume of the Narrative.

Year.	Jan.	Feb.	March.	April.	May.	June.	July.	Aug.	Sept.	Oct.	Nov.	Dec.
1853	...	...	...	...	...	...	...	...	29.662	29.815	29.713	29.821
1854	29.458	29.654	29.798	29.977	29.937	29.714	29.736	29.689	29.645	29.686	29.792	29.675
1855	30.089	30.032	29.693	29.820	...	...	...	...	...	...	...	...
Means	29.773	29.843	29.745	29.898	29.937	29.714	29.736	29.689	29.653	29.750	29.753	29.748

According to the resulting values, the height of the barometer is above the mean in the months of January, February, March, April, and May, and descends below the mean in the remaining summer and autumn months. The maximum pressure

[1] Although a long series of hygrometric observations were made, yet, owing to the peculiar delicacy which such observations require in a latitude of such low temperature, they proved, on close examination, too uncertain to be relied on in their results.

was observed in May, the minimum in September. The range between these two months is 0.284 inch.

ANNUAL VARIATION.

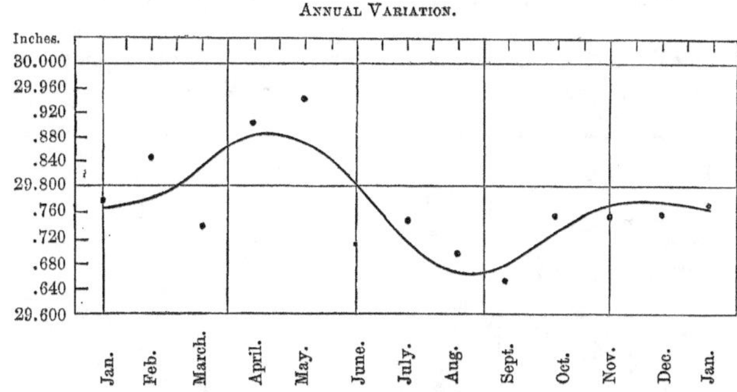

According to the above diagram, in which the dots indicate the mean monthly readings, the law of the annual fluctuation does not, perhaps, as plainly appear as we might expect from a longer-continued series of observations. In the month of January, for instance, we have a difference in the height of the barometer in the two years (1854 and 1855) of not less than 0.631 inch.

The general law that the height of the barometer is less in summer than in winter, is here prominently brought out. In the following expression, I have attempted to exhibit the course of the annual variation:—

$$B = \overset{\text{Inches.}}{29.770} + \overset{\text{Inch.}}{0.079}\ sin\ (\theta + 4^\circ) + \overset{\text{Inch.}}{0.044}\ sin\ (2\ \theta + 194^\circ),$$

the angle θ counting from January 1st, and is expressed in degrees at the rate of 30° a month.

The computed annual range is 29.875 — 29.668 = 0.207 inch. If we add 0.005 as correction to the constant 29.770, to refer it to the level of the sea, we find the mean barometric height, in the latitude 78° 37′ N., 29.775 inches.

Irregular Oscillations of the Pressure; Monthly and Annual Extremes.—The irregular changes in the atmospheric pressure are, like those of the temperatures, much greater in winter than in summer, of which an instance has already been given (see the means for the months of January and February of 1854 and 1855). If we deduce the average difference, irrespective of sign, in the barometric height between any two consecutive days, we obtain the following table of mean diurnal change, as made out from 17 months of observations:—

	Inch.		Inch.
January	0.17	August	0.10
February	0.26	September	0.11
March	0.17	October	0.15
April	0.12	November	0.17
May	0.14	December	0.26
June	0.10		
July	0.09	Mean . .	0.15

In the months of December, January, and February, the variability between successive diurnal means is a maximum, and in the months of June, July, and August, it reaches a minimum value; the ratio of the highest and lowest being as 2½ to 1.

The following table contains the maxima and minima of atmospheric pressure as observed in each month, and the extreme ranges for each month of the year:—

Month.	Maxima.			Minima.			Range.
	1853.	1854.	1855.	1853.	1854.	1855.	Inches.
September	30.06	30.25	...	29.07	29.01	...	1.11
October	30.50	30.16	...	29.11	29.00	...	1.28
November	30.26	30.41	...	29.05	29.01	...	1.30
December	30.50	30.37	...	29.01	28.89	...	1.48
January	...	29.92	30.97	...	28.86	(29.30)	1.36
February	...	30.45	...	...	28.84	...	1.61
March	...	30.49	...	...	29.18	...	1.31
April	...	30.37	...	...	29.28	...	1.09
May	...	30.49	...	...	29.19	...	1.30
June	...	30.19	...	...	29.41	...	0.78
July	...	29.97	...	...	29.40	...	0.57
August	...	30.05	...	...	29.22	...	0.83

Mean range of monthly extremes 1.17 inch; the maxima rise, on the average, to 30.31 inches, and the minima fall to 29.14 inches. As in the preceding table of the diurnal fluctuation, the greatest monthly range takes place in December, January, and February (1.48 inch), and the least in June, July, and August (0.73 inch). The ratio of highest and lowest values is as 2¼ : 1. Between the extremes, both tables show a regular progression.

The absolute highest reading was 30.97 inches; it occurred in the morning of January 22st, 1855. The absolute lowest reading was 28.84 inches, and occurred near noon of February 19th, 1854. Extreme range observed 2.13 inches.

Of the gales noted in my discussion of the winds at Van Rensselaer Harbor,[1] only the following ones were accompanied by a notable amount of change of atmospheric pressure:—

Before the setting in of the gale of December 28th, 1853, the barometer fell 0.35 inch in nine hours, or at a rate of 0.04 inch an hour. For three days preceding the gale of October 15th, 1854, the barometer was very low, and reached its lowest point at the hour when the gale was at its height; after this time, it rose 0.77 inch in eighteen hours, or at a rate of 0.04 inch an hour. Before the gale of December 18th, 1854, the barometer fell 0.36 inch in five hours, or 0.07 inch an hour; and before the setting in of the gale of January 13th, 1855, it fell 0.26 inch in eleven hours.

State of the Barometer during the Fall of Snow (or Rain).—To ascertain whether there is any change in the barometric pressure caused by the fall of snow, I have tabulated the readings during the hours of precipitation, and compared them with an equal number of readings, half immediately preceding, half immediately follow-

---

[1] See record and results of my discussion of the observations of winds at Van Rensselaer Harbor, in Vol. XI. of the Smithsonian Contributions to Knowledge.

ing, each fall of snow. If snow fell for less than three consecutive hours, I have taken no notice of it in this investigation. The mean result from 563 hours of comparison, gave only a difference of 0.006 inch, by which quantity the barometer is lower during the fall of snow than otherwise.

Variability of Atmospheric Pressure with the Direction of the Wind.—The connection of the atmospheric weight with the direction of the wind requires, in order to find its average effect, a great number of observations, particularly on account of the irregular oscillations of the barometer in the winter months. The following results are derived from a comparison of the barometric readings at the hours 6 A. M., noon, 6 P. M., and midnight, for each day, with the respective mean monthly reading during 17 months of observations. These difference were then arranged according to the directions of the wind. The result is as follows (± indicating {above / below} the mean):—

Magnetic direction.	Inch.	
N.	—0.022	
N. E.	+0.072	On account of the comparatively small number of observations for these directions, they may be combined: E. N. E. —0.044 in.
E.	—0.100	
S. E.	0.000	
S.	+0.038	
S. W.	+0.045	
W.	—0.031	
N. W.	—0.031	

From 1050 comparisons of calms and barometric readings, the latter were found 0.005 inch above their mean value.

It is only during S. and S. W. (magnetic) winds that the barometer rises above the mean value; during all other winds it is depressed.

Relation of the Atmospheric Pressure to each Wind and to the Temperature of the same.—To show this dependence, it is best to put the relation of the atmospheric pressure, as well as that of the temperature, to the winds, in an analytical form. In my discussion of the observed temperatures at Van Rensselaer Harbor, a table was made out showing the dependence of the temperature on the direction of the wind. If we deduct the mean elevation of temperature by the winds from each separately, we obtain the following table of the effect of each wind on the temperature (± indicating an {elevation / depression} of temperature):—

Magnetic direction.		Magnetic direction.	
N.	—1°.4	S.	+0°.6
N. E.	0.0	S. W.	+0.4
E.	—0.1	W.	+0.1
S. E.	+0.9	N. W.	—1.4

Counting θ from the north (or belonging to a (magnetic) north wind) round by E. to 360°, we obtain, by using Bessel's formula,

$$T = +1^{\circ}.02 \sin (\theta + 286^{\circ});$$

or, for the true directions,

$$T = +1^{\circ}.02 \sin (\theta + 34^{\circ});$$

and similarly, from the barometric relation to the winds,

$$B = +0.018 \text{ in. } \sin (\theta + 354^{\circ}).$$

A comparison of the angular constants in these two expressions does not show a correspondence of the wind of maximum temperature with a minimum pressure; on the contrary, there is a much nearer correspondence of the wind of maximum temperature with maximum pressure. According to the first formula, the hottest wind is from the direction N. E. ½ E. (true); and, by the second formula, the maximum atmospheric pressure is from the direction E. (true) nearly.

www.ingramcontent.com/pod-product-compliance
Lightning Source LLC
LaVergne TN
LVHW021423110826
845150LV00007B/2057

* 9 7 8 1 4 2 5 5 0 8 5 2 4 *